GARY L. FL(

MW01610429

UNDERSTANDING LIFE INSURANCE and RETHINKING POLICY MANAGEMENT and EVALUATION

EXPLAINING THE UNEXPLAINABLE

AMERICAN**BAR**ASSOCIATION

Real Property, Trust and
Estate Law Section

IMPORTANT DISCLAIMERS AND NOTICES

These materials are intended for educational purposes **only**. They are designed to provide accurate and authoritative information in regard to the subject matter covered. However, Gary L. Flotron is not offering any type of legal, accounting, insurance, investment, or other professional advice in these materials. If legal advice or other expert assistance is required, the services of a competent professional person should be sought.

These materials are provided solely for educational purposes. These materials cannot be sold, copied, reproduced, or distributed in any form or manner whatsoever without the express written consent of the author.

Internal Revenue Service Circular 230 Disclosure:

To ensure compliance with requirements imposed by the U.S. Internal Revenue Service, we inform you that any tax advice contained in this document (including any attachments) was not intended or written to be used, and cannot be used, by any taxpayer for the purpose of (1) avoiding tax-related penalties under the U.S. Internal Revenue Code or (2) promoting, marketing, or recommending to another party any tax-related matters addressed herein.

Contents

Foreword   xv
Preface   xvii
   Some Background on the Book   xx
Acknowledgments   xxi

CHAPTER 1
Introduction   1

CHAPTER 2
Toward Understanding Life Insurance and the Risk Transfer Paradigm Shift—Some Life Insurance Basics   7

The Building Blocks of Life Insurance   7
   Life Insurance Pricing   7
   Lack of Transparency   9
   Life Insurance Pricing and Costs Must Be Viewed Integrated
   as a Whole and Not Separately   13
   Pricing Assumptions of Life Insurance and Risk Transfer   14

Understanding Mortality Tables and Life Expectancy   16
   Mortality Tables   16
   Life Expectancy   17
   Two Additional Points about Life Expectancy   20

Mathematics of the Cost of "Pure" Term Insurance   20
   Characteristics of Term Insurance   20
   "Pay as You Go" Life Insurance   22
   Mathematics of the Cost of "Pure" Term Insurance   22

Mathematics of "Permanent" Types of Life Insurance—
Part 1: Fixed Guaranteed and Constant Assumptions   23
      Creation of Permanent Life Insurance   23
      Mathematics of Permanent Life Insurance Policies   25

Mathematics of "Permanent" Types of Life Insurance—
Part 2: Constant Assumption versus Reality   27
      Policy Interest or Earnings Crediting   27
      Effect of Rate of Return on Net Amount at Risk
      and Cost of Insurance   32
      Lessons Learned   36

CHAPTER 3
Risks of Life Insurance Policies   39

Background, History, and Perspective on the Risk Transfer   39

Trust-Owned Life Insurance Is an Example of Adverse Risk Transfer
Consequences   41

What Is the Definition of Risk and What Are Life Insurance Policy
Expectations?   42

Carrier Insolvency Risk   43

Purchasing Power Risk   45

Risks by Product Types   47
      Term Insurance   50
      Participating "Par" Whole Life   51
      Universal Life   52
      Variable Universal Life   55
      No-Lapse Guarantee Universal Life   57
      Indexed Universal Life   59
      Blended Base Whole Life with Combination Paid-Up Additions
      and Decreasing Term Insurance Dividend Option and/or Paid-Up
      Additions Rider   62

Product Suitability Risk   64

Diversification Risk   68

CHAPTER 4
Process of Managing Life Insurance Policies   71

Traditional Investment Management versus Life
Insurance Management   71

Life Insurance Policy Management Statement   73

Delegation of Life Insurance Management Duties   73

Best versus Predatory Practices in Life Insurance Trust Management   74

Duration Planning with Universal Life Policies and Using
Personalized Life Expectancy Reports   75

CHAPTER 5
Creditable Evaluation of Life Insurance   81

The Extreme Disconnect   81

Improper Policy Evaluation Methods   82

Monte Carlo Simulation and Actuarially Certified Policy Standards
Analysis   82

Creditable Evaluation of Life Insurance in Perspective   87

CHAPTER 6
Practical Questions and Guidelines to Acquiring and Managing Life Insurance to Avoid a Client Crisis   91

First Things First   91

Planning Horizon and Need for Either a Level, Increasing, or Decreasing
Face Amount—The Nature of the Goals, Objectives, and Needs   93

Need for Cash Value Accumulation Considerations   95

Beneficiaries and Policy Ownership   96

Underwriting Considerations   98

Selecting the Appropriate Life Insurance Product Type or Types—
Temporary or Term Insurance   100

Selecting the Appropriate Life Insurance Product Type or Types—
Permanent Insurance   102

Selecting the Appropriate Life Insurance Carrier   110

Selecting Life Insurance Professionals   112

Ongoing Policy Monitoring, Risk Management, Verification, and Creditable
Evaluation   123

Determining the "What Ifs"   127

Life Expectancy   141

Life Insurance Policy Management Statement   141

Summary   142

CHAPTER 7
Conclusion   145

About the Author   149

CONTRIBUTED ARTICLES   151

Introduction   151

Format for the Contributed Articles   152

The BOX   153

Guy E. Baker, M.B.A., M.S.F.S., Ph D., CLU®, ChFC®, CFP®, AEP® (Distinguished)

Introductory Comments by Gary Flotron   153

About Guy E. Baker   153

The BOX   155

   What Is Life Insurance?   156

   The Key to Understanding Life Insurance   157

   Determining the Cost of Insurance   159

   How Do You Determine The Cost of Life Insurance?   161

   What Does Life Insurance Cost?   162

   The Natural Consequences of Aging   163

   Introducing The BOX   164

   Are There Different BOX Designs?   165

   A Quick Summary   167

   The Factors That Impact Pricing   168

   What Happens If the Assumptions are Incorrect?   168

   A Closer Look at the Four Pricing Factors   169

   The Dynamics of The BOX   171

   How Much Can You Put in The BOX?   172

   What is a MEC?   174

   Retail Insurance Pricing   174

   Putting Money in The BOX   175

   Conclusion   177

Between a Rock and a Hard Place: NAIC Regulators— Life Insurance Intermediaries—State and Federal Regulators   179

Ben G. Baldwin, Jr., M.S.F.S., M.S.M., CLU®, ChFC®, CFP®, AEP® (Distinguished)

Introductory Comments by Gary Flotron   179

About Ben G. Baldwin, Jr.   180

Between a Rock and a Hard Place: NAIC Regulators—Life Insurance Intermediaries—State and Federal Regulators   181

NAIC Regulators Mandate Linear Paper Illustrations Be Used in the Sale of Life Insurance   181

How You Ask for an Illustration for UL and VUL Policies Is Very Important   182

Life Insurance Litigation Creates Pressure for New Regulation   183

Credible Life Insurance Advisors Agree—Today's Regulated Illustrations Mislead   183

NAIC Life Insurance Illustrations Model Regulation, Section 1   185

State & Federal Regulators and the Courts Can Impose Severe Penalties for Using NAIC Regulated LI Illustrations   186

Life Insurance Intermediaries Are Between Regulatory Rocks   186

Buying Life Insurance to Fund Estate Taxes: Toward a More Objective Decision   189

Jonathan G. Blattmachr, J.D., AEP® (Distinguished) and Marc A. Pasquale, CPA

Introductory Comments by Gary Flotron   189

About Jonathan G. Blattmachr   190

About Marc A. Pasquale   192

Buying Life Insurance to Fund Estate Taxes: Toward a More Objective Decision   192

Why Large Policies?   192

Timing of Death   193

Other Factors   194

Buy Term Insurance Instead? 195

Other Limitations 196

Funding Estate Taxes 196

Role of Insurance 197

Type of Policy 197

Policy Comparisons 199

Weighing the Options 199

The Miracle (and Disaster) of Compound Interest— Universal Life Insurance Edition 201

Christopher H. Hause, FSA, MAAA, CLU®

Introductory Comments by Gary Flotron 201

About Christopher H. Hause 202

The Miracle (and Disaster) of Compound Interest—Universal Life Insurance Edition 203

Explanation of "On the Curve" 207

Explanation of "COI Leveraging" 207

"Middling" Universal Life Policy Specifications 208

TOLI Trustee Tread Tactfully 209

Donald O. Jansen, J.D., LL.M., AEP③ (Distinguished)

Introductory Comments by Gary Flotron 209

About Donald O. Jansen 210

TOLI Trustee Tread Tactfully 211

The Days of Unmonitored ILIT Policies 211

Advent of Universal and Variable Life Policies 212

Enactment of UPIA 213

Conclusion 214

Adopting A Two-Dimensional Risk Tolerance Assessment Process
The Sorry State Of Risk Tolerance Questionnaires For Financial Advisors   215

Michael E. Kitces, M.S.F.S., M.TAX, CFP®, CLU®, ChFC®, RHU®, REBC®, CASL®

Introductory Comments by Gary Flotron   215

About Michael E. Kitces   218

Adopting A Two-Dimensional Risk Tolerance Assessment Process   219

    Executive Summary   219

    Separating Risk Tolerance From Risk Capacity   220

    Aligning Two-Dimensional Risk Tolerance And Risk Capacity   221

    Assessing Two-Dimensional Risk Tolerance And Risk Capacity (Separately)   222

The Sorry State Of Risk Tolerance Questionnaires For Financial Advisors   226

    Executive Summary   226

    PlanPlus Searches For Global Best Practices In Investment Risk Profiling   227

    Breaking Apart the Risk Profile—Tolerance, Capacity, and Risk Perception   228

    The Challenge Of Designing Good Risk Profiling Tools And Assessments   230

    The Sorry State Of Current Risk Tolerance Questionnaires (RTQs) And Risk Profiling Tools   232

    The Future Of (Better) Assessments Of Risk Tolerance   233

When to Hold Life Insurance in Trust; What Type of Trust   235

Martin M. Shenkman, CPA, M.B.A., PFS, J.D., AEP® (Distinguished)

Introductory Comments by Gary Flotron   235

About Martin M. Shenkman   236

When to hold Life Insurance in Trust; What Type of Trust   238

Introduction   238

Trusts Should Still Own Life Insurance   238

Use of Grantor Trusts   239

Life Insurance and Grantor Trusts   240

Burgeoning Use of Non-Grantor Trusts   240

The Insurance Planning Complexity Scale   241

Conclusion   241

Was Your Client Sold the Most Expensive Life Insurance Policy on the Planet? High Net Worth (HNW) Access to Institutionally-Priced Life Insurance for Personal Asset Diversification   243

Charles M. "Mark" Whitelaw and E. Randolph Whitelaw, AEP® (Distinguished)

Introductory Comments by Gary Flotron   243

About Charles M. "Mark" Whitelaw   247

About E. Randolph Whitelaw   248

Was Your Client Sold the Most Expensive Life Insurance Policy on the Planet?   249

Equivalent Return Disclosure to the S&P 500 Total Return   250

IUL Interest Bonus/Return Enhancements   251

Applying AG 49 Principles to Consumer Planning Assumptions   251

MA-200—200 Day Moving Average management.   252

Best Interest   252

What's Coming Down The Pipe?   254

High Net Worth (HNW) Access to Institutionally-Priced Life Insurance for Personal Asset Diversification   255

Overview   255

Evolution of the ILI Value Proposition   256

Agents/Advisors Can Finally Address Structural Suitability   257

Investment Container Comparison   258

Different Perspective of Dispute Defensible and Exposures   261

Conclusion   261

The Lapsing Life Insurance Policy Crisis—The Need for Dispute Defensible Advisor Practices And A Glidepath to Safety, Especially for Seniors   263

E. Randolph Whitelaw, AEP® (Distinguished), and George P. Whitelaw

Introductory Comments by Gary Flotron   263

About E. Randolph Whitelaw   264

About George P. Whitelaw   266

The Lapsing Life Insurance Policy Crisis—The Need for Dispute Defensible Advisor Practices And A Glidepath to Safety, Especially for Seniors   266

How Could This Happen?   266

What is The Purpose of This Article? To Provide Practical Advice and Explain the Obligations of the Parties.   267

What is "Illustration Abuse"?   269

Why is there a Lapsing Policy Crisis?   269

What is Actuarially Defensible Policy Evaluation?   271

The History of Flexible Premium Non-Guaranteed Policies (aka The Buy Term and Invest the Difference Transition)   271

Life Insurance Distribution Channels   272

Policy Performance Review and Risk Management Process   273

Actuarial Evaluation (AE) Reports   274

New Department of Labor Guidelines   276

Conclusion   276

Index   279

Foreword

Are you intimidated by life insurance? Do your eyes glaze over as you review pages of illustrations? How much coverage do you need? What types of policies should you buy and which carriers should you choose? Do you understand both the credit risks and the investment risks inherent in life insurance policies? Do you understand the differing management requirements of different types of policies? Once the policy is issued, can it be tossed into a drawer and not be worried about until the insured's death? Where can you get help with these issues?

All of these questions and more are answered in plain and understandable language in *Understanding Life Insurance and Rethinking Policy Management and Evaluation: Explaining the Unexplainable*. This book indeed makes the unexplainable understandable. It is an excellent resource for individuals seeking insurance coverage and lawyers, CPAs and other advisers trying to plan for their clients' personal and business needs, and trustees since they have fiduciary obligations to manage these policies owned by their trusts. Life insurance professionals should find this book useful too.

Many books in this field cover narrow areas and sometimes are so technical that they are not understandable to the general audience. Not so with Gary Flotron's book. It covers all of these fields with many helpful tables and charts.

In Chapter 2, he explains the building blocks of life insurance, including mortality charges, life expectancy, and the mathematics of term and permanent insurance. Chapter 3 describes the risks, advantages, and disadvantages of the various life insurance policies, including term, whole, universal, and variable life policies. Chapter 4 shows how to manage your policy after it is purchased, particularly with regard to universal life policies. The process of monitoring and evaluating policies is discussed in Chapter 5; this area is essential but all too often overlooked, sometimes with disastrous consequences. Finally, Chapter 6 answers those questions posed at the beginning of this foreword plus many more.

While life insurance has been around for many years and has benefits granted under the Internal Revenue Code that are not available to other assets, newer forms of policies raise issues of management that older types of policies (whole life and term) never did. Most people need coverage for personal needs (e.g., income replacement at premature death; children's college education; payment of estate taxes, mortgages, or other debts), for business needs (business succession, deferred compensation, key person coverage), or for charitable goals of providing large endowments or contributions at death to a favorite charity. This exceptional book will be a trusted guide to accomplishing these goals efficiently and effectively.

Donald O. Jansen, JD, LLM, AEP® (Distinguished)
Lawrence Brody, JD, LLM, AEP® (Distinguished)

Preface

The majority of writings on life insurance fall into three categories: Category one positively advocates the needs for life insurance, explains the benefits of differing product types, and attempts to demonstrate the economic advantages of permanent life insurance products—both guaranteed and non-guaranteed—through the use of traditional, constant crediting rate (and current cost of insurance) assumption policy illustrations. This first category is designed to be a friendly, helpful guide to the prospective life insurance purchaser. Category two, on the other hand, takes the approach that the needs for life insurance are a necessary temporary evil that should be met with term life insurance coverage and that coverage should cease at retirement, at the very longest, if not well before that time. This category is the classic theory of "buy term and invest the difference," with the difference intended to accumulate to an amount that negates the need for life insurance. Category three tends to take the form of educational textbooks intended either to provide the requisite life insurance knowledge to prepare the reader to sit for the state insurance license exam, or to provide the fundamental life insurance basics for a college course in either risk management, insurance, or financial planning. These educational publications, although generally presented in a neutral manner, tend to espouse the life insurance industry traditional marketing approaches, nomenclature, and positions.

By comparison, this book takes an entirely different approach. The author sincerely believes that life insurance is a form of intangible personal property that is designed to solve financial needs and problems—primarily the economic loss upon the death of the insured or insureds—in many cases in the most effective and efficient manner. There are many legitimate needs for life insurance in both personal and business planning situations. Some of these needs are truly temporary and are best funded with term insurance. Alternatively, planning needs of a more permanent nature tend to be funded with policies designed for long-term or life-long permanent protection. There are a variety of permanent life insurance products available in the marketplace. Some products guarantee the premium payment amount, duration period of the payment amount, cash value, and death benefit to the maximum age of the mortality table prescribed by law at the issuance of the policy, which is generally age 100 or 120. Other products contain maximum cost guarantees and, maybe, minimum crediting rates, and are not guaranteed performance products but rather are based on the insurance carrier's current non-guaranteed assumptions that will definitely change over time and market conditions. With guaranteed products, the performance risk is retained by the life insurance carrier. With non-guaranteed products, the performance risk is transferred to the policy owner. However, this risk transfer shift for non-guaranteed products, which commenced in 1979 with the introduction of the first universal life policy, is either unknown or has been completely ignored.

Like all financial products and instruments, all life insurance products have risks, particularly non-guaranteed flexible premium policies. Like other financial vehicles, life insurance needs to be periodically performance monitored, creditably evaluated, and risk managed. Yet all too often these tasks are completely ignored for life insurance. Unlike most writings in category one, the author does not advocate the use of the traditional, constant assumption policy illustrations for evaluating non-guaranteed life insurance products. In fact, all policy illustrations for non-guaranteed products disclaim the predictability of non-guaranteed policy values. Further, non-guaranteed policy illustrations should not be used to compare one life insurance policy to another, which, unfortunately, is common practice among many life insurance professionals and financial planners. Creditable evaluation for a non-guaranteed life insurance product requires actuarial evaluation and related practices that will be described and analyzed in the book.

Besides explaining the basics of understanding life insurance, the risk transfer paradigm shift, and the risks of life insurance policies, this book discusses a dispute defensible process for risk managing life insurance policies. Additionally, it is firmly believed by the author that life insurance should first be selected based on the true, real duration of the need for life insurance. If the need is permanent, the life insurance product type selected should be based first on the policy owner's risk tolerance and, second, on either the need to have increasing death benefit and cash values (to protect purchasing power) or minimum premium outlay. This is opposed to selecting the product *de jure* or "hot product" that does not take fully into account what is suitable for the policy owner based on the owner's risk tolerance and other personal preferences (such as investment objectives, asset allocation, and purchasing power protection).

As a practical matter, all permanent forms of life insurance are internally a "buy term and invest the difference" proposition. Universal life policies annually report to the policy owner the cost of insurance (based on annual mortality rates similar to annually renewable term rates) and the excess premium amounts (based on premium less the cost of insurance and other policy expenses) and earnings credited to the cash account value. As a result, the "buy term and invest the difference" aspect of the policy is readily transparent to the policy owner. However, while certainly opaque, internally whole life product values are calculated actuarially by an identical method utilized by universal life products. Thus, it can be questioned if you are going to "buy term and invest the difference," is it more effective and efficient to do such internally with either a universal life or whole life product-type or externally by actually buying a one-year renewable term life insurance product and investing the difference in mutual funds, stocks, bonds, and so on? Based upon an informed and honest analysis that considers all issues, the tax-deferral, economics of scale, and diversification aspects of the "difference" being invested internally in a permanent life insurance product, most consumers would unhesitatingly conclude it is far more favorable, effective, and efficient to invest the "difference" internally in the permanent life insurance product.

To understand life insurance and its risks, particularly the risk transfer associated with non-guaranteed flexible premium products, it is necessary to examine the basic pricing elements, or building blocks, that comprise every life insurance policy and how these elements interact to produce policy values. To a certain extent, most life insurance textbooks do explain the basic life insurance pricing elements and the rudimentary aspects as to how these elements react. Unfortunately, these textbooks ignore the risk aspects of life insurance and how to creditably risk manage life insurance policies. A discussion of creditable (dispute defensible) policy risk identification and management is a fundamental departure from the typical academic publication. While this writing does present academic justification for the presented materials, it also provides helpful questions and guidelines for acquiring and managing life insurance.

This book addresses basic product suitability, policy performance monitoring, and policy risk management considerations that are quite different (and long overdue) from the three described categories of life insurance publications. The book's objective is to help the reader become more informed in understanding the nature and mechanics behind various life insurance products in a simple, noncomplicated, practical, easy to follow, clear manner. More importantly, this book brings into perspective the risks involved with the most popular types of life insurance policies sold today, particularly the risk paradigm shift triggered by non-guaranteed flexible premium products that, in many cases, precipitated a policy crisis due to risk management inattention. Just as important, the easy-to-apply process to risk managed life insurance policies—that has been utilized in the professional portfolio investment and trust administration industries for years—is presented and described to enable policy owners to take prudent and informed control of these significant assets. Equally significant and valuable to the process of managing life insurance policies is the creditable evaluation of life insurance, particularly non-guaranteed flexible premium policies. The tome explores and analyzes the technique of actuarial evaluation, which applies benchmarking and statistical methods to the probabilities of favorable outcomes with non-guaranteed flexible premium policies. If the described approach of this book sounds like a financial planning and investment management approach to life insurance, it is. The author believes this is a practical, refreshing, different, and unconventional way to handle the topic of life insurance, which is long overdue, to help explain the unexplainable. Hope you find the book interesting, helpful, useful, beneficial, practical, and enjoyable!

Some Background on the Book

The thoughts and ideas expressed in this book are in many ways the accumulation of knowledge from either selling, advising, consulting, writing, speaking, or teaching on the college or university level life insurance over the past 40 years. There are many professional friends and colleagues who have influenced these thoughts either by the author reading their various writings, hearing their presentations and having conversations with them, or by working together or in collaboration. These friends and colleagues will be rightfully credited for their help and influence in the Acknowledgements section that follows. Suffice it to say for right now that the incubation for this book started sometime in 2011 with the conception of the idea of forming an alliance with four nationally prominent practitioners, each from a different professional discipline and perspective, with expertise on the Uniform Prudent Investor Act and trust-owned life insurance to speak at national conferences as a group around the country. In many ways, the gentlemen that comprised this group were kindred spirits that influenced each other. At least, they certainly highly influenced the author. This led to the author developing his own presentation and PowerPoint slide materials that have been used in numerous speaking engagements—both national and local conferences—around the country. The bulk of the material in this book represents the written, elaborated, and fully documented portions of these presentations.

One could say the content of the book is sort of like the time-honored wedding tradition of "something old, something new, something borrowed," without the "something blue." In any event, this writing represents cumulative thoughts on life insurance developed over an entire career and particularly over the past few years. It is written to provide a plain understanding of life insurance for both professional advisers—attorneys, accountants, trust officers, financial planners, and life insurance professionals—and laymen and laywomen who are either prospective policy owners or existing policy owners for personal or business needs, or are decision-making executives and administrators who oversee and have to manage life insurance policies for either public or private businesses or nonprofit and charitable institutions.

With that, it is time to start the journey of "Explaining the Unexplainable."

Acknowledgments

It is virtually impossible to write a book without the help of others. Such is the case for this author. However, that help comes in many different forms whether it is influences in thinking, actual support in proofreading, typing, editorial suggestions, or just plain support from many friends and loved ones while the author is in the process of composing the writing.

This author has been blessed by many wonderful individuals who have influenced, in one way or another, the author's perceptions, thoughts, philosophies, conduct, and methods of practice both from a life perspective and from a professional perspective. Of course, for purposes of this book, acknowledgements will be primarily limited to those who have been an influence or support in my professional life and within the profession of a financial and estate planner and life insurance professional. The great fear is that inadvertently someone is omitted who made a significant contribution to the attributes mentioned above or for my professional career. But, having said such, the best that one can do is hope memory does not fail in listing salient contributors that have influenced this author.

This career path would never have existed—particularly in attitudes and methods of practice—without the tutoring, mentoring, and encouragement of the late Richard W. Bartels, CLU®, the agency manager for the Bankers Life Company of Des Moines, Iowa—now the Principal Financial Group—who recruited me into the profession in late 1979. Dick was an extremely unique and rare manager who, after the basic required learning essentials, customized training based on an individual's background, education, experience, qualifications, aptitudes and natural inclinations, and markets as opposed to a "one size fits all" approach. Having come from a business and entrepreneurial background, Dick saw the potential for me to operate in the business and estate planning areas from the very beginning. For this I am most extremely grateful! Additionally, Dick was emphatic about doing things the right way and was extremely ethical. In fact, a life insurance policy replacement, even of a competitor's product, had to be justified to him or he would not allow it. While I think I had these values before I met Dick, he certainly further imbued these values into me. Unfortunately, Dick was diagnosed with Lou Gehrig's disease in 1981 and passed away in 1987.

To a tremendously large extent, this author has been highly influenced by his membership in the Society of Financial Service Professionals (FSP)—formerly the American Society of CLU and ChFC—and the National Association of Estate Planners & Councils (NAEPC) of which the Estate Planning Council of St. Louis is an affiliated Council. Both of these organizations have as their core values exceedingly advanced continuing education, and the development and fostering of quality professional relationships and the team approach to financial and estate planning. Of course, it is the individual members who make up these organizations that have made these professional societies great incubators for collaborative innovative thoughts and professional growth and development that leads to delivering the best professional services to our clients.

While many of the members of these professional societies have influenced the thoughts and practices of this author, there are a few who have had a profound effect on my career, thinking, and philosophies that should be particularly mentioned. One of those individuals is Richard M. Weber, M.B.A., CLU®, AEP® (Distinguished), an insurance fiduciary and managing member of Ethical Edge Solutions, LLC. In 1993, Dick conducted a vast series around the country of Life Insurance Due Care Workshops that were sponsored by the FSP. I attended one of those workshops in Kansas City, Missouri. This seminar introduced the Society of FSP's Life Insurance Illustration Questionnaire (IQ) as well as suggesting a more fundamental, ethical, and educational form of selling life insurance products. This meeting was an eye-opening, transformational event in my career. It taught me that for non-guaranteed products, the life insurance policy illustration was a complete illusion. Additionally, it taught me that among different life insurance products, and among different life insurance carriers, there are numerous, completely different assumptions behind each of the pricing elements in a life insurance policy that further makes the use of different life insurance policy illustrations incomparable. Subsequent to this Kansas City meeting, in 1995 I would later organize a joint meeting in St. Louis combining four professional organizations for Dick to do his workshop. With more than 350 people in attendance, that meeting turned out to be the largest ever for Dick's presentation.

Along with Christopher H. Hause, FSA, MAAA, CLU® (one of the contributing authors for this book), Dick co-invented and developed around 1996 the process of applying Monte Carlo simulation with actuarially certified policy benchmark standards to come up with a probability analysis of outcomes for a planned funding premium for a universal or variable universal life policy. Dick asked me to be a beta tester for this system that was then called the Dynamic Illustration System. The author considers Mr. Weber to be the conscience for the life insurance profession and is extremely grateful for his contributions to the author's career, thinking, and philosophies, as well as to the professionalism of the life insurance industry. In fact, if not for Dick, this book would not exist.

Ben G. Baldwin, Jr., M.S.F.S., M.S.M., CLU®, ChFC®, CFP®, AEP® (Distinguished) (also a contributing author for this book), is another individual the author met through the FSP whose analytical thoughts and graciousness have been nothing but inspiring. I met Ben in July 1993 where he was one of the presenters of what was then called the CLU Institute, a five-day program held at that time in Boulder, Colorado, at the University of Colorado. Mr. Baldwin did a three-hour presentation on the process and practice of comprehensive financial planning that was vastly insightful, profound, and useful. Subsequently, I attended a couple of years afterwards an all-day seminar he conducted on the same topic that was even more helpful and filled with more valuable insights.

But it is Ben's writings that have been extremely beneficial in my thinking and career. One of his amazing and perceptive publications is his book *The NEW Life Insurance Investment Advisor* (second edition published in 2002). Ben very thoughtfully sent me a copy of this book with an inscription that I will forever cherish. I had been a National Board Member of the FSP for one year when Ben became a member of the Board. In his inscription he called me his mentor. Talk about a true overstatement; that was it. At that time, Ben was truly a superstar in the financial planning field and highly respected by all. At best I was just a rookie. But his kind words in that inscription still stick with me.

As a columnist for Wolters Kluwer CCH *Estate Planning Review—The Journal*, Ben provides thoughtful analysis, vision, and astute commentary on life insurance. These discerning articles demonstrate why he is considered such a thought leader for our profession. In addition, he is truly a humble, kind man with tremendous humanity.

Another individual who is indeed a national thought leader in our profession who has inspired me is John L. Olsen, CLU®, ChFC®, AEP®. John is a fellow St. Louisan who I first met in a singing group we were both members of and through the local professional organizations including the FSP. In my humble opinion, John is the leading expert on annuities in the country. He has particular expertise in their risk management attributes, structure, design, mechanics, types, and distribution and tax planning aspects of this financial planning tool. His four books on annuities are state-of-the-art publications that should be on every financial advisor's desk. His dedication to professionalism, education, and the pursuit of knowledge in his chosen field is extraordinary and should be emulated by all practitioners.

But perhaps the individual who most profoundly changed the direction of my career was the late Robert G. Alexander, J.D., LL.M., AEP®, EPLS, known as Bob or Bobby to his many friends. Bob was the catalyst that got me started with writing and publishing. This started in late 2008 when he had me review an article he had written with Richard A. Oshins, M.B.A., J.D., LL.M., AEP® (Distinguished), and Kristen E. Simmons, J.D. Then he asked me to review and to be the technical editor for a long article he co-authored with the now late Michael W. Halloran, M.S F.S., M.S.M., CLU®, ChFC®, CFP®, REBC®, RHU®, AEP® (Distinguished), that was published in the *New York University Review of Employee Benefits and Executive Compensation 2009*. I suggested some other aspects of the 2009 article that I thought should be covered in addition to the material that Mike and Bobby wrote on and Bob solicited me to be a co-author along with Lawrence Brody, J.D., LL.M., AEP® (Distinguished), on a subsequent article published in the 2010 version of the same book. In fact, my portion of the draft of that "article" was 95 pages double spaced, with the total draft being 245 pages. Bobby and I subsequently went on to write another eight articles that were published.

Bob was a gregarious, affable, extremely bright, erudite attorney who, besides his study of the law, was a concert-level classical and jazz pianist who you could never get to play for you or anyone else. He also deeply loved his three daughters—who also studied piano, and Bob would attend every lesson with them—and the study of theology, although he was not one to ever wear his religion on his sleeve. Despite Bob having an undergraduate degree in English and myself having an undergraduate degree in engineering, we approached writing and the process in doing the writing in the same way. We unbelievably complemented each other and immensely enjoyed writing together. Bob was diagnosed with cancer of the lymph nodes in late 2011. After two separate bone marrow transplants in 2013 he was declared cancer free by his doctors in April of that year. Bobby planned to not return to his practice of law but instead to devote his life to writing and speaking on estate planning. We made very ambitious plans to do all kinds of writing on estate planning together and were both looking forward to doing such. Unfortunately, the cancer raised its ugly head in July and he was only given a few months to live. In August, that turned into less than two weeks. I knew that Bob was pretty bad when he asked me to finish editing the article we were writing for the 2013 *New York University Review*, co-authored with Larry Brody and E. Randolph Whitelaw, AEP® (Distinguished), using the Word software editing function as opposed to our conversations where we would do our editing over the phone. I finished the editing—this was well over a 100-page draft—that Bob would never see the day before he died in August 2013. I miss him so much!

After the 2010 *New York University Review* article I started researching the fiduciary duties to prudently manage and evaluate life insurance in an irrevocable life insurance trust (ILIT). Specifically, the relationship between the Uniform Prudent Investor Act (UPIA) and trust-owned life insurance (TOLI). While there were a variety of articles on the subject, all of the articles were only from the perspective of the author's specific discipline and none seemed to have an integrated or coordinated approach among the various professional disciplines involved with TOLI. It dawned on me to form a national group of experts from each of the respective professional disciplines involved with TOLI to do a series of presentations at various national conferences that would integrate the practical, how-to aspect of applying UPIA to TOLI. I refer to this group as the UPIA-TOLI Group and we did several presentations together at various national conferences and venues between 2012 and 2014. Each of the members of this group were kindred spirits that certainly had great influence on me with regards to my professional thinking, philosophies, and career, as I believe we all had influenced each other as well. In other words, this was a synergistic relationship.

This all started when I contacted E. Randolph Whitelaw, AEP® (Distinguished), after reading a couple of articles he wrote, either by himself or with co-authors, on the UPIA-TOLI topic that I was extremely impressed by. Randy has an extensive background in banking and trust operations, having been an Executive Vice President for a large bank holding company managing the holding company's middle market business and private client group, including the cross marketing of trust, investment, and life insurance markets. He was also the bank's interface with the Office of the Comptroller of the Currency (OCC) bank examiners. In addition, Randy was an expert witness for the plaintiff in the watershed and infamous *Cochran v. KeyBank* case that was the first case on UPIA and TOLI.

When I called Randy, I thought he would have no idea who I was. To my surprise, he said he knew me and that we had already met and that I was the one who introduced him to Dick Weber. It turned out that we met at the joint meeting I organized in 1995 where Dick Weber conducted his five-hour IQ Workshop seminar. It was such a delight to talk with Randy and I discovered that our thoughts and philosophies were completely aligned. I told him of my idea for the national group of experts from the different disciplines to jointly present a seminar on UPIA and TOLI at various national conferences and asked if he would be the trust and fiduciary expert member of the panel. He readily agreed. Then I told him who I had in mind for the attorney member and the financial advisor/life insurance expert. Randy similarly agreed with my choices. The only other member we needed was an actuary.

The choice for the attorney member was simple: Lawrence Brody, J.D., LL.M., AEP® (Distinguished). When it came to the premier estate planning attorney with expertise in life insurance, Larry was the man! When I called Larry and explained the proposed arrangement, I think it took him all of 30 seconds to say yes. Of course, my choice for the financial advisor/life insurance expert was Dick Weber and I think he even said yes to the arrangement faster than Larry.

So far, this was one hell of an unbelievable group of superstars! But I felt we also needed an actuary. One very serious consideration who would have done a superb, excellent job was Dick's actuarial partner, Chris Hause. There is no doubt that Chris would have been an excellent choice but I was concerned that we needed an actuary who was independent of any of the panel members, and with Chris being Dick's partner that was not the case. Dick Weber suggested Richard A. Schwartz, FSA, MAAA, CLU®, the former Executive Vice President and Chief Actuary for the very prestigious M Financial Group based in Portland, Oregon, and co-author of the American Bar Association's The Insurance Counselor book, *Life Insurance Due Care: Carriers, Products, and Illustrations Second Edition* (published in 1994). Like the other three gentlemen, Dick S. also agreed to be part of the panel. While I had known Larry Brody and Dick Weber for a very long time, and over the period of a couple of months had gotten to know Randy quite well, I had never met

Dick Schwartz. However, it did not take long before Dick S. and I became good and close friends. He is truly an outstanding gentleman, salt-of-the-earth type of fellow whom I am proud to call my good friend.

I served as the generalist on the UPIA-TOLI topic and moderator for the panel. My purpose in sharing this story was to tell how this amazing group came together and to acknowledge their influences on the development of my thinking, philosophies, and career. I am very grateful to each of these wonderful gentlemen!

Many colleagues and fellow faculty members at the University of Missouri–St. Louis (UMSL) have given me unbelievable support and encouragement in my speaking and writing endeavors, as well as in the classroom and my professional career. Professor Edward C. Lawrence, Ph.D., then Chair of the Finance Department, hired me in January 1997 to teach one life insurance course. Ed and I hit it off right from the beginning and it was probably the easiest job interview I ever had. He has been extremely helpful and supportive over the years and has become a great friend. Somewhere around ten years ago Ed stepped down as department chair but still remains a professor. His successor was Professor Hung-Gay Fung, Ph.D., a Curators' Distinguished Professor of Finance and Dr. Y.S. Tsiang, Professor of Chinese Studies. Like Ed, Hung-Gay treated me as a colleague and provided much encouragement and support for my endeavors. He also nominated me for a major *university*-wide faculty teaching award that I was fortunate to win in 2014. Hung-Gay, besides being a great scholar, is truly a great friend that I am very fortunate to know.

I met Professor Thomas H. Eyssell, Ph.D., when he asked me if he could audit my estate and trust planning class in the early 2000s. One day I handed out a pop quiz for the class and Tom refused to take the quiz. I kidded him about not taking the quiz as a Ph.D. and full professor of finance. After a while he stopped coming to my class and I thought I might have offended him. It turned out that he was named Interim Dean for the College of Business Administration (COBA). He later sent me an extremely kind note explaining why he could no longer come to class. Tom subsequently became associate Dean and the Director of Graduate Studies for the COBA. In either 2005 or 2006, Tom started a Preparatory Course Certificate Program for the Certified Financial Planner® (CFP®) designation and became the Director of the UMSL Financial Planning Programs. I was extremely honored when he called me and asked me to be the first faculty member for this program. Subsequently, I became the Associate Director for the UMSL Financial Planning Programs and I immensely enjoy working with Tom. Roughly four years ago Tom succeeded Hung-Gay as department chair when Hung-Gay wanted to return more of his attention to his research. Like all my other "bosses," Tom has encouraged and supported me and it has been a pleasure to work with him and have his friendship.

Tom was probably wearing too many hats and he turned over the department chair duties to Professor Gaiyan Zhang, Ph.D., a Finance Board Scholar and

Professor of Finance. (As of this writing Tom has semi-retired and is now Associate Dean Emeritus.) Like all my other department chairs, Gaiyan has been an absolute delight, giving me support, backing, and encouragement. I am lucky to have her as a chair and thank her so much.

Associate Dean Michael T. Elliott, Ph.D., Director of Undergraduate Studies and Associate Professor of Marketing, has also been of tremendous help to me over the years and a good friend. He keeps our undergraduate program running smoothly. That is not always an easy job.

The last of my UMSL colleagues that I want to pay tribute to and acknowledge is Dean Charles E. Hoffman, M.B.A. I sincerely believe we have the most awesome dean of any college of business administration anywhere. Charlie is a UMSL graduate (B.S.B.A. and M.B.A.) who has served many years as a Fortune 500 CEO. What a great concept for a business school: have a successful businessman as dean of the school. Like my other colleagues, he has been nothing but appreciative and supportive. I am extremely grateful to work with such great colleagues at UMSL and wish to thank them for their friendship and all they have done for me in supporting my career and this book.

At the end of the book there is a series of 11 Contributed Articles from 11 different authors and co-authors who are nationally known practitioners and advisors from the legal, actuarial, financial, and trust fields with extraordinary expertise in life insurance. These articles from notable, knowledgeable authors and co-authors are designed to give diverse insights that either reinforce, expand, or provide different perspectives than those of the author. While each author is acknowledged in the introduction to the Contributed Articles section and before each of their respective articles, I feel it is only appropriate to acknowledge them in the Acknowledgements section as well. They are: Guy E. Baker, M.B.A., M.S.F.S., M.S.M., Ph.D., CLU®, ChFC®, CFP®, AEP® (Distinguished); Ben G. Baldwin, Jr., M.S.F.S., M.S.M., CLU®, ChFC®, CFP®, AEP® (Distinguished); Jonathan G. Blattmachr, J.D., AEP® (Distinguished), and Marc A. Pasquale, CPA; Christopher H. Hause, FSA, MAAA, CLU®; Donald O. Jansen, J.D., LL.M., AEP® (Distinguished); Michael E. Kitces, M.S.F.S., M.TAX, CFP®, CLU®, ChFC®, RHU®, REBC®, CASL®; Martin M. Shenkman, CPA, M.B.A., PFS, J.D., AEP® (Distinguished); Charles M. "Mark" Whitelaw and E. Randolph Whitelaw, AEP® (Distinguished); and E. Randolph Whitelaw, AEP® (Distinguished), and George P. Whitelaw.

The author is extremely humbled that this group of contributing authors so graciously have contributed articles for this book. I extremely appreciate the contributions and works of this group of top-notch professionals.

An extra special tribute and acknowledgement to my very good and close friend and colleague E. Randolph Whitelaw, AEP® (Distinguished), for "peer" reviewing and making copious editing suggestions for this book! Randy is also the author of three contributed articles for this book. In addition, as mentioned earlier, he is part of the UPIA-TOLI Group, and we now have co-authored together at least several articles and have done numerous presentations together. I had the honor to be selected by the American Bar Association as the technical editor and "peer" reviewer for Randy's great book (co-authored with Henry Montag, CFP®, CLTC) *The Life Insurance Policy Crisis: The Advisors' and Trustees' Guide to Managing Risks and Avoiding a Client Crisis*, published by the American Bar Association in 2016. Randy views my book as a complement to his book and he has referred to it as an "under the hood" view of the material and topic of his book. I look very much forward to doing other future endeavors with Randy.

When I asked Donald O. Jansen, J.D., LL.M., AEP® (Distinguished), to write a contributed article for this book and sent him a copy of the draft, I was delightfully and pleasantly surprised when he "peer" reviewed the book with a fine-tooth comb before agreeing to do the article. The results of his review were finding about 20 typos undetected previously and a suggestion to update the number for the estate tax exemption. Other than that, apparently the book passed his muster. I am extremely grateful to Don, one of the nation's best and most highly respected estate planning attorneys, for his review, contributed article, and friendship.

An extra special thank you and tribute is also due to Don Jansen and Lawrence Brody, J.D., LL.M., AEP® (Distinguished), for being so kind and gracious to co-write the Foreword for this book. How could any author writing a book on life insurance be so lucky to have a Foreword to his book written by two of the most—if not the most—prominent estate planning attorneys in the country when it comes to knowledge about life insurance? I sincerely appreciate all that Larry and Don have done, and thank them both so much for the honor of having them write the Foreword to this book! I am, indeed, humbled, honored, grateful, and thrilled!

Two other close friends and associates also reviewed drafts of this book. James L. Butler, M.S.E.E., M.S.F.S., CLU®, ChFC®, CFP®, AEP®, of Butler Associates Financial Planners, Inc. in St. Louis told me that he thought the book provided valuable insights and he would make the book required reading for all of his planners. I am thankful and indebted to Jim for these very kind comments.

Bill Boersma, CLU®, AEP®, of OC Consulting Group in Grand Rapids, Michigan—who at age 50 represents the next generation with more than the prerequisite expertise in life insurance creditable evaluation to do an excellent job in succeeding my generation—gave me some very positive feedback. He commented:

> The information contained in this book is invaluable to the advisor and consumer market. While I wish the wisdom of these words could be distilled into a pill a prospective life insurance consumer could take before making decisions, we know this isn't possible. The best alternative is for the professional advisor market to internalize this information and deal it out liberally for the benefit of their clients.

Bill further noted:

> In my line of work, I get to see firsthand the ramifications of life insurance deci-
> sion making in the absence of this information and knowledge and it isn't pretty.
> The inability for the typical consumer—and too often the advisor and agent—to sit
> still, pay attention and learn enough before moving forward with such an important
> decision is well known. The value the educated advisor can bring to the situation
> cannot be overestimated. Unfortunately, the point in time when the conscientious
> adviser is counseling the client and proactively minimizing the chances of future
> disappointment—an end game the client never expects at the onset of the insurance
> transaction—is also the point when the value to the consumer isn't readily apparent.
> It is only with the benefit of a time machine or the ghost of life insurance future,
> that the consumer could understand where his fate lied without this guidance.

Bill picked up on exactly what this book is all about and I cannot thank him enough
for his very thoughtful and kind remarks!

Besides having drafts of the book reviewed by practitioners with knowledgeable expertise in life insurance, I wanted a student with no knowledge of life insurance to review the book in order to ascertain the readability, understandability, and
comprehensibility of the material. Finance student—now a graduate of UMSL—
Bradley D. Rempala undertook as an independent study the task as "guinea pig" to
test the qualities mentioned above of the book. Brad did an extremely thorough and
excellent job of reviewing and going over with me in detail every page that I wrote
in the book. According to Brad, the book passed the tests and could be used by both
students and laymen and lay-women in addition to the professional audience. I am
immensely thankful to Brad for his very positive feedback and a lot of hard work!

Special friend and my volunteer associate coach with the UMSL FSP Industry
Issues Competition teams, Emily A. Donaldson, read the entire manuscript. Emily
is a very intelligent and financially knowledgeable and astute woman but had no
previous knowledge of life insurance prior to reading the manuscript of this book.
She was surprised to learn about the risks embedded in life insurance products. She
also felt that none of these risks were conveyed to the policy owner and maybe not
understood by the person selling the life insurance policy. Emily also immensely
enjoyed reading Michael Kitces's contributed articles on risk tolerance. Her insights
and impressions were extremely helpful to me in confirming that the theme and
message for the book comes through loud and clear. I am extremely appreciative
and thankful to Emily for reading the book, her comments, and for all she does!

Finally, last but certainly not least, I want to thank close friend and colleague
Robert E. Fox, CLU®, AEP®, for all his support and encouragement while I have
been writing this book. Bob is a retired estate planner and life insurance professional who lives in Ocala, Florida, and is very active in serving on committees with

the NAEPC organization. One of the committees he serves on for NAEPC is the Accredited Estate Planner (AEP®) Designation Committee and he has more than served as the conscience and protector of the integrity of the AEP® designation. Bob has reviewed certain parts of the book, but, more importantly, he has certainly kept me on track in the completion of such for which I am more than appreciative and grateful.

Gary L. Flotron, M.B.A., CLU®, ChFC®, AEP®
University of Missouri–St. Louis
G.L. Flotron & Associates
February 2020

Chapter 1

Introduction

In the late 1970s and early 1980s, a far-reaching and profound paradigm shift occurred within the life insurance industry that drastically affected how life insurance is perceived, managed, and evaluated. Yet this paradigm shift and its potentially adverse policy owner implications went almost completely unnoticed and resulted in and precipitated the life insurance policy crisis that exists today.[1] The great divide, cross over point, and risk transfer to the policy owner occurred in 1979 with the introduction of life insurance policies where the pricing of the life insurance product was no longer based upon long-term guarantees and fixed schedules of premiums but was based on current non-guaranteed assumptions and flexible premium payments—the essence of what is referred to now as the family of universal life products.

This is not to say that this paradigm shift was necessarily a bad thing. Quite the contrary. All paradigm shifts have good and bad, and positive and negative aspects. However, change to a new paradigm requires adaptation and, quite frequently, a new support system. The problem with the life insurance paradigm shift that occurred was the almost complete lack of adaptation to the risk transfer precipitated by current assumption non-guaranteed flexible premium products, and the corresponding non-developed risk management and evaluation practices and support systems[2] necessitated by the new paradigm.

---

1. For an excellent exposé on the life insurance policy crisis see E. Randolph Whitelaw and Henry Montag, *The Life Insurance Policy Crisis: The Advisors and Trustees Guide to Risk Management and Avoiding a Client Crisis*, The American Bar Association, Chicago, Illinois, 2016.

2. Noted visionary, celebrated actuary, and former president of Tillinghast, James C.H. Anderson, was one of the pioneers who conceived and developed variable and universal life insurance products in the 1970s and early 1980s.Mr. Anderson strongly felt that universal life insurance was a consumer-oriented product that required the complete revamping of the traditional distribution system of life insurance carriers to make it cost competitive and in-line with other savings institutions. He envisioned that the "original agency organization will be disbanded and replaced by a new service-oriented organization designed to maintain its established customer relationships." *The Papers of James C.H. Anderson*, Actuarial Education and Research Fund, Schaumburg, Illinois, 1997, "The Universal Life Insurance Policy," page 217.]

Unfortunately, in reviewing universal life insurance ten years later in 1989, Anderson noted:

> *Distribution Costs.* Beginning around 1983, new versions of Universal Life began to emerge. These products featured a return to traditional commission rates coupled with "concealed loads" of various types. This change represented a return by the life insurance industry to its traditional

The new product was touted as being "transparent" and described as, in effect, the equivalent of "buy term and invest the difference," with the difference being invested internally within the policy.[3] Policy owners were never told how to prudently risk manage the performance of the policy, especially the changing premium payment risk to prevent policy lapse. Pricing that is based on a "current" non-guaranteed crediting rate and cost of insurance assumptions has required increased premium payments. Unfortunately, most policy owners as well as many sales agents were neither aware of these changes and the requirement to monitor these changes, nor how to obtain correcting premium information to avoid policy lapse.[4]

As already noted, sales agents had minimal familiarity with how the non-guaranteed features of this new product could interact to adversely affect policy performance. Additionally, questionable marketing practices with these non-guaranteed flexible premium product types over the past 35-plus years has adversely impacted how life insurance is perceived, sold, administered, and risk managed.[5] Ironically, because of the dramatic changes brought about by this

---

distribution-based philosophy and a rejection of the consumer-based philosophy which Universal Life was intended to promote.

The Papers of James C.H. Anderson, Actuarial Education and Research Fund, Schaumburg, Illinois, 1997, "1989/1 Universal Life 10 Years Later," page 619.

However, in that same 1989 commentary Anderson observed in a section titled "What Next?": *"Distribution.* It may not be possible to distribute an unbundled product in the conventional, high-cost way. Universal Life may become the product of nonconventional distributors, while others offer it only as the product of last resort." *The Papers of James C.H. Anderson*, Actuarial Education and Research Fund, Schaumburg, Illinois, 1997, "1989/1 Universal Life 10 Years Later," page 619.

By the way, in that same section, Anderson fully acknowledges the risk paradigm shift of variable universal life insurance:

Investments. The cash management problems of a product without fixed premiums are inherently different from those of traditional products. When the next interest rate spike occurs, consumers demand for new money investment returns on in-force Universal Life policies may give rise to significant new financial problems for the insurers. Variable Universal Life effectively addresses this problem by passing the investment risk back to the policyholder.

The Papers of James C.H. Anderson, Actuarial Education and Research Fund, Schaumburg, Illinois, 1997, "1989/1 Universal Life 10 Years Later," page 619.

3. Whitelaw and Montag, *supra*, note 1, page xiv.

4. Ibid, pages xiv, 5, and 11. Whitelaw and Montag also note:

[T]he scheduled policy owner premium payment amount is not adjusted annually, based upon crediting rate and cost of insurance changes. In a declining interest market, the originally calculated and scheduled premium must be increased to sustain the policy to its original maturity. *The policy owner solely is responsible to communicate with the issuing carrier and request this adjustment. If the adjustment is not requested, and the scheduled premium is not subsequently increased, the duration of coverage will be shortened. Unfortunately, few policy owners understand this responsibility and how to undertake it. Most owners mistakenly rely upon the sales agent to communicate and coordinate this adjustment.*

Ibid, page xiv.

5. Ibid, pages xiv, 4, 11–12.

type of life insurance product, "creative destruction"[6] of the life insurance retail distribution channel was predicted but never really materialized.[7]

Unfortunately, performance risk, questionable sales and policy management practices, and confused purchasers still persist today. The probability of policy lapse due to performance risk inattention continues to increase for reasons resolved long ago. The problem with the life insurance paradigm shift remains product feature awareness and product suitability based upon policy purchaser's objectives. Over time, the needed risk identification and management have been made available by independent policy administration and risk management firms usually introduced by the policy owner's legal and tax advisors. Said for emphasis purposes, the "dispute defensible"[8] sales, administration, risk management, and evaluation practices, and support systems necessitated by the new paradigm are available today but not from the traditional agent and carrier providers.[9]

Many factors contributed to the inauguration of this new type of life insurance product that resulted in the dramatic paradigm shift. In fact, the economic and marketing environment of the times provided the perfect storm for the launching of this new breed of life insurance. As noted so accurately by Professor Edward E Graves in *McGill's Life Insurance, 9th Edition*:

> The economic conditions of the early 1980s were a perfect incubator for the universal life variation of whole life. The economy was experiencing extremely high inflation rates and very high nominal rates of investment return. The real rate of return, however (nominal rate of return minus inflation rate), was quite low. Inflationary expectations were so rampant that investors were avoiding long-term investments, and the demand for short-term investments was outstripping the supply of funds, leading to what is known as a reverse yield curve (the cost of borrowing short-term funds is actually higher than the cost of borrowing for long-term mortgages). During more normal economic conditions, higher rates for borrowing are associated with longer-term investments, and lower rates are associated with the shortest investment durations.

---

6. In 1942, Austrian economist Joseph Schumpeter in *Capitalism, Socialism, and Democracy* used the term "creative destruction" to label the process of mutation that incessantly revolutionizes the economic structure from within, destroying the old one and creating a new one. Innovation creates obsolescence and replaces it. Joseph A. Schumpeter, *Capitalism, Socialism, and Democracy*, Harper & Brothers, New York, New York, 1942.

7. Anderson, *supra*, note 2, "The Universal Life Insurance Policy," page 217, and "1989/1 Universal Life 10 Years Later," page 619; Whitelaw and Montag, *supra*, note 1, pages xiv and 3.

8. "Dispute defensible" is a term coined and used by E. Randolph (Randy) Whitelaw, AEP® (Distinguished), the Managing Director of Trust Asset Consultants, LLC, to describe proper or best practices in the evaluation of life insurance and administration of the trust estate in the irrevocable life insurance trust (ILIT). Randy is a national expert and consultant in this subject matter and has served as an expert witness in litigation on these matters, including the watershed case *Cochran v. KeyBank*.

9. Whitelaw and Montag, *supra*, note 1, pages 7–9, 14, and footnote 4 on page 14.

Both short-term investment returns and inflation were hovering near 20 percent annual rates. This prompted many policyowners with traditional life insurance contracts to pull the cash value out of their existing life insurance contracts via policy loans or policy surrenders and invest the funds directly in these new high-yield investments. This process is commonly referred to as disintermediation.

Life Insurance companies were looking for a way to stem this outflow of funds that was forcing many of them to liquidate some of their long-term investments at a loss in order to honor policyowner requests. In such an inflationary environment the traditional fixed dollar life insurance contract lost much of its appeal.

Stock insurance companies were the first ones to introduce universal life policies. . . . . The real advantage was that nearly every insurance company introducing a universal life policy did so through a brand-new company that invested all of its assets into a new money portfolio and earned very high short-term investment yields. These yields seemed astronomical when compared with the yields being earned by traditional life insurance companies with long-term investment portfolios. Although the tremendous immediate advantage of higher yields could not persist over the entire duration of the life insurance contract, it was successfully **exploited** in the marketplace for the few years it lasted. [Emphasis added by the author.] After normal investment conditions returned and yields dropped to lower levels, the universal life policies decreased in popularity. Insurers selling universal life insurance started investing in longer term assets to increase their returns, and the total portfolios associated with universal life policies became very similar to those of seasoned insurance companies with large blocks of traditional whole life policies in force.[10]

In the above quoted paragraphs, Professor Graves is referring to the first type of universal life policies. All of the original non-guaranteed flexible premium products had portfolios backing up the cash value reserves of the policy consisting of mostly fixed income securities that are part of what is referred to as the general asset account of the insurer. Subsequent variations of the universal life product— such as variable universal life and indexed universal life—further exacerbated the risks associated with non-guaranteed flexible premium products.

In order to develop a thorough understanding of the nature of the risk-transfer paradigm shift problem, Chapter 2 will first examine the basic pricing elements of life insurance—mortality costs (rates), operation expenses, and interest (or earnings)—and the interaction between these pricing elements that, all too often, tends to be ignored. This chapter will include a discussion of the concepts behind mortality tables that are the basis of all life insurance policies. The simplest application of mortality tables to life insurance products is to term life insurance. Hence, this product will be examined and discussed, including the limitations of term insurance

---

10. Edward E. Graves, Editor, *McGill's Life Insurance, 9th Edition*, The American College, Bryn Mawr, Pennsylvania, 2013, pages 5.17–5.19.

that led to the development of permanent or whole life insurance that will also be examined and discussed.

In the general examination—and evolution—of permanent life insurance products, this book will explore the purely guaranteed whole life product design in addition to the non-guaranteed design elements of universal life-type products. The effect of assuming a constant rate of interest on non-guaranteed policy cash value reserves—or the earnings on policy sub-accounts in variable universal life-type products—used in life insurance policy illustrations are graphically compared and analyzed to rates of returns that vary but average the same overall return as the constant assumption used in the policy illustrations, and all too often used to determine the funding premium level of universal life products. The effect of the results of the difference from assuming a constant rate of return versus the more realistic varying rates of return on the interplay between the pricing elements of the life insurance policy will be graphically demonstrated and explained.

Risks inherent with life insurance will be considered and explained in Chapter 3, including the risks associated with some of the more common product types such as:

- Purchasing power risks, which are all too often ignored with the emphasis on minimum premium types of product.
- Product suitability that will explore the changing needs for life insurance over the life of a policy, product type appropriateness based on risk tolerance and the preference for either the lowest possible premium or growth in the death benefit and cash values of the policy, and the effect of changing premium paying capacity. Part of the product suitability discussion will consider the need for policy replacement and/or the option of a life settlement.
- Since life insurance by itself is a concentrated asset, the need for diversification by either multiple life insurance carriers or by different product types, or both, will be considered.

Risk management requires a process and life insurance is no exception. Hence, in Chapter 4, the process of managing life insurance policies will be discussed, particularly noting the need for a life insurance policy management or investment policy statement. Part of the management process will explore the value and need to use personalized life expectancy report assessments.

Chapter 5 of this book will analyze the creditable evaluation of life insurance, particularly non-guaranteed flexible premium life insurance policies. In 1992, a Society of Actuaries task force on policy illustrations presented their findings and report on the use of policy illustrations with non-guaranteed elements and values.[11] Similarly, the Financial Industry Regulatory Authority (FINRA) promulgated

---

11. *Final Report of the Task Force for Research on Life Insurance Sales Illustrations under the Auspices of the Committee for Research on Social* Concerns, Transactions of the Society of Actuaries 1991–92 Reports, Society of Actuaries, 1992.

FINRA Rule 2210, part of which dealt with the use of hypothetical policy illustrations in variable life products to project or predict values, or to compare products.[12] Both the Society of Actuaries and FINRA rule made it clear that policy illustrations could not be used to project or predict, or compare, non-guaranteed policy values. Despite these authoritative pronouncements against the use of policy illustrations to project or predict non-guaranteed policy values, or to compare one life insurance policy to another, too many financial planners and life insurance professionals are ignoring these directives and are improperly using policy illustrations to evaluate non-guaranteed life insurance.[13] After describing what are not acceptable methods of evaluation for non-guaranteed life insurance products, we will explore the criteria that is required and the methods for acceptable evaluation of non-guaranteed life insurance products. Finally, we will present the application of a method that meets such criteria to a real-life example to demonstrate the creditable evaluation of non-guaranteed flexible premium products.

Last before the conclusion in Chapter 7, but certainly not least, Chapter 6 will discuss and provide practical questions and guidelines to acquiring and managing life insurance in order to avoid a client crisis. Life insurance needs to be properly acquired and managed through a process. The practical questions and guidelines in Chapter 6 are designed to assist policy owners in developing a thoughtful life insurance program by implementing prudent systematic procedures for purchasing and managing their life insurance policy or policy portfolio, to maximize the probability of successful long-term outcomes tailored to their individual unique goals, needs, and objectives.

Additionally, to give diverse insights that either reinforce, expand, or provide different perspectives than those composed by the author, the end of the book contains a section of Contributed Articles from nationally known practitioners and advisers from the legal, actuarial, financial, and trust fields with extraordinary expertise in life insurance. These articles from notable, knowledgeable authors illustrate and offer unique viewpoints and thoughts on the topics covered. They truly expand the concepts and ideas of "Explaining the Unexplainable."

---

12. FINRA Rule 2210—IM-2210-2, Communications with the Public about Variable Life Insurance.
13. Whitelaw and Montag, *supra*, note 1, page 4 and footnote 8 on page 4.

Chapter 2

Toward Understanding Life Insurance and the Risk Transfer Paradigm Shift— Some Life Insurance Basics[14]

The Building Blocks of Life Insurance

Life Insurance Pricing

One of the first things taught to new life insurance professionals about any life insurance policy are the three basic pricing elements that determine the cost of life insurance:

1. Mortality, or the rate of death claims for a given age, sex, and other demographic characteristics such as occupation risk, income, smoking status and other health characteristics
2. Expenses, or the overhead and cost involved in the setup and management of a life insurance policy that include administration expenses, ongoing service expense, and the cost of initiating the life insurance policy that includes marketing, underwriting, and the paying of commissions
3. Interest, or the investment returns that can be either an interest credited or earned on premiums paid, or the earnings of the separate sub-account investments in variable life insurance products

---

14. While the material on life insurance policies primarily centers around single life insurance products, the principles and concepts discussed are just as relevant and germane to joint and survivorship life insurance products.

Life insurance is a "group thing." By that it is meant that when actuaries price out and design a new life insurance product, it is done in the aggregate considering prospective groups of insured individuals as a whole, and the product as a complete "block" or separate group of business, as opposed to each individual policy. In fact, it is the application of the "law of large numbers"—a large sample or a large group of individuals—that makes the mathematics of life insurance, and other types of insurance, work so well to the economic benefit of society.

In addition, there are two other important pricing elements. The first is the profit margin that is added into the expense element, and can be added to the other two pricing elements. The second is really associated with the profit margin and is referred to as persistence or the lapse rate. Persistence refers to the total number of policies that were underwritten in year "X," and how many of those policies are on the books at the end of each policy year. Or, in other words, what is the rate of lapse for each policy year. Because of the extremely high expenses of putting the business on the books in the first policy year, generally, it takes about three years before the typical policy breaks even on a yearly basis, and from seven to 15 years to fully amortize the first year's expenses. Thus, high persistency (a low lapse rate) in the early policy years is extremely important and crucial to profitability.

However, it can be argued that at a certain point in the block or book of life insurance policies, a high lapse rate is desirable in order to avoid paying future death claims. Of course, there is always the phenomenon known as adverse selection, meaning less healthy individuals tend to maintain their life insurance longer than healthy individuals. This is particularly true with yearly renewable term insurance policies wherein the premium increases each year and rises exponentially at older ages. Mortality tables (discussed below) build in safety factors and cushions to safeguard against the occurrence of adverse selection. Nonetheless, it is interesting to note that according to a study that is rather old, only 1 percent of term insurance policies result in a death claim.[15] In a more recent research study, Richard M. Weber and Christopher Hause constructed a model to access the payout ratio for 20-year level term insurance on a 45-year-old non-smoking male. Using 2001 Valuation Basic Table (VBT) mortality rates and assuming a level 10 percent lapse rate that was derived from recent Society of Actuaries and Life Insurance Marketing Research Association data on term lapse rates, Weber and Hause concluded "that approximately 85% of policy owners lapse their policy before the end of the twenty-year term period, meaning roughly 2.5% collect a death benefit, and the remaining 12.5% survive to the end of the term period."[16] Those surviving to the end of the

---

15. Arthur L. Williams, "Some Empirical Observations on Term Life Insurance," *The Journal of Risk and Insurance, Vol. 31 No. 3* (September 1964), pages 445–450.

16. Richard M. Weber and Christopher Hause, *Life Insurance as an Asset Class: A Value Added Component of an Asset Allocation*, Ethical Edge Insurance Solution, LLC, Pleasant Hill, California, 2009, endnote 29, pages 102–103.

20-year level term period who are now 65 and experiencing prohibitively high premium renewal rates would probably lapse the term coverage unless they are uninsurable and unable to purchase another policy. The author could find no compatible statistics or research for permanent insurance (i.e., whole life and universal life).[17]

As noted previously, profit margins can be embedded into each of the three basic pricing elements. For example, a profit margin can be part of mortality costs, gross interest or returns earned on general account assets and separate accounts net of that credited to the policy owner, and expense charges. In fact, positive variations in the pricing elements of life insurance represent surplus or profit for the insurer. In mutual insurance companies that write participating whole life insurance and other participating policies, these favorable deviations comprise the components for dividend payments to policy holders.

Lack of Transparency

Unfortunately, when it comes to the itemization of these three basic pricing elements that make up the cost of a life insurance policy, there is a considerable lack of transparency. Granted, perhaps, that the cost of one-year term insurance represents the cost most closely related to the probability of death within a year—hence, replicating the "true" mortality cost element—the one-year term life insurance purchaser has no way of knowing what part of this premium cost is the carrier's actual pure mortality cost; what part of the premium cost is due to contingency margins, reserve requirements, and margins for adverse selection; the effective interest rate that represents the time value of money on premiums paid, plus earnings over and above the time value of money; and what portion of the premium cost is allocated to expenses that would include profit margins, commissions, underwriting costs, premium taxes, the deferred acquisition charges tax (known as the DAC tax), overhead charges, and the effect of lapsed policies, all of which can vary by policy year or duration.

Gross premiums[18] paid into whole life insurance policies and the embedded internal costs of such policies have long been criticized for a complete lack of

---

17. In an article published by Marianne Purushotham, FSA, a Research Actuary in the Products Research department of the Life Insurance Marketing Research Association, referred to as LIMRA International, it was argued that such statistics as the amount of policies that resulted in a death claim were a misuse and misrepresentation of statistics for various reasons cited in her article. When the author asked LIMRA to furnish such data, LIMRA refused, referencing the article of Ms. Purushotham of which they graciously sent the author a copy. In the author's humble opinion, this is just part of the lack of transparency of the life insurance industry. See Marianne Purushotham, FSA, "Industry Statistics: Use and Misuse," *LIMRA's Marketfacts Quarterly/Summer 2006*.

18. In traditional term and whole life insurance, gross premiums are the premiums actually charged and paid by the policy owner. The gross premium is the net premium plus expenses, contingency, and profit margins. For statutory legal reserve purposes, and actuarial parlance, in traditional whole life policies the net premium is derived using only the statutory guaranteed mortality tables—such as the 2001 Commissioners Standard Ordinary (CSO) Mortality Table—and the minimum guaranteed interest rate specified in the policy. Thus, no expenses or contingency or profit margins—other than contingency margins that are contained in the statutory guaranteed mortality

transparency. All of the aforementioned internal cost elements for one-year term insurance are compounded with issues concerning the cash value reserve. The interest rate credited to the cash value reserve is guaranteed and stated in the policy. The guaranteed cash value calculation method is also stated in the policy but the calculations to derive the cash value[19] are not shown in either the policy contract or the policy illustration accompanying the whole life policy. What is shown is the cash surrender value for each year of the policy, and after somewhere between the first eight to 15 years is equal to the cash reserve value of the policy. During the first eight- to 15-year duration of the policy, the cash value internally is reduced by surrender charges. The surrender charges are generally reduced each year on a straight-line basis equaling zero at the end of the surrender charge period. The actual surrender charges and their specific composition are unknown to the policy owner but represent the recovery of the heavy up-front first-year acquisition expenses and charges to set up the policy, such as first-year commissions paid including overrides to managers and general agents; marketing costs; underwriting costs such as medical exams and attending physician statements and so on. This amortization of what amounts to contingent deferred sales charges over the first eight to 15 years of the policy is also referred to as back-end loading of the first-year expenses.

Similarly, in participating whole life policies that are generally issued by mutual insurance companies and pay dividends to the policy owner, the calculations and specific methods used to determine policy dividends are completely unknown to the policy owner, other than some companies may mention the interest earnings factor used to calculate the dividends. Dividends in life insurance—which are not and cannot be guaranteed—are legally a return of premium based on favorable experience over that guaranteed in the policy such as higher than expected investment returns and/or lower than expected mortality and/or expenses of operation;[20] but the itemization and calculation of this favorable experience is totally unknown to the policy owner.

---

table—are used to derive the net premium. The gross premium can be less than the net premium, which could be the case for competitive reasons and when the actual experience of the issuing carrier relative to mortality and/or interest earnings is more favorable than that of the guaranteed values. However, the net premium and the guaranteed mortality and interest rate are used for all statutory legal reserve calculations.

19. In actuarial parlance, the cash value is referred to as the terminal reserve. It is calculated based on the net premium—not the gross premium—the guaranteed interest rate specified in the policy, and the guaranteed mortality rates specified in the statutory mortality table used to calculate the net premium and stated in the policy.

20. Because legally dividends are a return of premium they are nontaxable until the total dividends received exceed the policy owner's basis (essentially the total premiums paid) in the policy. IRC § 72(e)(5); Treas. Reg. § 1.72-11(b)(1). Dividends received in cash decrease the basis in the policy. However, dividends received and applied to reduce premiums or purchase paid-up additional insurance have no effect on basis because the dividend received that would reduce the basis is applied, or contributed, back into the policy and, therefore, increases the basis in an amount equal to the dividend. Thus, the effect of the reduce premium or paid-up additional insurance dividend option is a "wash" resulting in no basis increase or decrease in the policy.

One unique feature of universal life policies is the "unbundling" and "detailed" itemized accounting of the expense components, including cost of insurance (mortality) and other expenses, crediting rates to the cash value of the policy, and loans and withdrawals from the cash value of the policy. Unlike whole life policies, the cash value, more commonly referred to as the account value in universal life policies, is shown separately from the cash surrender value. Thus, the surrender charges for the first eight to 15 years of the policy are known. Whole life insurance does not have this "transparency" and operates as a "bundled" package.

Unfortunately, this "transparency" and disclosure of the "actual" cost and earnings elements is not as transparent or comparable among universal life policies. The actual interest rate credited to a regular universal life policy is a discretionary decision of the insurer, over and above the guaranteed crediting rate specified in the policy, and may not reflect the actual earnings on the portfolio of mostly fixed-income securities backing any particular block of universal life policies. As noted by Professor Edward E. Graves in *McGill's Life Insurance, 9th Edition*:

> There have been times when some insurers were reluctant to credit the current interest rate to the policy's cash value. As interest rates were dropping gradually and steadily over the last decade, many insurance companies were hesitant to allow their current interest crediting rate to drop below 10 percent, and interest crediting rates seemed to stick around that point. Eventually, the economic folly of crediting interest rates in excess of actual earnings on the invested assets became apparent, and single-digit interest rates replaced double-digit rates in the crediting formula.[21]

On a similar note, many universal life policies in the 1980s and 1990s had a guaranteed minimum interest crediting rate of 4 to 5 percent, yet the portfolios backing these blocks of universal life policies are now only yielding 2 to 3 percent. Insurance companies can make up this spread between the interest credited and interest actually earned by raising the current mortality rates applied to the cost of insurance and/or raising current expenses. Of course, the insurance companies cannot raise the current mortality rates or current expenses above the maximum rates specified in the policy.

The allocation of operating expenses, contingency margins, and profit margins among the three basic pricing elements of life insurance of mortality, expenses, and interest or earnings is nothing more than a cost accounting decision. "The exact allocation formula is always arbitrary and to some extent guided by the philosophy of the insurance company management team."[22] Because of different cost accounting assumptions and differences in allocation methods used among universal life insurance policies and insurers, without further detailed information and

---

21. Graves, *supra* note 10, page 5.30.
22. Ibid, page 5.32.

itemization of each of the pricing elements, there is, generally, no direct comparability of the pricing elements.[23]

As noted by Kathryn Ballsun, Patrick Collins, and Dieter Jurkat in "Standards of Prudence and Management of the Insurance Portfolio," which was part two of their four-part series on the administration of life insurance as an asset of trust that was published in the *ACTEC Journal*:[24]

> You cannot, for example, assume that the interest rate crediting component in a universal life policy illustration reflects only interest earnings on underlying assets. Although clear disclosure regarding important policy elements was a marketing promise made by insurance carriers when Universal Life products first appeared,

---

23. The purpose of "The Building Blocks of Life Insurance" section is to give an overview of the main pricing or cost elements of a life insurance policy and how because of different cost accounting assumptions and differences in allocation methods, used among various life insurance policies and insurers, various operating expenses, contingency margins and profit margins, etc. may be allocated among the three main pricing elements quite differently. The effect of these differences in allocation of various cost factors is that there is, generally, a complete lack of consistency and no direct comparability of the pricing elements of different life insurance policies; not to mention a complete lack of transparency. The net effect is that life insurance pricing and costs must be viewed as an integrated whole and not separately as individual components.

In an excellent article by Christopher P. Cline and Barry D. Flagg, titled "The Prudent Investor and Trust Owned Life Insurance (TOLI)—Part 2," published in the March/April 2007 *ABA Trusts & Investments*, Cline and Flagg discussed in great detail the individual pricing and cost elements of a life insurance policy and specifically the various methods to charge the policy owner the expenses of a life insurance policy. Essentially there are three types or categories of policy charges in addition to cost of insurance (COI) charges: fixed administration expenses, cash value wrap fees, and premium loads.

Fixed expense fees are generally a flat dollar charge per period or transaction but can also include the surrender charges in the early years of the policy. Cash value-based fees fall into two general categories—investment fund fees and insurance fees—and are charged as a percentage of the cash or account value. Examples of investment fund fees are investment management and advisory fees, and fund operating expenses. These fees are typical in separate account funds with variable universal life insurance. The most common insurance cash value wrap fee is the mortality and expense (M & E) charges intended to cover contingency risk charges not allocated to COIs. Lastly, premiums loads are charges as a percentage of the premium paid and are designed to cover state premium taxes, the federal DAC tax, sales loads, and expenses.

Additionally, the Cline and Flagg article discusses the determination of the rate of policy earnings by pointing out it is necessary to deduct from the gross rate of return not only the investment fund fees, such as fund management and advisory fees, to determine the net rate of return, but to also deduct from the net rate of return the insurance wrap fees, such as M&E charges, to determine the "net net" rate of return. See Christopher P. Cline and Barry D. Flagg, "The Prudent Investor and Trust Owned Life Insurance (TOLI)—Part 2," published in the *ABA Trusts & Investments*, March/April 2007, Institute of Certified Bankers a subsidiary of the American Bankers Association, Washington, D.C., pages 34–49. See also Parts 1 and 3 of that same article published in the January/February 2007 and May/June 2007 issues, pages 38–43 and pages 42–48, respectively, of the same *ABA Trust & Investments* publication.

24. Kathryn A. Ballsun, Patrick J. Collins, and Dieter Jurkat, "Standards of Prudence and Management of the Insurance Portfolio (Part 2 of 4)," ACTEC Journal, Volume 32, The American College of Trust and Estate Counsel, Washington, D.C., 2006, pages 66–90. While written primarily for attorneys and trustees of irrevocable life insurance trusts, the four-part series of articles on the administration of life insurance as an asset of trust is of benefit for prudent management of life insurance for any policy owner. In fact, the author believes that this watershed series of articles should be mandatory reading for life insurance policy owners and their professional advisors. The other parts of the series are "Trustee Administration of Life Insurance (Part 1 of 4)," ACTEC Journal Volume 31, pages 280–301; "Evidencing Care, Skill, and Caution in the Management of ILITs (Part 3 of 4)," ACTEC Journal Volume 32, pages 145–158; and "ILIT Asset Management: The Written Investment Policy Statement (Part 4 of 4)," ACTEC Journal Volume 32, pages 229–259.

"not only are high early expenses now covered by a surrender charge, but mortality charges may frequently include expense or income tax, and interest rates credited may even be reduced by expense costs other than investment expense."[25]

Weber and Hause succinctly summed up the transparency issues with universal life policies as follows:

Transparency—when UL [universal life] policies were first introduced, one of the most appealing aspects of this new policy style was the *transparency* of policy expenses and credits. Unlike whole life policies, UL had discrete elements of expenses, cost of insurance charges, and current interest credits. Consumers believed that each major expense/credit element "stood on its own." Unfortunately, the reality of independently setting crediting rates and expense and scales of COI [cost of insurance] quickly succumbed to market competition, and it was easier to illustrate the "best" product by currently paying a somewhat higher interest crediting rate than the competition (and compensating by somewhat increasing expenses and/or COI). Today there is virtually no comparability of interest crediting rates or expenses between seemingly comparable policy styles.[26]

Life Insurance Pricing and Costs Must Be Viewed Integrated as a Whole and Not Separately

Professor Graves best describes this concept as follows:

Interest crediting rates have been the focal point of most of the competition among companies selling universal life policies. There has been very little emphasis on the mortality rates charged or the expense charges levied against incoming premiums. In reality, all three concepts constitute the total cost of insurance. Interest rates can be (and have been) intentionally elevated to a level above what the investment portfolio actually supported, but they are still viable because of compensating higher levels of mortality charges and expense deductions. When consumers choose to focus only on one of the three elements, it is not surprising that the marketing efforts zero in on that element. The assessment of overall policy efficiency requires that all factors be considered in concert.[27]

Additionally, a change in one of the three pricing or cost elements affects at least one, if not two, of the other elements. For example, a decrease in the interest or earnings element has the effect of decreasing the cash value, which raises the

25. Ibid, page 89 (quoting Albert E. Easting and Timothy F. Harris, *Actuarial Aspects of Individual Life Insurance and Annuity Contracts*, ACTEC Publications, Winstead, Connecticut, 1999, pages 46–47).

26. Richard M. Weber and Christopher Hause, *Life Insurance as an Asset Class: Managing a Valuable Asset*, Ethical Edge Insurance Solutions, LLC, Pleasant Hills, California, 2010, pages 78–79.

27. Graves, *supra* note 10, pages 5.30–5.31.

pure protection element—commonly referred to as the net amount at risk[28]—of the policy. This in turn raises the cost of insurance (COI), which is the product of the net amount at risk multiplied by the mortality rate for that particular attained age of the insured. Similarly, an increase in current mortality rates would increase the COI, which would in turn decrease the cash value and increase the net amount at risk going forward.

In summary, the three pricing elements do not operate separately but must be considered together in total as an integrated whole. Or, as so succinctly stated by Ballsun, Collins, and Jurkat, "[t]he determinants of illustrated policy dollar values cannot be disentangled."[29]

Pricing Assumptions of Life Insurance and Risk Transfer

All pricing and cost elements in life insurance policies are based on assumptions—that is, the mortality experience, expenses incurred, and earnings on premium dollars all have to be assumed in designing and constructing a life insurance product. The time frame for these assumptions is mind-boggling. The 2001 and 2017 Commissioners Standard Ordinary (CSO) Mortality Tables, which are the statutory tables that define maximum guaranteed mortality rates, extend to an age of 121, at which point it is actuarially assumed everyone is dead. Thus, if a life insurance policy is underwritten on an infant, that policy could be in force for 121 years. A policy written on a 25-year-old life could easily be in force to at least age 85 or 90, or a time span of at least 60 or 65 years.

Assumptions in the design of life insurance policies fall into two categories: The first category is where the benefit results of the assumptions are guaranteed by the insurer—that is, for a guaranteed premium payment amount over a guaranteed specified premium payment period, the death benefit is either guaranteed for a specific period, or to be paid either at the death of the insured or to the policy owner for the face amount of the policy at a point that is the end of the mortality table, such as age 121; and, a cash value amount at various durations of the policy may also be guaranteed. In other words, with life insurance product types in this category, the insurer is **guaranteeing the results** of the assumptions and the **performance risk is retained by the insurance carrier**.

---

28. The concept of the net amount at risk and its effect on permanent life insurance policies will be discussed in detail in subsequent sections of this chapter. Suffice it say for now that the net amount at risk is equal to the face amount of the insurance policy less the cash value of the policy at any particular attained age or duration of the policy. In the design of permanent life insurance products, over time the cash value increases and the net amount at risk decreases. This phenomenon is what makes permanent, level premium life insurance affordable to cover an insured individual to the end of the maximum age on a mortality table. At this maximum age of the mortality table used in a life insurance policy—either age 100 or age 121 depending on the issue date of the policy—if the insured has not already died, the policy will mature, and endow and pay to the insured the face amount of the policy. At this point in the policy the cash value will equal the face amount and the net amount at risk is zero.

29. Ballsun, Collins, and Jurkat, *supra* note 24, page 89.

The second category of assumptions for life insurance product types is where "current" assumptions—not guaranteed assumptions—are used to price and project the benefits of the policy. Current assumptions are based on recent experience of the insurance carrier with respect to mortality experience, expenses for the product type, and earnings on the portfolio of assets that back the reserves of the policy type. The premiums and premium-paying period for these types of products are not fixed or guaranteed but are "indeterminate" and flexible. Thus, other than a minimum required premium for the first year of the policy, the determination of the premium funding amount is up to the policy owner. Generally, with these types of products, the premium payments are based on these current pricing assumptions, but the adequacy and sufficiency of the premium to sustain the policy to a point desired by the policy owner and receive the benefit results originally projected for the policy is not guaranteed by the insurance carrier. Current assumptions can and do change in the life of the policy that will affect the amount of the premium payment needed to achieve the policy owner's desired results and objectives. Thus, if the assumed earnings on premium dollars decrease and/or the current mortality rates used to determine the COI increase, additional premium payments will be needed to achieve the original objectives of the policy. However, all of these products have guaranteed maximum mortality rates, generally based on statutory mortality tables such as the 2001 Commissioners Standard Ordinary (CSC) Mortality Table, and guaranteed maximum expense charges. Additionally, some product types have a guaranteed minimum interest crediting rate on cash values. There is, however, a lot of wiggle room between the maximum guaranteed mortality rates and expense charges. For example, it is not unusual for current mortality rates to be half of the maximum mortality rates. With life insurance products in this category the **method of calculating the results** of the current assumptions **is guaranteed but not the results** and the **performance risk is transferred to the policy owner and not retained by the insurance carrier**.

Product types that have fixed guaranteed premiums include term insurance, whole life insurance, and no-lapse secondary guarantee universal life insurance, the latter of which is also referred to as guaranteed universal life insurance. In **fixed premium guaranteed products**, the **performance risk is retained by the carrier**.

Product types that have indeterminate, flexible premiums include universal life insurance, variable universal life insurance, and indexed universal life insurance, the latter of which is also referred to as equity indexed universal life insurance. In other words, all of the universal life insurance-type products except the no-lapse secondary guaranteed universal life or guaranteed universal life. In **indeterminate flexible premium products**, the **performance risk is transferred to the policy owner**.

It should be noted that there are certain "blended" types of products that have part guaranteed and part non-guaranteed elements. The most common example of this type of product is a product with a base whole life policy in combination with a paid-up additions and decreasing term dividend option and/or paid-up additions rider. In this product, the base whole life is fully guaranteed. But the dividend option of paid-up additions and decreasing term insurance—where the term insurance face amount decreases by the face amount of each paid-up additional insurance dividend—is not guaranteed and is based on favorable experience of the insurance carrier of either increased earnings above guaranteed interest rates and/or mortality or expenses less than what is guaranteed in the contract. Here the non-guaranteed dividend declared by the insurance carrier could be insufficient—particularly in the later years of the policy—to support the decreasing term dividend face amount, with the result that the face amount of the policy supported by paid-up additional insurance and the decreasing term could be less than the original total face amount of the policy. In **blended part-guaranteed products, some of the performance risk is retained by the carrier (the guaranteed part) and some of the performance risk is transferred to the policy owner.**

Understanding Mortality Tables and Life Expectancy

Mortality Tables

The "cost" of life insurance is most dramatically and predominately affected by the probability of death for any insured in any given year of a life insurance policy. These probabilities of death are contained in various tables that are referred to as mortality tables.

Mortality tables are constructed by actuaries based on the ages of death of various members of large population groups over a period of years. These tables may be for aggregate groups—such as the set of United States Life Tables published as a by-product of the decennial census for the total population and each of several subpopulations—or tables may be for groups with specific characteristics and criteria—such as insured preferred risk, non-smoking females earning more than $100,000 per year. Additionally, the National Association of Insurance Commissioners (NAIC) has developed what are known as statutory tables for the purposes of calculating the legal reserves or liabilities required to be reported on an insurer's balance sheet, and to calculate guaranteed mortality rates and minimum surrender values contained in insurance policies, an example of which are the 2001 CSO Mortality Tables. Various private actuarial firms and insurance companies create proprietary tables with specific characteristics and purposes. All life insurers use proprietary tables to calculate gross premiums and mutual life insurers use these proprietary tables to calculate policy dividends.

Using the data from either the aggregate population group or groups chosen with specific characteristics, the probability of death at any age is derived. The probability of death increases with age, although there have been "blips" at young ages, and some smoothing of the data can occur. One of these blips, or humps, occurred in the 1980 CSO Mortality Table death rates for males between ages ten and 29.[30] In this table for males, because of deaths due to auto accidents, homicides, drug overdoses, and suicides, death rates reached a low at age ten and rose to a high at age 21—the hump—then decreased to age 28, at which point thereafter the rates rose for each age.[31] Because of the sample data size relative to the theoretical population of the group, there may be instances in the data where the probability of death does not increase for each attained age. In these instances, actuaries have developed methods, called graduation techniques, to produce a smooth set of rates from the initial non-smooth set where the probability of death increases with each age. This is done for both theoretical and practical reasons. From a theoretical standpoint, resistance to disease declines as we age and the degeneration of the body system over time increases in continuous and minute graduations. From a practical standpoint, it is not desirable to have a pattern of mortality rates that are irregular by age because then the premiums and reserves based on those rates would also have to be irregular.[32]

In every mortality table constructed an age must be assumed in which death by that age is a certainty. In other words, by a certain age death has to occur and the probability of death at that age is 100 percent. For official tables constructed prior to 2001 that maximum age, or terminal age, was 100. For official tables constructed in 2001 and 2017 the maximum age is 121. With increases in longevity, could the next generation of mortality tables have a maximum age of 150?

Life Expectancy

"Life expectancy" is often a misunderstood term. All life expectancy is measured, and has to be measured, from a specified starting age, such as age 0, 25, 35, and so on. Life expectancy also increases as the starting point age increases. Life expectancy is also generally measured with respect to specific groups with common characteristics or risks (i.e., preferred risk females age 50 non-smokers, standard risk males age 25 smokers). However, life expectancy can be measured with respect to large aggregate groups, such as all males age 45.

Life expectancy represents, for a particular group with a stated starting point age, the medium age or midpoint where half of the group members from the common starting point are deceased and half of the group members are survivors. Life expectancy, therefore, represents the 50-percentile mark.

---

30. This pronounced blip did not occur in prior CSO tables and in the 2001 and 2017 CSO tables that succeeded the 1980 CSO Mortality Table.

31. See Graves, *supra* note 10, at page 9.20.

32. Ibid, page 9.9.

Figure 2.1 is a graphical representation of the expected number of deceased and expected number of survivors, by attained age, for a group of 10,000,000[33] preferred risk age 50 female non-smokers based on the 2001 CSO Mortality Table[34] using select and ultimate mortality rates.[35] The curve running from the bottom left of the graph to the upper right of the graph represents the total number of deceased individual members of the group at each attained age. The curve running from the upper left of the graph to the bottom right of the graph represents the total number of surviving individual members of the group at each attained age. The point, or attained age, where the two curves intersect—that is, where the total number of deceased individuals of the group equal the total number of the surviving individuals of the group—is the life expectancy for this group of preferred risk age 50 female non-smokers, which is approximately 86 years of age.

The 2001 CSO Mortality Tables were the first tables to include rates that were broken down into five separate "standard" risk classifications, as well as composite rates for the five classifications. The five risk classifications, in order of life expectancy, are residual standard smoker, preferred smoker, residual standard

---

33. The starting point of the number of lives in a mortality table is called the "radix." The radix is an arbitrary number chosen such that the number of lives dying near the end of the maximum ages on the mortality table is a whole number.

34. The examples and graphical figures representing mortality and/or policy values in this book, unless otherwise stated, were prepared and written primarily in 2017 and 2018 utilizing the 2001 CSO Mortality Tables, and prior to the mandatory use of the 2017 CSO Mortality Tables. For all policies issued on, or after, January 1, 2020, NAIC requires the use of the 2017 CSO Mortality Tables in computing guaranteed mortality rates and values that include the net premium reserves, nonforfeiture determinations, and the caps for universal life cost of insurance charges.

The 2017 CSO Mortality Tables reflect improvements in longevity since the 20-years-plus data used in the preparation of the 2001 CSO Mortality Tables. Additionally, the statistical data collected for the 2017 CSO Mortality Tables, as opposed to the 2001 CSO Mortality Tables, encompasses larger sample populations and experiences from a greater number of insurance carriers. Like the 2001 CSO Mortality Tables, the 2017 CSO Mortality Tables have a terminal age of 121; have the same five "Preferred Structure Tables" with underwriting classifications of super preferred, preferred non-smoker, residual standard non-smoker, preferred smoker, and residual standard smoker, plus a composite table; and have a 25-year period for select rates before reaching ultimate rates (see subsequent footnote). The derived net premiums for whole life policies using the 2017 CSO Mortality Tables are, naturally, lower than the 2001 CSO Mortality Tables due to the improvement in longevity reflected in mortality rates for younger attained ages. Similarly, net premium reserves are also, generally, lower. See Joint American Academy of Actuaries' Life Experience Committee and Society of Actuaries Preferred Mortality Oversight Group CSO Development Subgroup, "Report on the 2017 CSO Preferred Structure Table Development," October 2015, https://www.soa.org/Files/Research/Exp-Study/research-2017-cso-report.pdf.

Conceptually the ideas, concepts, and principles espoused in this book are not affected by whatever mortality table is used, and are the same regardless of the mortality table used. Actuarial evaluation, discussed in Chapter 5, would not be affected since actuarially certified policy benchmark standards are derived utilizing current experience data and not guaranteed mortality rates as reflected in the CSO Mortality Tables.

35. "Select" mortality rates are those mortality rates used for individuals who have recently provided evidence of insurability. However, the effects of providing evidence of insurability at the issuance of an insurance policy wear off and diminish over time such that they become equal to the "ultimate" mortality rates. Ultimate mortality rates are those rates where the effects of the initial selection process have completely worn off and the mortality experience is the same as for individuals who have not provided evidence of insurability. In the 2001 and 2017 CSO tables, select rates are shown for the first 25 years after the issuance age of a policy. The select rates diminish or amortize over a 25-year period to then equal the ultimate rates. The previous 1980 CSO tables were the first tables to provide select and ultimate mortality rates. However, the 1980 CSO tables only provided for a five-year select period before the select rates equaled the ultimate rates.

non-smoker, preferred non-smoker, and super preferred non-smoker; with life expectancy for females age 50 of approximate ages of 76, 80, 83, 86, and 87, respectfully. The composite life expectancy for the group was approximately age 84. Figure 2.2 depicts the cumulative deaths by age for groups of 10,000,000 insured age 50 females for these five risk classifications, as well as the composite of the five risk classifications, and the respective life expectancies.

Figure 2.1 Mortality Tables and Life Expectancy

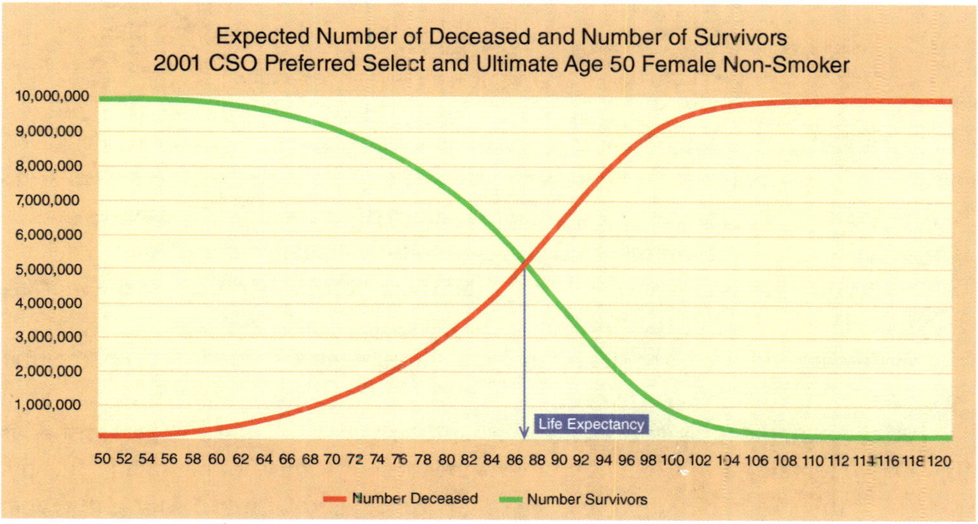

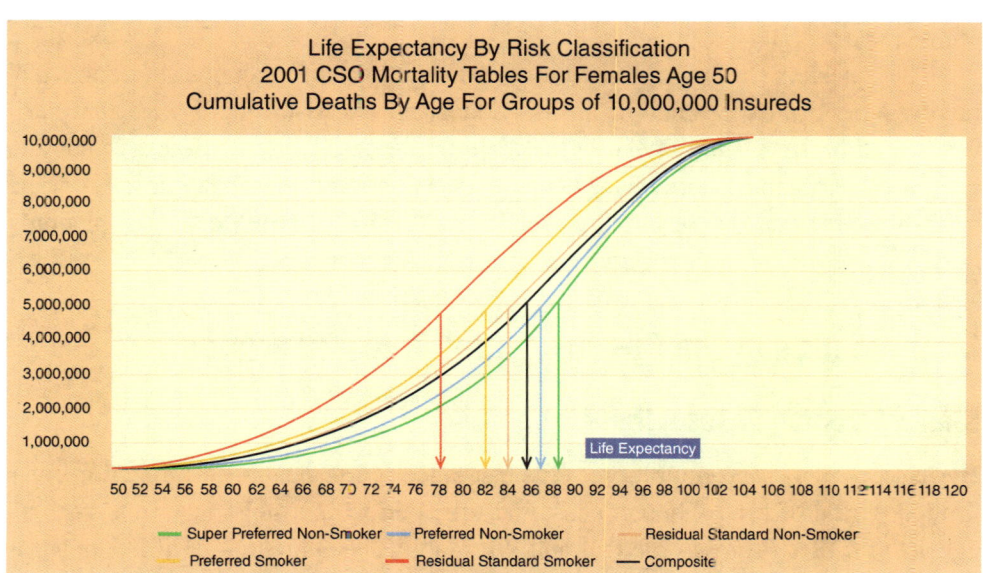

Figure 2.2 Life Expectancy by Risk Classification

Two Additional Points about Life Expectancy

The life expectancy for an individual and the resulting mortality curve over time can shift due to changes in the individual's health, occupation, and/or avocation. For example, one of the individual females who at age 50 would be classified as a preferred non-smoker, at age 60 either has developed a health condition that is not immediately life threatening but that has the effect of shortening her life expectancy, or has decided to become a competitive race car driver. Obviously, either one of these circumstances at age 60 would have the effect of reducing her life expectancy and shifting her to a less favorable mortality curve than the one she experienced at age 50.

As stated previously, life expectancy represents the medium age or midpoint where half of the group members from a common starting point are deceased and half of the group members are survivors. Thus, life expectancy represents the 50-percentile mark. However, for planning and risk management purposes—such as retirement benefit planning or funding premium management of universal life insurance policies—we may wish to consider other percentile points on the mortality curve. Depending on risk tolerances for planning horizon purposes, a planner may wish to consider a 70-percentile point, a 90-percentile point, or a 95-percentile point in life expectancy.

As an example, going back to our preferred age 50 non-smoker group of 10,000,000 females, Figure 2.3 reproduces the mortality curve of cumulative deaths by age for this group based on the 2001 CSO Select and Ultimate Mortality Table for this risk classification. As shown on the graph, and previously mentioned, the 50-percentile life expectancy age is 86. However, as also shown on the graph, the 70-percentile life expectancy point is age 91, and the 90-percentile life expectancy point is age 96.

The question becomes, based on various types of planning horizons that involved the life expectancy of an individual, and the risk tolerance of that individual and/or the planner, what is the appropriate percentile of life expectancy to use for these planning horizons? Once that decision has been made, the appropriate mortality table can be consulted to determine the age to be used for the planning horizon time period of the desired percentile life expectancy.

Mathematics of the Cost of "Pure" Term Insurance

Characteristics of Term Insurance

By its very name and definition, term insurance is life insurance protection for a limited period of time. Theoretically that time period can range from one year till age 100 or 121. From a practical and affordability standpoint—term insurance is ridiculously expensive at older ages—term insurance is generally issued with level

Figure 2.3 Life Expectancy—Percentile

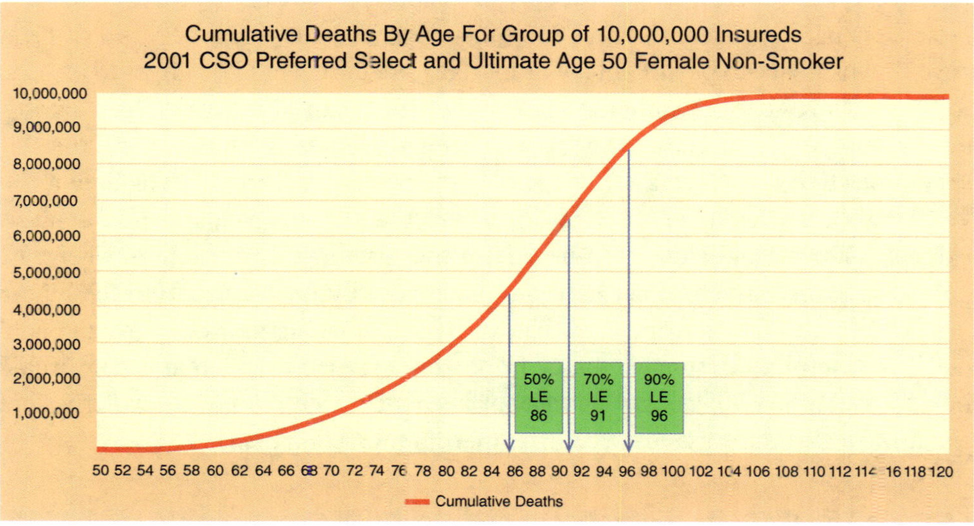
Cumulative Deaths By Age For Group of 10,000,000 Insureds
2001 CSO Preferred Select and Ultimate Age 50 Female Non-Smoker
10,000,000
9,000,000
8,000,000
7,000,000
6,000,000
5,000,000
4,000,000
3,000,000
2,000,000
1,000,000
50% LE 86
70% LE 91
90% LE 96
50 52 54 56 58 60 62 64 66 68 70 72 74 76 78 80 82 84 86 88 90 92 94 96 98 100 102 104 106 108 110 112 114 116 118 120
Cumulative Deaths

premium payments for periods of one, five, ten, fifteen, twenty, or thirty years, or to ages 55, 60, 65, 70, or 75. To a limited extent, term insurance is guaranteed renewable—generally not past ages 60, 65, or 70—for the same time period as the original term period, but at higher premiums, which because of adverse selection[36] and increased age can be substantial. Most term policies also have a feature—known as the convertibility feature—that allows for the term life insurance policy to be converted to a permanent type of life insurance plan—permanent life insurance will be discussed later in this chapter—offered by the insurance carrier without providing evidence of insurability. However, this right to exercise and convert the policy to a permanent policy generally expires a few years before the maximum period of coverage, with renewals, and/or at a specific age—such as age 55 or 60—which would be at least a few years less than the maximum age covered by the policy.[37] Traditionally, a term life insurance policy owner could convert the term life insurance into any permanent plan offered at the time of conversion by the insurance carrier. However, some insurance carriers are now severely limiting the permanent policy in which the term life insurance can be converted to a permanent policy with premium rates loaded for a heavy factor of adverse selection.[38]

---

36. When premiums increase on term life insurance policies—or for that matter on health and medical insurance policies—there is a tendency for healthy insureds to either drop the coverage or seek lower cost insurance. Less healthy individuals, or those individuals who are uninsurable, renew the coverage at the higher premiums. This phenomenon where unhealthy individuals renew and healthy individuals tend to drop the coverage is referred to as adverse selection.

37. This restriction in the time limit to convert the term insurance policy into a permanent policy before the end of the renewal period is for the purposes of limiting and discouraging adverse selection.

38. This has been done with conversion privileges for group term life insurance coverage for years.

Term life insurance is best to use in two situations: The first situation is where the need for life insurance protection is a temporary need and not a long-term or permanent need for life insurance. Some examples of a temporary need would be to have life insurance to pay off a loan or mortgage in the event of death, or to provide for a child's college education in the event of the death of a parent. What constitutes a "temporary" need time period is debatable. Clearly if the need for life insurance protection is ten years or less, term insurance is ideal, possibly as long as 30 years, but clearly less than life expectancy, which will become clear in a subsequent example. The second situation where term life insurance is suitable is where the policy owner has a permanent need but is temporarily unable to afford the higher initial premiums for permanent protection. In this situation, the policy owner could purchase a term life insurance policy from a highly rated carrier that is convertible into a suitable plan of quality permanent insurance once the policy owner is in a situation to afford the premiums of a permanent protection plan.

"Pay as You Go" Life Insurance

Essentially the annual cost of term life insurance is based on the probability of death for each year. Obviously, because the probability of death increases each year, and escalates exponentially at older ages, the premiums for term insurance increase each year and escalate exponentially at older ages. Term insurance premiums that are a reasonable cost at "younger" ages become an unaffordable cost at "older" ages.

Mathematics of the Cost of "Pure" Term Insurance

The premiums for one-year term insurance represent the cost most closely related to the probability of death within each year of coverage. Thus, the policy owner is directly paying each year the cost associated with the probability of death for each year. That means the policy owner is literally paying the direct costs each year associated with the curve of the mortality table. As stated previously, this premium cost will naturally increase each year and will escalate exponentially at older ages to become unaffordable.

To demonstrate the costs and mathematics of pure term insurance, let's take as an example a 50-year-old female, who is a preferred non-smoker risk classification, who wishes to purchase coverage for a face amount of $1,000,000 of one-year renewable term life insurance. Figure 2.4 graphically depicts, by attained age, the annual and cumulative term premiums to her life expectancy of 86 years, and ten years beyond life expectancy, for the $1,000,000 of term life insurance, with the term insurance premiums based on the 2001 Valuation Basic Table (VBT) rates.

Figure 2.4 Mathematics of the Cost of "Pure" Term Insurance

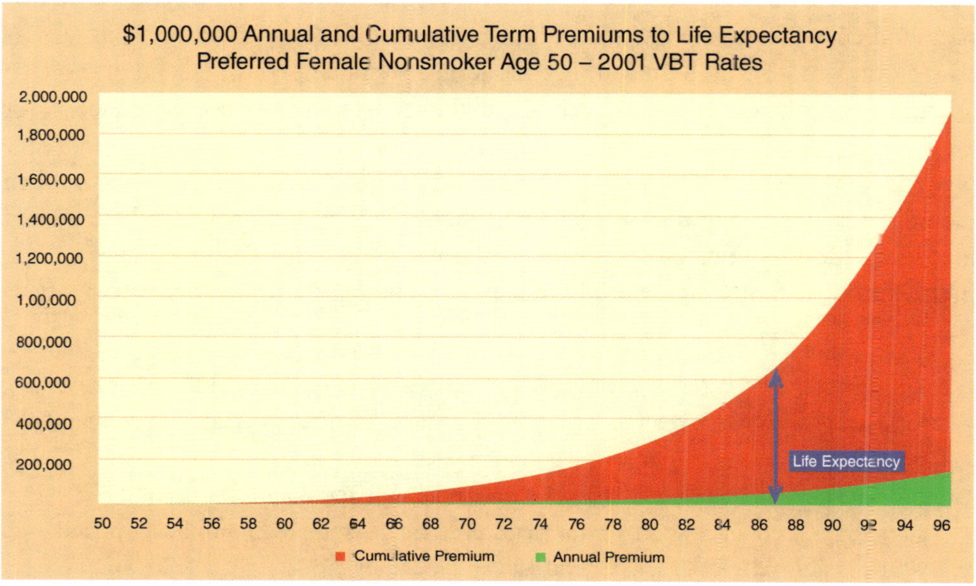

$1,000,000 Annual and Cumulative Term Premiums to Life Expectancy
Preferred Female Nonsmoker Age 50 – 2001 VBT Rates

The total cumulative annual term premium costs (non-interest adjusted) for this $1,000,000 of one-year renewable term life insurance coverage for this 50-year-old female preferred non-smoker risk based on the 2001 VBT rates to her life expectancy of 86 years is $640,900. To her life expectancy plus ten years, or age 96, the total cumulative premium costs is $1,948,420, and to her age 100 the total cumulative premium costs is $2,879,620. You do not want to hear the total cumulative premium costs for beyond age 100.

The obvious conclusion of the mathematics of the cost of pure term life insurance, as demonstrated by the above example, is that for life insurance needs close to life expectancy or beyond life expectancy, clearly term insurance is not the answer and does not work.

Mathematics of "Permanent" Types of Life Insurance— Part 1: Fixed Guaranteed and Constant Assumptions

Creation of Permanent Life Insurance

Recognizing that for needs for life insurance for long periods of time, or close to life expectancy or beyond life expectancy, term insurance is not the solution, actuaries came up with "permanent" life insurance that could cover an insured individual for long-term needs and for "the whole of life." The goal was to make permanent insurance affordable for the insured's entire or "whole life" by levelizing the annual premium cost. Where the payment of a death claim for term insurance is an uncertainty, unless the insured dies during the term insurance period, receiving the face amount of permanent life insurance is a certainty because the life insurance is for the insured's whole life.[39]

The simplified explanation of how actuaries do the calculations to accomplish the objective of making life insurance affordable for the lifetime of the insured and levelizing the premium payment, using the mortality rates for each attained age in the mortality tables—essentially the annual one-year term insurance cost—is as follows:

> The first step is to compute the net present value of all annual mortality (term) costs for each year to the maximum age used in a mortality table to create a "net single premium."
>
> The next step is to take the net single premium and amortize—level it out—taking into account deaths over the year, over the desired premium-paying period, which is generally to the maximum age at the end of the mortality table (i.e., age 100 or 121 under the latest mortality table) to create the "net level annual premium."
>
> The final step is to add policy expenses—which include first-year policy expenses of underwriting and commissions, operating expenses, contingencies, and profit margins—levelized by the same above process taking into account deaths over the years and policy surrender and lapses to create the "gross level annual premium" or "annual gross level premium."
>
> All of the above steps are to be done with a constant assumed rate of interest or earnings.

The first form of this permanent life insurance was called whole life—because it protected the insured for his or her entire life—and the premiums and death benefit, plus the interest rate to calculate such values, were all guaranteed; as is the same case with whole life policies today. In fact, whole life insurance dates back in the United States to 1759 with the formation of the Corporation for Relief of Poor and Distressed Presbyterian Ministers, which became known as the Presbyterian

---

39. The mortality tables that are the basis for life insurance policies have a maximum assumed age at which point it is actuarially assumed that the insured is dead whether or not the insured is actually dead or alive. If the insured is still alive at that maximum assumed age the policy is said to have matured and the total face amount can be paid to the policy owner. Prior to the 2001 CSO Table of Mortality, the maximum age on all prior CSO tables was 100. The 2001 and 2017 CSO Tables of Mortality have a maximum age of 121.

The terms "mature" and "endow" have been used interchangeably in insurance parlance. Endow essentially means to pay off the face amount of the policy. This is not to mean the whole life or universal life policies are endowment policies. Endowment policies act as savings vehicles that pay off the face amount at a specified age, such as age 65, if the insured has not died prior to that age, in which case the face amount would have been paid to the policy beneficiary. Endowment policies while popular in other countries have been eliminated in the United States due to the tax code.

Ministers' Fund.[40] Whole life insurance is derived and calculated based on guaranteed mortality, expenses, and interest rates. However, the same calculation procedure used to create a whole life policy with guaranteed values can be applied to calculate policy values that are not guaranteed but that are based on either current or assumed experience of mortality, expense, or earnings for the life insurance policy. The most prevalent forms today of "current assumption" non-guaranteed "permanent" life insurance are universal life insurance, variable universal life insurance, and indexed universal life insurance.

Mathematics of Permanent Life Insurance Policies

To demonstrate the costs and mathematics of permanent life insurance, let's go back to our example of a 50-year-old female, who is a preferred non-smoker risk classification, who wishes to purchase coverage for a face amount of $1,000,000. However, now instead of purchasing one-year renewable term life insurance, because she has a permanent need for the life insurance coverage, she wishes to consider purchasing, for a $1,000,000 face amount, either a whole life or universal life insurance policy. Using the 2001 CSO Mortality Table and a **constant** interest earnings assumption of 3 percent, and assuming no loading for policy expenses,[41] the calculated net annual premium would be $17,135 to endow the policy at age 121. Figure 2.5 is a graphical depiction of the life insurance policy illustration. If this was a guaranteed whole life policy, or if all the assumptions for the non-guaranteed universal life policy remained constant and did not change throughout the duration of the policy, then this would be an accurate depiction of the policy.

In all life insurance policies where a premium payment is leveled out over a period of years, in the early years of the life insurance policy the premium is greater than the actual mortality COI protection. In the later years of the life insurance policy the actual mortality COI protection is far greater than the level premium payment. The excess premium over the actual mortality costs in the early years of the insurance policy is put into a "reserve" that creates the cash value of the policy.[42] In

---

40. "The Oldest Life Insurance Company in the United States," *The New York Times*, column published November 19, 1905.

41. The annual gross level premium, which is the premium a policy owner pays on a whole life policy, or the planned funding premium for a universal life policy derived based on the linear, constant assumptions for the universal life policy, is generally set using the current versus guaranteed mortality assumptions of the 2001 or 2017 CSO Mortality Tables, and current expenses that include a margin for profit. The annual gross level premium for a whole life policy or the planned funding premium for a universal life policy may be more or less than the net annual premium for a whole life policy derived on only the guaranteed 2001 or 2017 CSO Mortality Tables and a constant assumption guaranteed interest rate, or a planned funding premium based on the 2001 CSO table and an assumed constant interest rate. However, for purposes of demonstrating the effect of a constant interest rate or earnings assumptions and volatile interest or earnings assumptions, we will use the guaranteed mortality rates of the 2001 CSO Mortality Table with no factor for expense or profit loading.

42. In fact, anytime a premium is levelized a reserve is created. This includes term life insurance policies. This reserve, or cash value, in term insurance policies of 20 years or longer, is available to the policy owner similar to permanent life insurance policies. However, in term insurance policies, the reserve reaches a peak and declines to zero at the end of the term policy term.

Figure 2.5 Mathematics of "Permanent" Types of Insurance—Fixed Guaranteed and Constant Assumptions

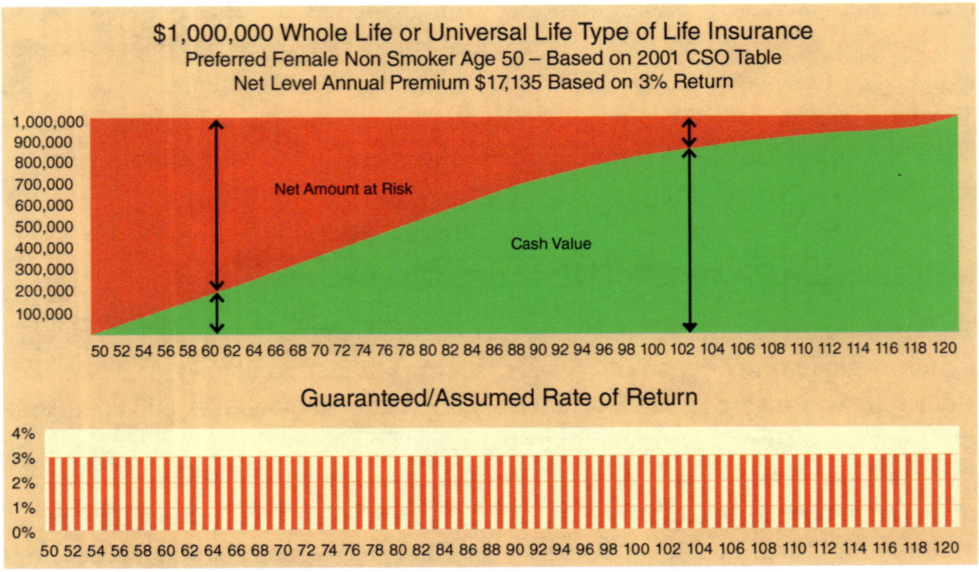

$1,000,000 Whole Life or Universal Life Type of Life Insurance
Preferred Female Non Smoker Age 50 – Based on 2001 CSO Table
Net Level Annual Premium $17,135 Based on 3% Return

Net Amount at Risk

Cash Value

Guaranteed/Assumed Rate of Return

permanent life insurance policies, over time with additional premium payments and earnings on the cash value, this cash value grows to the point at the maximum age of the mortality table—age 121 under the 2001 and 2017 CSO tables—where the cash value is equal to the death benefit of the policy.[43] At any attained age in the life insurance policy this cash value, or reserve, is part of the death benefit. Since the cash value is part of the death benefit at any attained age, the other part of the death benefit payment is represented by what is called the "pure" insurance risk, or more commonly referred to as the "net amount at risk." Thus, at any particular attained age, the death benefit is the sum of the cash value plus the net amount at risk.

As depicted in Figure 2.5, over time the cash value increases and the net amount at risk, or pure insurance protection, decreases. The actual cost of this pure insurance protection at any attained age—referred to as the COI—is equal to the net amount at risk multiplied by the mortality rate for the particular attained age. While the mortality rates increase each year—and increase exponentially at older ages—the net amount at risk decreases each year in a permanent life insurance policy. Thus, because of the cash value increase, and the decrease in the net amount at risk that is applied to increasing mortality rates, the COI protection at advanced ages becomes manageable. It is this relationship that makes permanent life insurance affordable. However, this relationship is a **very delicate** balance. As mentioned previously, all life insurance is based on assumptions. If the assumptions are guaranteed, as in a

---

43. Remember at the maximum age in a mortality table the probability of death is 100 percent. Therefore, since death is considered a certainty according to the mortality table, whether or not the insured is actually dead, a reserve, or cash value, has to be created at the face amount of the policy to meet this certain obligation of the insurance carrier.

whole life product, then the policy owner does not have to be concerned with the delicate balance in the relationship between the cash value of the policy and the net amount at risk. Similarly, if all of the assumptions remain constant in deriving the values and funding premium for a non-guaranteed current assumption life insurance product, then the very delicate balance will remain in check.

Thus, if the life insurance product depicted in Figure 2.5 is a guaranteed product, or all of the assumptions—the policy earnings, COI, policy expenses, and premiums—in a non-guaranteed product remain constant, then Figure 2.5 is an accurate representation of the $1,000,000 life insurance policy for our age 50 preferred non-smoker female. Note that Figure 2.5 represents a graph, or picture, of a constant assumption policy illustration. However, what if in a non-guaranteed life insurance product the assumptions are not constant but volatile—particularly policy earnings—what happens in our **very delicate relationship** with the life insurance policy?

Mathematics of "Permanent" Types of Life Insurance—Part 2: Constant Assumption versus Reality

Policy Interest or Earnings Crediting

While mortality costs and expenses are an integral component and determinate in the performance of a permanent life insurance policy, interest and earnings on premium dollars and cash value reserves have the most profound and dramatic effect on the overall results and outcome of a life insurance policy.

Even though there is a minimum guaranteed interest crediting rate to the cash values in whole life and universal life policies, policy dividends in participating[44] whole life policies—which are largely determined based on favorable investment results over and above the guaranteed interest rate, but also determined, in part, on favorable experience of mortality and expenses over the guaranteed mortality and expenses—and excess interest crediting rates in universal life are dependent on returns of the

---

44. Almost all whole life policies issued today are offered through mutual insurance companies, which are companies owned by the policy owners as compared to stock life insurance companies that are owned by stockholders. Similarly, almost all whole life policies sold by mutual insurance companies are "participating" policies. Participating policies are policies that pay dividends to the policy owner. As stated by Dan M. McGill and revised by Edward E. Graves: [Graves, *supra* note 10, at page 4.11.]

> Whole life policies issued on a participating basis anticipate charging a small extra margin in the fixed premium with the intent to return part of the premium in the form of policy owner dividends. This approach allows the insurer to maintain a stronger contingency margin and still adjust the cost downward after periods of coverage have been evaluated. Policy owner dividends are based on favorable experience such as higher than expected investment returns or lower than expected expenses of operations and/or mortality.

Legally, dividends are a return of premium, and are nontaxable until the total dividends received under the policy exceed the policy owner's basis (essentially the total premiums paid) in the policy. IRC § 72(e)(5); Treas. Reg. § 1.72-11(b)(1).

portfolios backing these policies. The portfolios for these two types of policies are part of the general asset accounts of the insurance carrier. These general accounts, which are subject to the claims of the insurer's creditors, are invested primarily in high-grade fixed-income securities, mostly corporate or government bonds.[45]

Older indexed universal life insurance policies, also referred to as equity indexed universal life insurance policies, had a minimum interest crediting rate of about 100 to 150 basis points less than the insurance carrier's regular universal life policies. Most indexed universal life policies issued today now have a 0 percent minimum interest crediting rate. The policy cash value crediting rate in an indexed universal life policy is the greater of the minimum interest crediting rate, or is based upon a percentage—or as it is referred to a participation rate, with generally a maximum cap of 10 percent or 12 percent—of some market type index, without including dividend returns, measured on a point-to-point basis[46] over some period that can vary most commonly from one to three years. The most commonly used index is the Standard and Poor's® (S&P) 500® Index, again not including dividend returns. However, even though crediting rates for indexed universal life insurance policies are based on a formula using some market index without dividend returns, the portfolio of general account assets backing these policies is still invested primarily in high-grade fixed-income securities but with some put and call options.

---

45. In fact, according to the American Council of Life Insurers' *2016 Life Insurers Fact Book*, in 2015, 70 percent of general account assets of life insurers were invested in corporate or government bonds, 11 percent of general account assets were invested in mortgages and real estate, including occupied real estate, 3 percent in policy loans, and 14 percent in miscellaneous assets. Only 2 percent of the assets were invested in stocks. American Council of Life Insurers, 2016 Life Insurers Fact Book, Chapter 2, at page 8, 2016, *available at* https://www.acli.com/-/media/ACLI/Files/Fact-Books-Public/2016LIFactBook.ashx?la=en.

46. A point-to-point basis of measurement is done by taking the selected market index, without dividend considerations, on the starting point of the measuring period, usually the policy anniversary date, and comparing it to the selected market index, again, without dividend considerations, on the exact date of the end of the measuring period. After calculating, if any, increase in the selected market index, the increase percentage on the market index is multiplied by the participation rate. If the product of the increase percentage of the market index multiplied by the participation rate is less than the maximum cap allowed for the measuring period, then that rate is the crediting rate for the cash value account. If the product of the increase of the market index percentage multiplied by the participation rate is greater than or equal to the maximum cap allowed for the measuring period, then the crediting rate for the cash value account is equal to the maximum cap rate for the measuring period. If the selected market index had a decrease over the measuring period, or if the selected market index was the same at the end of the measuring period as it was at the start of the measuring period, then the crediting rate for the cash value account is zero, because in indexed universal life insurance negative returns are not recognized. However, if the indexed universal life policy features a minimum guaranteed crediting rate, the cash value of the policy would be credited with that rate in the measuring period if the minimum guaranteed crediting rate were greater than the crediting rate derived from the index crediting formula.

As an example, where we are assuming that the index crediting rate formula derives a crediting rate that is greater than the minimum guaranteed crediting rate contained in the policy, suppose the Standard and Poor's® (S&P) 500® Index, without dividend considerations, was 2,150.00 on August 14, 2016, the start of the measuring period, and the S&P 500® Index was 2,450.00 on August 14, 2017, the one-year end of the measuring period. The percentage increase of the S&P 500® Index over that measuring period was 13.95 percent. Let's suppose this particular equity indexed universal life policy had a 75 percent participation rate and a cap of 10 percent. The product of multiplying the S&P 500® Index increase for the measuring period by the participation rate of 75 percent is 10.46 percent. Since this amount is greater than the 10 percent cap, 10 percent would be the crediting rate for the cash value account. If, however, the cap were 12 percent with the same participation rate, then 10.46 percent would be credited to the cash value account in the policy.

Unlike whole life, universal life, and indexed universal life insurance policies that are backed by portfolios that are part of the general asset accounts of the insurance carrier and consist primarily of high-grade fixed-income securities, variable universal life insurance policies are backed by separate sub-accounts of the insurer, which are very similar to mutual funds, and that are beyond the reach of the insurer's general creditors.[47] As noted by Weber and Hause, "[a] variable universal life policy typically provides a variety of proprietary and non-proprietary mutual fund-like sub-accounts across a spectrum of fixed and equity accounts."[48] It is not unusual for a variable universal life policy to have a choice of more than 100 mutual fund-like accounts of every variety in which the policy owner can allocate and reallocate his or her premium dollars over and above the mortality COI and expenses—as well as the existing accumulated cash account value—according to his or her risk tolerance. Thus, the earnings crediting in variable universal life policies are based on the performance of each of the individual sub-accounts chosen by the policy owner.

It should be obvious that the economy and the financial markets determine the rates of return on the separate mutual fund-like sub-accounts and portfolios in the general asset accounts of the insurance carrier; and, that these rates of return and earnings are not constant over time but volatile. Figures 2.6 and 2.7 graphically demonstrate, for the period from 1977 till 2017, the fixed account volatility of corporate and government bond yields, and the equity account volatility represented by the S&P 500® Index rate of return, respectively.

Figure 2.6 Constant Assumption vs. Reality—Fixed Account Volatility

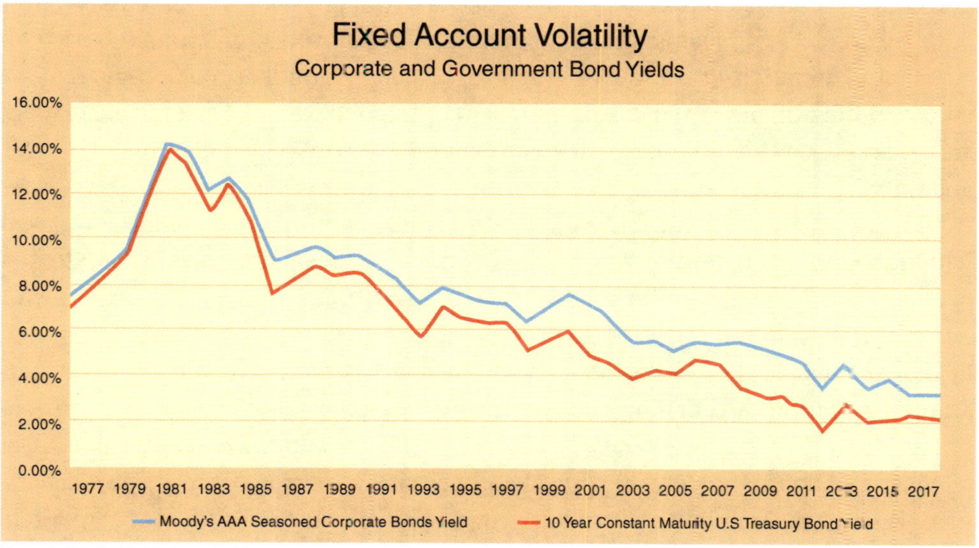

---

47. The U.S. Securities and Exchange Commission requires that the separate accounts for variable life insurance and annuities "not constitute part of the insurance company's general investment fund and put such assets beyond the claims of its general creditors." Edward E. Graves, Editor, *McGill's Life Insurance, Seventh Edition*, The American Collage, Bryn Mawr, Pennsylvania, 2009, at page 5.7.

48. Weber and Hause, *supra* note 16, at page 22.

Figure 2.7 Constant Assumption vs. Reality—Equity Account Volatility

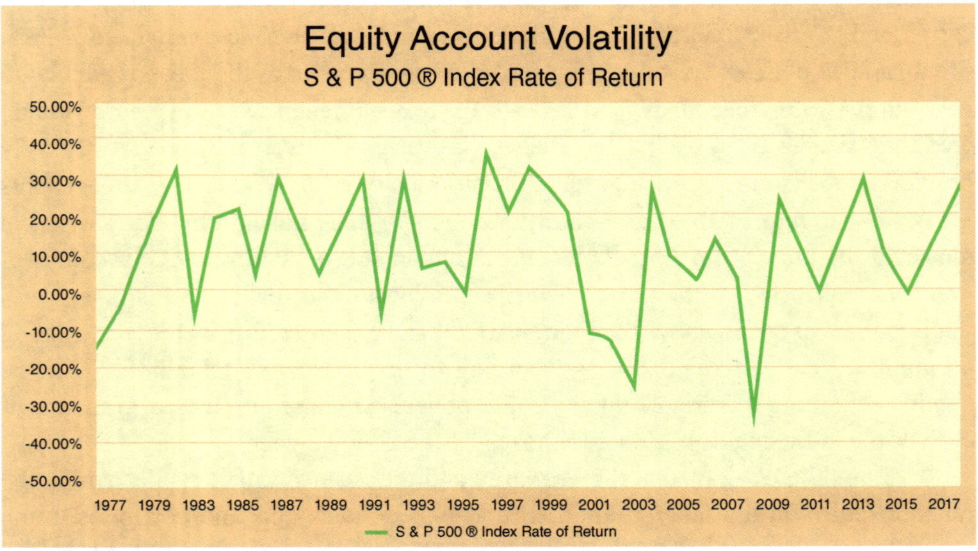

Given the volatility of the various securities that back up the cash value accounts and reserves of non-guaranteed universal life products,[49] does assuming a constant rate of return in any type of universal life policy illustration or calculation of policy values make sense? In other words, do constant rates of return assumptions reflect reality in universal life insurance illustrations and calculations? What is the effect of deriving planned funding premiums for universal life policies based on constant assumption of returns calculations? Recognizing that for non-guaranteed universal life policies that the assumptions for the policy do not remain constant but are volatile—particularly the policy earnings—how do we manage the risk of this volatility?

To demonstrate the effect of volatility on policy earnings, and the risks involved with assuming **constant** earnings assumptions in designing and calculating a planned funding premium for a universal life policy, let's return to our example of our 50-year-old female who has a preferred non-smoking risk classification and desires to have $1,000,000 of permanent coverage. After a risk tolerance and suitability evaluation, it is determined that a variable universal life policy is an appropriate choice for our prospective insured, with a premium and cash value asset allocation of approximately 70 percent equities and 30 percent fixed-income securities, which is an apt choice given her growth risk tolerance profile. The target rate of return for this asset allocation is 8 percent, which is the **constant assumed rate**

---

49. In addition, the interest or earnings component of non-guaranteed participating whole life policy dividends.

of return that will be used to determine the funding premium for her variable universal life policy.

Figure 2.8 represents a $1,000,000 hypothetical variable universal life insurance policy using our same age 50 female preferred non-smoker risk. Assuming a **constant earnings assumption** of 8 percent, which is typical in variable universal life policy illustrations, the 2001 CSO Mortality Table, and no loading for expenses, the calculated net annual premium is $7,888, to endow the policy at age 120. Figure 2.8 represents a graphical depiction of a hypothetical universal life insurance policy illustration with **assumed constant earnings** of 8 percent. (Note that if we had assumed a 10 percent constant rate of return, the derived premium would have been $6,056. Compare the premiums derived using constant assumed earning of 8 percent and 10 percent to premium derived of $17,135 for the guaranteed whole life or non-guaranteed universal life illustration using the same mortality and expenses assumptions but with an assumed constant rate of return of 3 percent.)

Figure 2.8 Mathematics of "Permanent" Types of Insurance—Constant Assumption of Returns

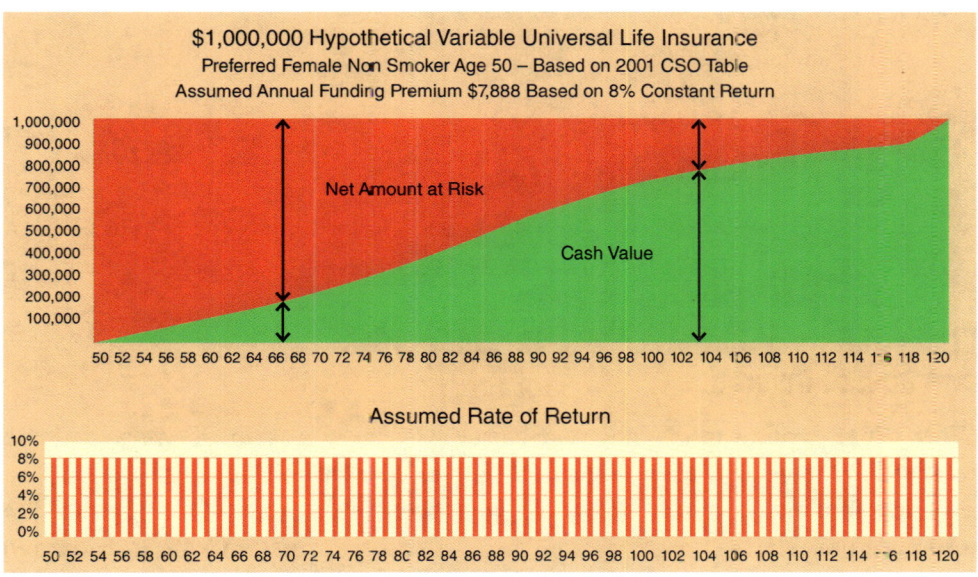

Of course, for variable universal life policies, and other non-guaranteed products, the policy rates of return are **not constant** but **volatile** and changing constantly. Thus, the constant average return life insurance policy illustration for non-guaranteed products **does not** reflect reality, let alone provide any predictive value. Keeping all other assumptions constant except the assumed rates of return, let's look at the effect of volatile rates of return on the previous hypothetical variable universal life policy using a premium projected at an 8 percent constant rate of return.

In Figure 2.9 the earnings rate varies by year but results in an **average** over-all rate of return just short of 9 percent. However, note that the assumed funding premium of $7,888, based on a **constant** rate of return of 8 percent, is **inadequate** to sustain the policy beyond age 90 given the pattern of assumed varying rates of return shown in Figure 2.9. Thus, the insufficient premium causes policy insolvency and lapse.

Figure 2.9 Mathematics of "Permanent" Types of Insurance—Volatile Rates of Returns

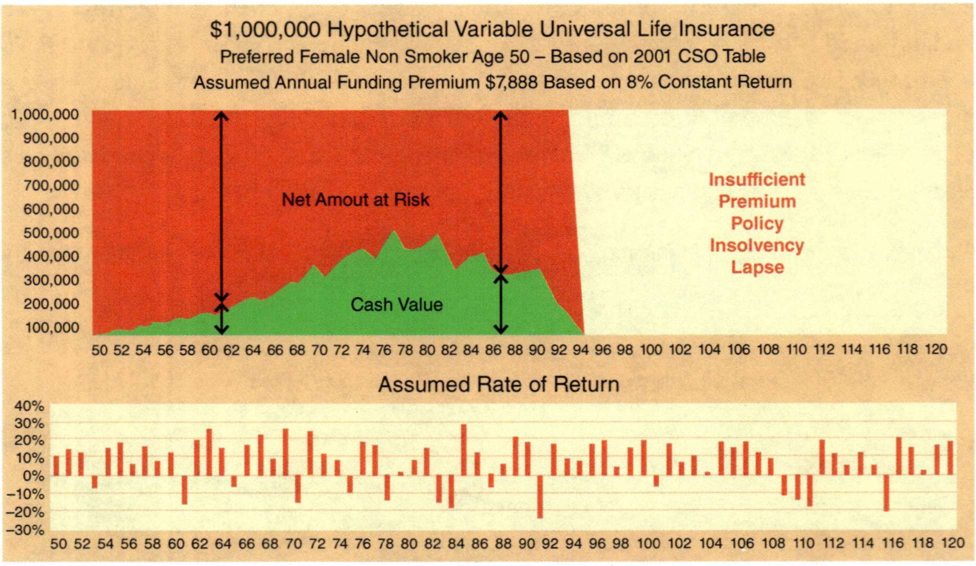

$1,000,000 Hypothetical Variable Universal Life Insurance
Preferred Female Non Smoker Age 50 – Based on 2001 CSO Table
Assumed Annual Funding Premium $7,888 Based on 8% Constant Return

Effect of Rate of Return on Net Amount at Risk and Cost of Insurance

What causes policy insolvency and lapse? The answer is in the **very delicate** relationship between the net amount at risk and the cash value of the policy. The assumed funding premiums for non-guaranteed, flexible premium universal life insurance policies are typically calculated assuming a **constant rate of return** to endow the policy at contract maturity, generally at or near the end of the mortality table used for guaranteed mortality rates such as the 2001 or 2017 CSO Mortality Table. As long as actual rates of return remain at or above the assumed **constant** rate of return and there is no change in premiums, mortality rates, or expenses, the policy will endow or mature as projected using the **constant** rate of return. How-ever, if the rate of return falls below the assumed **constant** rate of return, the **very delicate balance** between the net amount at risk and cash value **is compromised**, thus causing the policy to become insolvent or to lapse unless sufficient additional premiums are added.

Actual rates of return lower than the assumed **constant** rate used initially to calculate the policy premium cause a decrease in cash value and an increase in the net amount at risk, which increases the COI determined by the net amount at risk multiplied by the mortality rates for the insured's attained age in any particular policy year. (Note that mortality rates increase constantly each year and exponentially at older ages.) The COI is deducted from the cash value for each period, generally monthly, and the increased amount further reduces the cash value. With volatile rates of return and no increase in the funding premium, the result can be a "death spiral" causing the policy to become insolvent and lapse (i.e., the policy can die long before the insured).

Figures 2.10 and 2.11 duplicate the cash value and net amount at risk relationships for the constant assumed rate of return and the varying assumed rates of returns for Figures 2.8 and 2.9, respectively. However, for Figures 2.10 and 2.11, two additional graphs are added depicting the mortality rates and COI for the policies shown in Figures 2.8 and 2.9. The mortality rates for both graphs are the same, as the mortality rates used to determine the COI would remain constant whether or not the rates of return were constant or varying. COI is, of course, determined by multiplying the net amount at risk—which is affected by the amount of the cash value that is affected by either the constant or varying rates of return applied to the cash value—by the mortality rates for each attained age of the policy.

Figure 2.10 Effect of Rate of Return on Net Amount at Risk and Cost of Insurance—Variable Universal Life Policy—Constant 8% Rate of Return

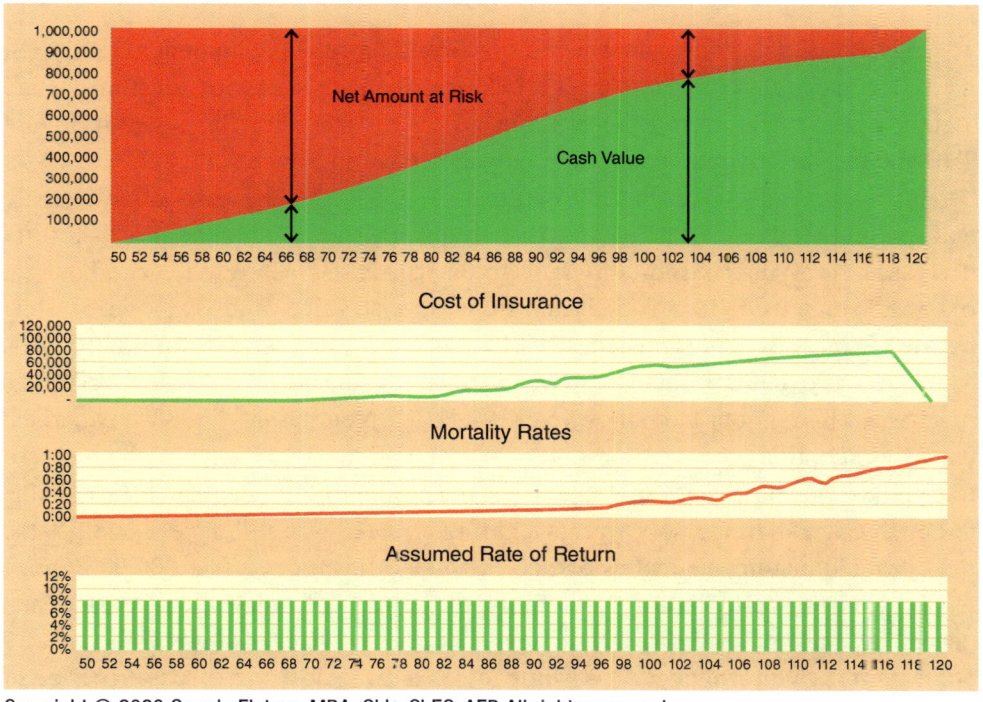

Figure 2.11 Effect of Rate of Return on Net Amount at Risk and Cost of Insurance—Variable Universal Life Policy—Average Rate of Return 8%

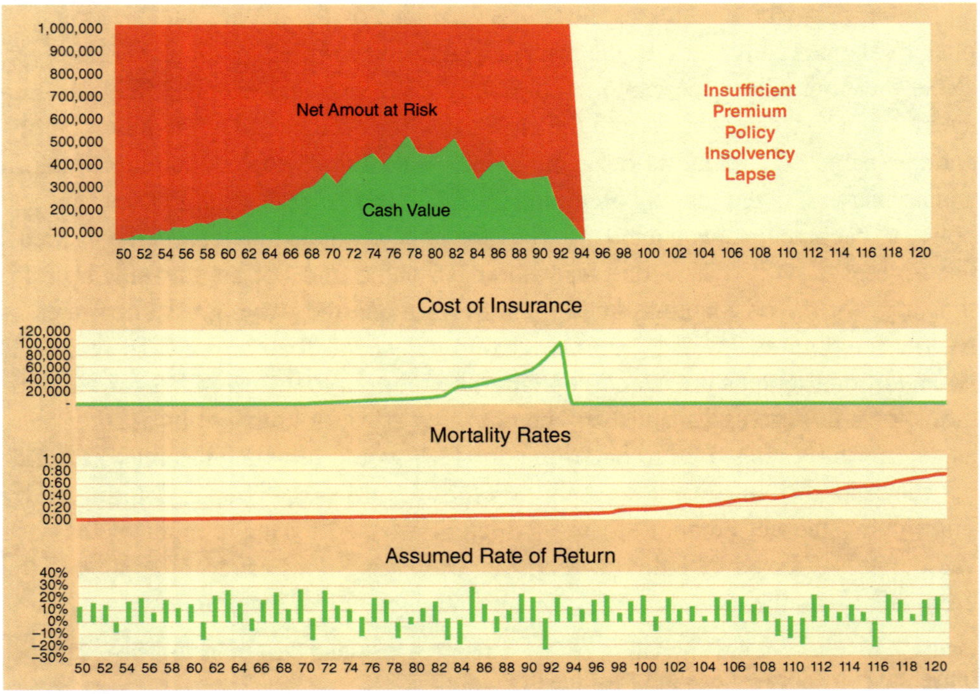

Figure 2.12 is a composite showing an overlay for the net amount at risk, COI, mortality rates (which, again, remain identical for both scenarios illustrated), and assumed rates of return, for the constant rate of return policy illustrated in Figure 2.10 and the varying rates of return policy illustrated in Figure 2.11.

In Figure 2.10, with constant earnings of 8 percent, the cash value steadily and smoothly increases each year and subsequently the net amount at risk steadily decreases. Applying the mortality rates to the steady decrease in the net amount at risk results in a COI—that is deducted from the cash value each year—with a slow but steady increase that is considerably less than the increase in the mortality rates. Thus, the **very delicate** balance between the cash value and net amount at risk was maintained throughout the policy years. Since the premium of $7,888 was derived on the assumption of a constant rate of return, and in Figure 2.10 all the assumptions remained constant through the years, the premium was adequate to sustain the policy through all of the policy years and if the insured was still alive at age 120 the policy would mature and endow the face amount of insurance of $1,000,000.

In contrast with Figure 2.10, in Figure 2.11 with varying increasing and decreasing rates of return—even though these varying rates average just short of 9 percent through the policy years—while the cash value does increase for a period of time, the increase in the cash value over time is not at the same pace as if the cash value were increasing at a constant 8 percent and eventually the cash value starts declining and subsequently is exhausted at age 90 of the insured.

Figure 2.12 Effect of Rate of Return on Net Amount at Risk and Cost of Insurance—Variable Universal Life Policy—Constant vs. Average Rate of Return of 8%

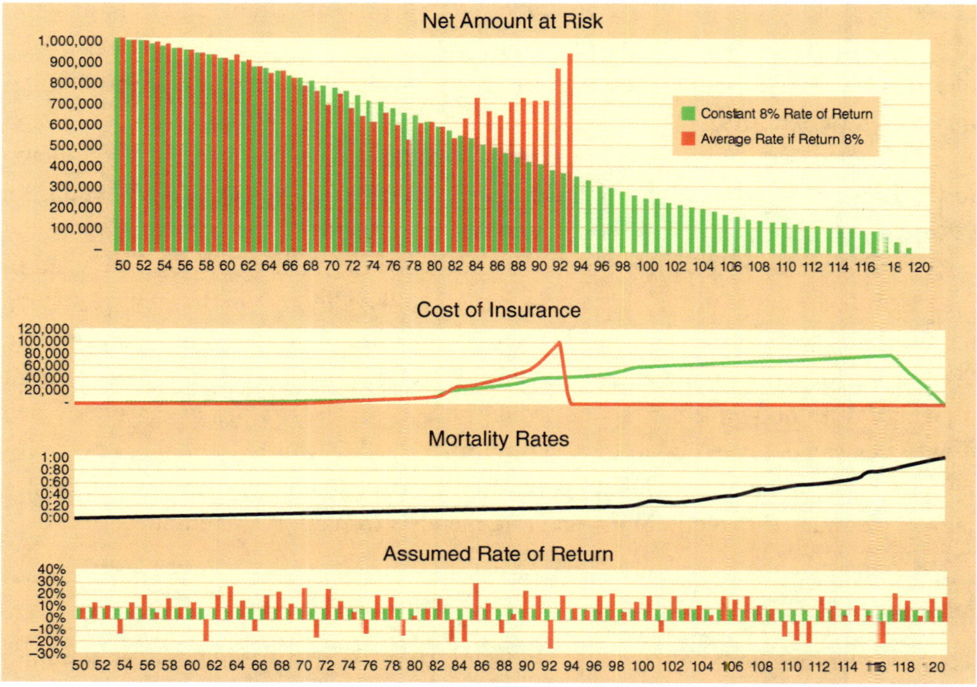

Given the varying assumed rates of return for each policy year, the difference for the net amount at risk compared to if a constant rate of return was applied to the cash value each year, as shown in Figure 2.12, is negligible in the earlier attained ages of the policy, actually is less from around attained age 65 to around attained age 80, but increases substantially after age 80 until the policy is insolvent at age 90 and the policy lapses. Applying the mortality rates to the pattern of the net amount at risk, given the assumed rates of return each year, results in a COI—that is deducted from the cash value—difference, when compared with the constant rate of return assumption, that is negligible in the earlier attained ages of the policy, actually is less from around attained age 65 to around attained age 80, but, because of the higher mortality rates of older ages applied to a substantial increase in the net amount at risk, skyrockets after age 80. As these costs of insurance increases rise faster than the growth of the cash value, they drain the cash value, causing the cash value to be completely exhausted, resulting in policy insolvency and lapse.

The effect of the volatile increases and decreases in the assumed rates of return was to **compromise** the **very delicate balance** of the cash value and net amount at risk. Additionally, the planed funding premium of $7,888 that was based on a **constant return** assumption was **inadequate** to sustain the policy to maturity, and the policy barely made it to a little over the life expectancy of our 50-year-old preferred non-smoking risk female.

However, since this is a variable universal life policy, additional premium funding could prevent the lapse of the policy, and, alternatively, the death benefit could be reduced. However, assuming no reduction in the death benefit, and this "danger" of the policy lapse was not discovered until the insured was in her very late 80s, then a very, very substantial additional premium would be required to properly fund this policy to maturity.

Of course, the varying assumed rates of return could be different than shown in the illustration, and definitely the actual rates of return for the policy would be different than those shown in the illustration, with results of the performance of the policy being more or less favorable to the policy owner than what was illustrated in the example for our 50-year-old female. Additionally, although in the example above the mortality rates set for the policy were the maximum guaranteed rates using the 2001 CSO Mortality Table and no expense loading was assumed, in reality current mortality rates and expense factors would be used in the pricing of the policy and those rates can change—up to the maximum 2001 CSO Mortality Table rates, or for policies issued January 1, 2020, or thereafter the 2017 CSO Table rates, and expense factors guaranteed in the policy—and affect the performance of the policy.

Lessons Learned

The first lesson learned from the above example is that with flexible premium non-guaranteed life insurance products we cannot rely on the use of **constant and continuous** assumptions in predicting the performance of the policy. Yet the main vehicle used in setting the planned funding premium for these types of policies is the **constant assumption** traditional policy illustration. Obviously, the traditional policy illustration does not account for volatility in rates of returns and the effect of the volatility on policy performance. Any creditable evaluation of flexible premium non-guaranteed life insurance products must take into consideration and account for the volatility of varying rates of return.

The second lesson learned from the above example is that the performance of the non-guaranteed life insurance policy must be monitored and managed on a continuous basis, similar to the management of a stock or bond portfolio or a portfolio of mutual funds, or any other type of financial asset. This monitoring and management must be on a continuing basis and performed at least annually.

The broader picture here is that this is a prime example of the **risk paradigm shift** that resulted from the introduction in the late 1970s and early 1980s of indeterminate, flexible premium non-guaranteed life insurance products. That is, the **performance risk of the life insurance policy was transferred from the insurance carrier to the policy owner**. For the most part, this performance risk has gone unnoticed, but it certainly did precipitate a huge policy crisis when the risk paradigm shift was discovered by the policy owner, generally after many years of being ignored. When the risk transfer paradigm was discovered it became obvious that there needed to be rethinking of policy management and the creditable evaluation of life insurance policies.

In the next chapter we will discuss the risks of life insurance policies. This is followed by an examination of the process of managing life insurance policies. Later, we will examine how to address the volatility issue and properly and creditably evaluate non-guaranteed flexible premium life insurance products, and derive a premium that, while certainly not guaranteed, can accurately reflect the effect of volatility in rates of return with statistical probabilities of confidence.

Chapter 3

Risks of Life Insurance Policies

Background, History, and Perspective on the Risk Transfer

Talking about risks in life insurance policies may seem a bit ironic since life insurance is a risk transfer device. Prior to 1979, the only risks associated with life insurance policies were carrier insolvency, purchasing power, product suitability, and diversification. Prior to 1979, life insurance products were all guaranteed products with the risk of guaranteed performance, premium sufficiency, and sustainability all retained and maintained by the insurance carrier. The attitude of policy owners was that they could buy the insurance policy and place it in a sock drawer or safety deposit box. As long as they paid the premium when due, policy owners could forget about the policy since there was no perceived need to manage the policy.

The only performance risk for the policy owner was with participating policy dividends—participating policies are policies that pay dividends that are non-guaranteed and are legally a return of the guaranteed premium—and the amount of the dividend or whether dividends would be paid. However, dividends are an "enhancement" to the benefits of the participating policy, and the guaranteed premium amount paid by the policy holder is a guaranteed payment amount that is sufficient to sustain the policy and provide all of the guaranteed benefits of the policy.

In 1979, the life insurance world changed when E.F. Hutton Life Insurance Company introduced universal life insurance, the first indeterminate, flexible premium non-guaranteed product. With this type of product, the risk of policy performance and premium sufficiency and sustainability was transferred from the insurance carrier to the policy owner. With this risk paradigm shift, the policy owner could not just buy the universal life policy, put it in the sock drawer, and forget about it. Rather, the policy owner was now responsible for monitoring the policy performance and managing the sufficiency and sustainability of the policy premium. The "new generation" policy required attentive policy management to achieve original policy purchase objectives and avoid lapse due to inattention. The key word with life insurance now became "managing."

This "new" product now has been aggressively marketed for more than 40 years. However, the risk transfer associated with this product has been for the most part either completely unnoticed, misunderstood, or thoroughly ignored. Life insurance sales agents usually do not communicate the risk transfer responsibility or how creditable risk management can be provided. Life insurance carriers do not offer creditable risk management services.[50] The life insurance industry and profession has completely failed in assisting the policy owner in adapting to this risk transfer paradigm shift and in developing proper and creditable risk management procedures. Why? There is not a simple answer to the question and no one knows for certain the complete answer.

Part of the answer might be a complete lack of policy risk identification[51] and management understanding by issuing carriers, their contracted sales agents, and policy purchasers who relied upon sales agent disclosures and suitability determinations.[52] Part of the answer might be a complete lack of imagination: no one just plain ever thought about it or perceived any problems with, now, an indeterminate, flexible premium non-guaranteed life insurance product. In other words, during the time it was first happening, and being in the middle of it at the time, there was no realization that there really was a risk paradigm shift, let alone realizing the implications of the risk transfer. Linear thinking was rampant with the belief that the high—particularly short-term—interest rates[53] were the "new normal" and that interest rates would never return to their historic average levels of around 3 percent. In addition, the universal life policy illustration looked pretty much the same as a traditional policy illustration with its constant assumption projections; although both types of illustrations had the normal caveats and disclaimers with regard to the non-guaranteed values. To the policy owner the universal life illustration and life insurance policy looked the same as all the other traditional life insurance, and the policy owner had the mental paradigm that it would act and perform the same, even if told otherwise.

From the author's personal perspective and observations, the marketing arms of the life insurance profession also fell into the linear thinking mentality and certainly made no heroic effort to explain the risk transfer or the necessary policy monitoring and management required of the policy owner. The universal life policy was a "hot" new product to sell. It was being priced using current assumption costs and high interest crediting rates—with the resulting derived calculated premium from

---

50. Whitelaw and Montag, *supra* note 1, page 9.
51. Ibid, page 4.
52. Ibid, page xiii, footnote 2, and page 6.
53. For an excellent discussion of the effect of interest rates on indeterminate premium non-guaranteed life insurance in the late 1970s and early 1980s and into the 21st century, see Whitelaw and Montag, *supra* note 1, pages 4–5. Also see Graves, *supra* note 10, pages 5.17–5.18.

such current assumptions—that were known or should have been known not to be sustainable. This new product had competitive advantages over traditional products and appeal to the consumer who was never made aware of the risk transfer. The consumer's view was to buy life insurance at the least possible premium cost without consideration of the non-guaranteed aspects or the risk transfer. If the policy monitoring and risk management requirements were properly explained fully by the life insurance agent or broker—which was mostly not the case because the agent or broker never thought that it needed to be emphasized—the client ignored these requirements because, after all, he or she was now paying less money for life insurance coverage.

However, the insurance company actuaries and executives had to understand this risk transfer as well as the policy risks needed to be monitored and managed. But little effort, if any, was made to communicate these risk management issues to the marketing field force, let alone the consumer. Did competitive advantage and sales take precedence over full disclosure of risks to the policy owner and consumer?

Trust-Owned Life Insurance Is an Example of Adverse Risk Transfer Consequences

Reliable data concerning life insurance policies owned in irrevocable life Insurance trusts (ILITs) is unavailable. Since 1993, trust-owned life insurance (TOLI) risk management articles have suggested that unskilled trustees administer up to 90 percent of in-force TOLI policies. The TOLI Center, LLC (TTC) has provided fee-based policy administration and risk management services to skilled and unskilled trustees, attorneys, affluent family groups, and ILIT beneficiaries since 1992. TTC has maintained portfolio statistics since TOLI-specific statistics are unavailable from traditional life insurance sources. As of October 2013, approximately 40 percent of in-force universal and variable-universal life products administered by TTC are carrier illustrated to lapse prior to the insured's estimated life expectancy or within five years of the insured's estimated life expectancy.[54] Further, approximately 12 percent of whole life and guaranteed universal life policies have compromised guarantees.[55]

If TTC statistics—whose clientele are extremely sophisticated, mostly skilled professionals—suggest a 40 percent insolvency or lapse rate[56] with TOLI policies,

---

54. Whitelaw and Montag, *supra* note 1, footnote 4, page 3.

55. E. Randolph Whitelaw, "The Need for a Fresh Look at Irrevocable Life Insurance Trust (ILIT) Fiduciary Practices," *Estate Planning, August 2014,* Society of Financial Service Professionals, endnote 1, page 7.

56. E. Randolph Whitelaw, Co-Managing Director of The TOLI Center, has told the author that if creditable policy evaluation is employed—as will be described subsequently in this book—instead of the carrier in-force illustration lapse rate of 40 percent, the expected lapse rate by life expectancy or within five years of life expectancy would probably be 60 percent.

what is that statistic for the vast majority of unskilled, accommodation trustees? Sixty percent? Seventy percent? Ninety percent? Should professional advisors be concerned?

Of course, professional advisors should be concerned if their clients' ILITs might be at risk of insolvency due to a TOLI policy lapse. Advisors are all fiduciaries and owe a duty to act in the best interest of their clients. Additionally, advisors are held to a standard of competency and some advisors to a suitability standard as well. To fulfill that standard, the advisor is expected to be aware of the risks and related causes involved with non-guaranteed life insurance policies. Further, they are expected to know the proper process of managing the risks and evaluating non-guaranteed life insurance products. Otherwise, the advisors could potentially expose themselves to unnecessary reputation and litigation risks where they could potentially be held liable.

What Is the Definition of Risk and What Are Life Insurance Policy Expectations?

For the purposes of this writing, "risk" is defined as a variation from expectations. What are expectations with respect and regard to life insurance? The author believes that life insurance policy owners have the following expectations for the life insurance policies they own:

- The life insurance policy carrier will remain solvent and financially viable.
- The life insurance product performs according to the policy illustration; that is, the premium is sufficient and the policy will sustain itself for the lifetime of the insured, which may be defined as either a specific age or until the policy matures and endows.
- The life insurance product will remain suitable for the policy owner.
- For some policy owners, purchasing power will remain constant.

The first expectation, that the carrier will remain solvent and financially viable, is a very reasonable expectation. The second expectation, that a non-guaranteed policy performs according to the policy illustration, is a **completely** unrealistic expectation. The third expectation, that the life insurance product remains suitable, is reasonable at the start of the program but, as we all know, situations change and so the suitability of the life insurance policy can change as well. The fourth expectation, that purchasing power will remain constant, assumes that the inflation rate is zero, and is, of course, unrealistic. However, if a policy owner purchases a policy with a constant level death benefit that cannot increase in any way but will remain the same nominal face amount throughout the life of the policy, isn't the policy owner assuming that either the inflation rate is zero or the needs for the life insurance will decrease over time? More will be addressed on this topic later in this chapter.

These basic expectations can vary and, therefore, constitute risks that need to be annually monitored and managed. We will discuss each of the expectations, or risks, in the next parts of this chapter. We will first address the expectation and risk that the carrier will remain solvent. Next, because subsequent discussion requires that we first address inflation, or purchasing power, we will address the expectation of the purchasing power remaining constant. While we have already addressed the expectation that the life insurance policy performs according to the policy illustration, we will explore risks specific to the main types of life insurance product types. Finally, we will explore the questionable expectation that the policy will remain suitable for the policy owner. Additionally, we will consider the issue of diversification among life insurance policies.

Carrier Insolvency Risk

The guaranteed and non-guaranteed performance of any life insurance policy is dependent on the financial strength, solvency, and viability of the insurance company that underwrites the policy. Yet as stated by Kathryn Ballsun, Patrick Collins, and Dieter Jurkat, predicting life insurance carrier insolvency can be a precarious and daunting task:

> Academic evidence suggests that there does not yet exist a model that, with a high degree of accuracy, can predict insurance company insolvency. Furthermore, although the past decade has seen a great improvement in solvency monitoring systems on the part of both regulators and independent rating agencies, the nature and scope of such activities are, for all practical purposes, beyond the skill set of most ILIT trustees. Solvency monitoring is no longer a spreadsheet exercise drawing data from accounting and actuarial performance results. Rather, it is a sophisticated process that entails the necessity to develop and test intricate stochastic valuation models as well as to make insightful predictions regarding the likely future consequences of current business strategies in an increasingly competitive marketplace. Bankruptcy prediction for insurance carriers is difficult because of constant changes in the economic, tax and regulatory environments under which carriers operate. Much of traditional credit-risk analysis opines on the quality of assets owned by the carrier. However, when the carrier's general asset portfolio contains a significant amount of private placement securities and surplus note financing, opinion shades quickly towards mere guess. It is no longer adequate to assume that carriers owning risky investments, such as "junk bonds," pose a higher insolvency risk than carriers with portfolios of "safe" assets. High quality private placement bonds that lack marketability because they are not registered for sale in public markets can turn

from blue-chip assets into accounting nightmares, as insurance companies holding Enron bonds discovered to their great dismay.[57]

Life insurance company solvency, viability, and true financial and competitive position evaluation is beyond the capabilities of the policy owner, unless the policy owner is a highly trained financial analysis specializing in the insurance industry. The alternative may be "to rely primarily on the summary conclusions and grades of independent ratings and company evaluation services that conduct both a qualitative as well as quantitative examination of insurance carrier assets, liabilities and management policies."[58] There are four such independent rating services that meet this criterion: A.M. Best Company, Fitch Rating Company, Moody's, and Standard & Poor's. The criteria and purpose of each rating service varies but, generally, each is evaluating creditworthiness, claims paying ability, and financial strength. Each rating service has a number of different ratings, or grades, that they assign to the companies they evaluate. Additionally, not all life insurance companies are rated by each of the four firms;[59] although all life insurance companies are rated by A.M. Best and most of the major carriers are rated by all four services.

Given the differences in the number of rating scales and inconsistencies in the rating criteria between the four rating services—plus, the rating "curve" or percentage distribution of each rating grade differs by the different rating services—it is difficult to compare the relative ratings of one service to another. This led to the creation of the Comdex, which has also been referred to as the Comdex Index or the Comdex rankings. The Comdex is not a rating itself, but rather a composite of all the ratings that a life insurance company has received. It is an attempt to rank life insurance companies relatively by the average of percentile distribution of ratings received from the different rating services. The Comdex rankings range from 0 to 100, with 100 being the top ranking. For example, if a life insurance carrier received the highest ratings from each of the four rating services, their Comdex index would be 100. The theory behind the Comdex rankings is that it is not the letter grade of rating that is important but rather the percentiles that each rating represents. The percentile gives the percent of carriers that are ranked lower than a particular company. For example, if a company is in the 90th percentile, 10 percent of companies ranked are ranked higher and 90 percent are ranked lower.

From a practical standpoint, the author personally recommends that a prospective policy owner choose a life insurance carrier with at least a Comdex ranking of 85, and preferably a carrier with a Comdex ranking of 90 or better.

---

57. Kathryn A. Ballsun, Patrick J. Collins, and Dieter Jurkat, "ILIT Asset Management: The Written Investment Policy Statement (Part 4 of 4)," ACTEC Journal, Volume 32, The American College of Trust and Estate Counsel, Washington, D.C., 2006, page 239. See also Ballsun, Collins, and Jurkat, *supra* note 24, pages 71–82, particularly pages 78–82, for a more detailed discussion of the fallacy of predicting life insurer carrier solvency and insolvency.

58. Ibid, page 240.

59. The life insurance company must pay a fee to be rated by the rating services.

Carrier ratings and Comdex rankings should be monitored annually. Ratings and Comdex rankings vary over time. Occasionally, the life insurance industry outlook as a whole is downgraded, which would affect the ratings and Comdex rankings of all carriers. In fact, the relative rankings of the Comdex vis-à-vis the various insurance carriers in this scenario would remain relatively stable. However, a carrier with a significant and sudden downgrade, or a series of sequentially smaller downgrades, could be a signal of serious financial difficulties[50] that would require attention and possibly action on the part of the policy owner.

There is, however, a partial safety net for insurance company insolvency. Each of the 50 states and the District of Columbia have a guaranty association to provide protection and continuing coverage, and help keep the promises of the insurance industry when a company fails. However, such guarantees are limited to a total of $300,000 to $500,000 cash value or face amount per insured depending on the particular state.[61]

Perhaps the best way to manage and protect against the risk of life insurance carrier insolvency, as advocated by Kathryn Ballsun, Patrick Collins, and Dieter Jurkat, is diversification of coverage among multiple insurance carriers and cost control of high commissions and acquisition costs.[62] Having life insurance coverage concentrated in one insurance carrier is analogous to having an investment portfolio with only one company stock. Like an investment portfolio, diversification is the key to mitigate risks. However, depending on the amount of insurance coverage required, the economics of purchasing life insurance due to fixed policy fees and the banding of rates per 1,000 of coverage by policy size, may make the transaction cost of diversification unfeasible. The flip side of keeping transaction costs low is to allow management flexibility if it becomes necessary to replace a life insurance policy. Of course, this is providing that the insured is still insurable. High commissions and other acquisition costs generally result in higher and longer periods of surrender charges, or lesser or inadequate cash value accumulation, which can make life insurance policy replacement an unsuitable alternative.

Purchasing Power Risk

Inflation has been relatively low for the past couple of years, with inflation rates of 0.8 percent, 0.7 percent, and 2.1 percent for the years 2014, 2015, and 2016,

---

60. Ballsun, Collins, and Jurkat, *supra* note 57, page 240. Ballsun, Collins, and Jurkat also succinctly point out through various examples the short time frame in which a carrier can go from high ratings from the rating services to insolvency. *See* Ballsun, Collins, and Jurkat, *supra* note 24, pages 71–75.

61. See the National Organization of Life & Health Insurance Guaranty Associations website, which provides links to the individual state guaranty associations, for more detailed information at https://www.nolhga.com/ (last visited Oct. 31, 2019).

62. Ballsun, Collins, and Jurkat, *supra* note 57, pages 240–241.

respectfully, as measured by the consumer price index for all urban consumers (CPI-U).[63] The compounded annual rates of inflation ending in the year 2014 for the past 10, 20, and 30 years has been 2.2 percent, 2.3 percent, and 2.7 percent, respectfully.[64] In fact, the compounded annual rate of inflation for the 89-year period from the end of 1925 to the end of 2014 has been 2.9 percent.[65] During that same 89-year period, "[i]nflation rates ranged from a high of 18.2% in 1946 to a low of negative 10.3% in 1932."[66]

A life insurance policy is purchased to provide death benefit protection over a ten-to-50-year time horizon. Given the examples of the long-term average rates of inflation mentioned above, the expectation that purchasing power will remain constant is an unrealistic and unattainable expectation. Yet, if a policy owner purchases a policy type with a constant level death benefit that cannot increase in any way but will remain the same nominal face amount throughout the life of the policy, the owner is either assuming a decreasing need for the amount of life insurance required over time or he or she is thoroughly ignoring the erosion of purchasing power caused by inflation.

To demonstrate the erosion of purchasing power over time due to inflation, consider the following example: Assume that the rate of inflation is 2.5 percent per year. Also, assume we have a 55-year-old female, with a life expectancy of age 91, who purchases a level death benefit type of policy with a face amount of $1,000,000. Assuming this 55-year-old female dies at her life expectancy age of 91, what is the purchasing power of the $1,000,000 policy at her life expectancy? With 2.5 percent inflation, the answer is $411,094. In fact, with a level death benefit type of life insurance product, she would have had to purchase a policy at age 55 for $2,432,535 to have $1,000,000 of purchasing power at her life expectancy of age 91.

Tables 3.1, 3.2, and 3.3 show the purchasing power risk for a $1,000,000 level death benefit life insurance policy with 2.5 percent inflation for various insureds at their respective life expectancy. Table 3.1 shows the value of $1,000,000 at life expectancy, and the amount of insurance that would have had to be purchased at the insured's issue age in order to have $1,000,000 of purchasing power at life expectancy, for female insureds of various select ages. Tables 3.2 and 3.3 show the same data for male insureds of various select ages, and for joint female and male insureds for second-to-die policies, with the life expectancy of that of the second to die, for various select ages, respectively.

---

63. Bureau of Labor Statistics, Southwest Information Office—Consumer Price Index, Calendar Year Historical, 2014–2018, U.S. City Average, https://www.bls.gov/regions/southwest/data/consumerpriceindexcyhistorical_southwest_table.htm (last visited Oct. 31, 2019).

64. *2015 Ibbotson® Stocks, Bonds, Bills, and Inflation® (SBBI®) Classic Yearbook*, Morningstar, Inc., Chicago, Illinois, 2015, Table C-7 (page 6 of 6)-b, page 297, Table C-7 (page 6 of 6)-a, page 297, and Table C-7 (page 5 of 6), page 296.

65. Ibid, page 63.

66. Ibid, page 63.

Table 3.1 Purchasing Power Risk for Female Insureds: Effect of 2.5% Inflation on $1,000,000 Life Insurance Policy

Issue Age Female	Life Expectancy @ Issue Age	Value of $1,000,000 @ Life Expectancy	Needed Now for $1M Purchasing Power @ L.E.
45	90	$329,174	$3,037,903
55	91	$411,094	$2,432,535
65	91	$526,235	$1,900,293
75	92	$657,195	$1,521,618

Table 3.2 Purchasing Power Risk for Male Insureds: Effect of 2.5% Inflation on $1,000,000 Life Insurance Policy

Issue Age Male	Life Expectancy @ Issue Age	Value of $1,000,000 @ Life Expectancy	Needed Now for $1M Purchasing Power @ L.E.
45	88	$345,839	$3,037,903
55	88	$442,703	$2,258,853
65	89	$552,875	$1,808,726
75	91	$673,625	$1,484,506

Table 3.3 Purchasing Power Risk for Joint Female/Male Insureds: Effect of 2.5% Inflation on $1,000,000 Life Insurance Policy

Issue Age Joint Female/Male	Life Expectancy @ Issue Age	Value of $1,000,000 @ Life Expectancy	Needed Now for $1M Purchasing Power @ L.E.
45/45	95	$290,942	$3,437,109
55/55	95	$372,431	$2,685,054
65/65	95	$476,743	$2,097,558
75/75	96	$595,386	$1,679,582

The solution to the purchasing power risk is to purchase types of life insurance policies wherein the death benefit face amount has the potential to increase over time in order to attempt to keep pace with inflation. This would suggest the purchase of either participating whole life policies, with dividends applied to purchase paid-up additional insurance, or substantially funded variable universal life policies. The purchasing power risks, as well as other policy risks, for various types of life insurance policies will be explored in the next section.

Risks by Product Types

The discussion in this section is limited to what the author believes are the seven main types of life insurance policies purchased in today's insurance marketplace. Since carrier insolvency risk was covered previously, this section assumes that the life insurance company underwriting the policy types discussed is financially strong, solvent, and viable. Thus, the discussion will concentrate only on the risks of the specific product type.

Risks vary by product type. Risks are first affected by what is guaranteed and what is not guaranteed in the life insurance policy. Assuming a financially strong and solvent carrier, the guaranteed aspects of a life insurance policy are riskless or risk-free. Of course, the non-guaranteed elements of the life insurance policy are not without risk and cause policy performance variance. These non-guaranteed elements include the interest credited or earnings of the accounts backing the cash value reserve; the mortality rates that are a component of the cost of insurance at each attained age; and policy expenses. In other words, all the pricing elements of a life insurance policy discussed previously in this book. Policy lapses can also affect these non-guaranteed pricing elements.

Additionally, policy funding adequacy is crucial for the performance, sufficiency, and sustainability of universal life, variable universal life, and indexed universal life policies. After the first policy year where there is a minimum required premium amount, there is no premium requirement for these products nor any fixed carrier-calculated periodic premium. The premium amount paid into the policy[67] and the timing when the premium is paid is determined at the discretion of the policy owner. The indeterminate premium policies that are minimally funded or underfunded pose serious risks of sustainability and lapse of the policy, and are extremely susceptible to policy performance variance.

While all the base policy elements of a whole life policy are guaranteed, including the death benefit, cash value, premium payment amount, and duration of the premium payment, dividends on participating whole life policies are not guaranteed. Dividends are effectively enhancements to the whole life policy over and above the base guaranteed policy. Among other choices, dividends can be used to reduce premium payments or applied to purchase paid-up additional amounts of guaranteed whole life insurance, which also pays non-guaranteed dividends. While there is no sufficiency or sustainability risk with a participating whole life policy, there is the risk that dividends turn out to be less than expected. This risk is particularly troublesome if the policy owner contemplated using the dividends from paid-up additional insurance to pay future premiums due on the policy by surrendering part of the paid-up additional insurance cash value and using the current dividend to reduce premiums, or was relying on an expected dividend amount to provide a stated amount of supplemental retirement income.

The risk of dividend performance is particularly critical on blended whole life policies. Blended whole life policies consist of a base whole life policy where

---

67. Of course, for administrative expense purposes, carriers impose a minimum premium payment amount. Also, IRC § 7702 corridor amount requirements for the life insurance policy impose a maximum premium that will be accepted by the insurance carrier.

dividends are applied to a combination of paid-up additional insurance and purchasing decreasing term life insurance. These policies may also feature a rider where a set dollar amount of premium is applied each year to purchase an amount of paid-up whole life insurance that that premium will purchase at each attained age of the insured—of course, dividends are also paid on this paid-up whole life insurance.

The concept here is to purchase life insurance coverage where the total amount of the coverage consists of the base whole life protection and decreasing term life insurance that decreases by the amount of total death benefit associated with the paid-up additional insurance dividends and, if the paid-up additions rider is also included, the amount of coverage that rider has purchased. At some point it is contemplated that the total amount of life insurance coverage from the paid-up additions dividends will equal the initial amount of term insurance included with the base whole life insurance when the policy was purchased. At that point the term insurance ceases and future dividends that are applied to the paid-up additional insurance option will increase the face amount of the life insurance policy.

As an example of the use of this blended whole life-type product, assume an insured has a need for $1,000,000 of life insurance coverage but does not want to pay the premiums for the $1,000,000 policy. Alternatively, the insured is willing to pay the premium cost of a $700,000 whole life policy. The solution for the $1,000,000 coverage is to purchase a $700,000 base whole life policy with an initial amount of decreasing term life insurance coverage of $300,000 provided by the dividend option that is applied to a combination of paid-up additional insurance and decreasing term life insurance. The term insurance decreases by the total face amount increases from the paid-up additions. Assuming the non-guaranteed dividends are paid as projected, the policy owner will have the desired $1,000,000 of coverage but will have paid the premium for a $700,000 whole life policy Again, at some point it is contemplated that the total amount of life insurance coverage from the paid-up additions dividends will equal the $300,000 initial decreasing term insurance. At that point the term life insurance coverage would cease and future dividends that are applied to the paid-up additional insurance option will increase the total face amount of the life insurance policy.

The purchasing power risk associated with life insurance policies varies by both product type and, in the case of universal life, variable universal life, and indexed universal life, the premium funding adequacy and whether or not the level death benefit or the increasing death benefit option is chosen.

Assuming life insurance carrier financial strength, solvency, and viability, the risks of life insurance product types can be divided into the risk-free guaranteed elements of the particular product type and the non-guaranteed elements of the particular product type whose results will vary and, therefore, constitute the risks of that particular product type. Also, while the discussion that follows primarily is centered around single life insurance products, the concepts and risks are just as relevant to joint and survivorship life insurance products. Below we examine and summarize the risks of the main seven types of life insurance products in today's insurance marketplace.

Term Insurance

The simplest and, perhaps, the "purest" form of life insurance protection is term insurance. Term insurance is good for definite short-term needs for life insurance or when the policy owner cannot temporarily afford the premiums for permanent life insurance protection. By its very name, term insurance is protection for a maximum period of time that is, generally, less than life expectancy. Term insurance is available in a variety of terms from one-year term insurance, wherein the premium is increased each year, to level premium term insurance payments of 5, 10, 15, 20, or 30 years, or to age 55, 60, 65, or 70.

What's guaranteed? The premium is guaranteed for a stated period of time. Other than decreasing term life insurance associated with mortgages and other debts where after each payment the principal of the debt and the face amount of the policy is reduced by a like amount, term life insurance has a level death benefit that is guaranteed for the period of the term insurance. Additionally, term insurance is guaranteed renewable with each premium payment without the insured having to furnish evidence of insurability each time the term is renewed. Similarly, most term insurance products, for a time period that is less than the maximum length of the term policy, offer the right to convert the term insurance policy into a permanent insurance policy offered by the carrier without proving evidence of insurability. Traditionally, the conversion feature is applied to any permanent type of policy currently offered by the insurance carrier. Some newer policies with this term insurance conversion feature have restricted the conversion to specific insurance products that more than likely account for adverse selection factors of those who convert their term insurance product.[68]

What's not guaranteed? What are the risks? The biggest risk with term life insurance is whether or not the insured is insurable at the end of the term period. This is a huge risk that could lead to the insured being unable to purchase any life insurance at an affordable price or any life insurance at all. For levelized premium term products, current rates that are based on the insured providing evidence of insurability are guaranteed for at least the period of the level term payments, such as 30 years. The policy may be technically renewable at the end of the level term payment period at guaranteed rates to a maximum term period, but those rates will assume heavy adverse selection and will be the maximum term insurance rates that can be charged. The issue is whether or not the insured can purchase any term

---

68. This conversion restriction has existed for years with group term life insurance.

insurance at the more favorable current rates at the end of the level premium term period. Lastly, because the death benefit of most term life insurance policies is level, there is purchasing power risk. The amount of purchasing power risk varies from the time of the purchase of the policy until the insured's death.

Table 3.4 summarizes the risks of term life insurance.

Table 3.4 Risks by Product Types—Term Insurance

What's Guaranteed	What's Not Guaranteed—Risks
• Premium for a Period • Death Benefit • Renewability for a Period • Conversion for a Period	• Current Rates at End of Term Period • Insurability at End of Maximum Term of Term Insurance • Purchasing Power of Death Benefit

Participating "Par" Whole Life

As mentioned previously, whole life insurance is the oldest form of life-long permanent life insurance protection dating back to 1759.[69] Participating, or par, whole life policies today are almost exclusively sold by mutual insurance carriers. Participating whole life policies pay dividends to policy owners, which return to policy owners a pro rata share of gains for the life insurance policy block that is based on investment returns and mortality and expense experience that is more favorable than the guaranteed pricing elements incorporated in the policy. Dividends are legally a return of premium.[70] According to Richard Weber and Christopher Hause, "[h]istorically, dividend-paying policies have generally provided greater long-term value than those policies that did not pay dividends."[71]

What's guaranteed? The premium payment amount, the premium payment duration, the policy cash value (minimum guaranteed amount), and the death benefit are all guaranteed. Therefore, policy sustainability and premium sufficiency are also guaranteed.

What's not guaranteed? What are the risks? Policy dividends are not guaranteed. As stated previously, there is the risk that dividends may be less than expected. This risk is particularly troublesome if the policy owner contemplated either using the dividends from paid-up additional insurance to pay future policy premiums due by surrendering part of the paid-up additional insurance cash value and using the current dividend to reduce premiums, or, alternatively, was relying on an expected dividend amount to provide a stated amount of supplemental retirement income.

---

69. See footnote 40 and accompanying text.
70. See footnote 20.
71. Weber and Hause, *supra* note 16, page 21.

The purchasing power risk of a participating whole life policy is dependent on the dividend option chosen by the policy owner. If the policy owner elects to either receive the dividends in cash or have the dividends applied to reduce the next premium payment, there would be purchasing power risk since the policy death benefit will remain level. The amount of purchasing power risk varies from the time of the purchase of the policy until the insured's death. If the policy owner elects to have the dividends accumulate at interest it can be argued that the "side fund" held by the insurance company would provide some minimal purchasing power protection. However, the interest accumulated on the side fund is taxable at ordinary income tax rates. The best dividend option to protect the purchasing power of the death benefit—at least in the long run—is to apply the dividends to purchase paid-up additional insurance.[72] While there may be short-term timing mismatches, particularly with short-term bursts of inflation in the initial policy years, historically, in the long run, paid-up additions have more than kept pace with inflation.

Table 3.5 summarizes the risks of par whole life insurance.

Table 3.5 Risks by Product Types—Par Whole Life

What's Guaranteed	What's Not Guaranteed—Risks
• Premium • Premium Paying Period • Cash Values (Minimum Guarantee) • Death Benefit • Policy Sustainability • Premium Sufficiency	• Dividends • Purchasing Power Depending on Dividend Amount and Option, Some Purchasing Power Protection can be afforded with Paid-Up Additional Insurance Dividend Option

Universal Life

First introduced in 1979, universal life insurance offers tremendous flexibility to the policy owner that was not available with whole life-type products. The policy owner, after paying, at least, a minimum required premium amount in the first year of the policy, can increase, decrease, or even skip payments of policy premiums at any time, and control when premium payments are paid.[73] The policy owner can also increase (with evidence of insurability) or decrease[74] the face amount of the policy at any time. Two death benefit options are available with universal life insurance: a level death

---

72. There are other additional dividend options offered by the various carriers who sell participating whole life insurance. For this discussion, we have chosen the main dividend options offered. However, many carriers do offer what is referred to as the fifth dividend option, which is to purchase term insurance equal to the guaranteed cash value. This obviously increasing term insurance dividend option is primarily used in what is referred to as a split-dollar arrangement that is beyond the scope of this book.

73. See footnote 67.

74. Decreasing the face amount of the policy could produce tax problems with a force out of cash value during the first 15 policy years because of the IRC § 7702 corridor or cause the policy to be treated as a modified endowment contract (MEC).

benefit option, which makes the policy design similar to a whole life policy with an increasing cash value account and decreasing net amount at risk; and an increasing death benefit option, in which the cash value account is added to a constant amount at risk death benefit amount. In lieu of, or in addition to, policy loans, a policy owner can make cash withdraws from the policy.[75] One of the goals of universal life insurance was to make the policy more transparent by unbundling and reporting to the policy owner the interest credited and the costs deducted from the cash account of the policy.[76] Another goal of universal life, because of its flexibility and its ability to change as the policy owner's needs changed throughout life, was to make just one universal life policy the only life insurance policy the policy owner ever needed. Universal life is the answer to and effectively functions as a method of buying term and investing the difference, with the difference accumulated tax deferred (and very possibly tax free) in the cash value account. However, universal life shifted the risks of policy sustainability, premium sufficiency, and creditable policy performance monitoring from the insurance carrier to the policy owner.

What's guaranteed? The first policy year death benefit is guaranteed along with a first-year minimum premium requirement. A minimum cash value account interest crediting rate; a maximum cost of insurance, or more technically correct a maximum mortality rate for each attained age generally based on the Commissioners Standard Ordinary (CSO) Mortality Table when the policy was issued; and maximum policy expenses are all guaranteed.

What's not guaranteed? What are the risks? Premium sufficiency and policy sustainability are the main risks associated with universal life policies. However, both are a function of the amount of premium funding paid into the policy. All too often, the planned funding premium for a universal life policy is based on the minimum annual premium that will cause the policy to mature assuming that the current interest rate credited, cost of insurance, and expenses remain constant as shown in a life insurance policy illustration. Unfortunately, assuming that all current pricing elements remain constant is a very dangerous assumption because the effect of assuming a constant interest, or earnings rate, and determining a premium from such rate, was demonstrated in the section "Mathematics of 'Permanent' Types of Life Insurance—Part 2: Constant Assumption versus Reality" in Chapter 2 as a substantial risk. Not surprisingly, a high planned funding premium close to the amount of premium allowed under the IRC § 7702 corridor regulations substantially mitigates the risk of premium sufficiency and policy sustainability by allowing the universal life policy to "absorb" volatility in the interest rate credited and changes to the cost of insurance and expenses.

---

75. However, withdrawals greater than the policy owner's basis in the policy—generally total premiums paid—are taxable at ordinary income tax rates.

76. See subsection "Lack of Transparency" in Chapter 2 for a discussion of lack of transparency in life insurance pricing elements.

Current interest crediting rates that are higher than the guaranteed minimum interest crediting rate can definitely change as fixed-income securities rates of return change in the economy. In fact, many policies sold in past decades having crediting rates in double digits are now only paying the minimum guaranteed interest crediting amount. A drop in the current crediting rate can require an increase in the planned funding premium (depending on the level of premium funding but particularly if the policy is minimally funded) in order to sustain the policy to either contract maturity or the planned duration of the policy owner.

While there is generally considerable wiggle room between the current cost of insurance, or more correctly mortality rates, and the current expenses of the policy and the guaranteed maximum mortality rates and expenses of the policy, changes in these elements can occur. Negative changes do adversely affect policy performance, particularly with older attained ages and/or minimally funded policies. Several carriers just recently announced increases in the current cost of insurance, or mortality rates, for insureds over the age of 70.[77]

The purchasing power risk of the death benefit of a universal life insurance policy depends on four factors: whether the death benefit option is level or increasing, funding adequacy, policy performance, and the IRC § 7702 corridor. A minimally funded level death benefit option offers no purchasing power risk protection. In this case, the amount of purchasing power risk will vary from the time of policy purchase until the insured's death. On the other hand, depending on policy performance, an adequately funded universal life policy, particularly with premiums at the maximum amount allowed by the IRC § 7702 corridor regulation, can provide some purchasing power protection. The IRC § 7702 corridor rules demand that certain ratios between the cash value account and the death benefit at different attained ages must be maintained. In other words, these cash value account-to-death benefit ratio rules force the death benefit to increase, particularly at older attained ages, causing some purchasing power risk protection.

Inherent in the design of the increasing death benefit option universal life policy is that the death benefit of the policy will increase by the amount of the cash value account in the policy. However, the growth of the cash value account is dependent on policy funding adequacy. Minimally funded universal life policies will experience very little growth and will not offer much purchasing power protection.[78] If the policy is adequately funded as described above, and depending on the performance of the cash value account plus the effect of the IRC § 7702 corridor ratio rules, purchasing power protection can be attained, particularly at older ages. It should be pointed out that due to the increasing high cost of insurance charges at older

---

77. This action on the part of the carriers has resulted in several class action lawsuits, plus some very negative publicity.

78. These policies will also be in danger of lapsing considering changes and volatility of the interest crediting rates and/or increases in the cost of insurance and other policy expenses without significant premium increases.

insured ages with the increasing death benefit option, many policy owners switch from the increasing death benefit option to the level death benefit option at some point in the life of the policy.

Table 3.6 summarizes the risks of universal life insurance.

Table 3.6 Risks by Product Types—Universal Life

What's Guaranteed	What's Not Guaranteed—Risks
• First Year Death Benefit and Minimum Required Amount of Premium • Minimum Interest Crediting Rate • Maximum Cost of Insurance • Maximum Policy Expenses	• Premium Sufficiency • Policy Sustainability • Current Interest Crediting Rates • Current Costs of Insurance • Current Policy Expenses • Purchasing Power • Depends on Factors Such as Level or Increasing Death Benefit Option, Policy Performance, Funding Adequacy, and Section 7702 Corridor

Variable Universal Life

Variable universal life has all the characteristics, aspects, features, and benefits of universal life but with one additional significant element. This variation of the universal life policy design allows the policy owner the opportunity to invest and allocate his or her premiums in mutual fund-like sub-accounts as opposed to in the general asset account that is primarily composed of investment grade corporate and government bonds and commercial mortgages (as is the case with whole life and universal life insurance). Most universal life insurance carriers provide a wide variety of proprietary and non-proprietary mutual fund-like sub-accounts to choose from ranging across a spectrum of fixed and equity account funds. As with all life insurance cash values, the growth of the sub-accounts is tax deferred (and very possibly tax free), plus the sub-accounts may be rebalanced or reallocated without any capital gains taxes. This type of life insurance product has the most volatility and, therefore, the greatest investment risk. All non-guaranteed life insurance products need to be creditably managed; however, with variable universal life, policy management is imperative. Depending on the market returns of the sub-accounts chosen, as well as proper funding and management, variable universal life has the long-run potential for outstanding performance results.

What's guaranteed? Like universal life, the first policy year death benefit is guaranteed along with a first-year minimum required amount of premium. A maximum cost of insurance, or more technically correct, a maximum mortality rate for each attained age generally based on the CSO Mortality Table when the policy was issued; and maximum policy expenses are all guaranteed. However, unlike universal life, there are no minimum guarantees on earnings or a minimum interest crediting rate. In fact, some of the sub-accounts can have negative returns.

What's not guaranteed? What are the risks? Premium sufficiency and policy sustainability are the main risks associated with variable universal life policies. However, both are a function of the amount of premium funding paid into the policy. All too often, the planned funding premium for a variable universal life policy is based on the minimum annual premium that will cause the policy to mature assuming that the assumed policy earnings rate credited—which is generally projected at either a constant 6 percent, 8 percent, 10 percent, or 12 percent—cost of insurance, and expenses remain constant as shown in a life insurance policy illustration. Unfortunately, assuming all current pricing elements will remain constant is a very dangerous and unrealistic assumption. Of course, the effect of assuming a constant interest or earnings rate as the basis for determining a premium was demonstrated in the section "Mathematics of 'Permanent' Types of Life Insurance—Part 2: Constant Assumption versus Reality" in Chapter 2 as a substantial risk. Not surprisingly, a high funding premium close to the amount of premium allowed under the IRC § 7702 corridor regulations substantially mitigates the risks of premium sufficiency and policy sustainability by allowing the variable universal life policy to "absorb" volatility in the earnings rates credited, both positive and negative, and the changes to the cost of insurance and expenses.

Earnings crediting rates will definitely fluctuate as rates of return of various investments change in the economy. Earnings on sub-accounts that are less than anticipated by the assumed earnings crediting rate, and the volatility of such, can require an increase in the planned funding premium—depending on the level of premium funding but particularly if the policy is minimally funded—in order to sustain the policy to either maturity or the planned duration of the policy owner.

While there is generally considerable wiggle room between the current cost of insurance, or more correctly mortality rates, and the current expenses of the policy and the guaranteed maximum mortality rates and expenses of the policy, changes in these elements can occur. Negative changes do severely affect the performance of the policy, particularly with older attained ages and/or minimally funded policies.

The death benefit purchasing power risk of variable universal life, like a universal life insurance policy, depends on four factors: whether the death benefit option is a level or increasing death benefit, funding adequacy, policy performance, and the IRC § 7702 corridor. A minimally funded level death benefit option offers no purchasing power risk protection. In this case, the amount of purchasing power risk will vary from the time of the purchase until the insured's death. On the other hand, depending on policy performance, an adequately funded variable universal life policy—particularly with premiums at the maximum amount allowed by the IRC § 7702 corridor regulation—can provide some purchasing power protection due to the IRC § 7702 corridor rules that demand certain ratios between the cash value account and the death benefit at different attained ages must be maintained. In other words, the cash value account-to-death benefit ratio rules force the death benefit to increase, particularly at older attained ages, causing some purchasing power risk protection.

Inherent in the design of the increasing death benefit option universal life policy is that the policy death benefit will increase by the amount of the policy cash value account. However, the growth of the cash value account is dependent on policy funding adequacy. Minimally funded universal life policies will have very little growth and will not offer much purchasing power protection.[79] If the policy is adequately funded as described above, and depending on the performance of the cash value account plus the effect of the IRC § 7702 corridor ratio rules, purchasing power protection can be attained, particularly at older ages. Sub-account investment experience may not keep pace with inflation in the short run in the beginning years of the policy or due to short-term bursts of inflation. However, in the long run, "the investment-induced increases in coverage should equal, if not exceed. general increases in price levels."[80] It should be pointed out that due to the increasing high cost of insurance charges at an insured's older attained ages with the increasing death benefit option, many policy owners switch from the increasing death benefit option to the level death benefit option at some point in the life of the policy.

Table 3.7 summarizes the risks of variable universal life insurance.

Table 3.7 Risks by Product Types—Variable Universal Life

What's Guaranteed	What's Not Guaranteed—Risks
• First Year Death Benefit and Minimum Required Amount of Premium • Maximum Cost of Insurance • Maximum Policy Expenses	• Premium Sufficiency • Policy Sustainability • Earnings • Current Costs of Insurance • Current Policy Expenses • Purchasing Power • Depends on Factors Such as Level or Increasing Death Benefit Option, Policy Performance, Funding Adequacy, and Section 7702 Corridor

No-Lapse Guarantee Universal Life

No-lapse guarantee universal life is also referred to as no-lapse secondary guarantee universal life and guaranteed universal life. In reality, no-lapse guarantee universal life is guaranteed level premium term insurance to a stated age—older policies were generally age 100 but some newer policies may be age 75, 80, 85, 90, or 95—built on a universal life insurance "chassis." The "guarantee" is either

---

79. These policies will also be in danger of lapsing considering changes and volatility of the earnings crediting rates and/or increases in the cost of insurance and other policy expenses without significant premium increases.

80. Graves, *supra* note 10, page 5.43.

in the form of a rider to the policy or is built into the policy contract, and is subject to stringent conditions on the part of the policy owner. The most common form of this guarantee is that for the continuous timely payment of a stipulated premium amount the policy will not lapse even though the cash value account is zero, which would normally cause a universal life policy to lapse. However, part of the requirements of the no-lapse guarantee provisions is no changes can be made to the universal life policy, and premium payments must be received by the insurance carrier continuously before or on the due date at the specified amount and payment interval stated in the policy. Unlike all other life insurance policies, which allow the policy owner to pay the premium within 31 days after the premium due date, there is no grace period allowed with no-lapse guarantee universal life. If the conditions as stated in the policy are not met by the policy owner, the guaranteed coverage can be lost. These policies provide premium sufficiency to a stated age for a very modest premium cost. Because of the low premium outlay, cash values will most likely be the relatively small guaranteed minimum amount listed in the policy contract and at some point in the mid to later years of the guaranteed period this nominal cash value account will decrease and become zero.

What's guaranteed? Subject to the no-lapse guarantee provision of the policy contract, the death benefit of the policy and the premium amount and duration, if paid on the timely basis with no grace period, are guaranteed to the stated age in the policy. Therefore, subject to the conditions in the policy, premium sufficiency and policy sustainability are guaranteed to the stated age in the policy contract.

What's not guaranteed? What are the risks? One of the biggest risks with the no-lapse guarantee universal life policy is that the policy owner does not live up to the required policy provisions in order to maintain the guaranteed coverage. This is especially true of the requirement to make the exact stipulated premium payment on the exact required interval due date. Because the cash value and reserves backing these policies are minimal, and at certain points zero, carrier financial strength, solvency, and viability is extremely important and should be considered at the selection of the insurance carrier and monitored throughout the life of the policy.

Because of a lack of policy reserve requirements for the secondary no-lapse guarantee at the inception of these policies, there was concern whether the secondary no-lapse guarantee aspect of the policy would be covered by the various state guarantee fund associations. These concerns have now been alleviated. Actuarial Guideline XXXVIII (AG 38) was promulgated by the National Association of Insurance Commissioners in 2003 and further revised in 2012. AG 38 decreed certain reserve account requirements for "shadow account" types of policies such as no-lapse guarantee universal life policies.

No-lapse guarantee universal life has the same purchasing power risks as level death benefit term insurance, since the death benefit of no-lapse guarantee universal life is a constant level amount. Of course, like level term insurance coverage, the amount of purchasing power risk varies from the time of the purchase of the policy until the insured's death.

Table 3.8 summarizes the risks of no-lapse guarantee universal life insurance.

Table 3.8 Risks by Product Types—No-Lapse Guarantee Universal Life

What's Guaranteed	What's Not Guaranteed—Risks
• Premium Amount if Paid Timely and Other Conditions • Death Benefit Subject to Premium Conditions Above • Policy Sustainability Subject to Premium Conditions Above • Premium Sufficiency Subject to Premium Conditions Above	• Policy Owner Fails to Comply with the Conditions of the Guarantee, Especially Not Making Premium Payments on Time • Carrier Solvency • State Guarantee Fund Coverage • A.G. 38 • Purchasing Power

Indexed Universal Life

Indexed universal life, also referred to as equity indexed universal life, is a variation on universal life insurance. Rather than the policy having a minimum guaranteed interest crediting rate with excess interest crediting rates declared at the discretion of the life insurance carrier's board of directors, "index policies employ an elaborate formula and matrix of criteria to determine how much of the gains in a broad index of stocks (such as a S&P 500® Index) [or a portfolio of broad indexes of stock market indices as allocated by the policy owner] will be credited to the cash value."[81] All of the stock indices used in these policies are without dividends. Unlike variable universal life policies where the sub-accounts can have a negative return, the floor index crediting rate is zero. Older indexed universal life policies may have a minimum crediting rate that was typically at least 100 basis points lower than the minimum crediting rate offered on the carrier's universal life products. Newer policies tend to have a zero-minimum crediting rate. The appeal for these policies is the ability to participate in part of the gains of equity markets without incurring the risk of any losses. In other words, the crediting rate for these policies is collared for a measuring interval or period—such as one to five years—of a point-to-point comparison of some market index (without dividends) with a percentage participation rate of the gains in the index—such as 75 percent or 100 percent—and with a maximum cap for the gains—typically 10 percent or 12 percent; and zero. However, with most indexed universal life policies, the participation rate and maximum cap can change at the beginning of each measuring period. "Equity indexed products

---

81. Weber and Hause, *supra* note 16, page 22.

have a number of investment attributes, but under current regulation can be sold by agents with and without securities licensing."[82]

What's guaranteed? The first policy year death benefit is guaranteed along with a first-year minimum required amount of premium.

With regard to the crediting rate formula, on single stock market index policies the use of the index is guaranteed, without dividends, for a point-to-point comparison over a specified interval, such as a yearly or three-year interval. Some policies allow the policy owner to choose among several—generally international—market indices, and, in some cases, allow the policy owner to make a crediting allocation among the different indices. This type of index crediting choice is generally guaranteed. While the overall cap for increases in the index, or indices, and the participation rate for the increase in the index are guaranteed for the current measuring interval, the cap and participation rate may be changed for subsequent measuring intervals. While more recently issued policies tend to have a zero-minimum guaranteed crediting rate, older policies may have a minimum guaranteed crediting rate that is generally at least 100 basis points less than the minimum guaranteed crediting rates on universal life policies offered by the insurance carrier, typically 1 percent or 2 percent.

A maximum cost of insurance, or more technically correct a maximum mortality rate for each attained age generally based on the CSO Mortality Table when the policy was issued; and maximum policy expenses are all guaranteed.

What's not guaranteed? What are the risks? Premium sufficiency and policy sustainability are the main risks associated with indexed universal life policies. However, both are a function of the amount of premium funding paid into the policy. All too often, the planned funding premium for an indexed universal life policy is based on the minimum annual premium that will cause the policy to mature assuming that the assumed policy earnings rate credited—that is generally projected at a constant rate with the maximum assumed crediting rate determined by Actuarial Guideline XLIX (AG 49), which is based on back-tested actual crediting results for the policy—cost of insurance, and expenses remain constant as shown in a life insurance policy illustration. Unfortunately, assuming all current pricing elements remain constant is a very dangerous assumption, as the effect of assuming a constant earnings crediting rate, and determining a premium from such rate, was demonstrated in the section "Mathematics of 'Permanent' Types of Life Insurance—Part 2: Constant Assumption versus Reality" in Chapter 2 as a substantial risk. Not surprisingly, a high planned funding premium close to the amount of premium allowed under the IRC § 7702 corridor regulations substantially mitigates the risks of premium sufficiency and policy sustainability by allowing the indexed universal life policy to "absorb" volatility in the indexed increase rates credited and the changes to the cost of insurance and expenses.

---

82. Ibid, page 22.

Index crediting rates will definitely fluctuate as rates of return of various investments change in the economy. Index increases credited that are less than anticipated by the assumed earnings crediting rate, and the volatility of such, can require an increase in the planned funding premium—depending on the level of premium funding but particularly if the policy is minimally funded—in order to sustain the policy to either maturity or the planned duration of the policy owner.

While there is generally considerable wiggle room between the current cost of insurance, or more correctly mortality rates, and the current expenses of the policy and the guaranteed maximum mortality rates and expenses of the policy, changes in these elements can occur and negative changes do affect severely the performance of the policy, particularly with older attained ages and/or minimally funded policies.

The purchasing power risk of the death benefit of an indexed universal life policy, like a universal life insurance policy, depends on four factors: whether the death benefit option is a level death benefit or increasing death benefit, funding adequacy, policy performance, and the IRC § 7702 corridor. A minimally funded level death benefit option offers no purchasing power risk protection. In this case, the amount of purchasing power risk will vary from the time of the purchase of the policy until the insured's death. On the other hand, depending on policy performance, an adequately funded indexed universal life policy—particularly with premiums at the maximum amount allowed by the IRC § 7702 corridor regulation—can provide some purchasing power protection due to the IRC § 7702 corridor rules, which demand that certain ratios between the cash value account and the death benefit at different attained ages must be maintained. In other words, these cash value account-to-death benefit ratio rules force the death benefit to increase, particularly at older attained ages, causing some purchasing power risk protection.

Inherent in the design of the increasing death benefit option indexed universal life policy is that the death benefit of the policy will increase by the amount of the cash value account in the policy. However, the growth of the cash value account is dependent on policy funding adequacy. Minimally funded universal life policies will have very little growth and will not offer much purchasing power protection.[83] If the policy is adequately funded as described above, and depending on the performance of the cash value account plus the effect of the IRC § 7702 corridor ratio rules, purchasing power protection can be attained, particularly at older ages. It should be pointed out that due to the increasing high cost of insurance charges at older attained ages of the insured with the increasing death benefit option, many policy owners switch from the increasing death benefit option to the level death benefit option at some point in the life of the policy.

---

83. These policies will also be in danger of lapsing considering changes and volatility of the indexed crediting rates and/or increases in the cost of insurance and other policy expenses without significant premium increases.

Table 3.9 summarizes the risks of indexed universal life insurance.

Table 3.9 Risks by Product Types—Indexed Universal Life

What's Guaranteed	What's Not Guaranteed—Risks

• First Year Death Benefit and Minimum Required Amount of Premium
• Crediting Rate Formula
  • Based on Some Index Such as S&P 500® **Without** Dividend Component, with non-guaranteed Participation Rate and Caps; and Minimum Interest Crediting Rate (Typically 100 Basis Points or More Below UL Min. Rate but can be Zero)
• Maximum Cost of Insurance
• Maximum Policy Expenses
	• Premium Sufficiency
	• Policy Sustainability
	• Adequacy of Earnings
	• Participation Rate
	• Maximum Caps on Increase in Index
	• Current Costs of Insurance
	• Current Policy Expenses
	• Purchasing Power
	  • Depends on Factors Such as Level or Increasing Death Benefit Option, Policy Performance, Funding Adequacy, and Section 7702 Corridor

Blended Base Whole Life with Combination Paid-Up Additions and Decreasing Term Insurance Dividend Option and/or Paid-Up Additions Rider

Blended whole life policies are whole life policies with a dividend option that is a combination of paid-up additional insurance and decreasing term insurance, and/or a paid-up additions rider. Such a policy is not technically a separate product type but rather a variation, or use, of a base whole life policy in combination with dividend options and riders causing some additional product risks not associated with just the base whole life policy. As stated previously, blended whole life policies consist of a base whole life policy where dividends are applied to a combination of paid-up additional insurance and purchasing decreasing term life insurance. These policies may also feature a rider where a set dollar amount of premium is applied each year to purchase an amount of paid-up whole life insurance that that premium will purchase at each attained age of the insured—of course, dividends are also paid on this paid-up whole life insurance. The concept here is to purchase life insurance coverage where the total amount of the coverage consists of the base whole life protection and decreasing term life insurance that decreases by the amount of total death benefit associated with the face amount of paid-up additional insurance dividends and, if the paid-up additions rider is also included, the amount of coverage that rider has purchased. At some point, it is contemplated that the total amount of life insurance face amount coverage from the paid-up additions dividends will equal the initial amount of decreasing term insurance included with the base whole life insurance when the policy was purchased. At that point, the term insurance ceases and future dividends that are applied to the paid-up additional insurance option will increase the face amount of the life insurance policy. The appeal of the blended whole life policy is to purchase a total amount of insurance protection for the premium amount afforded by a lesser amount of the base whole life policy, typically around 70 percent or more of the total protection.

What's guaranteed? Of course, for the base whole life policy the premiums, premium paying period, cash values (minimum guaranteed), death benefit, premium sufficiency, and policy sustainability are all guaranteed. If the base whole life policy contains the paid-up additions rider, the right to purchase on a continuous ongoing basis at a fixed-dollar premium amount, single premium paid-up whole life insurance at the insured's attained age for each policy year, and the face amount purchased at each year's attained age is guaranteed. The paid-up additions rider cash values (minimum guaranteed), death benefit, policy sustainability, and sufficiency are also all guaranteed.

What's not guaranteed? What are the risks? Dividends for both the base whole life policy and the paid-up additions rider are not guaranteed and can be less than anticipated. Since dividends are used both to purchase decreasing term insurance and paid-up additional insurance, inadequate dividends—particularly at older attained ages and with the initial base whole life coverage at a relatively low percentage compared with the total initial amount of coverage—could fail to cover the decreasing term insurance cost, resulting in additional premium contributions by the policy owner that probably could also increase in subsequent years of the policy.

Purchasing power risk depends on the dividend performance and amount. Prior to the point where the decreasing term insurance amount is equal to zero and the death benefit increases because at that point the dividends are devoted to only purchasing paid-up additions, the death benefit of the policy is level and, of course, the purchasing power risks vary from the time of policy purchase until that point. Thereafter, some purchasing power can be attained with the paid-up additions dividend option, particularly if combined with the paid-up additions rider.

Table 3.10 summarizes the risks of a blended base whole life with the combination paid-up additions and decreasing term dividend option, and/or the paid-up additions insurance rider.

Table 3.10 Risks by Product Types—Blended Base Whole Life with Combination Paid-Up Additions and Decreasing Term Dividend Option and/or Paid-Up Additions Rider

What's Guaranteed	What's Not Guaranteed—Risks
• Base Whole Life Premium • Base Whole Life Premium Paying Period • Base Whole Life Cash Values (Minimum Guarantee) • Base Whole Life Death Benefit • Base Whole Life Policy Sustainability • Base Whole Life Premium Sufficiency • Paid-Up Additions Rider—The Right to Purchase on a Continuous Ongoing Basis at a Fixed Dollar Premium Amount, Single Premium Paid-Up Whole Life Insurance at the Insured's Attained Age for Each Policy Year • Paid-Up Additions Rider Face Amount Purchased at Each Year's Attained Age • Paid-Up Additions Rider Cash Values (Minimum Guarantee) • Paid-Up Additions Rider Death Benefit, Policy Sustainability, and Sufficiency	• Dividends for Both Base Policy and Paid-Up Additions Rider • Inadequate Dividends Failure to Cover Term Cost Requiring Term Premium Contributions, Which Probably Could Increase in Subsequent Years • Purchasing Power Depends on Dividend Amount, Some Purchasing Power Protection Can Be Afforded with the Paid-Up Additional Insurance Dividend Option After Paid-Up Additional Insurance Face Amount Additions Are Equal to the Initial Decreasing Term Face Amount

Product Suitability Risk

Over time, circumstances and needs for life insurance change. First of all, the growth of the insured's, or policy owner's, assets—particularly with closely held business interests or real estate—can require an increase need for liquidity for, perhaps, buy/sell agreements or estate taxes that an increase in life insurance coverage can provide. Conversely, values of assets can decline and/or estate tax exemption amounts can increase, precipitating either a lesser need for the liquidity provided by life insurance or no longer a need for life insurance coverage. Of course, in the latter case a life settlement[84] should be considered.

Different product types are appropriate for different policy owners and different circumstances during the policy owner's life cycle. Similarly, product-type appropriateness can change with time and varying circumstances. The first criterion for selecting a product type[85] should be the risk tolerance of the policy owner. Policy owners with what would be considered a conservative to moderate risk tolerance would probably be more comfortable with guarantee-type products such as term, whole life, or no-lapse guarantee universal life insurance. Policy owners with a moderately aggressive to aggressive risk tolerance should consider universal life, indexed universal life, or variable universal life insurance. Very aggressive risk tolerance policy owners should consider variable universal life insurance. Of course, with variable universal life insurance policies, asset allocations may be made among the mutual fund-like sub-accounts in proportion to the policy owner's risk tolerance.

The second criterion for selecting a product type is the preference of the policy owner for either the lowest premium outlay or growth in the policy death benefit and cash values. Policy owners with a preference for the lowest premium outlay would either choose term insurance, hopefully, for temporary coverage, or for more permanent coverage, no-lapse guarantee universal life insurance. If the preference is for growth of the death benefit and cash values—which would be appropriate for protecting purchasing power, increases in death benefit needs for buy/sell

---

84. The life settlement industry provides a secondary market for life insurance policies that are no longer needed or affordable. Rather than surrendering a cash value life insurance policy with the life insurance carrier, the settlement market provides the policy owner the ability to sell an existing life insurance policy for an amount in excess of the policy's cash surrender value. Settlements take two forms: "viatical" (probability of death within 24 months if the insured is diagnosed as terminally or chronically ill) and "life" (if the insured has a life expectancy longer than 24 months). To qualify as a life settlement prospect, the insured should be age 65, preferably age 70 or older, and in declining health. It is essential for the policy owner to engage an experienced settlement broker who has access to the well-established, institutionally funded "providers." See Whitelaw and Montag, *supra* note 1, Chapter 10, pages 91–104.

85. For an excellent discussion on the selection of product types and the building of a life insurance portfolio see Weber and Hause, *supra* note 16, Chapter 10, pages 73–85.

agreements or estate tax liquidity, or retirement income supplement needs—participating whole life or variable universal life insurance would be the most appropriate choices. Universal life and indexed universal life could fall somewhere between these two choices.

Of course, a product type that is suitable and appropriate when purchased may not be suitable at a later point in time. Risk tolerances do and can change. As policy owners grow older, their risk tolerance tends to become more toward the conservative. Also, after a downturn in the equity markets, it is not surprising that a lot of investors' risk tolerances change from aggressive to conservative. The preference over the choice for the lowest premium outlay or the growth in the death benefit and cash values can also change. Similarly, the premium paying capacity of the insured or the policy owner can also change over time and make the initial product-type choice inappropriate.

Product suitability needs to be reviewed on a frequent basis—at least every two years—and appropriate or remedial action needs to be taken. This may entail increases or decreases in premium; increases (requiring evidence of insurability) or decreases in the death benefit with universal life, indexed universal life, and variable universal life; or a reallocation of the sub-accounts with variable universal life insurance. With participating whole life insurance, this may require changes in the dividend option, or surrendering paid-up additions to pay policy premiums; or the election of one of the "non-forfeiture" options of extended term insurance or reduced paid-up insurance,[86] both of which would terminate the premium payment requirements.

Policy replacement to a policy more suitable for the policy owner's needs is another option that can be considered. However, the paramount consideration with any policy replacement is whether or not the insured is insurable at the same risk classification of the original policy, or even insurable at all.

---

86. Whole life and endowment life insurance policies are required by law to contain under the Standard Non-forfeiture Law of all 50 states and the District of Columbia three forms of surrender options if the policy owner wishes to cease paying premiums. These surrender options are referred to as the nonforfeiture options. Besides including the option to surrender the policy for its cash surrender value, in which case the life insurance coverage is terminated, the policy owner may elect either a reduced paid-up insurance or an extended term insurance option.

The reduced paid-up insurance option applies the net cash surrender value—guaranteed cash value plus the cash value from the paid-up insurance dividend option less policy loans—to purchase a paid-up policy of the same type as the original policy but of a reduced face amount of protection.

The extended term insurance option applies the net cash surrender value to purchase a paid-up term insurance policy of a face amount equal to the original face of the policy, plus any face amount additions from paid-up insurance dividends, less policy loans, for a term length that that net cash surrender value can purchase at the insured's attained age as a net single premium.

See Graves, *supra* note 10, pages 8.8–8.16 and 27.12–27.13.

One interesting argument in favor of replacements was advanced by noted actuary Richard A. Schwartz during an educational program that included the author.[87] Schwartz commented that as long as you can keep commissions and other acquisition costs low, replacements would result in mortality cost savings—Schwartz suggested as much as 40 percent—because by the insured proving evidence of insurability, "select" mortality rates would be used for some period—varying from 15 to 25 years—instead of the "ultimate" mortality rates. Select mortality rates are those rates that reflect the experience of those insureds who have recently provided evidence of insurability. However, the effects of providing evidence of insurability diminish over a period varying from 15 to 25 years at which point ultimate mortality rates are used that are the rates that do not reflect providing evidence of insurability. The effect of select and ultimate mortality rates for a policy issued on a 50-year-old preferred female non-smoker using the 2001 CSO Mortality Table is shown in Figure 3.1. Schwartz's argument is based on the premise that the present value of the mortality cost savings during the duration of the select mortality rates period is greater than the present value of the new commission and acquisition costs and other expense differentials. While this argument may be theoretically correct, how would a policy owner get the data to calculate the replacement savings advantages—to say nothing as to whether or not the data is guaranteed?

Figure 3.1 Select and Ultimate Rate Comparison

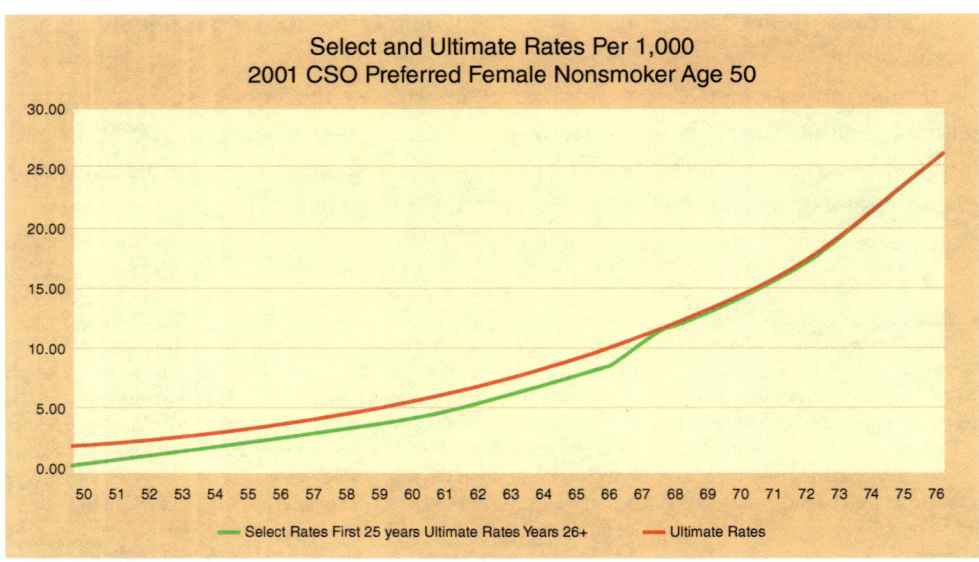

---

87. Gary L. Flotron, Lawrence Brody, Richard A. Schwartz, Richard M. Weber, and E. Randolph Whitelaw, "The Uniform Prudent Investor Act and Trust-Owned Life Insurance: The Impossible Dream or a Match Made in Heaven," *48th Annual Heckerling Institute on Estate Planning*, University of Miami School of Law, Orlando, Florida, Thursday, Special Session III-E, January 16, 2014.

In 1992, the Society of Financial Service Professionals[88] published an extremely useful questionnaire form to assist policy owners in the policy replacement decision that was titled "Replacement Questionnaire (RQ)—A Policy Replacement Evaluation Form." The Replacement Questionnaire has not been updated to reflect new products such as no-lapse guarantee universal life and indexed universal life, and appears to no longer be available from the Society of Financial Service Professionals. Nevertheless, if one can still find the form, it does provide a number of insightful issues that need to be considered with policy replacements. Noteworthy, however, is the cautionary first introductory paragraph to the form:

> **Replacing an existing life insurance policy with a new one generally is not in the policyholder's best interest**. New sales loads and other expenses, the new company's right to challenge a death claim during the suicide and contestability periods, changes in age or health and the loss of important grandfathered rights are some of the obvious reasons that **most replacements cannot be justified**. On the other hand, there may be circumstances where a replacement is in your client's best interest. The ethical agent will provide his or her client with the impartial information needed to make an informed decision, including reasons the client should not replace the current policy and/or how to modify the existing policy to accomplish their goals. The need for additional coverage is not, by itself, a justification for replacement. [Emphasis added by the Society of Financial Service Professionals.][39]

There are certain circumstances where a policy replacement is appropriately warranted, such as (1) where either the insured's risk classification has improved since the purchase of the policy but the insurance carrier refuses to amend the policy to reflect such an improvement; (2) the financial condition of the current carrier has dramatically deteriorated; or (3) circumstances have caused a change in budget and have made it difficult to maintain a large policy with significant premiums.

Nevertheless, all policy replacements should be approached with extreme caution and a thorough due process evaluation in order to make the proper decisions. If a policy is replaced, however, and the cash value from the replaced policy is not transferred to the new policy via an IRC § 1035 exchange,[90] then consideration should be given to disposing the replaced policy via a life settlement.[91]

---

88. At the time of publishing, the Society of Financial Service Professionals was known as the American Society of CLU and ChFC.

89. "Replacement Questionnaire (RQ)—A Policy Replacement Evaluation Form," Society of Financial Service Professionals, Newtown Square, Pennsylvania, 1992.

90. An IRC § 1035 exchange is a tax-free direct transfer of the cash value of one life insurance policy into another life insurance policy with the same insured or insureds made by the insurance carriers. The exception to the same insureds rule occurs with a second-to-die life insurance policy where one of the insureds is deceased. In this case, the surviving insured may have an IRC § 1035 exchange from the second-to-die policy into a single life policy.

91. See footnote 84.

Diversification Risk

Life insurance has been viewed as and can be considered as a separate asset class.[92] Individual policy owners normally have investment portfolios—either owned outright, in revocable living trusts, in individual retirement accounts (IRAs), or within qualified plans such as 401(k) plans—generally made up of various asset classes such as stocks and bonds in order to achieve diversification and lower overall investment risk as espoused by Harry Markowitz's modern portfolio theory (MPT).[93] In order to reduce unsystematic risk,[94] each asset class ordinarily should contain a variety of individual securities of that asset class. Having only one security causes concentration risk, or, to put it another way, the risk of having all your eggs in one basket. Having only one life insurance policy can be considered a concentration risk, at least within the asset class of life insurance. An extreme example of concentration risk is, perhaps, the typical ILIT in which the only asset of the trust is one life insurance policy.

Diversification within the life insurance asset class can be obtained by purchasing life insurance policies from different life insurance carriers and having life insurance policies of different product types. Having diversification by both multiple carriers and different product types helps mitigate against the risks of carrier insolvency[95] and product type performance, the latter analogous to having both stocks and bonds—or different asset classes—in an investment portfolio. A life insurance portfolio can be selected applying similar principles used in the construction of an investment portfolio. This would entail determining an asset allocation mix of life insurance product types based on the policy owner's risk tolerance and preference for either the lowest premium outlay or growth in the death benefit and

---

92. See Weber and Hause, *supra* note 16, Chapter 9, pages 63–72, and Lawrence Brody, Robert G. Alexander, and Gary L. Flotron, "The Cash Value Beneficiary Defective Inheritor's Trust: Advanced Planning Issues—Split-Dollar and Premium Financing Arrangements and Modern Portfolio Theory and Life Insurance," *New York University Review of Employee Benefits and Executive Compensation 2010*, Matthew Bender & Company, Inc., a Member of the LexisNexis Group, New Providence, New Jersey, 2010, §§ 17.13–17.20, pages 17.83–17.143.

93. Harry Markowitz, "Portfolio Selection," *The Journal of Finance*, Vol. 7, No 1, March 1952, pages 77–91.

94. The academic financial literature is replete with publications on risks and uncertainty, and investment risks and returns. Most textbooks on investments and portfolios contain chapters or sections on the topic. See for example: College for Financial Planning, CFP® Certification Professional Education Program: Investment Planning, Module 2—Invest Risk & Return, College for Financial Planning, Greenwood Village, Colorado, 2008 (or latest edition), Chapters 1 and 2; Hirt, Geoffrey, Block & Basu, Investment Planning for Financial Professionals, 1st Edition, The McGraw-Hill Companies, New York, New York, 2006, Chapter 5, pages 71–90; Summer N. Levine, Editor, The Financial Analyst's Handbook, Second Edition, Irwin Professional Publishing, Burr Ridge, Illinois, 1988, Chapter 37; Jack Clark Francis and Stephen H. Archer, Portfolio Analysis, Second Edition, Prentice-Hall, Inc., Englewood Cliffs, New Jersey, 1979, Section One: Risk Estimates, Chapters II, III, and IV.

95. See previous discussion on carrier insolvency risk.

cash values of the policies.[96] However, the benefits of a diversified portfolio of life insurance policies may be economically unfeasible where the total amount of life insurance protection is less than $1,000,000 to $3,000,000 of coverage due to the banding of premium rates, with higher face amounts of coverage having lower rates per $1,000 of coverage, and the multiple fixed policy fees incurred. In other words, the policy owner has to weigh the tradeoff between the benefits of diversification versus lower cost based on premium banding and multiple policy fees. Of course, this trade-off is highly dependent on the total face amount of life insurance involved in the decision.

---

96. The details of this selection process and life insurance asset allocation mixes based on risk tolerance and preference for the lowest premium outlay or growth in the death benefit and cash values of the policies is beyond the scope of this book. However, see Weber and Hause, *supra* note 16, Chapter 10, pages 73–85, and Brody, Alexander, and Flotron, *supra* note 92, §§ 17.18–17.19, pages 17.117–17.142, for a thorough discussion and analysis of the topic.

Chapter 4

Process of Managing Life Insurance Policies

Traditional Investment Management versus Life Insurance Management

It is accepted practice to set objectives, formalize a written plan of operation, execute the plan, monitor and risk manage the plan according to the objectives on a periodic basis, and take corrective action when needed. Corrective action may entail restructuring the plan and plan investments based on revised objectives. Indeed, the process just stated is the essence of not only financial and investment planning but professional fiduciary trust management. As part of this management process, owners of such portfolios realize the need for professional unbiased advice in management, legal and tax matters, and in other areas where the owner lacks expertise. Owners, and managers, also understand the importance of delegating certain functions to individuals and institutions when the owner or manager lacks either the capability, expertise, or resources to do those functions effectively and efficiently. Investment portfolios can consist of assets worth in the hundreds of thousands to multimillions of dollars range and for which the planning duration can span either decades or for generations.

However, this traditional management process, described for investment assets, securities, and portfolios above, is seldom applied to the management of life insurance. Yet, life insurance policies are a substantial asset and usually part of the policy owner's estate planning for the future of the insured's family, business associates, and charities. Life insurance policies typically have a planning duration of ten to 50 years or more. Additionally, as identified in the two previous chapters of this book, life insurance policies have risks that need to be prudently monitored and managed, particularly indeterminate premium non-guaranteed universal life insurance policies. As stated by E. Randolph Whitelaw and Henry Montag:[97]

---

97. Whitelaw and Montag, *supra* note 1, pages 62–63.

Why should life insurance not be managed with the same discipline as [a] $1 million investment in fixed income and/or equity investments? In other words, in order to avoid glazed eyes, protect against unpleasant surprises, and facilitate informed decisions, that maximize the probability of a favorable planning outcome, why not employ the same tools and prudent process as used for fixed income and equity investments, especially if the life insurance asset and its performance monitoring are linked to those asset types?

As depicted in Figure 4.1,[98] the process for risk managing life insurance is the same as risk managing traditional investments of fixed-income and equity securities. Both start with identifying the objectives of the investor/insured/policy owner/trust grantor in formulating a life insurance policy management statement or investment policy asset allocation and management statement. For life insurance, determining the product type suitability mix and design (asset allocation), based on the risk tolerance specified in the life insurance policy management statement, is critical to maximizing the probability of a successful planning outcome.

Figure 4.1 Life Insurance and Traditional Investment Management Processes

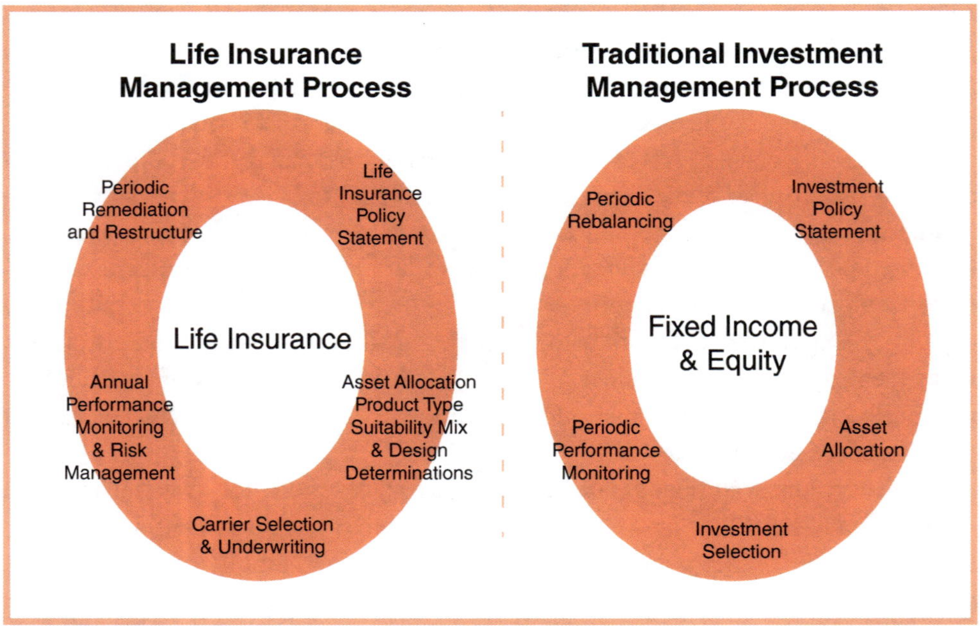

---

98. Figure 4.1 is a modification of a similar figure produced by E. Randolph Whitelaw, AEP® (Distinguished), Managing Director of Trust Asset Consultants, LLC (TAC), a trust-owned life insurance (TOLI) risk management consulting firm, and Co-Managing Director of The TOLI Center, LLC (TTC), a life insurance policy administration and risk management firm.

Life Insurance Policy Management Statement

Perhaps, the most crucial step in the life insurance risk management process starts with the creation of a life insurance policy management statement, which can also be called a life insurance policy risk management statement, life insurance management statement, or, in the irrevocable life insurance trust (ILIT) context, a trust-owned life insurance (TOLI) investment policy statement (TIPS). Some of the most important purposes of the life insurance policy management statement are to:

- Formalize the insured/policy owner/trust grantor's objectives and expectations
- Identify parties and their duties to the life insurance planning, monitoring and risk management, creditable evaluation, and remediation and restructure
- Specify risk tolerance pursuant to the objectives of the insured/policy owner/ trust grantor
- Provide for the delegation of life insurance expertise and creditable policy evaluation to a qualified fee-based life insurance consultant
- Summarize the risk management criteria to be annually evaluated, and the procedure to monitor and/or remediate and restructure underperforming or no longer suitable life insurance policies
- Confirm annual reporting, accounting, and communication schedule functions to various parties, such as trust beneficiaries

Delegation of Life Insurance Management Duties

As mentioned earlier, owners and managers of investment portfolios understand the importance of delegating certain functions to individuals and institutions where the owner or manager lacks either the capability, expertise, or resources to do those functions effectively and efficiently themselves. Most life insurance insureds, policy owners, and ILIT trustees lack life insurance expertise and creditable life insurance policy evaluation capabilities. Therefore, in order to properly monitor and risk manage either a life insurance policy or life insurance portfolio, delegation to an impartial, qualified fee-based life insurance consultant is essential. The key words here are impartial, qualified, and fee-based. Finding such individuals is not easy but can be accomplished by a prudent process involving referrals and a request for proposals (RFP) procedure requiring detailed information about the consultant's background, qualifications, and creditable life insurance policy evaluation methods.[99]

---

99. See Chapter 5, which deals with creditable actuarial policy evaluation (AE) using Monte Carlo simulation and actuarially certified policy benchmark standards.

4.1 illustrates,[100] in the context of managing life insurance policies in an spectrum of life insurance administration and management duties that can be de..._ .ted to an independent, impartial, qualified fee-based life insurance consultant. Most of these same delegated duties can be utilized by any insured or policy owner.

Table 4.1 Process of Managing Life Insurance Policies: TOLI Administration and Risk Management Duties May Be Delegated

- If ILIT Trustee Lacks Life Insurance Expertise and Policy Evaluation Ability, and/or Administration Capacity, These Functions May and Should Be Delegated to Independent Qualified Parties
- Delegation Must Follow a Prudent Process Which Should Include Requests for Proposals (RFP) and the Procedures and Process Should Be Written in the TOLI Investment Policy Statement (TIPS)

Spectrum of TOLI Delegation	
• Investment Policy Statement Review	• ILIT Client Administration
• Carrier/Product Suitability Analysis	• Policy Performance Evaluation
• Fact-Based Policy Risk Assessment	• Portfolio Risk Management Reporting
• Life Expectancy and Duration Analysis	• Policy Performance Management Reports
• Policy Underwriting Oversight	• Actuarial-Certified Policy Evaluation
• Policy Acceptance Oversight	• Premium Adequacy
• Portfolio "Watch List" Procedures	• Lapse Evaluation
• Policy Remediation Consulting	• Policy Cost Evaluation
• Policy "Rescue" Option Analysis	• Monte Carlo Simulation Analysis
• Requests for Proposal Oversight	• Remediation Option Evaluation
• Professional Adviser Communications	• Grantor/Beneficiary Communications

Best versus Predatory Practices in Life Insurance Trust Management

Table 4.2[101] illuminates and portrays the best versus predatory practices in the risk management of life insurance policies within the context of an ILIT. The practices for the process of properly managing life insurance policies for trustees are essentially the same for any policy owner and, thus, transferable. Just replace the term "Trustee" in the table below with the term "Policy Owner."

---

100. Table 4.1 is based on material and illustrations produced by E. Randolph Whitelaw, AEP® (Distinguished), Managing Director of Trust Asset Consultants, LLC (TAC), a TOLI risk management consulting firm, and Co-Managing Director of The TOLI Center, LLC (TTC), a life insurance policy administration and risk management firm.

101. Table 4.2 is based on material and illustrations produced by E. Randolph Whitelaw, AEP® (Distinguished), Managing Director of Trust Asset Consultants, LLC (TAC), a TOLI risk management consulting firm, and Co-Managing Director of The TOLI Center, LLC (TTC), a life insurance policy administration and risk management firm.

Table 4.2 Process of Managing Life Insurance Policies: Best versus Predatory Practices for Professional and Amateur Trustees

- Process the Same for Both Amateur and Professional Trustees
- Amateurs Can Use Best Practices of Professional Trustees
- Best Practices—Policy Acceptance, Management, and Restructure Decisions Based upon the ILIT Agreement, TOLI Investment Policy Statement, and TOLI-Specific Expertise
- Predatory Practices—The Conscious and Willful Inattention to, Avoidance of, and Disregard for the ILIT Agreement, Known ILIT Trustee Duties, and Known Life Insurance Guidance (Ignorance and Lack of Awareness Are Not Defensible Excuses.)

Spectrum of TOLI Risk Management Options			
	Predatory	**Questionable**	**Best**
Trustee	No Duties	Limited Duties	Active Oversight
IPS	No	No	Yes
Life Insurance Expertise	Unknown	Grantor Friend	Delegation per IPS
Policy Monitoring	No	Illustrations	Dispute Defensible per IPS
Annual Communication	No	Periodic	Yes per IPS
Restructure Evaluation	Unknown	Unknown	Yes per IPS

Duration Planning with Universal Life Policies and Using Personalized Life Expectancy Reports

The universal life, variable universal life, and indexed universal life policy "chassis" offers tremendous flexibility. While most policy owners and planners endeavor to select a planned funding premium that will endow the policy at either age 100 or 120, depending on the mortality table used at the time of policy issue, providing "true" permanent lifetime protection, it is possible to select a planned funding premium—using creditable actuarial policy evaluation that will be discussed in Chapter 5—that will provide protection for a duration time frame that is shorter than full permanent lifetime protection. The advantage of using a duration planning period shorter than the point the policy would endow is a significantly lower amount of required planned funding premium. Of course, the disadvantage and risk is that the insured outlives the planned duration selected. Proper policy monitoring and application of the risk management techniques described in the following can be utilized to reasonably determine a planned duration period.

As a prelude to duration period planning, recall from a previous section in Chapter 2 that life expectancy, in insurance and actuarial terms, represents for a particular group with a stated starting point age, the medium age or midpoint where half of the group members from the common starting point are deceased and half of the group members are survivors. Life expectancy, therefore, represents the 50-percentile mark. However, on that same mortality curve for a particular group with a stated starting age, we can also identify other percentile marks, such as the

90-percentile mark where 90 percent for a particular group with a stated starting age are deceased and 10 percent of the group are survivors. Of course, the 100-percentile mark is at the end of the mortality curve where actuarially everyone in the particular group with a stated starting age is deceased. Similarly, recall that life expectancy for an individual and the resulting mortality curve over time can shift due to changes in the individual's health, occupation, and/or avocation.

We will use Figures 4.2–4.6 to illustrate and demonstrate the issues and techniques involved with duration analysis planning. Figure 4.2 presents the mortality curve for a recently underwritten group of 50-year-old females in the preferred non-smoker risk classification. Notice that the life expectancy, or 50-percentile mark, for this group of age 50 females is age 86, and the 90-percentile mark is age 96. Figure 4.3 duplicates the graph in Figure 4.2 but adds the quintessential $64,000 question:[102] "To which LE [life expectancy] should a policy owner manage a policy?"

The effect of the duration period, or percentile life expectancy, chosen on the actuarially evaluated planned funding premium for a $1,000,000 variable universal life policy is demonstrated in Figure 4.4. As shown in the figure, managing the policy to age 86, which is the 50-percentile life expectancy for this 50-year-old group of females, requires a planned funding premium of $8,000 per year. Whereas, managing the policy to age 96, which is the 90-percentile life expectancy, requires a planned funding premium of $11,000 per year.

Figure 4.2 Duration Analysis Planning—Underwritten Mortality and Life Expectancy Percentiles

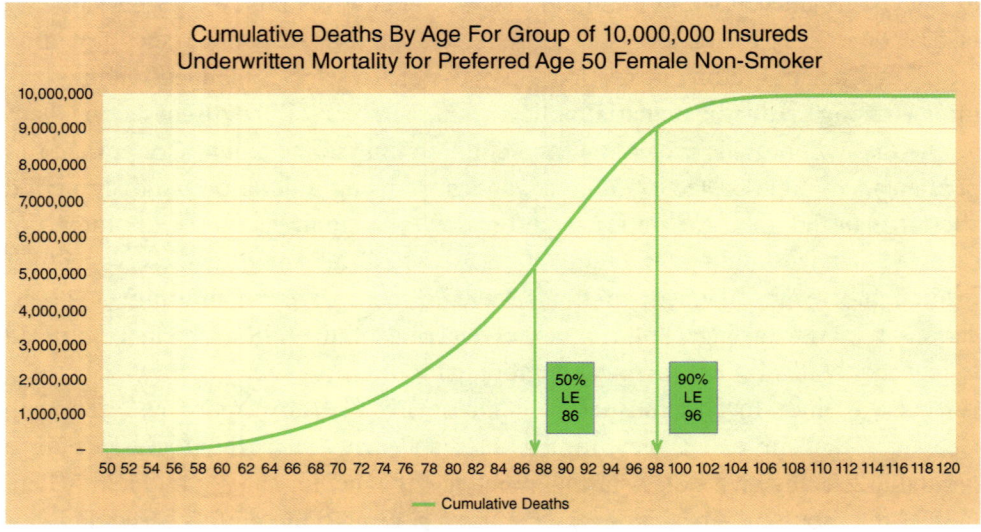

---

102. The author is showing his age.

Figure 4.3 Duration Analysis Planning—The $64,000 Question about Life Expectancy

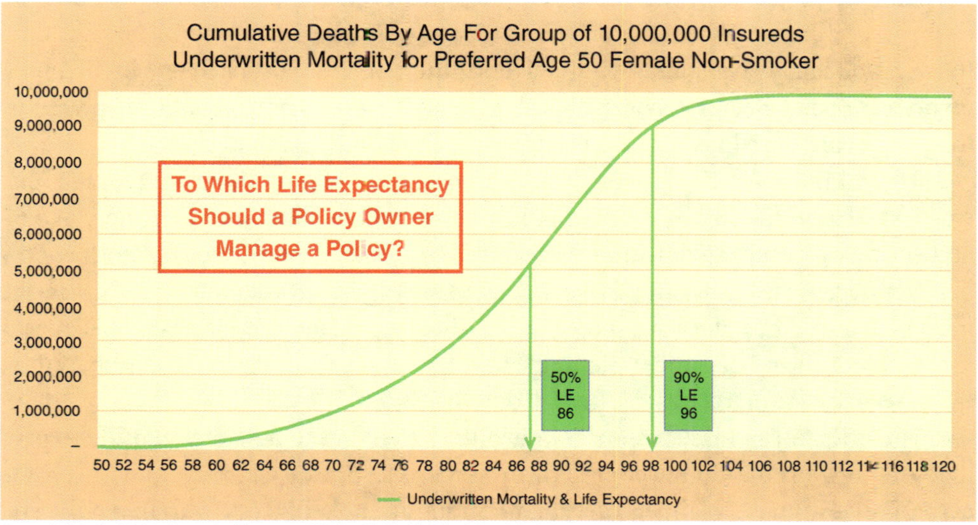

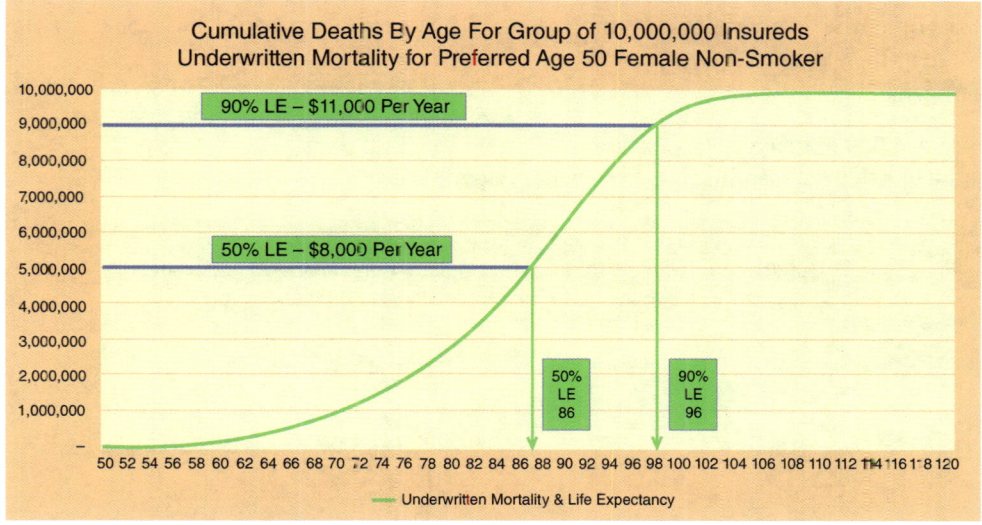

Figure 4.4 Duration Analysis Planning—Effect of Life Expectancy Objective on Universal Life Premium Requirements

Carriers use separate mortality tables for each particular group of risk-classified insureds, such as preferred non-smoker females, to estimate the life expectancy, or other percentile of life expectancy marks, for the group as a whole. These tables, therefore, represent the life expectancies of a group of insureds and are not individual-insured specific. As a by-product of the development of the life settlement industry, it is now possible to obtain an individualized, personalized life expectancy report at a reasonable cost—ranging from $250 to $500 depending on the provider—based upon an individual's medical records. These reports are particularly accurate and relative for planning purposes for individuals in their 60s or individuals who have a chronic or terminal illness. The life expectancy reports can be particularly useful not only for duration analysis planning with universal life policies, but for longevity planning involving Social Security benefit starting periods, retirement income distributions, long-term care decisions, reverse mortgages, and annuity planning.

Returning to the duration analysis planning example for an insured female that was issued a preferred non-smoker policy at age 50, let's assume she is now age 62 and obtains a personalized life expectancy assessment report. Her health has now deteriorated, shifting her life expectancy curve. Figure 4.5 depicts this shift in the mortality curve based on her personalized life expectancy report. Her life expectancy based on the 50-percentile mark has decreased from 86 to 78, and based on the 90-percentile mark, has declined from 96 to 90.

The effect of her deterioration in health, based on the personalized life expectancy report, on the duration period, or percentile life expectancy, chosen on the actuarially evaluated planned funding premium for a $1,000,000 variable universal life policy is demonstrated in Figure 4.6. As shown in the figure, if the variable universal life policy is just managed to the point of the revised life expectancy, or 50-percentile mark, of age 78, premiums could be decreased from $8,000 per year to $5,900 per year. If the variable universal policy is managed to the revised 90-percentile life expectancy mark of age 90, premiums could be reduced from $11,000 per year to $9,200 per year.

Figure 4.5 Duration Analysis Planning—Shifting Mortality and Life Expectancy from Updated Personalized Life Expectancy Report

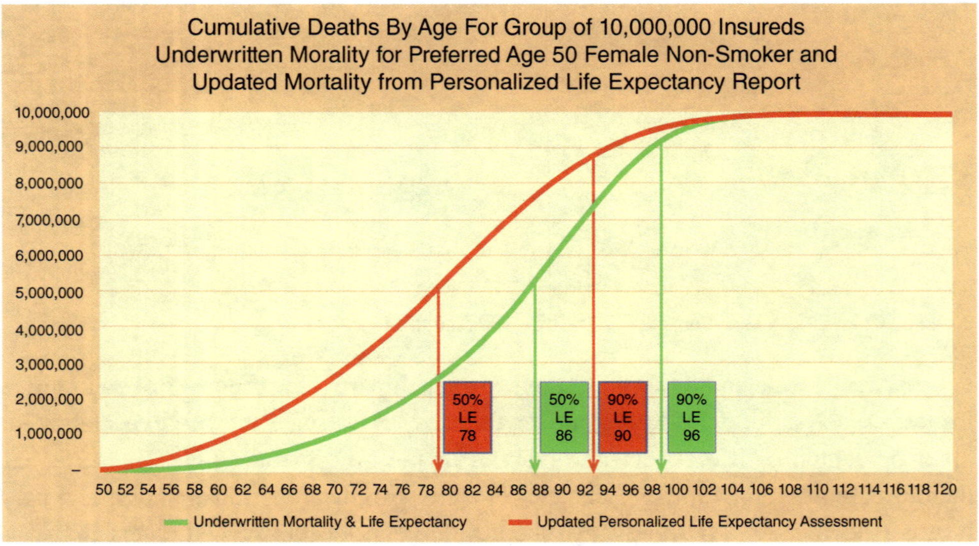

Figure 4.6 Duration Analysis Planning—Effect of Updated Personalized Life Expectancy Report on Management of Universal Life Premium Requirements

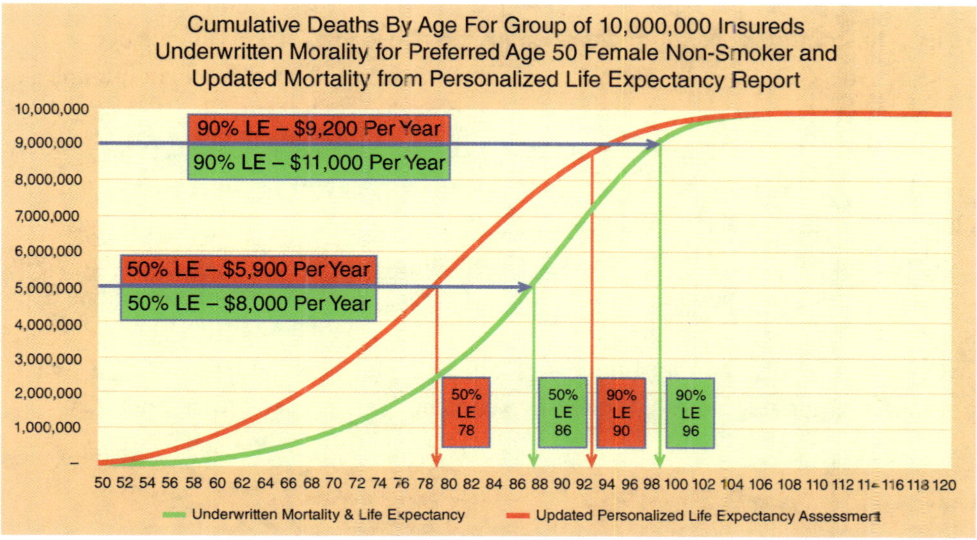

Cumulative Deaths By Age For Group of 10,000,000 Insureds
Underwritten Morality for Preferred Age 50 Female Non-Smoker and
Updated Mortality from Personalized Life Expectancy Report
10,000,000
9,000,000
8,000,000
7,000,000
6,000,000
5,000,000
4,000,000
3,000,000
2,000,000
1,000,000
90% LE – $9,200 Per Year
90% LE – $11,000 Per Year
50% LE – $5,900 Per Year
50% LE – $8,000 Per Year
50% LE 78
50% LE 86
90% LE 90
90% LE 96
50 52 54 56 58 60 62 64 66 68 70 72 74 76 78 80 82 84 86 88 90 92 94 96 98 100 102 104 106 108 110 112 116 118 120
Underwritten Mortality & Life Expectancy
Updated Personalized Life Expectancy Assessment

While the above example shows the effects of duration planning analysis for an insured whose health deteriorated since her policy was issued, with medical science advances and insureds who maintain a healthy lifestyle with proper diet and exercise, a personalized life expectancy report can result in showing life expectancies much greater than that shown for a group of individuals with the same risk classification. Thus, longevity risk needs to be taken into consideration in any type of planning. With respect to duration planning for universal life policies, insureds whose personalized life expectancy reports indicate high life expectancy expectations will naturally require higher premium contribution levels at whatever the life expectancy percentile mark is chosen by the policy owner.

Duration analysis planning must first take into account the policy owner's objectives and risk tolerance as, hopefully, contained in a life insurance policy management statement. Purchasing power risks need also to be taken into consideration. Universal life duration analysis generally implies an emphasis on level death benefits with minimum premium outlay. If the policy owner's objectives are to maximize the cash values in the policy for retirement income purposes, or to have increasing death benefits due to increasing needs for life insurance and protection from purchasing power erosion, then the maximum premium contribution levels should be considered.

Duration analysis planning exhibits the amazing versatility of universal life policies. The actual duration period chosen and the planned funding period are dependent on two very important factors: First, the risk tolerance of the policy owner.

Absent a personalized life expectancy report that shows an extremely short life span, not too many policy owners would choose life expectancy, or the 50-percentile mark, as the duration period. Most policy owners would like a cushion of at least a few years. The comfort zone of the duration period chosen is a risk tolerance decision.

Second, after choosing the planned actual duration period, it is paramount that the planned funding premium be actuarially evaluated by an independent, impartial, fee-based life insurance consultant for the sustainability and sufficiency of that scheduled premium to the chosen duration period. As will be discussed in the next chapter, actuarial evaluation is based on the risk tolerance of the policy owner.

Personalized life expectancy reports enhance and provide greater accuracy to the life expectancy percentile duration decision. Like all risk management decisions, the duration planning period needs to be reviewed annually, in consideration with all the aspects of the monitoring and risk management process, and, where appropriate, updated personalized life expectancy reports need to be obtained.

Chapter 5

Creditable Evaluation of Life Insurance

The Extreme Disconnect

There is an extreme disconnect between the most commonly used method of flexible premium, non-guaranteed policy evaluation used today and what a 1992 report by the Society of Actuaries[103] and Financial Industry Regulatory Authority (FINRA) regulations[104] say is an improper method of policy valuation. That is, the majority of financial planners and life insurance professionals are evaluating non-guaranteed life insurance products by comparing the different carriers' life insurance policy illustrations. Yet the 1992 Society of Actuaries Task Force on Policy Illustrations makes it clear that "[i]llustrations which are typically used, however, to portray the *numbers* based on certain fixed assumptions—and/or are likely to be used to compare one policy to another—are an improper use of a policy illustration."[105]

So, what is the problem with the use of policy illustrations in evaluating non-guaranteed life insurance policies? Again, the Society of Actuaries Task Force on Policy Illustrations says it best:

> How credible are any non-guaranteed numbers projected twenty years in the future, even if constructed with integrity? How does the consumer evaluate the credibility of two illustrations if they are from different companies? Or even if they are from the same company if different products with different guarantees are being considered? Most illustration problems arise because the illustrations create the illusion that the insurance company knows what will happen in the future and that this knowledge has been used to create the illustration.[106]

---

103. *Final Report of the Task Force for Research on Life Insurance Sales Illustrations under the Auspices of the Committee for Research on Social Concerns*, Transactions of the Society of Actuaries 1991–92 Reports. Society of Actuaries, 1992.

104. FINRA Rule 2210—IM-2210-2, Communications with the Public about Variable Life Insurance.

105. Society of Actuaries, *supra* note 103, pages 159–60.

106. Ibid, page 140.

The problem is the number of "moving parts" in a non-guaranteed life insurance policy and the interaction of these moving parts. Stated differently, it is the volatility of these moving parts, particularly interest or earnings credited, that do not stay stagnant, and the interaction of the cost of insurance with the volatility of the earnings.

Improper Policy Evaluation Methods

From the discussion in Chapter 2, it should be evident that we cannot use traditional **constant** rate policy illustrations to either predict non-guaranteed policy values or to compare one policy to another, even if it is the same type of policy. In the past several years, many independent life insurance brokerage operations and some producer groups have marketed what is commonly called policy audit reports or premium optimization reports that purport to unbiasedly compare various policies, generally of the same policy type, issued by different insurance carriers. The problem with these "optimization" reports is that they are all based on the individual carriers' **constant** assumption policy illustrations. Thus, the policy audit reports or optimization reports have the same lack of credibility problems as individual policy illustrations. In fact, any policy evaluation methodology system that uses non-guaranteed **constant** earnings or interest crediting rates to predict future policy performance or to compare policies or to rank policies based upon "subjective" non-disclosed criteria, such as a one to five scale, is not a valid method of policy evaluation and is not "dispute defensible"[107] in a court of law.

Monte Carlo Simulation and Actuarially Certified Policy Standards Analysis[108]

It is clear that any acceptable form of non-guaranteed, flexible premium life insurance policy evaluation must address this volatility of earnings issue and calculate a premium that, while not guaranteed, can reasonably evaluate the effect of volatility in rates of return with statistical probabilities of confidence. The evaluation must be unbiased, creditable, impartial, and fact-based. Similarly, as a certified public accountant uses generally acceptable accounting principles to prepare financial statements,

---

107. "Dispute defensible" is a term coined and used by E. Randolph (Randy) Whitelaw, AEP® (Distinguished), the Managing Director of Trust Asset Consultants, LLC, to describe proper or best practices in the evaluation of life insurance and administration of the trust estate in the irrevocable life insurance trust (ILIT). Randy is a national expert and consultant in this subject matter and has served as an expert witness in litigation on these matters, including the watershed case of *Cochran v. KeyBank.*

108. Full and very grateful acknowledgement needs to be given to Richard M. Weber, M.B.A., CLU®, ChFC®, AEP® (Distinguished), and Christopher Hause, FSA, MAAA, CLU®, of Ethical Edge Insurance Solutions, LLC who are the inventors and developers of the Historical Volatility Calculator software and pioneers in the Monte Carlo simulation and actuarially certified policy standards technique.

the evaluation of a non-guaranteed, flexible premium life insurance policy should be an actuarial-certified evaluation using generally accepted actuarial methods.

In all reasonable types of evaluation, a comparison must be made to a known, objective (non-subjective), quantitative measurable standard or benchmark. Is such a comparison available for non-guaranteed life insurance and, if yes, what can be used as the policy standard or benchmark model? To answer this question, consider the three main pricing components of life insurance policies: (1) cost of insurance (mortality costs); (2) administration and operation expenses including start-up costs and commissions; and (3) investment returns, whether the interest credited to the policy or the earnings of separate accounts.

Is a benchmark model available for life insurance? Yes. The Society of Actuaries accumulates and annually publishes actual, current and past, experience data from life insurance companies that represent almost 80 percent of all life insurance sold in the United States. This data includes mortality experience and policy expenses, including lapse experience. Further, other statistical-type studies are available from credible sources used to derive industry norms. The data is broken down by not only issue age of policies and sex but also by smoking status, underwriting classifications, policy type, policy size, and so on. This readily available data facilitates construction of statistical expectations for mortality costs and policy expenses from which policy standards can be created as well as policy pricing benchmark models. In fact, Asset Share model software programs used by actuaries to design and price life insurance products have incorporated this type of benchmark model for these two components in life insurance pricing.

That said, what can be used as a benchmark for investment returns, taking the form of either interest credited or separate accounts earnings? We know that policy investment returns are not constant and, therefore, inappropriate. Rather, we need to consider the volatility of investment earnings over time. This can be accomplished by employing a technique adopted by corporate trust companies and large investment portfolio managers over the past 40 years to statistically estimate probable portfolio returns, known as Monte Carlo simulation. It statistically evaluates an unknown future outcome based on numerous random samples of prior experience.

Insurance company reserves that back up a policy's cash value is nothing more than a portfolio of securities. If the policy is a whole life or traditional universal life policy, the general asset account backing up those policies is mostly a fixed-income portfolio made up of government and corporate bonds and securities. If the policy is a variable universal life policy, the separate sub-accounts—which themselves are portfolios of types of securities—make up the account value of the policy and depend on the asset allocation chosen by the policy owner based on the policy owner's risk tolerance.

As a result, actuarially certified policy standards for cost of insurance and expenses can be combined with the use of Monte Carlo simulation to derive expected returns that account for volatility. The result is a benchmark model that can predict results to which a statistical probability of confidence can be attached. This benchmark is in effect a generic life insurance policy standard. It cannot be purchased but nonetheless represents industry norms and expectations that can be reasonably compared to life insurance company-generated policy illustrations.

To create one hypothetical "trial illustration," we start with the actuarially certified policy standards database for the cost of insurance and policy expenses. Depending on the type of universal life insurance policy, we create a database of past rates of investment returns ranging from the 1920s to the present. For example, in the case of an all equity asset allocation variable universal life policy, there is a database of the Standard and Poor's® (S&P) 500® Index returns, with dividends, by month from the 1920s to the present. Since regular and variable universal life policies are credited each month with investment earnings, we do the same with the "trial illustration," except the rate of investment return for each month will be randomly selected.

To understand the monthly investment return randomization calculation process, think of all these rates of returns as electronic bingo cubes with a single bingo cube for each monthly return data. To calculate policy values for the first month we randomly select an investment rate of return bingo cube from the database that acts like an electronic drum cage holding the bingo cubes. We calculate the policy values at the end of the first month using the randomly selected "bingo cube" rate of investment return and applying it to the proposed premium payment, face amount of the policy, and the cost of insurance and expenses from the actuarially certified policy standards database. We replace the first bingo cube back into the electronic drum cage and repeat the entire process for the second policy month, then the third month, and so forth, accumulating policy account values along the way. This is done until either the policy matures—or reaches the planned policy duration period—or the policy lapses due to insufficient policy account values. For example, if we have a 50-year-old insured and a policy maturing at age 100, the above process would be repeated 600 times to create one hypothetical trial policy illustration assuming the policy does not lapse. That is, 12 months in a year times 50 years. For variable universal life policies, asset allocations are rebalanced every 12 months. This is how one "trial illustration" is created.

However, one created hypothetical policy trial illustration—even though the investment returns have been randomized for each month of the policy—has no creditability. In order to be statistically creditable, we generate 1,000 separate hypothetical trial illustrations. We note the number of times each trial illustration made it to the testing point for premium adequacy and policy sustainability—such as life expectancy, life expectancy plus five years, or policy maturity—and count that as a "success." We also note the number of times the trial illustrations did not make it to the testing point and count that as a "failure." Thus, with these 1,000 hypothetical trial illustrations—each with randomized investment rates of return by month—we are able to compute the probability of a proposed premium's success in adequately sustaining the policy to the chosen testing point.

As an example, assume an irrevocable life insurance trust (ILIT) has been created by Ms. Toli Ilit, now a 62-year-old female who has a calculated life expectancy of age 91. Twelve years ago, the trust purchased a $1,000,000 variable universal life insurance policy with a preferred non-smoker underwriting risk classification from GLF Life Insurance Company when the insured was age 50. Ms. Ilit is an aggressive investor with a relatively high-risk tolerance and, hence, has an asset allocation for the policy of 80 percent equity investments and 20 percent bond or fixed-income investments, which she wants to continue throughout the life of the policy. Based on an original policy illustration projected at 8 percent, the planned and current annual funding premium is $7,888.15 with premiums being payable to age 119, with the policy maturing at age 120. The account value for the 12th policy year was originally illustrated to be $118,465; however, the actual account value in the 12th policy year is $114,280. An in-force policy re-illustration projected at 8 percent and assuming continuation of the current funding premium shows that the policy will lapse at age 97, six years past Ms. Ilit's life expectancy.

Given the past 12 years of market volatility, the trustee is concerned with the policy's performance. The trustee wants to know what the probability of the timely payment of the current scheduled premium would be to sustain the policy to the insured's life expectancy and to age 100. The trustee's premium adequacy risk tolerance is a 90 percent sustainability probability confidence. If the current funding premium is inadequate, what is the correcting premium to achieve a 90 percent probability of success? Tables 5.1 to 5.3 provide a data and assumptions summary.

Table 5.1 Creditable Evaluation of Life Insurance: Example of Actuarial Evaluation of In-Force Policy

Insured Information	
Name:	Ms. Toli Ilit
Current Age:	62
Gender:	Female
Risk Classification:	Preferred Non-Smoker
Life Expectancy (Calculated):	91

Table 5.2 Creditable Evaluation of Life Insurance: Example of Actuarial Evaluation of In-Force Policy (Continued)

In-Force Policy Information	
Carrier:	GLF Insurance Company
Year of Policy Issue:	2008
Issue Age:	50
Face Amount:	$1,000,000
Policy Type:	Variable Universal Life
Asset Allocations (Equity/Bond):	80%/20%
In-Force Policy Account/Cash Value:	$114,280 (Originally Projected $118,465)

Table 5.3 Creditable Evaluation of Life Insurance: Example of Actuarial Evaluation of In-Force Policy (Continued)

In-Force Policy Illustration Data & Risk Tolerance	
Current Annual Funding Premium:	$7,888
Premium Paying Years:	58
Illustration Interest/Crediting Rate:	8.00%
Illustrated Lapse Age:	97
Premium Adequacy to Sustain Policy— Risk Tolerance (Confidence Level):	90%

We generate 1,000 randomized hypothetical illustration trials to determine the probability of the policy sustaining to the insured's life expectancy of age 91. Of those 1,000 trial illustrations 840 of the illustrations sustained the policy to age 91 and 160 failed to sustain the policy to age 91, resulting in an 84 percent probability the current premium will successfully sustain the policy to life expectancy.

The earliest lapse occurred at age 82 and the highest concentration range of lapses was between ages 89 through 93. By comparison, the GLF Life Insurance Company in-force illustration projected lapse at age 97.

The same process was used to solve for the correcting funding premium to sustain the policy to the predetermined testing points. For example, the correcting funding premium to sustain the policy to insured life expectancy, assuming a 90 percent probability in this example, is $9,089, which represents a 15 percent increase over the current funding premium of $7,888. Additionally, based upon actuarially certified policy standards, the cost of insurance and expenses obtained from the GLF Life Insurance Company in-force policy illustration were calculated to be slightly (−4 percent) less favorable than the policy standards benchmark. The average rate of return of the 1,000 randomly generated hypothetical illustration trials was 9.32 percent but, like a policy illustration, does not account for volatility. However, the correcting funding premium, using 1,000 randomly generated hypothetical policy illustration trials, does take into account volatility, and, hence, results in the significant correcting funding premium increase.

In testing whether the illustrated GLF Life Insurance Company variable life insurance policy will sustain to the insured's age 100, we again generate 1,000 random hypothetical illustration trials. Of those 1,000 trial illustrations 620 of the illustrations sustained the policy to age 100 and 380 failed to sustain the policy to age 100. Thus, from this we derive a 62 percent probability of successfully sustaining the policy to age 100 with the current premium.

Of these 1,000 randomly generated hypothetical illustration trials the earliest lapse occurred at age 82 and the highest five-year concentration range of lapses was between ages 88 through 92, statistically comparable to the lapse data derived from testing for sustaining to life expectancy for the current funding premium.

Using the process to solve for the correcting funding premium to sustain the policy to age 100, such that there is a 90 percent probability that the premium will sustain the policy to the testing point, we find that premium to be $13,008, or an increase of 65 percent over the current funding premium of $7,888. The pricing deviation of the actuarially certified policy standards for the cost of insurance and expenses from the GLF Life Insurance Company in-force policy illustration remains at −4 percent as previously calculated in the testing for sustaining the policy to life expectancy. The average rate of return of the 1,000 randomly generated hypothetical illustration trials in testing the premium adequacy of the policy sustaining to age 100 was 9.34 percent, again statistically comparable to the average rate of return derived from testing for sustaining to life expectancy for the current funding premium. A summary of the actuarial evaluation of the in-force policy example results is contained in Figure 5.1.

It is important to note that the goal of the Monte Carlo Simulation and Actuarially Certified Policy Standards analysis is to objectively determine the relative credibility of an illustration as opposed to predicting the actual performance of a specific policy. In addition, the correcting premium is not a guaranteed premium but rather a suggested premium that meets, in the example above, the 90 percent statistical confidence level requirement to help the client set more reasonable expectations for ongoing policy review and management.

All statistical analysis has margins of error, generally in the range of plus or minus 5 percent or less as is the case with this analysis process. While this tool and technique is not perfect—and improvements and sophistication of the technique and the data behind the technique will improve over time—it is the best method available to set benchmarks for policy expectations that are actuarially certified. Further, it is a far superior tool to the linear, constant assumption policy illustration, which is known to be neither credible nor appropriate for predictive value determinations.

Creditable Evaluation of Life Insurance in Perspective

Since the purpose of policy illustrations for flexible premium non-guaranteed death benefit products is to explain how a policy works, they cannot be relied upon or should not be used to predict or project policy performance, nor used to evaluate or compare one policy to another. Such a use of the policy illustration is improper and clearly not "dispute defensible."

Having described the criteria required to properly evaluate non-guaranteed flexible premium life insurance products, an analysis of the actuarially certified policy standards combined with the Monte Carlo simulation method of policy evaluation was presented and shown ideally to meet the criteria of proper evaluation for non-guaranteed flexible premium life insurance products. An example demonstrated the ability of this actuarially certified evaluation technique to access the probability—within a confidence probability of a successful outcome, or risk tolerance, set

Figure 5.1 Creditable Evaluation of Life Insurance—Example of Actuarial Evaluation of In-Force Policy (Continued)—Probability of Current Funding Premium Sustaining Policy To:

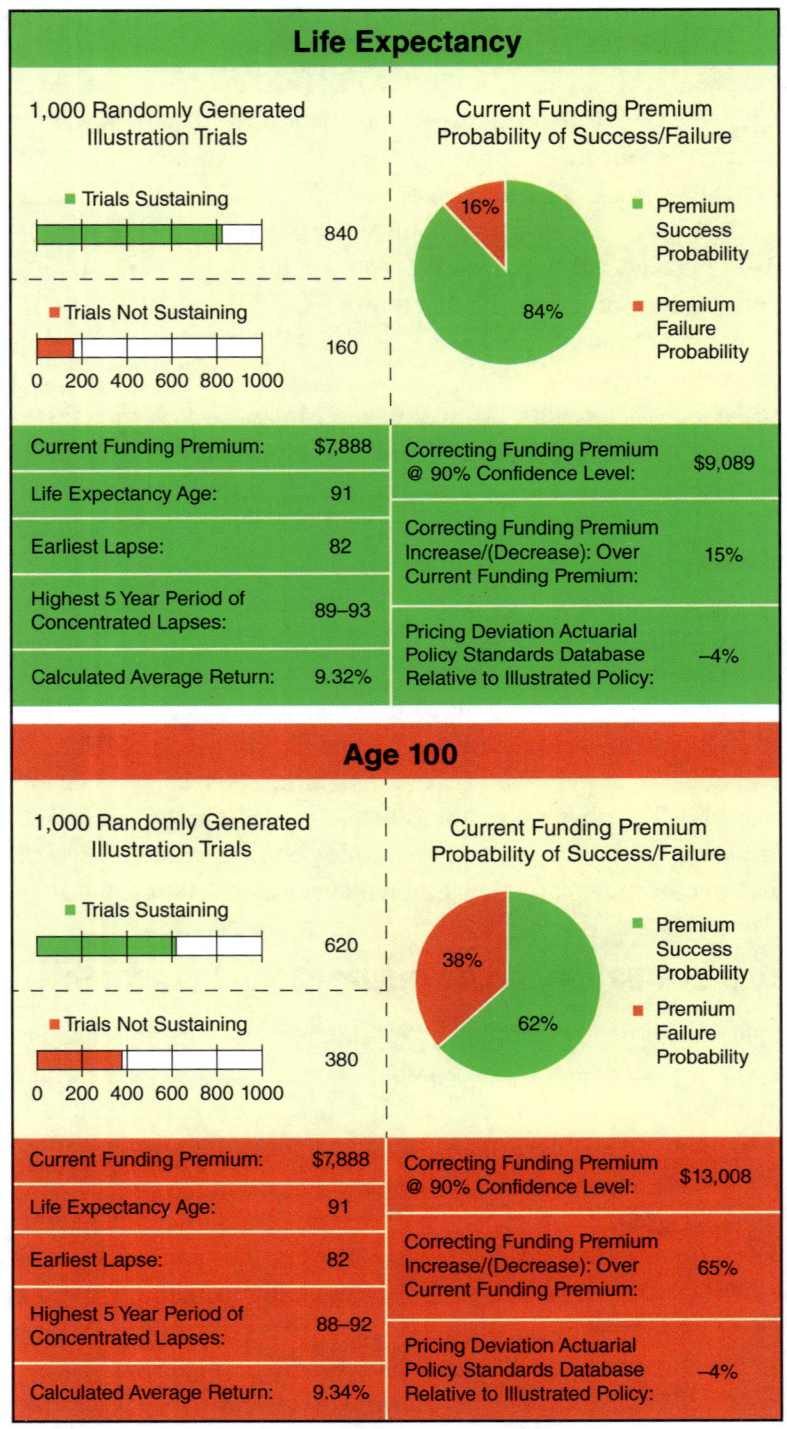

by the policy owner or trustee of a life insurance trust—that a carrier's illustrated scheduled premium could adequately sustain the policy to contract maturity or other desirable testing points such as life expectancy or life expectancy plus five years. Furthermore, the actuarially certified evaluation provides the most likely five-year range of policy lapse given the current scheduled premium, as well as the earliest possible lapse; an evaluation of the competitiveness of policy pricing of cost of insurance and policy expenses relative to the benchmark policy standards; and the correcting premium to sustain the policy to the desired age or to contract maturity given the policy owner/trustee's risk tolerance.

Policy performance monitoring and prudent risk management is a continuous process that requires an **annual** actuarially certified policy evaluation. Further, prudent risk management includes **annual** suitability of the selected life insurance product, plus the suitability and solvency of the life insurance carrier.

In summary, the proper evaluation of non-guaranteed, flexible life insurance products is available, is affordable, and is "dispute defensible."

Chapter 6

Practical Questions and Guidelines to Acquiring and Managing Life Insurance to Avoid a Client Crisis

Previous portions of this book have delved into an understanding as to how life insurance works, the risk paradigm shift, and the causes of the life insurance policy crisis; risks of life insurance policies; the process of managing life insurance policies; and the creditable evaluation of life insurance. Given this knowledge, how can it be correctly applied to financial planning situations that require the use of life insurance? What are the checklist types of questions and guidelines to acquire and then manage a life insurance policy or policies in order to maximize the probability of a successful outcome and avoid a policy crisis?

The following material, while not meant to be a complete and comprehensive source, provides some checklist-like questions and guidelines to acquire and maintain—if suitable and appropriate—a life insurance policy or policies. These questions and guidelines apply to both single life insurance policies as well as joint and survivorship life insurance policies. Where differences exist, they will be noted.

First Things First

What is the purpose for the life insurance policy(ies)?
What goals, objectives, and needs does the life insurance policy meet?

The above questions, while very basic, are fundamental to obtaining a successful outcome with any life insurance program. These questions should not only be employed in the initial acquisition of a life insurance policy but also should be reexamined annually to reaffirm the suitability of and appropriateness for life insurance.

Typical goals and objectives for a life insurance program can include the following:

- Provide income and support to the family in the event of early death
- Provide for payment of debt, such as mortgages, loans, and credit cards at the time of death
- Provide an education fund for children or grandchildren
- Provide for a special needs child
- Provide funds for a charity or to create an endowment for a charity
- Provide for supplemental retirement income
- Provide for estate liquidity to pay federal and state estate taxes, estate administration expense, and other estate settlement costs
- Provide funds for business continuity purposes such as funding cross purchase buy/sell agreements, stock redemption agreements, and employee stock ownership plan (ESOP) purchases
- Provide key person protection for business entities to either repay loan agreements, replace and train a key person, or extend indemnity to the business for possible lost profits and earnings
- Provide for key person executive benefit plans such as section 162 bonus plans, non-qualified deferred compensation that includes supplemental executive retirement plans (SERPs), stock appreciation plans, phantom stock plans, and split-dollar plans

Could these goals and objectives be satisfied through other means or other financial products?
Is life insurance the most effective and efficient means of accomplishing the planning goals and objectives?

Generally, when there is a need for cash or an income stream because of premature death, there is not another financial product that effectively and efficiently provides for that need as well as life insurance. An honest analysis of the alternatives usually concludes that life insurance is either the best or the only solution for the objective of providing an income stream immediately upon the death of a beloved person or key employee who other individuals, businesses, or institutions depend upon for support, or whose death prompts an immediate need for cash.

Additionally, the tax-favored advantages of life insurance—tax-deferred accumulations of cash value, the ability to take withdrawals up to the tax basis of the policy, and distributions by policy loans income tax-free, income tax-free, and possibly estate tax-free nature of the death benefit—may make life insurance an excellent vehicle to accumulate supplemental retirement income. Of course, in all financial planning scenarios various alternatives need to be analyzed and compared to determine the appropriate financial product solutions.

Planning Horizon and Need for Either a Level, Increasing, or Decreasing Face Amount—The Nature of the Goals, Objectives, and Needs

What is the anticipated duration period of the need for life insurance? Is the need for life insurance temporary or permanent?

The duration or length of the need for life insurance is a determinate of the type of life insurance product required to properly fund that need. In general, term insurance is designed to accommodate temporary needs for life insurance from one to 30 years. By comparison, permanent needs are best funded with either participating whole life, no-lapse secondary guarantee universal life, universal life, indexed universal life, or variable universal life products. Clearly, if the need for life insurance is ten years or less, then term insurance is the appropriate solution. If the need is 30 or more years, then clearly one of the listed permanent policies could be the appropriate choice, unless the policy owner lacks the funds to purchase a permanent product, in which case the policy owner could purchase a convertible term insurance product and consider conversion to a permanent product once funds are available. Sometimes a duration period grey area can exist between ten and 30 years where, depending on circumstances and the probability for the insurance need being longer than planned, either a term insurance product or permanent product could be utilized effectively and efficiently.

The experience of financial planners and life insurance professionals strongly suggests that many clients significantly underestimate the duration need for life insurance protection. What was envisioned as a need for life insurance for ten years or less turns into a permanent need quite frequently.

The author personally worked with two business owners who wanted to fund a buy/sell agreement. Both swore for a decade that they would only need term insurance because the business would not last longer than ten years and, hence, would be sold within that time frame. After a little more than a decade, the owners finally decided funding was a long-term need and their buy/sell policies are now permanent policies. By the way, the business is now well over 30 years old.

Further, while the goals and objectives for life insurance may change, the need for life insurance may not. For example, a couple that purchased life insurance for family income protection or to fund college education for their kids may now wish to use the protection to either provide for a charity, grandkids, or estate liquidity needs. In the business context, a policy once purchased to provide funds to pay off a bank loan could be used to fund a SERP. The point is that, while purposes and needs for life insurance change over time, there are still needs for life insurance protection, suggesting that the choice of a permanent type of policy may be prudent.

Is the need for life insurance a level amount, increasing amount, or decreasing amount (remember the effects of inflation on purchasing power)?

The amount of life insurance protection needed can definitely change over time. Thus, the need for life insurance protection is not generally static but rather dynamic. All too often in analyzing future life insurance needs, purchasing power (erosion caused by inflation) is ignored. As an example, with 2.5 percent) inflation per year over 10, 20, 30, and 40 year periods a life insurance policy with a level $1,000, 000 death benefit is worth in purchasing power $781,198, $610,271, $476,743, and $372,431, respectively. Thus, while the need for life insurance protection may remain constant, the nominal face amount of the policy must increase to support the need for constant purchasing power.

This discussion would suggest that, in order to keep purchasing power constant, the policy owner should consider a permanent policy wherein the face amount would increase such as a universal life-type policy with an increasing death benefit option, that is properly premium funded to support the increasing death benefit; or, instead, a participating whole life insurance policy is an option with dividends applied to purchase paid-up additions, or, better yet, with a paid-up additions rider also added to the base policy.

Alternatively, because of the section 7702 requirements to maintain a certain ratio of cash value to death benefit that increases with age, a maximum funded level death benefit universal life-type product would be an excellent choice to provide increasing death benefit protection. For example, with policy owners who have a more conservative risk tolerance, a maximum funded level death benefit universal life policy is an acceptable option. However, a participating whole life policy with dividends applied to purchase paid-up additions may be a better choice with more guarantees and an equal or better chance of policy performance. Similarly, policy owners having a less conservative and moderate risk tolerance may wish to choose a maximum funded level death benefit indexed universal life policy. Further, policy owners with a more aggressive risk tolerance would be very comfortable with a maximum funded level death benefit variable universal life policy with appropriate asset allocations among the sub-accounts corresponding to the policy owner's exact risk tolerance. Term insurance, minimally funded level death benefit universal life, indexed universal life, and variable universal life policies, and no-lapse secondary guarantee universal life policies will not increase in face amount, and, therefore, will not provide for purchasing power protection.

Besides keeping purchasing power needs constant—or to prevent the erosion of inflation—other purposes and goals for life insurance may require an increasing face amount of protection. For example, with a growing business value, the need for insurance for cross purchase buy/sell agreements or entity purchase agreements would increase. Similarly, with an estate that is growing in value—despite estate freezing techniques—liquidity needs would increase to pay increasing federal and state death taxes.

Conversely, there are situations where the need for life insurance decreases. A prime example—no pun intended—is a bank loan where the principle balance on the loan that is covered by life insurance decreases after each loan payment. Likewise, a business decreasing in value may require less life insurance. Estate tax legislation over the past several years has caused some decrease in the liquidity needs to pay estate taxes because of increased exemption amounts and decreases in rates on the federal and sometimes the state level. At the time of this writing, there are proposals to eliminate the estate and generation-skipping transfer taxes. However, these same proposals are replacing the estate tax with a capital gains tax at death similar to what is done in Canada.

In all of these decreasing needs for life insurance, unless there is some other goal or purpose for the life insurance need, the insurance may be decreased or eliminated. If the decision is made to eliminate the life insurance policy, a life settlement should be considered.

How much flexibility is required to accommodate changing needs for life insurance and funding ability?

Lastly, depending on a variety of circumstances, there may be a need for flexibility in the life insurance program to more easily adapt to changes in the face amount of life insurance needed, cash accumulations, and premium funding amount due to circumstances and cash flow availability of the policy owner. This need for flexibility can best be accommodated by either a universal life, indexed universal life, or variable universal life type of policy.

Need for Cash Value Accumulation Considerations

Is the policy being purchased primarily for the death benefit, primarily for the tax-favored buildup of cash value accumulations, or a combination of the death benefit and cash value accumulation?

How important is the buildup and access to the cash value in the life insurance policy?

Is the ability to develop excess or increasing death benefit amounts an important consideration?

To a certain extent, the three questions above are loaded questions. That is, the cash value reserve of a life insurance policy serves multiple purposes and you cannot have level premium long-term term insurance or permanent insurance without a cash value reserve. Besides being available for lifetime needs for cash and income—such as to fund a child's college education or to provide supplemental retirement income—the cash value is what supports the level death benefit in a level premium permanent life insurance policy. Additionally, excess growth in cash values is what supports increasing death benefits.

The relative importance to the policy owner of the death benefit or cash value accumulation depends on the planning purposes, objectives, and goals for the life insurance program. For example, on the surface, a life insurance policy that is to be owned by the typical irrevocable life insurance trust (ILIT) in order to provide estate liquidity upon the insured's death would have little need for cash value accumulation as the trust purpose is not to provide lifetime benefits to the insured (and affect the estate tax-free nature of the ILIT) or beneficiaries of the trust. This would be a correct assumption if—despite purchasing power erosion—the objectives for the trust were to maintain a level death benefit policy for a duration somewhere—depending on duration planning analysis objectives—between sometime greater than life expectancy and the maximum age assumed by the life insurance policy mortality table, or, if in terms of purchasing power, the death benefit need were a decreasing need. On the other hand, if the objective for the life insurance policy is for the ILIT to provide an increasing death benefit over time, then cash value accumulations would be highly important so that the cash value accumulations provide for the increasing death benefit.

Obviously, if the purpose and objectives of a life insurance policy are to either fund a child's college education expenses or to provide supplemental retirement income, then cash value buildup and accumulation is extremely important. However, what about a policy designed to fund a cross purchase buy/sell agreement? Here, the policy design would depend on whether or not there was an increasing need for the death benefit to keep pace with the increasing value of the business interest, plus whether cash value accumulation may also be desired for a buyout during the lifetime of the insured, perhaps upon the retirement of the insured. Clearly, the need for cash value accumulation must be considered carefully.

Beneficiaries and Policy Ownership

Who is (are) the beneficiary (beneficiaries) of the life insurance policy?

The basic purpose of a life insurance policy is to provide a death benefit to some person(s) or institution that suffers an economic loss upon the death of the insured. For most families, that beneficiary is the spouse followed by the children born or adopted of the marriage. However, the beneficiary could also be other relatives such as one's parents or siblings. The beneficiary could also be a charitable institution such as a hospital, zoo, church, or university. In business situations, the beneficiary is the business entity for key person insurance, entity purchase agreements, and non-qualified deferred compensation plans such as supplemental executive retirement plans (SERPs). For cross purchase buy/sell agreements, the beneficiary would be the other co-owner(s) of the business entity.

It is possible to name more than one "primary" beneficiary. If that is the case, unless the proportional share of each beneficiary is specified, then each of the primary beneficiaries would share equally. If one of the named beneficiaries predeceases the insured, the remaining named beneficiaries would split the predeceased beneficiary's share proportionately, unless per stirpes distribution is specified.

Have contingent beneficiaries been considered, identified, and named?

When the only beneficiary named is a person who predeceases the insured—or if no beneficiary is named—then the insured's estate is the default beneficiary. In general, the estate of the insured is the worst beneficiary choice because the death proceeds will be subject to estate administration expenses and the claims of the creditors of the estate. By contrast, in most states, death benefit proceeds are—up to a maximum amount in some states—not subject to the claims of creditors. The all too uncommonly used solution to avoiding having the death benefits paid to the insured's estate is to always name a contingent, or secondary, beneficiary. In fact, it is also possible to name a tertiary beneficiary if the primary beneficiary and secondary beneficiary predecease the insured.

Rather than directly naming individuals as beneficiaries, would it be prudent to consider creating a trust for these beneficiaries and naming the trust as the policy beneficiary?

Rather than leaving large amounts of money directly to individual beneficiaries—especially young beneficiaries or beneficiaries who either are unfamiliar with or incapable of managing money or who have or may have creditor problems—consideration should be given to naming a trust for the benefit of the intended beneficiaries of the life insurance proceeds as the beneficiary of the life insurance proceeds. A trustee of the trust can be named—whether individuals, a corporation, or a combination—to manage the life insurance proceeds and distribute either the income of the trust and/or the principal of the trust according to instructions provided by the insured/grantor of the trust. A close estate planning attorney friend of the author once told him that the trust advantages to the trust beneficiaries was that it was "creditor proof, spouse proof, business associate proof, and stupid proof."

Who will be the owner of the life insurance policy?

Should a trust or other third-party owner be considered?

In most situations, the owner of the life insurance policy is the insured. A life insurance policy contains a bundle of economic rights and options that are exercisable by the policy owner. Two of the primary rights in a life insurance policy are the right to name the policy beneficiary and the right to access and use the cash value of the policy during the insured's lifetime. Although beyond the scope of this writing, either all of the ownership or some of the ownership rights in a policy may be transferred.

There are certain situations where the insured should not be the owner of the life insurance policy, nor possess any incidents of ownership. This is particularly true with individuals who would be subject to estate taxes—those individuals whose assets and previous taxable gifts total more than $11,580,000 in 2020 or married couples with total assets or taxable gifts in excess of $23,160,000 in 2020. While life insurance proceeds are free of income taxes, they are not estate tax-free if the insured owns the policy. If either an irrevocable trust, with no incidents of ownership in the policy retained by the insured, owns the life insurance policy or a third party owns the life insurance policy, then the proceeds of the life insurance policy will not be subject to estate taxes, unless the life insurance policy is transferred by gift within three years prior to the insured's death.

In business situations, to avoid various tax traps, the business entity should be the policy owner and beneficiary for key person insurance, entity purchase agreements, and non-qualified deferred compensation plans, such as SERPs. For cross purchase buy/sell agreements, the person or entity purchasing the business interest from the insured should be the policy owner and beneficiary of the life insurance policy.

One last very important point about third-party life insurance policy ownership. In order to avoid a serious tax trap—known in the insurance tax literature as "the unholy triangle"—it is important that the third-party owner also is the beneficiary of the life insurance policy proceeds. The following real example will demonstrate the tax trap problem caused when the third-party owner named a beneficiary different than the third-party owner: mother was the owner of a large life insurance policy on her husband's life and named her daughter as the beneficiary. The result was that the Internal Revenue Service imposed a gift tax upon the mother for the indirect gift of the life insurance policy proceeds to her daughter.[109] Not a good result. Similar problems also occur when a corporate-owned life insurance policy names the spouse of a key employee as policy beneficiary.

Underwriting Considerations

What is the health status of the proposed insured or insureds?
Do the proposed insured or insureds have any type of hazardous occupation or occupation that could involve or expose the insured to any type of hazardous risks?
Do the proposed insured or insureds have any type of what could be perceived as a hazardous avocation such as parachute jumping, scuba diving, flying, motorcycle racing, and so on?
Do the insured or insureds use any type of tobacco products?

The main pricing determinate of life insurance is the mortality rates used in the cost of insurance calculation. The specified mortality rates charged the insured are determined by the life insurance company's underwriters whose job it is to determine the risk classification of the proposed insured. This risk classification is based on many factors, not the least of which is the health status and condition of the proposed insured. Of course, use of tobacco products and recreational drugs play a vital part, as well as the occupation and avocations, financial considerations such as income, net worth and credit rating, and moral habits of the proposed insured.

---

109. See *Goodman v. Commissioner of Internal Revenue*, 156 F.2d 218 (2d Cir. 1946).

In general, most insurance carriers now have five risk classifications that are considered "standard" classifications, as follows: super preferred (a non-smoking individual), preferred non-smoker, preferred smoker, standard non-smoker, and standard smoker, the latter sometimes referred to as residual standard smoker. There are additionally several substandard risk classifications more commonly referred to as table ratings. The table ratings are denoted either by the alphabet or a whole number starting at either A or 1, respectively, with each table representing an incremental 25-percentage higher surcharge of mortality rates based on standard rates increasing as to position in the alphabet or number of the table. Carriers may charge a flat extra rate per $1,000 of death benefit for certain risks. This flat extra charge is mostly associated with certain occupation and avocation risks. For example, depending on total hours flown and hours flown each year, an airplane pilot may be given an extra flat-rate charge.

While most of the large, major carriers tend to equally classify proposed insureds—both in terms of the risk classification assigned and the nomenclature used to describe the risk—this is not always a case with all carriers. For example, carrier A may use the classification of preferred and carrier B may use the classification of standard for the same proposed insured. Similarly, carrier X may give a risk classification of table D while carrier Y may give a risk classification of standard for the same proposed insured. This is not to say that carrier A would be a better choice for the proposed insured than carrier B, or that carrier Y would be a better choice for the proposed insured than carrier X. Nor is this an indication of the competitiveness of policy pricing. What it does mean is that different carriers have different nomenclature and different ranges for each risk classification.

Some carriers may be more aggressive and competitive in pricing different impaired health conditions such as cancer or heart conditions. The same applies toward the treatment of different hazardous occupations or avocations.

Too many people with various health conditions assume that they are uninsurable or that their health condition may make a life insurance policy an economically unviable planning choice. It never ceases to amaze the author how easy it is for life insurance agents representing multiple carriers to acquire a competitively priced life insurance policy despite various health issues. While the mortality rates or cost of insurance for these policies are obviously higher than the mortality rates in a policy insuring an Olympic athlete, this does not mean life insurance is an unaffordable or uneconomical planning option. What it means is that the life insurance option priced for the appropriate insurance risk needs to be explored along with other planning options. In most cases, the life insurance still remains the most viable planning option despite the increased mortality rates.

It is quite common in life insurance policies that will be owned by an ILIT designed to provide money for estate taxes and estate settlement costs to use a second-to-die life insurance policy—also called a survivorship life insurance policy—as the funding vehicle. This policy insures the lives of two people—generally a husband and a wife—and pays a death benefit on the death of the second insured to die (i.e., the survivor). In underwriting these types of policies, it is not unusual to have one of the two insureds completely uninsurable. Therefore, in certain underwriting situations the survivorship policy may be an appropriate choice.

An old insurance adage says that "you buy insurance with your health [and other underwriting risk factors] and you pay for it with money." The point here for planning purposes is that the potential risk classification of the proposed insured or insureds must be taken into account in the pricing of insurance products and the selection of insurance carriers. The more detailed and thorough information a life insurance consultant has on the underwriting factors of the proposed insured, the more helpful the consultant can be in the process of selecting appropriate insurance carriers and in negotiating the underwriting classification with these carriers.

Selecting the Appropriate Life Insurance Product Type or Types—Temporary or Term Insurance

If the need for life insurance is temporary and the planning duration has been determined, is the best option one-year renewable term insurance or a level premium for "X" number of years, with "X" equal to or greater than the planned duration of need purpose?

Term insurance is available in a variety of forms from one-year term insurance, where the premium is increased each year, to level premium term insurance payments of 5, 10, 15, 20, or 30 years, or to age 55, 60, 65, or 70. While virtually all term insurance is guaranteed renewable, the question becomes at what guaranteed price depending upon either a year-to-year basis with annually renewable term insurance or at the end of a level term premium payment period or age? Additionally, with term insurance, there becomes a maximum number of years or insured age in which term insurance is no longer renewable and the term life insurance coverage expires, assuming, of course, that premiums are even affordable at older ages near the policy expiration period.

The decision as to whether to purchase one-year annually renewable term insurance or a level premium payment term insurance product for a certain period depends on the desired duration of coverage and consideration of the time value of money (i.e., buy one-year term insurance and invest the difference). In certain instances, the duration of coverage desired does not match up perfectly with available level premium paying periods for term insurance. For example, the duration period desired is seven years and level premium payment term insurance is only available for either a five-year period or ten-year period. In this circumstance, the policy owner would have three options: (1) purchase annually renewable term insurance, (2) purchase a five-year level premium term policy that is renewable either for an additional five-year period or on a yearly term insurance basis, or (3) purchase a ten-year level premium term policy and drop the coverage in the eight-policy year. The consideration as to which of the three options to choose, again, comes down to a time value of money question. Generally, in choosing between one-year term insurance and some level premium paying period term insurance, the better option for most policy owners is the level premium paying period even if the level premium paying period extends a bit beyond the duration of coverage desired.

In a level premium term insurance policy, at what premium rate(s) and for how long can the policy be renewed if the duration of need actually turns out to be greater than the original duration of need planned?

The experience of financial planners and life insurance professionals strongly suggests that many clients significantly underestimate the length of need for life insurance protection. What was envisioned as a need for life insurance for ten years or less turns into a permanent need quite frequently.

The situation that needs to be drastically avoided is to have coverage for less than the desired duration of coverage. The big risk with term life insurance is always whether or not the insured remains insurable at the end of the term period. This is a huge risk that could lead to the insured being unable to purchase any life insurance at an affordable price or any life insurance at all. For levelized premium term products, current rates that are based on the insured providing evidence of insurability are guaranteed for at least the period of the level term payments, such as 30 years. The policy may be technically renewable at the end of the level term payment period at guaranteed rates to a maximum term period, but those rates will assume heavy adverse selection and will be the maximum term insurance rates that can be charged. The issue is whether or not the insured can purchase any term insurance at the more favorable current rates at the end of the level premium term period.

One note of caution with regard to purchasing level premium term insurance products. In the 1980s, carriers introduced a level premium term insurance product that was commonly referred to as "re-entry term insurance." Premiums were level and guaranteed for certain periods such as either five or ten years. At the end of the initial guaranteed period, the insured would receive another period of the same length of very favorable rates on the condition that the insured furnish satisfactory evidence of insurability at that time—this is referred to as select mortality rates, which are given for a period of time to an insured who has recently furnished evidence of insurability. However, if the insured failed to provide satisfactory evidence of insurability, rates for the policy would increase drastically. To the best of the author's knowledge, this product is no longer issued. Thank God. However, if re-entry term insurance is somehow still around, never, never, never buy such a policy, and never do business with any life insurance professional who tries to sell you such a product.

What is the maximum number of years or age after which the term insurance product can no longer be converted?

Most term policies have a convertibility feature, which allows for the term life insurance policy to be converted to a permanent type of life insurance product offered by the insurance carrier without providing evidence of insurability. However, this right to exercise and convert the policy to a permanent policy generally expires either at a specific age—such as age 55 or 60—or a few years before the maximum period of coverage of the term insurance policy.

Can the policy owner convert the term insurance policy into any permanent insurance product the insurance carrier offers or is conversion limited to specific policies and/or blocks of insurance products strictly reserved for the purpose of converted policies?

Traditionally, a term life insurance policy owner could convert the term life insurance into any permanent plan offered at the time of conversion by the insurance carrier. However, some insurance carriers are now severely limiting the permanent policy in which the term life insurance can be converted to a permanent policy with premium rates loaded for a heavy factor of adverse selection—this has been done with conversion privileges for group term life insurance coverage for years.

If term insurance is being purchased because permanent insurance is unaffordable at this time, what are the conversion provisions of the term insurance policy?

For a policy owner who is purchasing a term life insurance policy at this time because either a permanent life insurance policy is not affordable or the purchaser wants to maintain the option to convert at a future time, it is important to choose a term insurance product from a quality life insurance carrier that allows conversion and also offers a competitive range of permanent conversion products.

Selecting the Appropriate Life Insurance Product Type or Types—Permanent Insurance

What is the policy owner's risk tolerance?

Like various investment products, permanent life insurance product types have different characteristics. For example, is policy performance risk retained by the insurance carrier or transferred to the policy owner? Is the product suitable based upon policy owner risk tolerance and the product's degree of the risk and potential volatility considering the assets backing up the policy's cash value reserve; the relative premium outlay required; and the potential for increasing death benefits and cash value accumulations? Each life insurance product type has a mix of these characteristics, or elements. Likewise, the suitability of any product type for a particular policy owner is determined by the policy owner's preferences or choices of the mix of policy characteristics.

Like an investment product, the starting point to selecting an appropriate life insurance product type is to determine the risk tolerance and where the selected life insurance policy will fit into the asset mix of the portfolio of the perspective policy owner. Determining the risk tolerance of a policy owner is both an art and a science. Most financial advisors have risk tolerance questionnaires to use as a starting point in helping a client to assess his or her risk tolerance.[110]

Is the risk tolerance for life insurance products any different than for investment products?

While it may not make completely logical sense, some clients may have a different risk tolerance perspective for life insurance as opposed to financial investments, for no other reason than because it is life insurance. That is, these clients have a more conservative approach to life insurance than investment products because in life insurance they seek more certainty and guarantees. This may also be due to clients having an aggressive and more risky approach to investments, feeling that their life insurance program needs to be a safeguard or safety net to counterbalance the investment program.

Where will the life insurance policy fit into the asset mix and total portfolio of financial products held by the policy owner?

Many policy owners view their life insurance program in isolation, separate from their portfolio of investments and other financial interests. A more holistic and balanced approach is to view life insurance as part of an overall asset mix component, or asset class, of an entire portfolio consisting of all financial assets. After all, the cash values of permanent life insurance products take on the investment characteristics of the assets backing up either the general asset account of the life insurance carrier or the separate sub-accounts that back up variable universal life policies. For example, the general asset accounts of life insurance companies that back up whole life and universal life products, other than variable universal life policies, consist primarily of fixed-income securities of corporate and government bonds. The assets backing up the cash values of variable universal life insurance policies consist of separate sub-accounts that are analogous to various types of mutual funds that can range from aggressive growth funds to international funds, balance funds, and bond funds. Why not treat the asset classes of the cash values backing up various types of life insurance policies as part of the overall portfolio asset mix and asset allocation structured to the risk tolerance of the policy owner?

---

110. One such simple system to determine asset allocations based on risk tolerance was developed by Professor William G. Droms of Georgetown University and is called the Portfolio Allocation Scoring System (PASS). PASS has been used by major insurance companies, banks, and Certified Public Accountant firms and is included in *The American Institute of Certified Public Accountants' Personal Financial Planning Practice Management Handbook*. See William G. Droms, "Investment Asset Allocations for PFP Clients," *Journal of Accountancy*, April 1987, pages 114–118.

Does the policy owner prefer minimum premium outlay or the ability to develop increasing cash values and death benefit amounts?

After determining the appropriate life insurance policy that is suitable to the prospective policy owner's risk tolerance, the next step is to ascertain the policy owner's preference for either minimum premium outlay or the ability to develop excess or increasing cash values and death benefit amounts. This decision should be in line with the needs, goals, and objectives of the "suitable" life insurance program. **Given the policy owner's risk tolerance and preference for either minimum premium outlay or the ability to develop excess or increasing cash values and death benefit amounts, have the life insurance product type characteristics been compared and evaluated to select the most suitable product type for the policy owner?**

Considering the five major types of "pure" permanent life insurance policies primarily sold today and discussed previously, whole life and no-lapse guarantee universal life are more than suitable for a policy owner with a conservative risk tolerance for life insurance. Both policies provide certainty and guarantees and the policy performance risk is retained by the life insurance carrier; however, with no-lapse guarantee universal life insurance, the policy owner is responsible for the timely payment of life insurance premiums on or before the premium due date with no grace period or other conditions to maintain the policy guarantees. Additionally, in newer no-lapse guarantee universal life policies, the guarantee may only be to age 85 or 90 as opposed to age 100 or 120 with most older policies. While the relative premium outlay for participating whole life insurance is the highest, with dividends applied to the paid-up additions option, there is an excellent potential for increasing death benefit and cash value accumulation (this is not the case if dividends are applied to the cash option or reduce premium option). On the other hand, while the relative premium outlay for no-lapse guarantee universal life insurance is by far the lowest for any permanent type of protection, there is absolutely no potential for increasing death benefit or cash value accumulations. In fact, the policy will contain no cash value in the later policy years and very little in the earlier years. There is some flexibility with whole life products but nothing compared to regular universal life products. No-lapse guarantee universal life policies have no flexibility.

Traditional universal life policies are suitable policy choices for a policy owner with a conservative to moderate risk tolerance for life insurance, particularly if the policy owner desires the flexibility of the universal life policy design. Like whole life and no-lapse guarantee universal life insurance policies, the cash values of these policies are backed up by the general asset account of the insurance carrier, which consists primarily of fixed-income securities composed mostly of corporate and government bonds. Unlike whole life and no-lapse guarantee universal life insurance policies, policy performance risk is transferred to the policy owner and the policy's success/failure is primarily determined by the amount of planned funding premium for the policy. After the first policy year when a minimum amount of funding premium is required, the amount of the funding premium and decision to pay or not to pay the premium is determined by the policy owner. A minimally funded universal life policy requires a relatively moderate amount of premium outlay. However, with minimally funded universal life policies there is little or no potential—even with the increasing death benefit option—for the policy to have much of an increasing death benefit or substantial cash value, not to mention the risk of the policy lapsing. On the other hand, a more highly and aggressively funded universal life policy, which would require a relatively high premium outlay, would have a good potential for increasing death benefits and cash value growth. However, the relative premium outlay for a highly funded universal life policy is almost equivalent to the premium requirement for a whole life policy. Whole life policies are guaranteed products where the performance risk for the policy is retained by the insurance carrier. Given today's low-interest rate environment and the almost equivalent premium requirement of a highly funded universal life policy to a whole life policy premium, unless there is a need for the flexibility of premium payments or other flexibilities built into the universal life policy design, the whole life policy with dividends applied to purchase paid-up additions would appear to be the better option. Because performance risk is transferred to the policy owner, universal life policies require annual performance monitoring and risk management based upon updated planning objectives.

Indexed universal life insurance functions as a "hybrid" cross between traditional universal life insurance and variable universal life insurance. Unlike variable universal life insurance that is classified as a security and must be sold by a life insurance professional duly licensed to sell both securities and life insurance, indexed universal life insurance is not classified—at least for now—as a security and can be sold by a life insurance professional only licensed to sell insurance. Indexed universal life insurance attempts to allow the policy owner to participate in the gains of equity markets, without being subject to incurring any losses of the equity markets, by collaring the returns credited to the policy between a percentage of the increase in an equity index—without dividends—such as Standard & Poor's (S&P) 500® Index, subject to a maximum crediting rate typically 10 percent or 12 percent, and zero. However, although crediting rates for indexed universal life are determined by references to various market indices, primarily equity market-type indices, the assets actually backing up the policy's cash value reserves are still the issuing carrier's general asset accounts consisting primarily of fixed-income securities, such as corporate and government bonds, and may include call and put options.

Like universal life insurance policies, indexed universal life policies are suitable for a policy owner with a moderate, or slightly aggressive, risk tolerance. Policy performance risk is transferred to the policy owner and the success/failure of the policy is primarily determined by the planned premium funding amount. After the first premium payment and policy year, subsequent annual premium payment and amount decisions are determined by the policy owner. A minimally funded indexed universal life policy requires a relatively moderate amount of premium outlay; however, the result is minimal increasing death benefit and cash value accumulation, and increased lapse probability given the volatility of market indices. By comparison, a more aggressively, higher premium funded indexed universal life policy would have a good potential for increasing death benefits and cash value growth. Mindful that performance risk resides with the policy owner and that market volatility is to be expected, indexed universal life policies require attentive and creditable annual performance monitoring and risk management.

Variable universal life policies add to the flexibility of the universal life policy "chassis" by allowing the policy owner the opportunity to invest, allocate, and reallocate and balance his or her premiums to mutual fund-like sub-accounts per an asset allocation mix determined by the policy owner's risk tolerance. Variable universal life is ideally suitable for a policy owner having a more aggressive risk tolerance and who is sophisticated and familiar with investing in the financial markets. Policy performance risk is transferred to the policy owner, and the success/failure of the policy is primarily determined by the amount of planned funding premium for the policy. After the first policy year requiring a minimum amount of funding premium, subsequent funding premium amounts and payment schedules are determined by the policy owner. A minimally funded variable universal life policy requires a relatively moderate amount of premium outlay. However, with minimally funded variable universal life policies there is little or no potential—even with the increasing death benefit option—for the policy to have much of an increasing death benefit or substantial cash value. Further, given the volatility of the financial markets, there is a higher risk of the policy lapsing. On the other hand, a more highly and aggressively funded variable universal life policy, which would require a relatively high premium outlay, would have an excellent potential for increasing death benefits and cash value growth. Mindful of the performance risk transfer to the policy owner and the potential volatility of the mutual fund-like sub-accounts, variable universal life policies require careful annual monitoring and risk management.

Table 6.1 summarizes the major permanent life insurance policy type characteristics mentioned for participating whole life, no-lapse guarantee universal life, and both minimally funded and aggressively funded universal life, indexed universal life, and variable universal life, respectively.

Blended base whole life with the combination paid-up additions and decreasing term dividend option, and/or the paid-up additions rider, are left off this table but the degree of the blend would affect the characteristics of the policy. In this type of policy, the performance risk for the base whole life policy would be retained by the carrier. However, the policy owner bears the risk of the adequacy of the

Table 6.1 Permanent Life Insurance Product Type Characteristics

Permanent Product Type	Performance Risk Retained By	Suitable Policy Owner Risk Tolerance	Relative Premium Outlay	Potential for Increasing Death Benefit/ Cash Value
Participating Whole Life Dividends PUA	Carrier	Conservative	High	Yes—High
No-Lapse Guarantee Universal Life	Carrier	Conservative	Very Low	No
Universal Life Minimally Funded	Policy Owner	Conservative/ Moderate	Moderate	No
Universal Life Aggressively Funded	Policy Owner	Conservative/ Moderate	High	Yes
Indexed Universal Life Minimally Funded	Policy Owner	Moderate	Moderate	No
Indexed Universal Life Aggressively Funded	Policy Owner	Moderate	High	Yes
Variable Universal Life Minimally Funded	Policy Owner	Aggressive	Moderate	No
Variable Universal Life Aggressively Funded	Policy Owner	Aggressive	High	Yes—High

dividends to provide for the payment of the decreasing term insurance, and to eventually cause the elimination of the decreasing term insurance once the face amount of the paid-up additions reaches the total initial face amount of the decreasing term insurance. Of course, this is a function of the blend of the base whole life and initial decreasing term insurance, and whether or not there is a paid-up additions rider added to the policy. The higher the amount of decreasing term insurance relative to the base whole life policy, the more the risk of performance that is retained by the policy owner. This type of policy is suitable for a policy owner with a conservative to moderate risk tolerance. The relative premium outlay would vary from moderate to high, again depending on the initial blend of the base whole life to decreasing term insurance and whether or not there is an additional paid-up additions rider. Similarly, the potential for increasing death benefit and cash value depends on these same factors.

For diversification purposes, should there be a portfolio of life insurance policies with an asset mix of policy types based on the risk tolerance of the policy owner?

Having only one life insurance policy can be considered a concentration risk, at least within the life insurance asset class. An extreme example of concentration risk is, perhaps, the typical ILIT in which the only asset of the trust is one life insurance policy. Diversification can be obtained with having life insurance policies from different life insurance carriers and having life insurance policies of different product types. Having diversification by both multiple carriers and different product types helps mitigate against the risks of carrier insolvency and product type performance, the latter analogous to having both stocks and bonds—or different asset classes—in an investment portfolio. A life insurance portfolio can be constructed applying similar principles used in the construction of an investment portfolio. This would entail determining an asset allocation mix of life insurance product types based on the policy owner's objectives, risk tolerance, and preference for either the lowest premium outlay or growth in the policy death benefit and cash values. However, the benefits of a diversified life insurance policies portfolio may be economically unfeasible wherein the total amount of life insurance death benefit protection is less than $1,000,000 to $3,000,000 due to the banding of premium rates, with higher face amounts of coverage having lower rates per $1,000 of coverage, and the multiple fixed policy fees incurred. In other words, the policy owner has to weigh the trade-off between the benefits of diversification versus lower cost based on premium banding and not having multiple policy fees. Of course, this trade-off is highly dependent on the total face amount of life insurance involved in the decision. **Have policy riders such as disability waiver of premium or waiver of mortality costs, accidental death benefit, paid-up additional insurance, term insurance and long-term care (LTC) been considered and evaluated?**

Policy riders are important optional features and benefits that can be added to a life insurance policy. While all too often overlooked, they can play a significant role in the enhancement of policy design and risk management. Life insurance carriers continue to develop various types of riders to meet the changing needs of policy owners. While certainly not a complete list of available riders, some of the more common riders include disability waiver of premium or waiver of mortality charges, accidental death benefit, paid-up additional insurance, term insurance, and LTC. Following is a brief discussion of each of these riders:

> **Disability waiver of premium, or waiver of mortality costs**. The waiver of premium rider is more commonly found in whole life policies. This rider provides for the waiver of the entire policy premium once the insured has been totally disabled—as defined in the rider—for a period of six months and continues to be totally disabled. The rider is generally available for standard insureds less than 55 or 60 years old and the rider coverage generally ceases—unless the insured is totally disabled—at age 60 or 65. It is not uncommon for the rider to provide that for a continuous total disability that commences prior to age 60, that at age 65 the policy becomes a paid-up policy. The waiver of mortality costs rider is utilized in universal life-type policies and is similar to the waiver of premium rider. However, rather than waiving the entire premium, the waiver of mortality costs rider only waives the mortality costs of the policy. Given that the probability of becoming disabled prior to age 65 is at least three times greater than the probability of dying

before age 65, the waiver of premium or waiver of mortality costs riders need to be given serious consideration.

Accidental death benefit. This rider, also known as double indemnity, provides an additional death benefit—generally equal to the face amount of the base policy—if the insured dies—generally prior to a certain age—as a result of an accident. The author is not a fan of this rider because it insures the cause of the death and not death by itself. While the cost of the rider is relatively inexpensive, the author believes the money spent would be better utilized in either increasing the base policy face amount, purchasing some other rider, or in universal life policies, to increase the planned funding premium.

Paid-up additional insurance. The paid-up additional insurance rider is an enhancement to a whole life policy. This rider provides for the purchase of a single premium paid-up amount of whole life insurance. The rider is a constant dollar amount applied each year, but each year as the insured's attained age increases a lesser face amount of paid-up additional insurance is purchased. This rider has two main advantages: First, it significantly enhances the cash value of the policy. Second, the commission or loading charges on this rider are significantly low; thus, the more of the total premium of the policy devoted to the paid-up additional insurance rider, the lower the percentage of commission costs to the policy.

Term insurance. Term insurance riders can be utilized with each of the main permanent types of life insurance policies discussed, with the exception of no-lapse guarantee universal life policies. The rider may insure the insured on the base policy, the spouse of the insured, or the spouse and dependent children of the insured. Typically, the term insurance is a level face amount limited to the face amount of insurance on the base policy. Term insurance riders are utilized for two purposes: First, for additional amounts of life insurance that cover temporary needs. Second, where the insurance premium dollar is limited and the policy owner cannot afford to have all of the life insurance permanent insurance.

LTC. LTC riders are available for both whole life policies and universal life policies with the exception of no-lapse guarantee universal life policies. In fact, life insurance policies with LTC riders have become a very successful substitute for stand-alone LTC policies. The LTC benefits provide living benefits to the policy owner in the form of providing LTC payments once the insured either is unable to perform at least two of the six activities of daily living or suffers from a mental deficiency such as dementia. These payments reduce dollar for dollar the death benefit of the policy, and the total LTC payment benefits are generally limited to a percentage of the face amount of the policy such as 50 percent. The appeal of life insurance policies with this rider is that, unlike stand-alone LTC policies, it is not a use-it-or-lose-it proposition. That is, if the LTC payment benefits are not utilized, the insured's family receives the total death benefit. For older insureds, this rider needs to be seriously considered. However, the author strongly advocates not using this rider when the life insurance is acquired for estate settlement costs purposes and is owned either by an ILIT or another third-party owner. This is because the Internal Revenue Service could construe the arrangement as either retained incidents of ownership in the policy or retained interests in the ILIT in violation of either IRC § 2042 or § 2036.

If the desired life insurance product type is a non-guaranteed flexible premium policy (i.e., universal life, variable universal life, indexed universal life), has an actuarial evaluation incorporating actuarially certified policy benchmark standards and Monte Carlo simulation been performed to determine the probability of the planned funding premium sustaining the policy to the desired planned policy duration?

Carrier illustrations for flexible premium non-guaranteed death benefit products show how the policy works, and do not serve a predictive value purpose. This disclaimer is made in the illustration and policy contract as well as Financial Industry Regulatory Authority (FINRA) and Society of Actuaries guidance. In order to determine the probability of success of a planned funding premium sustaining a proposed policy to the desired planned policy duration (i.e., life expectancy plus five years or to contract maturity), it is imperative to have an actuarial policy evaluation that incorporates actuarially certified policy benchmark standards for the mortality and expenses of the policy combined with Monte Carlo simulation that takes into account the volatility of earnings on the policy. Additionally, this actuarial evaluation should include an analysis of the cost competitiveness of the mortality and expense charges of the proposed policy as compared to the actuarially certified policy benchmark standards; the earliest predicted lapse as well as the five-year range of the highest concentration of policy lapses based upon Monte Carlo simulation trials for the proposed funding premium; and the correcting funding premium for the policy to bring the probability of success of the proposed policy funding premium for the planned policy duration to the percentage confidence level—or risk tolerance—of the policy owner. For continued monitoring and risk management purposes necessary for non-guaranteed indeterminate flexible premium policies, this actuarial evaluation process should not only be performed at the time of policy purchase, but also on an annual basis thereafter.[111]

Selecting the Appropriate Life Insurance Carrier

What is the Comdex ranking of the proposed life insurance carrier?

Financial strength ratings by the four major independent rating services—A.M. Best Company, Fitch Rating Company, Moody's, and the Standard & Poor's—are an extremely important criterion in selecting a life insurance carrier. The criteria and purpose of each rating service varies but, generally, each is evaluating

---

111. See Chapter 5, Creditable Evaluation of Life Insurance.

creditworthiness, claims paying ability, and financial strength. Each rating service has a number of different ratings, or grades, that they assign to the companies they evaluate. Additionally, not all life insurance companies are rated by each of the four firms; however, all life insurance companies are rated by A.M. Best and most of the major carriers are rated by all four services.

Given the differences in the number of rating scales and inconsistencies in the rating criteria between the four rating services—plus, the rating "curve" or percentage distribution of each rating grade differs by the different rating services—it is difficult to compare the relative ratings of one service to another. This led to the creation of the Comdex, which has also been referred to as the Comdex Index or the Comdex rankings. The Comdex is not a rating itself, but rather a composite of all the ratings that a life insurance company has received. It is an attempt to rank life insurance companies relatively by the average of percentile distribution of ratings received from the different rating services. The Comdex rankings range from 0 to 100, with 100 being the top ranking. For example, if a life insurance carrier received the highest ratings from each of the four rating services, their Comdex index would be 100. The theory behind the Comdex rankings is that it is not the letter grade of rating that is important but rather the percentiles that each rating represents. The percentile gives the percent of carriers that are ranked lower than a particular company. For example, if a company is in the 90th percentile, 10 percent of companies ranked are ranked higher and 90 percent are ranked lower.

From a practical standpoint, absent any health, occupation, avocation, or any other underwriting issues and considerations that affect the proposed insured or insureds, the author personally recommends that a prospective policy owner choose a life insurance carrier with at least a Comdex ranking of 85, and preferably a carrier with a Comdex ranking of 90 or better.

The critical aspect about ratings and the Comdex rankings is that they must be monitored continuously. Ratings and Comdex rankings vary over time. Occasionally, the life insurance industry outlook as a whole is downgraded, which would affect the ratings and Comdex rankings of all carriers. In fact, the relative rankings of the Comdex vis-à-vis the various insurance carriers in this scenario would remain relatively stable. However, a carrier with a significant and sudden downgrade, or a series of sequentially smaller downgrades, could be a signal of serious financial difficulties that would require attention and possibly action on the part of the policy owner.

What is the proposed life insurance carrier's ranking based on admitted assets within the largest 25, 50, or 100 life insurance carriers?

While certainly not an absolute, the size of the life insurance carrier is another important consideration. The 100 largest life insurance companies by admitted assets represent more than 90 percent of the life insurance industry's capitalization. This measure of "staying power" would suggest choosing a life insurance carrier that is at least in the top 50 rankings by admitted assets and better yet the top 25 rankings.

What percentage of the proposed life insurance carrier's total premium revenue is based on first-year and in-force individual life insurance premium?

Is the focus of the proposed life insurance carrier primarily on individual life insurance? Not all life insurance companies concentrate solely on individual life insurance. Many may have an emphasis on other areas of the life insurance industry such as group life insurance, annuities, pension and retirement plans, and so on. So, in addition to raw size by admitted assets, consideration should be given to selecting a carrier that ranks in the top 25 as measured by first-year and in-force individual life insurance policy premium revenue.

Is the proposed life insurance carrier a stock or mutual insurance company?

Mutual life insurance carriers are owned by the policy holders, whereas stock life insurance carriers are owned by outside investors. It is interesting to note that the four major mutual life insurance companies are the top four insurers ranked by the Comdex Index. Obviously, this has to do, in part, with the high quality of the assets backing the general asset accounts of these insurers. On the other hand, it can be argued that mutual insurance carriers can be more focused on long-run results that are in the best interest of the policy owners as opposed to stock life insurance carriers that must focus their attention not only on the policy owners but on the next quarterly earnings report. While not an absolute, the author usually recommends a mutual insurance carrier over a stock insurance carrier.

Finally, it must be emphasized that underwriting issues and considerations of the proposed insured or insureds' health, occupation, avocation, or other factors can trump and change what would be the preferred selection criterion for a life insurance carrier.

Selecting Life Insurance Professionals

What life insurance professionals, advisers, and consultants will be involved in the decision and acquisition process for the life insurance policy or policies, and how are these life insurance professionals compensated?

Depending on the nature of the need for life insurance; the size, premium dollar, or face amount of life insurance contemplated; and other factors and circumstances, different types of life insurance professionals may be involved—as well as other professional advisers such as attorneys, accountants, trust officers, and financial planners—in the decision and acquisition of a life insurance policy or policies. Each adviser will be compensated either by a stipulated fee amount or hourly rate fee, a commission based on the premium dollars involved, an asset under management fee (arguably another form of commission), or some combination thereof. In other words, depending on the circumstances, there could be just one adviser who is a life insurance professional or a whole team of advisers consisting of not only life insurance professionals but other professional advisers. In some cases, the number of advisers involved depends on which adviser initiated the need for life insurance or if the need was initiated by the proposed insured/policy owner/client; although, more commonly, the need for life insurance is initiated by an adviser, or advisers, rather than the client himself or herself.

For example, the need for life insurance to cover a mortgage, provide for a child's college education, provide for supplemental retirement income, or to provide for a dependent spouse and/or child or children may be suggested by a single life insurance agent or broker, or a single financial planner, who then also handles the acquisition of the policy for the client. This would probably also be the case when the size of the face amount or premium dollars of the life insurance policy involved is a relatively small amount under, for example, $500,000 or $1,000,000 of permanent life insurance coverage. In these cases, the life insurance agent or broker or financial planner would be compensated via a commission amount based upon the premium dollar amounts of the life insurance policy or policies. The premium dollars involved would not necessarily justify the services of an independent fee-based life insurance consultant or adviser in addition to the commission paid to the life insurance agent or broker.

On the other hand, in a more sophisticated planning situation that could involve estate tax and settlement cost planning, business succession planning, non-qualified deferred compensation, or SERPs, the need for life insurance could be initiated by either an attorney, accountant, trust officer, financial planner, or life insurance professional, and involve relatively large face amounts and premium dollars for permanent life insurance. In these cases, a team of advisers could be involved in the planning situation needing or requiring life insurance. For example, the planning may require just an attorney and a life insurance professional who is either an agent or a broker. Alternatively, the planning may require an attorney, accountant, trust officer, financial planner, an independent fee-based life insurance consultant, life insurance agent or broker, and other advisers. Each adviser would be compensated on either a commission or fee basis as typically set out in an engagement letter.

It is important to understand the differences in the roles and limitations of various life insurance professionals, and how they are compensated. This would also include various financial planners involved in the life insurance transaction. Technically, a life insurance agent represents a life insurance company, or companies. A life insurance broker usually represents the life insurance client, although in taking and completing the life insurance application, the broker has to legally be an agent for the selected life insurance company. Agents and brokers are commission-compensated based on the life insurance product(s) sold. However, in practice, a life insurance agent could either function strictly as an agent for one life insurance carrier or represent several carriers and, in addition, have the freedom to represent an unlimited number of carriers. In the latter cases, the agent is functioning as a broker. In other words, the functions of agent and broker have become quite blurred, resulting in many states not having separate licenses for agents and brokers but only one license that is referred to as a life insurance producer license. Also, it is not uncommon to use the terms "agent" and "broker" interchangeably.

How a life insurance agent actually functions is determined by the life insurance agent's contract with the life insurance carrier, or carriers, the agent represents. With some life insurance companies, the life insurance agent, by contract, is a captive agent. That is, the agent may only represent that one life insurance carrier. Many of the multiline insurance carriers—such as State Farm and American Family Insurance—have only captive agents. Other life insurance companies have what is referred to as "career agent contracts" in which the agent is a captive agent. Some life insurance companies require the agent for the first three years of the agent's contract to be a captive agent, and thereafter modify the contract so that the agent only has to give the carrier a "right of first refusal." In practice, this arrangement can effectively allow the agent to function as a broker and place business with other insurance carriers but, generally, there are attractive incentives for the agent to place business with his or her primary carrier.

It is not unusual for some of the captive agent insurance carriers to have an arrangement whereby policies can be placed with other insurance companies where either the captive insurance company does not insure the particular risk, or have certain products, or the captive insurance company's product is not competitive. Generally, these arrangements are managed out of the captive insurance company's home office and the captive insurance agent will tell a client that he or she can "shop" the insurance market where necessary. Quite often, the captive insurance company's arrangement with other insurance carriers is limited to just a few companies and the home office personnel handling such arrangements is not skilled in negotiating with insurance companies to get the client the best deal.

The bottom line in dealing with a life insurance agent or broker is to request disclosure of the agent or broker's contractual life insurance carrier arrangements. This disclosure could also include compensation arrangements as to base commissions, expense allowances, overrides, bonuses, and service fees for both first-year premium and renewals, plus the length of the renewal compensation period, and persistency bonuses and other incentives such as company conferences and conventions based on production. If the agent or broker does not want to disclose these arrangements, engagement of another agent or broker is a consideration. There has to be trust and honesty in the relationship between an agent or broker and a client.

Agents and brokers perform a variety of essential roles and services in the procurement and acquisition of a life insurance policy or policies. In addition to helping clients clarify their need for life insurance and the various common uses for life insurance, agents can advise on the suitability of various life insurance products and assist in the selection of the specific life insurance product. By inquiring into and exploring the proposed insured's health, occupation, avocation, financial, and other statuses, the agent and broker can make an initial assessment of the risk classification the proposed insured could potentially be assigned by various carriers.

In some cases, the risk factors involved in underwriting classification may cause the broker—or agent who is functioning as a broker—to "shop" and negotiate among various life insurance companies. This quite frequently will involve taking a "trial application" that summarizes out the medical, occupational, avocational, financial, and other underwriting factors needed for carriers to make a preliminary underwriting risk classification assessment. It is imperative in this process that the broker is familiar with the underwriting practices of various life insurance carriers. It is not unusual for a broker to work with a firm that specializes in the placement of life insurance on insureds that have either medical or other risk factors that would cause a life insurance policy to be issued with less than a standard risk classification or involve some type of flat extra charge.

After taking the life insurance application, the agent or broker will help facilitate other underwriting requirements such as medical examinations, financial information, and attending physician statements sought by the life insurance company underwriting the policy. Finally, the agent or broker will deliver the policy to the owner along with an as-sold policy illustration and, hopefully, an agent suitability letter. Further, the first premium payment and any additional premium requirements need to be collected if they were not submitted with the life insurance policy application.

It is interesting to note, as espoused in the recent court case *UBS Financial Services, Inc. et al. v. Thompson et al.,*[112] that an agent or broker has no post-sales responsibilities or duties to the policy owner(s), and the duties of an insurance agent or broker are limited to using reasonable care, diligence, skill, good faith, and judgment in procuring the insurance requested. While it is typical for most agent contracts to require routine service to the life insurance policies sold—such as facilitating beneficiary changes when requested, policy loans, and death claims— the agent's contract does not impose or require any post-sale management duties. Typically, the agent or broker is unskilled and untrained in providing policy management services and, particularly, creditable policy evaluation.

An independent fee-based life insurance consultant is compensated purely on his or her advice and services. In most instances, the consultant (or agent serving in a consultant role) does not sell life insurance products or receive any type of commission or compensation based on the sale of life insurance products resulting from such advice and services as a fee-based life insurance consultant. Thus, the independent fee-based life insurance consultant's compensation is based on either

---

112. *UBS Financial Services, Inc. et al. v. Nancy Lee Kathryn Thompson et al.*, No. 0352, September Term, 2013, Court of Special Appeals of Maryland (June 25, 2014).

a set fee for the services rendered and/or an hourly rate based on the time involved in consulting, researching, and rendering such advice as required for the client. Independent fee-based life insurance consultants offer a degree of expertise that is impartial and unbiased, and adheres to a fiduciary standard. What makes the life insurance consultant's advice impartial and unbiased is the complete lack of "any skin in the game" from being compensated via a commission, or assets under management (AUM) fee, based on the procurement, acquisition, or placement of a life insurance policy or any other financial product.

The life insurance consultant can help the client clarify and verify the needs for life insurance protection, select suitable product type(s) to fulfill the needs for life insurance based on a risk tolerance assessment and the preference for either a minimum premium outlay or growth in death benefits and cash values, and determine the exact criteria for carrier selection based on the underwriting and risk characteristics of the proposed insured or insureds. After determining the life insurance needs including (1) the amount of the insurance need, (2) the appropriate product type or types, and (3) the carrier selection criteria, the life insurance consultant then oversees and works with various life insurance agents and brokers employing a request for proposal (RFP) process, to solicit "bids," underwrite, negotiate, creditably evaluate, and acquire the prerequisite life insurance coverage.

Additionally, unlike almost all life insurance agents and brokers, creditable life insurance consultants can assist the client in preparing a life insurance policy management statement—or, in the trust context, a trust-owned life insurance investment policy statement (TIPS)—and do the necessary ongoing life insurance policy risk management and ongoing creditable evaluation of the life insurance policy or policies. Some life insurance consultants also provide for the routine administration of life insurance policies that can entail monitoring premium payment and tracking non-guaranteed policy values, and, in the trust context, sending out routine Crummey withdrawal notices.

The term "financial planner" is used in many different contexts in the financial service professions. Some life insurance agents and brokers, and even some life insurance consultants, refer to themselves as financial planners. The use of the term financial planner by life insurance professionals can be more than justified by the broadening, expanding role and services provided by the life insurance professional. Sixty years ago, life insurance agents and brokers just sold life and health insurance, and stockbrokers just sold stocks and bonds. With the advent of equity-linked or variable life insurance products, life insurance producers had to become securities licensed, and now having security licenses, life insurance producers began selling mutual funds and other securities. Similarly, stockbrokers acquired insurance licenses and began selling life insurance. Consumers came to demand an integrated approach, as opposed to a separate approach, towards needs for financial products, thus resulting in the broadening role for both life insurance professionals and stockbrokers to that of a comprehensive financial planner.

In order to properly assess needs for life insurance, the life insurance professional must know all the personal, career, and financial goals and objectives of his or her client, the family situation and dynamics of the client, and the total financial picture and position of the client. Such information includes all current assets and liabilities, income currently and projected, investments, life and other insurance plans and coverages, retirement plans, estate plans, and, if applicable, business succession plans. In other words, the life insurance professional needs to utilize the same process and integrated approach as the financial planner. Thus, to be a good life insurance professional, the life insurance professional must be a good financial planner, and, similarly, to be a good financial planner, the financial planner must be a good life insurance professional.

Obviously, financial planners can also be life insurance agents or brokers, and even life insurance consultants, the difference being the role the financial planner plays in the decision and acquisition of life insurance and how the financial planner is compensated. Thus, depending on the role of the financial planner, the above comments for life insurance agents or brokers and life insurance consultants are applicable.

It should be pointed out that some financial planners—most of whom are also Certified Financial Planners® (CFP®)—are compensated not by commissions but rather primarily by assets under management (AUM) fees, and refer to themselves as fee-based financial planners. In directly placing and acquiring life insurance coverage for their clients, these "fee-based" financial planners will either receive a commission for the service like a life insurance agent or broker, or place the life insurance coverage with a carrier that issues a "no-load" policy. A no-load policy is a policy that does not pay any commissions to an agent, broker, or life insurance producer. This is not to say that the no-load policy has no policy expenses. Quite the contrary. In fact, overall expenses for the policy could be higher than commission-based policies because of other marketing expenses and low-volume sales for these policies. As mentioned in previous portions of this book, an analysis of a life insurance policy must take an integrated approach considering policy earnings, mortality charges, and all policy expenses.[113] Furthermore, especially with non-guaranteed flexible premium products, it is important to have the policy, either commission-based or no-load, creditably evaluated using Monte Carlo simulation and actuarially certified policy benchmark standards analysis.

---

113. See subsection titled "Life Insurance Pricing and Costs Must Be Viewed Integrated as a Whole and Not Separately" in the section "The Building Blocks of Life Insurance" in Chapter 2, Toward Understanding Life Insurance and the Risk Transfer Paradigm Shift—Some Life Insurance Basics.

What criteria will be used in the selection of life insurance professionals?

There are a wide variety of life insurance professionals and financial planners available to provide advice and services, each having various relationships with financial firms, life insurance carriers, different backgrounds and education, experience, professional credentials, personalities, and philosophies and methods of doing business. Choosing and selecting among these professionals as to who is the most suitable for life insurance expertise and with whom you will be comfortable working can be a daunting task. Perhaps the best starting point is to ask for referrals from friends, business associates, accountants, estate planning attorneys, and trust officers. However, do not assume that the referrer conscientiously chose a life insurance professional or a financial planner based on either a selection process or the criteria listed below. This means that the recommendation from the referrer is a starting point and it is necessary to use due diligence in finding out the background and other information about the referred as listed below. Another source to find life insurance professionals and financial planners is membership directories of the professional organizations listed below. This option depends on whether or not the professional organization makes the membership directory available to the public or only to the membership. The last option as a source is to do a Google search on the Internet.

In many circumstances and situations, clients do not consciously or methodically follow a selection process. Rather, an adviser approaches the client, or there is some type of relationship wherein the client feels obliged to work with an adviser such as a neighbor, fellow member of a church or social club, or family relationship such as the cousin or brother-in-law. But assuming a prudent process and methodology to "hire" the appropriate life insurance professional(s), the author offers the following selection criteria, which can also be applied in an RFP format utilizing specifications and questionnaires:

> **Experience**. Like many other professions, the life insurance profession has a "learning curve." For life insurance agents or brokers a minimum of five years' experience is recommended and ten years would be even better. Additionally, the vast majority and percentage of the experience in the insurance area should be with individual life insurance policies, not group insurance, medical insurance, or property and casualty insurance.
>
> If you have to work with your inexperienced neighbor, church member, cousin, or brother-in-law make sure that that person is actively working with an agent or broker who meets all of the requisite requirements stated herein. By actively working, it is meant that the senior agent or broker is present in all meetings with the inexperienced agent or broker and is actively engaged in the process.
>
> For fee-based life insurance consultants the minimum experience in the individual life insurance policy area should be at least ten years. Experience in providing expert opinion and expert witness litigation support is also desirable.

Background and education. Frankly, there is no "ideal" background and education for a life insurance agent or broker, or a life insurance consultant. The author has personally known extremely conscientious, competent, and knowledgeable life insurance professionals and financial planners having former occupations that included a symphony musician, engineer, banker, teacher, salesman, accountant, labor lawyer, and even a medical doctor—and having educational backgrounds as diverse as a high school diploma; undergraduate degrees in English, economics, history, music, education, business, accounting, finance, insurance, theology, engineering, political science, psychology, and biology; and graduate degrees, including master's and doctoral, in almost all of the previously mentioned undergraduate fields plus law (J.D.), medicine (M.D.), and a Ph.D. in nuclear physics.

Having said that, however, there is a degree of intelligence and sophistication required to practice in the more advanced areas—such as in estate planning, business succession planning, and executive benefit plans and non-qualified deferred compensation plans—and to work with high-net-worth clients that is demonstrated by educational background. The key is to have an individual with a thirst for knowledge who is continuingly learning new things, both professional and otherwise. All things being equal—which is rarely the case—the author would prefer to work with a professional that has at least an undergraduate degree and, maybe, preferably a graduate degree.

Professional educational credentials and designations. The above discussion addresses education obtained before entering the fields of life insurance and financial planning. This section is concerned with professional credentials and designations specifically for life insurance acquired after entering the profession. This is not addressing the required insurance and securities licenses necessary to provide insurance and financial advice. Rather, the focus is on professional educational credentials and designations the practitioner obtains voluntarily that demonstrate the highest standard of advanced knowledge and skill in the life insurance profession.

Over the past couple of decades there has been a proliferation in professional designations in the finance services arena. There are a number of prestigious and quality financial services designations that are not germane to the life insurance field—such as the Chartered Financial Analyst (CFA) and the Certified Employee Benefit Specialist (CEBS) designations. There are also financial services designations that are pejoratively referred to as "Holiday Inn" designations. That is, you attend an educational program for "X" number of days and, maybe, take a test at a Holiday Inn and you have a professional designation. A quality designation program requires the completion of college-level educational courses, experience requirements of at least three years, ethical and licenses background checks, and professional referrals, and has a substantial continuing education requirement.

The important designations in the life insurance and financial planning fields—that meet all of the above criteria for high-quality designation programs— are the Chartered Life Underwriter® (CLU®), Chartered Financial Consultant®

(ChFC®), and the Certified Financial Planner (CFP®). The Accredited Estate Planner® (AEP®) designation is also a tremendous plus. It is a graduate-level specialization designation in estate planning. However, to obtain the AEP® designation an individual must already possess either a CLU®, ChFC®, CFP®, J.D., Certified Public Accountant (CPA), or Certified Trust and Financial Adviser (CTFA) credential. Additionally, there are quality master's degree programs devoted to either life insurance or financial planning generally taken by individuals in the profession who already possess one of the above designations. Two of these programs include the Master of Science in Financial Services (MSFS) from The American College of Financial Services at Bryn Mawr, Pennsylvania, and the Master of Science from the College of Financial Planning of Greenwood Village, Colorado.

The gold standard for life insurance knowledge for a life insurance professional is the CLU® designation. The National Association of Insurance and Financial Advisors (NAIFA)—formerly the National Association of Life Underwriters—has espoused a designation program called Life Underwriter Training Council Fellow (LUTCF). While the LUTCF does contain multiple semester-long courses that do contain valuable technical information, the program itself is primarily designed to be a sales course and is not the same standard as the CLU® designation. Interestingly, The American College of Financial Services now sponsors the LUTCF in conjunction with NAIFA and is the sole provider and creator of the CLU®, ChFC®, and MSFS program, as well as the course provider for the AEP® designation.

The ChFC® and CFP® designations study programs do have a considerable bit of content on life insurance knowledge—more so the ChFC® program—but the emphasis on each of those designation programs is on financial planning. The AEP® designation program is primarily about estate planning and business succession planning. However, life insurance quite often plays a large role in both estate planning and business succession planning.

The author is biased towards working with life insurance professionals who have the CLU® designation. However, many life insurance and financial planning professionals today have more than one designation (i.e., CLU® and ChFC®, or CLU® and CFP®, or ChFC® and CFP®) and it is not hard finding individuals in the life insurance profession who are very serious about continuing education and have a thirst for knowledge who have three or more designations—such as CLU®, ChFC®, and CFP®, or CLU®, ChFC®, and AEP®. The designations are important and should be given considerable consideration in choosing a life insurance professional.

Professional memberships. There are many financial planning and life insurance professional organizations. From the author's standpoint, the two professional organizations that provide the most advanced knowledge about life insurance in their professional continuing education programs are the Society of Financial Service Professionals (FSP)—formerly the American Society of CLU and ChFC—and the National Association of Estate Planners & Councils (NAEPC) through their affiliated local estate planning councils. Both the FSP and NAEPC are national organizations with local chapters and councils around the county. Both the national organizations and the local chapters and councils provide high-quality continuing education programs. Both are professional societies that do not do any lobbying with governmental bodies.

There are three other major life insurance organizations for agents and brokers. The largest single life insurance organization is NAIFA. NAIFA is currently organized under state associations that each have numerous local chapters. NAIFA, on both the national and state levels, does considerable advocacy and lobbying with governmental bodies. Although NAIFA does considerable life insurance continuing education—particularly basic and intermediate—for its members, it functions primarily as a professional trade organization.

The Association for Advanced Life Underwriting (AALU) is a national organization that is affiliated with NAIFA and has two primary purposes: political advocacy (membership requires $1,000 in political contributions) and advanced knowledge on current and timely issues that are mostly legal and legislative developments. The organization has one annual meeting in Washington, D.C., and provides its members with ongoing current updates through the Internet and other publications.

The Million Dollar Round Table (MDRT) is an international organization whose membership is based upon qualifying levels of production of base commissions generated on sales of life insurance, both individual and group, and other financial products such as mutual funds. The MDRT has various suborganizations for higher level producers such as the Court of the Table and the Top of the Table. While the organization does provide some high-quality advanced education of life insurance and other financial products at its various annual meetings, the primary focus of the organization is on production, sales, and motivation.

The major trade organization for financial planners, particularly CFPs®, is the Financial Planning Association (FPA). The FPA is a national organization that has many local chapters. Both the national and local chapters provide high-quality continuing education meetings and programs in the area of financial planning, although occasionally the organization will have presentations on life insurance and annuities. Like NAIFA, the FPA, both on the national and state levels, does a considerable amount of advocacy and lobbying with governmental bodies.

Those financial planners that hold the CFP® designation are governed by the Certified Financial Planner Board of Standards® (CFP® Board) and must maintain membership in good standing with that organization. This includes complying with the CFP® Board's standards and continuing education requirements that the CFP®

Board administrates. The CFP® Board does a considerable amount of advocacy and lobbying with governmental bodies and a large portion of the CFP® annual membership fee goes to advertising.

In selecting life insurance professionals, the author recommends FSP membership plus membership in a local estate planning council. Membership in the other organizations mentioned is certainly a plus and demonstrates commitment to the life insurance and financial planning professions.

Company and/or firm the life insurance professional is associated with. In general, experienced life insurance agents and brokers tend to operate autonomously and independently. While many place the majority of their life insurance policies with a primary carrier or a number of select carriers, the majority of experienced agents and brokers have the freedom to place business with any carrier that does not operate as a captive system with exclusive agents. However, there are some experienced life insurance agents who are captive agents and represent one carrier. As already mentioned, it is important that the agent or broker disclose all contractual arrangements and relationships with various carriers and companies, including compensation arrangements.

The goal is to retain a life insurance agent or broker who works strictly on the client's behalf. The author strongly feels that independence and freedom to place business anywhere—except captive companies as mentioned above—is very important and, hence, does not recommend working with captive agents.

By definition, an independent fee-based life insurance consultant acts autonomously and independently.

Lists of services performed. The key in asking for a list of the services performed by the professional is to get an idea of the breadth of the professional's practice. For example, mindful that life insurance is a "buy and manage" asset, it is essential to inquire whether or not the professional will provide the post-sales ongoing policy management services and policy suitability evaluation. As stated previously, most life insurance agents and brokers do not perform ongoing policy management let alone creditable life insurance policy evaluation. Independent fee-based life insurance consultants are more likely to perform these services. From a "buyer beware" perspective, any life insurance agent or broker, or life insurance consultant, that uses a carrier illustration-based comparison system to evaluate non-guaranteed life insurance products should be avoided. Illustrations do not have any predictive creditability for non-guaranteed products and it is improper to use illustrations for this purpose. The proper way to evaluate non-guaranteed life insurance products is to utilize an actuarial evaluation employing Monte Carlo simulation and actuarially certified policy benchmark standards.

There are exceptions to all of the above recommendations, and there are not necessarily any absolutes. The key is to obtain thorough information on prospective life insurance professionals and use your best judgment in picking the appropriate individual. Seek references. Of course, a life insurance professional is not going to give you a reference that will speak poorly of him or her—nor would any other professional. It is important to speak with the references to determine personality and type of person the life insurance professional is, the process utilized by the professional, whether the professional is a good listener, and the philosophy and outlook of the professional. It may not be a bad idea to ask the reference to name the positive traits as well as the negative traits of the life insurance professional. The goal and objective is to find an experienced, qualified, consciences, competent, and knowledgeable individual who has your overall outlook and philosophy on the world, will work on behalf of your best interest, and is just a plain good fit and feels right.

Ongoing Policy Monitoring, Risk Management, Verification, and Creditable Evaluation

Once the life insurance policy is acquired, what ongoing required policy monitoring, risk management, verification, and creditable policy evaluation procedures and functions have been established and how frequently will these functions be performed?

Tables 6.2, 6.3, and 6.4 [14] summarize requirements for life insurance policy acceptance, monitoring, risk management, and verification for guaranteed products—participating whole life, no-lapse guarantee universal life, level premium term, and yearly renewable term—and non-guaranteed products—universal life, indexed universal life, and variable universal life. Table 6.2 contains acceptance considerations and policy management features that a policy owner needs to understand and contemplate in determining the suitability for the various life insurance product types before acquiring the policy and for ongoing policy risk management. Table 6.3 enumerates the various monitoring and risk management requirements, and the frequency of such, for the different product types. Finally, Table 6.4 lists the advisor or trustee annual verification requirements. Note that the critical policy management features, monitoring and risk management requirements, and annual verification requirements are highlighted in red in the three tables.

Premium adequacy, as itemized in both Tables 6.3 and 6.4 for universal life, indexed universal life, and variable universal life, needs to be determined by actuarial evaluation that employs actuarially certified policy benchmark standards

---

114. Tables 6.2, 6.3, and 6.4 are a modification of similar tables produced by E. Randolph Whitelaw, AEP® (Distinguished), Managing Director of Trust Asset Consultants, LLC (TAC), a trust-owned life insurance (TOLI) risk management consulting firm, and Co-Managing Director of The TOLI Center, LLC (TTC), a life insurance policy administration and risk management firm.

combined with Monte Carlo simulation in order for the policy evaluation to be creditable. Any type of policy evaluation utilizing policy illustrations for these non-guaranteed flexible premium products is thoroughly inappropriate and lacks any creditability. The actuarial evaluation process using actuarially certified policy benchmark standards and Monte Carlo simulation is a statistical technique that involves setting "confidence levels," generally expressed as a percentage. Confidence levels for premium adequacy are a risk tolerance determination. An extremely conservative policy owner may require a 100 percent confidence ratio, or risk tolerance, and some type of guaranteed product would probably be more suitable for that policy owner. More commonly used confidence levels for non-guaranteed flexible premium type of products range from 85 percent to 95 percent. The confidence level set, of course, depends on the risk tolerance of the policy owner.

Has the cost of policy monitoring, risk management, verification, and creditable policy evaluation—particularly with non-guaranteed flexible premium type of products—been budgeted and taken into consideration, and who is going to perform those functions?

The cost of the ongoing policy monitoring, risk management, verification, and creditable policy evaluation needs to be taken into consideration and budgeted. Of course, the first decision is to determine who is going to perform the various functions. The guaranteed products primarily require product suitability review and carrier solvency monitoring. These functions may be performed by the policy owner with assistance from his or her life insurance professional and financial advisers at either no or minimal costs. In addition to the management requirements of ongoing product suitability and carrier solvency monitoring, non-guaranteed flexible premium products require ongoing creditable policy evaluation of premium and death benefit adequacy. This evaluation needs to be performed using actuarially certified policy benchmark standards and Monte Carlo simulation techniques by an independent, fee-based life insurance consultant. The fees for such service typically range from $250 to $400 per policy.

The independent, fee-based life insurance consultant can assist the policy owner in accessing and performing the necessary monitoring and risk management requirements, annual verifications, and the creditable evaluation of the life insurance policy or policies, and in determining the cost of such services. In fact, anytime a policy owner lacks life insurance expertise it just makes good sense to employ, and in some cases delegate, these life insurance risk management functions to the life insurance consultant.

Table 6.2 Life Insurance Policy Acceptance, Monitoring, Risk Management & Verification: Acceptance Considerations & Policy Management Features

	Guaranteed Products				Non-Guaranteed Products		
	Participating Whole Life	No-Lapse Guaranteed Universal Life	Level Premium Term	Yearly Renewable Term	Universal Life	Indexed Universal Life	Variable Universal Life*
Premium Schedule	Fixed	Fixed	Fixed Period	Increasing	Flexible	Flexible	Flexible
Specified Death Benefit Amount	Fixed	Fixed	Fixed	Fixed	Flexible	Flexible	Flexible
Account Value Management	Carrier	Carrier	None	None	Policy Owner	Policy Owner	Policy Owner
Asset Allocation Required	N/A	N/A	N/A	N/A	No	Yes**	Yes
Illustration Credibility	Yes/No***	Yes	Yes	Yes	No	No	No
Actuarial Evaluation	N/A	N/A	N/A	N/A	Yes	Yes	Yes
Volatility Simulation	N/A	N/A	N/A	N/A	Yes	Yes	Yes

* Includes private placement life insurance (PPLI). Accredited investors have access to PPLI, which wraps investments similar to variable universal life but also includes options such as hedge funds, private equity, and complex derivatives. Also includes institutional life insurance (ILI), also referred to as corporate variable universal life.

** Some indexed universal life (IUL) policies allow selection and/or allocation along multiple indices.

*** Participation whole life policies have guaranteed specified death benefits, cash values, and premiums. All of these guaranteed values have full illustration credibility. However, dividends—which are a return of premium and enhancement to the policy—are not guaranteed and the dividend portion of the whole life policy illustration has no illustration credibility.

Table 6.3 Life Insurance Policy Acceptance, Monitoring, Risk Management & Verification (Continued): Monitoring & Risk Management Requirements

	Guaranteed Products				Non-Guaranteed Products		
	Participating Whole Life	No-Lapse Guaranteed Universal Life	Level Premium Term	Yearly Renewable Term	Universal Life	Indexed Universal Life	Variable Universal Life*
Investment Policy Statement	Yes	Yes	Yes	Yes	Yes	Yes	Yes
Trust-Owned Life Insurance (TOLI)-Specific Procedures	Yes	Yes	Yes	Yes	Yes	Yes	Yes
Product Suitability	Ongoing	Ongoing	Ongoing	Ongoing	Ongoing	Ongoing	Ongoing
Premium Adequacy Risk	No	No	No	No	Yes	Yes	Yes
Monitoring Cycle	N/A	N/A	N/A	N/A	Annual	Annual	Annual
Carrier Solvency Risk	Yes	Yes	Yes	Yes	Yes	Yes	Yes
Monitoring Cycle	Ongoing	Ongoing	Ongoing	Ongoing	Ongoing	Ongoing	Ongoing
Asset Allocation Review	N/A	N/A	N/A	N/A	N/A	Yes**	Yes
Conversion Review	N/A	N/A	As Directed	As Directed	N/A	N/A	N/A
Rating and Rider Review	Annual	Annual	Annual	Annual	Annual	Annual	Annual
Regulatory Review (Institutional)	Annual	Annual	Annual	Annual	Annual	Annual	Annual

* Includes private placement life insurance (PPLI). Accredited investors have access to PPLI, which wraps investments similar to variable universal life but also includes options such as hedge funds, private equity, and complex derivatives. Also includes institutional life insurance (ILI), also referred to as corporate variable universal life.

** Some indexed universal life (IUL) policies allow selection and/or allocation along multiple indices.

Table 6.4 Life Insurance Policy Acceptance, Monitoring, Risk Management & Verification (Continued): Advisor or Trustee Annual Verification

	Guaranteed Products				Non-Guaranteed Products		
	Participating Whole Life	No-Lapse Guaranteed Universal Life	Level Premium Term	Yearly Renewable Term	Universal Life	Indexed Universal Life	Variable Universal Life*
Product Suitability	Yes	Yes	Yes	Yes	Yes	Yes	Yes
Premium Adequacy	N/A	N/A	N/A	N/A	100%***	100%***	100%***
Death Benefit Adequacy	N/A	N/A	N/A	N/A	Yes	Yes	Yes
Carrier Solvency and Suitability	Yes	Yes	Yes	Yes	Yes	Yes	Yes
Investment Performance Rebalancing	N/A	N/A	N/A	N/A	N/A	Yes**	Yes

* Includes private placement life insurance (PPLI). Accredited investors have access to PPLI, which wraps investments similar to variable universal life but also includes options such as hedge funds, private equity, and complex derivatives. Also includes institutional life insurance (ILI), also referred to as corporate variable universal life.

** Some indexed universal life (IUL) policies allow selection and/or allocation along multiple indices.

*** Or to a risk tolerance percentage chosen by the policy owner or trustee as specified in the life insurance policy management statement (LIPMS) or TOLI investment policy statement (TIPS).

Determining the "What Ifs"

Has it been determined what options will be pursued if the life insurance policy or product chosen is no longer suitable?

A life insurance policy is purchased to provide death benefit protection (and living benefits) over a ten- to 50-year time horizon. During this time period, personal and business situations will more than likely change as well as tax rules. Risk tolerance will change and life happens. Because of various changes and circumstances the life insurance policy or policies purchased may become unsuitable. Additionally, the financial position of the carrier(s) may deteriorate or the policy or policies may not perform as expected. Therefore, it makes perfect sense to contemplate in advance the different options available under the various circumstances that can change over time and anticipate and plan for the risk management of the life insurance policy. This type of planning should be part of any life insurance purchase yet few advisers and life insurance professionals ever bring up the topic or discuss it with their clients.

The options available to the policy owner if the life insurance policy or product is no longer suitable depend on the cause of the unsuitability. If the policy becomes unsuitable because the original need for life insurance or a subsequent need for life insurance—or any other need such as electing an annuity income option with the cash value of the policy—no longer exists, then the options available are to either stop paying the premium on the policy and let the policy lapse, surrender the policy for its cash value (if any), or sell the policy on the secondary market (i.e., the life settlement market). The latter option is particularly viable if the policy face amount is greater than $250,000, underwritten by a carrier with a minimum of a BBB financial rating, and the insured has a life expectancy of two to 12 years and has experienced a deterioration in health since the policy was issued.[115] However, before considering sale of the policy in the life settlement market, Richard M. Weber and Christopher Hause suggest that the following question needs to be considered and assessed:

> If a life settlement funder is willing to offer me (hypothetically) 20% of the death benefit to assume the obligations and benefits of the policy until my death—and knowing that the funder assumes at least a 12% internal rate of return in calculating what it will offer for my policy—why wouldn't I keep this policy strictly for its comparable investment value?[116]

Of course, the question assumes the policy owner is able to pay the ongoing premiums of the policy and that this "investment" is appropriate for the policy owner's investment portfolio and/or the beneficiaries of the insured or trust.

Other causes for the life insurance policy or product to be unsuitable are deterioration in the life insurance carrier ratings and Comdex ranking, or carrier insolvency; underperformance of the policy as determined by actuarial evaluation; policy premiums for the non-guaranteed flexible premium life insurance become inadequate as determined by actuarial evaluation; the cost of insurance (mortality rates) and other policy expenses are too high as determined by actuarial evaluation; and the policy owner's (or beneficiaries of a trust) risk tolerance changes. Each of these issues will be addressed below.

---

115. Whitelaw and Montag, *supra* note 1, page 94.
116. Weber and Hause, *supra* note 26, page 87.

Has it been determined what options will be pursued if the life insurance carrier ratings and the Comdex rankings deteriorate or the carrier becomes insolvent?

Options available to the policy owner if the life insurance carrier's ratings by the four main independent rating services and the Comdex rankings deteriorate are dependent on the insurability of the insured, or insureds, and other underwriting considerations. If the insured is totally uninsurable there are really no options. On the other hand, if the insured's health or other underwriting considerations have deteriorated since the original issue of the policy, and a replacement policy would have a relatively higher risk classification, then an economic and risk management decision would need to be assessed based on the trade-off between increased cost of insurance and the risk and consequences of a possible carrier insolvency. Underwriting considerations set aside, the selection of the initial life insurance carrier should have been based on a Comdex ranking of at least in the 85-percentile range or higher, the carrier's ranking based on admitted assets being at least within the top 50 of the largest 100 life insurance carriers, and the carrier's ranking of individual life insurance first-year and renewal premium total income being within the top 25.

Comdex rankings can be lowered either based on risk and outlook factors facing the entire life insurance industry or because of rating downgrades due to an individual carrier's deterioration in financial condition or performance. Theoretically, in the former global scenario, the percentile ranking scores of all carriers would be lower and the relative order of the rankings should remain the same. This situation would probably not warrant any action on the part of the policy owner. Downgrades due to an individual carrier's change in financial condition or other factors do warrant consideration and assessment by the policy owner. The obvious questions to consider are the magnitude of the downgrades and whether or not the downgrade is a single occurrence or further deteriorations in ratings and the Comdex ranking are likely to occur. Part of risk management planning is to determine a risk tolerance for a carrier's decline in ratings by the four main independent rating services and the Comdex ranking. In terms of the Comdex ranking, what is the minimum percentile Comdex ranking that is acceptable before a policy replacement—assuming insurability and other underwriting factors—is executed? The author would suggest no less than a decline to the 80-percentile ranking as the minimum acceptable Comdex ranking.

If the ratings of the carrier and Comdex ranking have declined below the minimum acceptable risk tolerance level—and, again, assuming that either the insured's underwriting risk factors have remained the same since the issuance of the original policy, or the trade-off between the increase in cost of insurance due to the insured's increased underwriting risk factors and the risk and consequences of possible carrier insolvency is acceptable—then policy replacement can be accomplished by selecting a new insurance carrier based on carrier selection criteria previously determined and a product type that is the same as the original policy—or if risk tolerance and the desire for either increasing cash value and death benefit or minimum premium outlay has changed, a new product type reflecting the change in product type suitability. The cash value of the original policy can be transferred to the new policy via an IRC § 1035 tax-free exchange. Alternatively, the original policy could be sold in the secondary market if the conditions mentioned above for a viable life settlement exist and a new policy could be purchased.

If, unfortunately, either the carrier deterioration was very rapid or the policy owner failed to monitor the life insurance carrier and the carrier became insolvent and taken over by the state insurance department or commission, state guaranty associations provide some safety nets. The fundamental responsibility of the state guaranty associations—that exist in all 50 states and the District of Colombia and Puerto Rico—"is to assure the provision of insurance protection to consumers, up to a statutorily established maximum level of guaranteed protection, once the duties of the guaranty association have been 'triggered' by a judicial determination that an insurer is insolvent and should be liquidated."[117] The two principal set of duties to consumers for the guaranty associations are:

> First, the guaranty association must pay, up to coverage limits, any claims that are to become ripe for payment. Second, as to contracts that the failed insurer had no rights to cancel prospectively (e.g., annuities, most non-term life insurance contracts, and some types of health insurance contracts), the guaranty association must guaranty, assume, or reinsure the continuing insurance coverage. In other words, the association must make sure that the coverage continues, as long as the consumer pays any required premium.[118]

These duties are accomplished

> by the negotiation of an arrangement known as an "assumption reinsurance" transaction. In such a transaction, a healthy carrier agrees to assume all or part of the policy liabilities of the failed insurer in exchange for the transfer of assets to support the liabilities—assets that are usually provided in part by the receiver from the estate of the insurer, and in part by guaranty associations. In other cases, the guaranty associations simply assume the covered liabilities of the insolvent insurer for whatever period is required for the liabilities to run off.[119]

What this essentially means is that all guaranteed provisions and values—up to the coverage maximum—of the failed life insurance carrier will be covered by the guaranty association of the state where the policy owner resides. Since once either

---

117. *Testimony for the Record of the National Organization of Life and Health Insurance Guaranty Associations before the House Financial Services Subcommittee on Insurance, Housing, and Community Opportunity, Hearing Entitled "Insurance Oversight and Legislative Proposals," November 16, 2011*, page 2.

118. Ibid, page 4.

119. Ibid, page 5.

dividends have been paid in a participating whole life policy, or excess declared interest over minimum guaranteed interest credited in a universal life policy, or earnings amounts credited based on the specified formula in an indexed universal life policy, these amounts paid or credited, before the carrier's insolvency, become part of the guaranteed values of the policy, and are covered up to the coverage maximum by the guaranty association. However, after the insurance carrier's failure, only the guaranteed increase in values provided for in the insurance policy are covered, again, up to the coverage maximum of the particular state guaranty association. Variable life insurance products are eligible for guaranty association coverage, subject to certain exclusions and limitations. However, variable life insurance separate sub-accounts that are not guaranteed and where the policy owner bears the risk of returns are segregated assets not subject to the claims of an insurer's creditors and are, therefore, excluded from coverage by state guaranty associations.

The state guaranty association maximum coverage benefits can vary from state to state but most states are consistent with the NAIC Model Act and provide coverage of $300,000 in life insurance death benefits and $100,000 in cash surrender value or withdrawal values for life insurance. In most states, these benefit amounts are aggregate values for any one individual insured in any one insolvency.[120] For life insurance policy values over the maximum state guaranty association covered amounts the insured or policy owner has a priority claim against the assets of the insolvent carrier in liquidation. Interestingly, according to the National Organization of Life and Health Insurance Guaranty Associations (NOLHGA), in multi-state insolvencies between 1991–2009 claims on average for life insurance policies for both policy claims fully covered by the maximum coverage benefit amounts and for claims in excess of the maximum coverage benefit amounts have resulted in an average loss of only 3.79 percent. In other words, the average recovery for all policies after liquidation proceedings was 96.21 percent.[121] This is because the shortfalls in assets versus liabilities for most life insurance insolvencies for larger cases are seldom more than 15 percent and are more typically in the range of 5 percent to 10 percent.[122] However, NOLHGA neglects to mention the time frame to collect claims over the state guaranty association maximum coverage amounts.

Has it been determined what options will be pursued if the non-guaranteed life insurance policy is underperforming as determined by actuarial evaluation?

Whether or not a non-guaranteed flexible premium product is underperforming, the premium payments are inadequate, or the cost of insurance (mortality rates) and other policy expenses are too high can only be determined by an independent

---

120. See the National Organization of Life & Health Insurance Guaranty Associations website, which provides links to the individual state guaranty associations, for more detailed information at https://www.nolhga.com/ (last visited Oct. 31, 2019).

121. *Testimony for the Record of the National Organization of Life and Health Insurance Guaranty Associations, supra* note 117, pages 11 and 16–17.

122. Ibid, page 9.

actuarial evaluation that incorporates actuarially certified policy benchmark standards, for the cost of insurance and other policy expenses, and Monte Carlo simulation (stochastic analysis) to account for the volatility of non-guaranteed returns on policy cash values and premium dollars. This actuarial evaluation is performed to a statistical confidence level (risk tolerance) selected by the policy owner to determine the probability that the planned policy funding premium is adequate enough to sustain the policy to a certain duration period that is generally contract maturity but should be at least to life expectancy.

Policy underperformance is dependent on policy expectations and can be caused by either inadequate returns of policy cash values and premium dollars, inadequate policy premium funding—that is more than likely based on linear constant assumption policy illustrations—or the cost of insurance and other policy expenses are too high, or any combination of the aforementioned causes.

Returns on cash values and premium dollars are determined by the particular non-guaranteed flexible premium product type. Of course, the selection of product type should have been determined based on the policy owner's risk tolerance and other product suitability considerations. (See discussion below on risk tolerance changes.)

The cash value on a universal life policy is backed by the general asset account associated with the block of policies of which the policy owner's policy is a part and is invested in mostly fixed-income securities, primarily government and corporate notes and bonds. At a minimum, the cash value is credited with the guaranteed crediting rate specified in the policy but the board of directors of the insurance carrier can determine a non-guaranteed crediting rate greater than the minimum guaranteed rate. At the time of this writing, fixed-income security rates have been extremely low and are expected to remain as such for the foreseeable future. Thus, the policy owner should not expect a crediting rate much greater than the minimum guaranteed rate of the policy.

Indexed universal life policy cash values are credited based on a specified formula of an increase in some market index—such as the S&P 500™ Index—without dividends over a defined measuring period—such as one or three years. The formula generally contains a participation amount percentage—such as 75 percent of the increase in the index without dividends over the defined period—and a maximum rate of increase (cap rate) that can be credited—such as 10 percent or 12 percent. While older indexed universal life policies may have a minimum rate of return of 1 percent to 2 percent, newer policies have a minimum rate of return of zero. During each measuring period for the increase in the index—or in some policies a portfolio of indices, the asset allocation of each index chosen by the policy owner—the participation rate and the cap rate are guaranteed. However, in subsequent measuring periods for the index, or indices, the carrier can change the participation rate and/or the cap rate. Thus, for indexed universal life policies for each index measuring period the crediting formula is specified and is dependent on the market returns participation rate collared between a minimum return and maximum return cap.

Variable universal life policy cash values are determined by the returns of each of the individual mutual fund-type sub-accounts chosen by the policy owner based on an asset allocation for the policy owner's risk tolerance. Of course, the sub-account portfolio asset allocation needs to be rebalanced periodically—preferably annually—based on either the original policy owner risk tolerance or revised risk tolerance. With the majority of variable universal life carriers having a large variety of sub-accounts of various asset types and well in excess of 50 to choose from, it is not difficult for the policy owner to replace underperforming sub-accounts with other sub-accounts that have performed better and, hopefully, will continue such performance.

Has it been determined what options will be pursued if the non-guaranteed flexible premium life insurance policy premiums are inadequate as determined by actuarial evaluation?

If actuarial evaluation determines that policy premium funding is inadequate—assuming acceptable returns for the particular non-guaranteed flexible premium product type given the policy owner's risk tolerance, and that the cost of insurance and other policy expenses are reasonable compared to actuarially certified policy benchmark standards—the policy owner has two options: either increase the amount of premium funding or reduce the death benefit. If the universal life policy was initially set up with the increasing death benefit option—often referred to as option 2 or option B—changing the death benefit option to the level death benefit option—referred to as option 1 or option A—may be sufficient by itself to lower the future cost of insurance and bring the current premium funding in balance such that the funding is now adequate. Otherwise, without additional premium funding, the face amount will have to be reduced to sustain the policy. Conversely, if through actuarial evaluation the premium funding is more adequate than necessary the premium funding could be reduced or, if needed, by proving evidence of insurability, the death benefit could be increased.

Has it been determined what options will be pursued if the cost of insurance (mortality rates) and other policy expenses are too high as determined by actuarial evaluation utilizing actuarially certified policy benchmark standards?

Part of actuarial evaluation is to determine the variance between actuarially certified policy benchmark standards for cost of insurance (mortality rates) and other policy expenses—given the particular policy type, size, and the insured's underwriting classification—and the current cost of insurance and other policy expenses for the policy being evaluated. A variance in the range of plus or minus 10 percent is reasonable and acceptable. Deviations of 25 percent or more between the actuarially certified policy benchmark standards and the carrier's current cost of insurance and other policy expenses require serious investigation by the policy owner. If the current carrier's cost of insurance and other policy expenses are 25 percent or more greater than the policy benchmark standards then clearly the policy expenses are way too high and if the insured, or insureds, are insurable then policy replacement is warrantable and needs to be considered. On the other hand, if the current carrier's cost of insurance and other policy expenses are 25 percent or more less than the policy benchmark standards then this favorability becomes highly questionable and suspicious. This is because in the long run carrier cost of insurance and policy expenses approach the mean represented by the actuarially certified policy benchmark standards. Variations of between 10 percent and 25 percent would certainly require examination and continued monitoring and may lead to—if the deviation indicates higher carrier policy expenses than the benchmark standard—policy replacement.

Has it been determined what options will be pursued if the policy owner's (or beneficiaries of a trust) risk tolerance changes?

Part of the annual policy suitability review process is to assess the policy owner's current risk tolerance. Generally, the policy owner's risk tolerance tends to become more conservative as the policy owner ages. If risk tolerance changes, options available to the policy owner depend on the product type and the direction of the risk tolerance change, and may involve the insurability of the insured or insureds. (See Table 6.1, Permanent Life Insurance Product Type Characteristics, which depicts suitable policy owner risk tolerance for the various permanent product types.)

If somehow a policy owner who has either a participating whole life policy or a no-lapse guarantee universal life policy risk tolerance becomes significantly more aggressive, and the policy owner decides that cash values of the policy would be better off invested in a growth equity fund or funds as opposed to the fixed-income fund nature of the general asset account of the insurer that supports the cash values of every type of policy except variable universal life, then the policy owner's only option, if the insured or insureds are insurable, is to replace the more conservative policy types—and pay a significantly larger funding premium if the policy to be replaced is a no-lapse guarantee universal life—with a variable universal life policy. However, while changing asset allocation in security portfolios may involve capital gains taxes and a minor transaction cost, replacing one type of life insurance policy with another type of life insurance policy is not quite that simple. While the mortality rates could decrease by the insured proving evidence of insurability—and, thereby, being subject to "select" mortality rates with, perhaps, a decrease in mortality rates from the previous "ultimate" rates[123] by as much as 40 percent—the new select mortality rates will amortize to the ultimate mortality rates over a 15- to 25-year period. On the other hand, new policy acquisition costs

---

123. "Select" mortality rates are those mortality rates used for individuals who have recently provided evidence of insurability. However, the effects of providing evidence of insurability at the issuance of an insurance policy wear off and diminish over time such that they become equal to the "ultimate" mortality rates. Ultimate mortality rates are those rates where the effects of the initial selection process have completely worn off and the mortality experience is the same as for individuals who have not provided evidence of insurability.

can consume up to 100 percent of the first-year premium. Thus, the policy owner needs to weight whether replacing a policy for a policy more suitable for the policy owner's new risk tolerance, and possible mortality savings over a 15- to 25-year period, are worth the new acquisition costs that can be substantial.

If, on the other hand, the policy owner with an aggressive risk tolerance purchased a variable universal life insurance policy and now has a more moderate or conservative risk tolerance, then the policy owner just needs to do an asset reallocation among the available sub-accounts to balance the portfolio of sub-accounts to the policy owner's new risk tolerance. In the extreme case of a risk tolerance change to very conservative, most variable universal life policies offer a guaranteed principal and income fund sub-account option that the policy owner could reallocate all of the cash value and premium dollars to that emulates the guaranteed cash values of a universal life or whole life policy. Like a universal life policy, the variable universal life guaranteed principal and income sub-account guarantees the cash value but not the current cost of insurance and other current policy expenses. However, the maximum cost of insurance (mortality rates) and other policy expenses of a universal life policy would be equivalent to the guaranteed cost of insurance and policy expenses in a whole life policy. For a variable universal life policy owner having a conservative risk tolerance whose cash flow for premium payments has become more limited, it may be more suitable to replace the variable universal life policy with a no-lapse guarantee universal life policy providing, of course, insurability is not an issue and the replacement cost trade-offs make the effort worthwhile.

Universal life and indexed universal life policy owners who desire more equity participation, and whose risk tolerance becomes more aggressive, would be faced with the same options as the participating whole life and no-lapse guarantee universal life policy owner. Universal life policy owners whose risk tolerance remains relatively conservative are still suitable candidates for a universal life policy but may need to reconsider the funding premium amount. An indexed universal life policy owner whose risk tolerance has become more conservative may need to consider replacing the indexed universal life policy with either a universal life policy or a participating whole life policy, again considering insurability issues and replacement cost considerations. Depending on the funding premium for the indexed universal life policy, the latter option may require an additional premium amount that is, of course, a fixed premium requirement.

If the total death benefit face amount for the insured and total premium dollars involved made it feasible for diversification purposes—at least within the asset class of life insurance—to have a portfolio of different carriers and different policy types based on an asset allocation model of different policy types appropriate for the risk tolerance of the policy owner,[124] and that risk tolerance changes in the

---

124. See section titled "Diversification Risk" in Chapter 3, Risks of Life Insurance Policies. See also footnotes 92 and 96.

future, rebalancing the policies portfolio due to changes in risk tolerance depends on the product types and the direction of the risk tolerance change, and may involve the insurability of the insured or insureds.

If one of the policies in the portfolio is a variable universal life policy—depending on the percentage of the total death benefit the variable universal life policy represents, the asset allocation among sub-accounts, and the degree of risk tolerance change—rebalancing the portfolio of policies to the new risk tolerance of the policy owner may be simply a matter of changing only the asset allocation of the sub-accounts of the variable universal life policy. For example, if the policy owner originally had an aggressive risk tolerance with the variable universal life policy constituting 70 percent of the total death benefit of the portfolio of policies and the entire sub-accounts allocated to various growth equity type funds, and the policy owner's risk tolerance changes to a moderate risk tolerance, then by reallocating approximately 30 percent of the variable universal life growth equity sub-accounts into fixed-income securities or guaranteed principal and income sub-accounts the policy owner would now have a portfolio of policies more suitable to his or her moderate risk tolerance. Assuming the other 30 percent of total death benefit was represented by more conservative policy types—such as participating whole life, no-lapse guarantee universal life, and universal life—then with the variable universal life reallocation, approximately 50 percent of all policy cash values would be backed up by fixed-income and guaranteed principal and income securities and 50 percent represented by growth equity funds.

If the policies portfolio either only had a relatively small percentage of the total death benefit for the insured in a variable universal life policy or the policies portfolio did not contain a variable universal life policy, and the policy owner's risk tolerance changes, then the options available to adjust to the new risk tolerance of the policy owner are the same as the options available with the single policy types, other than variable universal life, mentioned above with the same concerns for insurability and replacement cost issues.

Has it been determined what options will be pursued if the insured(s)' health deteriorates (or conversely if the insured(s)' health or other underwriting risk factors improve)?

Once a life insurance policy is issued, the policy retains the original underwriting risk classification for the insured, or insureds, despite subsequent deterioration in the insured's health, or changes in avocations or occupations. On the other hand, if the insured's health improves after policy issuance, or the insured stops smoking and becomes a non-smoker, the policy owner may request the insurance carrier to change, or upgrade, the insured's risk classification to a more favorable risk classification.

Depending on the policy type, the insured's deterioration in health may provide some planning opportunities. There are limited opportunities with a participating whole life policy if the insured's health deteriorates. Most of the options involve the use of the various nonforfeiture features of the whole life policy such as electing extended term insurance or reduced paid-up insurance. These are the same options available if the premium payer stops paying premiums, which will be discussed subsequently below.

There are really no options if the insured's health deteriorates with a no-lapse guarantee universal life policy. The premiums on these policies are already remarkably low and with the design of the policy there is no wiggle room.

On the other hand, universal life, indexed universal life, and variable universal life policies have tremendous premium flexibility that allows correlation with life expectancy duration planning. Generally, when an insured's health deteriorates, his or her life expectancy decreases as well. Once the insured's health has deteriorated, or the insured is in his or her 70s, a personalized life expectancy report can be obtained. Individualized, personalized life expectancy reports are a by-product of the development of the life settlement industry. These reports range in cost from $250 to $500, depending on the provider, and are based upon an individual's medical records. Depending on the face amount of life insurance involved, it probably makes sense to obtain two personalized life expectancy reports from two providers for comparison purposes.

With this life expectancy information, it is possible to decrease universal life-type policies funding premium amount to an amount that would carry the policy to a lesser duration period than contract maturity or the original duration planning period. This type of planning, of course, needs to be combined with a personalized life expectancy report, actuarial evaluation employing actuarially certified policy benchmark standards and Monte Carlo simulation, and, most importantly, the risk tolerance of the policy owner with respects to statistical confidence levels and the length of the duration planning over life expectancy. The actuarial evaluation and risk tolerance review would need to be performed annually and the personalized life expectancy report would need to be updated periodically on a two- to three-year basis.[125]

Following policy issuance, if the insured's health has improved or the insured has stopped smoking for at least a year or dropped a hazardous avocation such as skydiving, changed occupations to a non-hazardous occupation, or has had any other changes that would more favorably affect his or her underwriting classification and premium payment amount, then the policy owner should request the issuing carrier change the original underwriting classification to a more favorable classification that reflects the insured's more favorable underwriting status and, subsequentially, either reduce the premium payment amounts or improve the policy benefits. If the carrier refuses to change the original underwriting classification,

---

125. See the section titled "Duration Planning with Universal Life Policies and Using Personalized Life Expectancy Reports" in Chapter 4, Process of Managing Life Insurance Policies, for a more complete discussion and analysis of the concept.

then policy replacement may be warranted to a carrier having more favorable underwriting guidelines that would either reduce premium payments or improve policy benefits.

Has it been determined what options will be pursued if the premium payer for the policy is either unable or unwilling to continue to make premium payments, or reduces premium contribution amounts?

For various sundry reasons, premium payers—whether the insured/policy owner, third-party policy owners, a trust grantor/insured, or some other party through a split-dollar arrangement—may either be unable or unwilling to continue to make premium payments, or may have to reduce premium contribution amounts. The options available in this situation depend on the permanent policy type. The option chosen depends on the objectives and needs of the policy owner.

One option that theoretically is always available is to find another source for the premium payments to continue the policy for the policy owner. Of course, this option could be rather difficult but potential sources for premium payments could be various family members or friends willing to donate the payments, or part of the premium payment, either outright or through a private spilt-dollar arrangement; a split-dollar arrangement between the policy owner and a business entity that the policy owner is associated with; or premium financing with a lending institution. It may also be possible to structure a life settlement agreement with a policy buyer who would agree to pay the premiums and allow the policy owner to retain part of the death benefit, and many life settlement companies are advertising the availability of this alternative. However, the author is of the opinion that this latter arrangement would constitute an endorsement split-dollar arrangement with tax consequences and this possibility is not, generally, disclosed by life settlement purchasers allowing a retained death benefit by the former policy owner.[126]

---

126. Although now repealed by the Tax Cuts and Jobs Act of 2017, Revenue Ruing 2009-13 addressed the income tax treatment of cash transactions in life settlements but did not address retained death benefit arrangements. Applying the definition of split-dollar life insurance arrangements from the Final Spit-Dollar Regulations promulgated in Internal Revenue Bulletin 2003-46 and effective as of September 17, 2003, many commentators believe the retained death benefit arrangement is an endorsement (economic benefit regime) split-dollar arrangement. In these regulations, a split-dollar arrangement is defined as

> any arrangement between an owner of a life insurance contract and a non-owner of the contract under which either party to the arrangement pays all or part of the premiums, and one of the parties paying the premiums is entitled to recover (either conditionally or unconditionally) all or any portion of those premiums and such recovery is to be made from, or is secured by, the proceeds of the contract.

This broad definition is not qualified by limiting the parties in any way to, for example, an employer and employee or a donor and a donee. Thus, it would appear to include a buyer and a seller; and it is well-known to include a lender and lendee under premium financed arrangements. The "economic benefit" of the retained death benefit would be income to the seller. But how this income would be treated and reported is not clear. Currently, there are no revenue rulings, private letter rulings, or cases on the entire issue of the tax effects of retained death benefits in life settlement arrangements. The bottom line is that life settlement sellers contemplating retaining a

In all the policy types, the life settlement option is available—either as a completed policy sale or a retained death benefit arrangement as mentioned earlier—for older insureds at least in their late 60s or for insureds whose health has deteriorated since the issuance of the policy. As mentioned before, this option is particularly viable with insureds who have experienced a deterioration in health and have a life expectancy of two to 12 years, and have a policy with a face amount greater than $250,000 that is underwritten by a carrier with a minimum of a BBB financial rating.

With participating whole life, universal life, indexed universal life, and variable universal life policies, there is always the option to surrender the policy for its cash surrender value or to apply the cash value towards an annuity income stream. Except, perhaps, in the early policy years, neither of these options would be available for no-lapse guarantee universal life policies since these policies generally have no cash values—or very little, in which case the cash value could be surrendered.

Whole life policies have guaranteed nonforfeiture values that can be elected—once cash values develop, which is generally at least by the end of the second policy year for the guaranteed portion of the cash values and the end of the first policy year for the cash values from paid-up additions dividends. In addition to surrendering the guaranteed cash surrender value (and cash surrender values from paid-up additions dividends), two other very important nonforfeiture options are reduced paid-up insurance and extended term insurance. Essentially, the policy owner can elect to have the net cash surrender value applied to either of these options. The net cash surrender value is the guaranteed cash surrender value plus the cash surrender value of paid-up additions dividends less policy loans and interest accrued on policy loans.

The reduced paid-up insurance option applies the net cash value to purchase a completely paid-up whole life policy of the same type as the original policy with a face amount equal to what the net cash surrender value can purchase with a single premium payment. Participating whole life policies continue to pay dividends on the reduced paid-up life insurance.

The extended term insurance option applies the net cash value to purchase term insurance with a face amount equal to the guaranteed face amount of the policy plus the face amount of paid-up additions dividends less policy loans and accrued interest on policy loans for a term duration, or length, equal to what the net cash surrender value can purchase as a single premium applied to purchase the net face amount of the policy. If a policy lapses for nonpayment of premiums and the policy owner does not elect another nonforfeiture option, the extended term insurance nonforfeiture option is the default option applied by almost all whole life policies.

---

portion of the death benefit need to consult with an attorney in their jurisdiction who is knowledgeable on split-dollar arrangements and tax law.

Participating whole life policies generally do not pay dividends on the extended term insurance option.

Another option available to whole life policy owners is to pay premiums via policy loans. Many whole life policies have an automatic premium loan feature—that is elected by the policy owner on the policy application—that functions to pay the premiums on the policy by borrowing the premium payment from the cash value of the policy. However, even without the automatic premium loan feature the policy owner could, of course, elect to execute the payment of premiums by policy loans. Paying premiums by policy loans does have the advantage of maintaining all of the policy riders, such as the disability waiver of premium rider, which is not the case with the reduced paid-up insurance or extended term insurance nonforfeiture options. If the curtailment of premium payments is only expected for a short time period then the premium loan payment method is probably a good option. Similarly, if only part of the premium payment is available, the policy owner could partially pay the premium and pay the balance by policy loan, or borrow the policy premium payment and apply the cash funds available to pay the policy loan interest and possibly repay part of the policy loan principal. The policy loan option to pay policy premiums can work very well in the short run but in the long run, with the accrued interest on the policy loans, the cash value—despite the crediting of the guaranteed interest crediting rate and cash value additions from paid-up additions dividends—will be depleted in a shorter time period, causing the policy to lapse, than the term duration of the extended term insurance nonforfeiture option.

No-lapse guarantee universal life policies are extremely inflexible and there are no options available, other than, perhaps, a very small cash value in the early years of the policy that could be surrendered or the sale to a life settlement buyer, once the full premium payment stops.

Universal life, indexed universal life, and variable universal life policies do not contain the nonforfeiture options of guaranteed reduced paid-up insurance and extended term insurance. Since after the first policy year no premium payments are required, there is no need for policy loans to pay premiums. However, the death benefit can be reduced to an amount such that the policy cash values can support the policy to either a chosen policy duration or to contract maturity, but the reduction amount of the death benefit to accomplish this objective must be determined by actuarial evaluation incorporating actuarially certified policy benchmark standards and Monte Carlo simulation. By the very nature of universal life-type policy design, if premium funding ceases, the policy continues with the same face amount—in either the level death benefit option or increasing death benefit option—until the monthly deductions for cost of insurance and other policy expenses, less earnings credited on the policy account values, exhaust the cash account value of the policy at which point the policy lapses. Actuarial evaluation would be required to determine the length of duration of the policy before the cash account value would be exhausted. Similarly, if premium contribution funding amounts are reduced, actuarial evaluation can determine the reduced death benefit amount that can support the reduced payments to either the chosen policy duration or contract maturity, or determine the policy duration time period maintaining the current face amount of insurance.

Life Expectancy

Has it been determined how life expectancy will be defined for purposes of creditable policy evaluation and duration planning and analysis?

Life expectancy forms the heart of creditable policy evaluation and duration planning and analysis. But how life expectancy is actually defined and calculated needs to be specified in order to have a common basis for the term. Life expectancy is also a moving target that changes as the insured ages—it generally gets greater with increases in age of a group because the surviving group gets smaller—and can drastically be affected by deterioration of health.[127]

Life expectancy can be defined as (1) determined by an independent firm that does personalized life expectancy reports, (2) the 2001 or 2017 Commissioners Standard Ordinary (CSO) Tables for the underwriting classification of the insured (i.e., the five "standard" risk classifications of super preferred, preferred non-smoker, preferred smoker, standard non-smoker, and standard residual smoker, plus the tables used for risk classification of medically impaired insureds), or (3) a mutually agreed alternative mortality table reflecting the insured's underwriting condition. Underwriting classifications as reflected by the 2001 or 2017 CSO Tables as noted above are acceptable in the early policy years. However, if the health of the insured deteriorates, or as the insured reaches his or her late 60s and 70s, the life expectancy as determined by a personalized life expectancy report should be utilized.

Life Insurance Policy Management Statement

Has a life insurance policy management statement been prepared?

By addressing all of the above questions, it should be a simple matter to document the thoughts and answers derived in a written life insurance policy management statement. This document is the equivalent for life insurance of an investment policy statement used in a security portfolio. It spells out the plan for managing the life insurance policy or portfolio of life insurance policies.

In addition to the information obtained by answering the above questions, the life insurance policy management statement should also specify and identify the roles of various parties and their duties with respect to life insurance planning, monitoring and risk management, creditable policy evaluation, and policy changes,

---

127. See the section titled "Understanding Mortality Tables and Life Expectancy" in Chapter 2, Toward Understanding Life Insurance and the Risk Transfer Paradigm Shift—Some Life Insurance Basics, for a more complete discussion and analysis of the concept of life expectancy.

restructure, and remediation. For example, the life insurance policy management statement would provide for the delegation of life insurance expertise and creditable policy evaluation to a qualified—and defining the qualification criteria—independent fee-based life insurance consultant. The functions of annual reporting, accounting, and communication among the various parties—including the policy owner and, possibly, or definitely if a trust is involved, the beneficiaries—should be specified and scheduled.[128]

Summary

Life insurance needs to be properly acquired and managed through a process. The practical questions and guidelines above for acquiring and managing life insurance are meant to be a start to the prudent development of systematic procedures that are aimed at providing successful outcomes for life insurance programs and avoiding a life insurance policy client crisis.

Just as mutual funds and investment securities need to be acquired and managed with the recognition of client needs and objectives and the risks associated with the particular investment choice, so too life insurance must be acquired and managed with the same criteria. Management is particularly required for any life insurance policy type or style where there are non-guaranteed pricing elements involved that will change over the duration of the policy. This would include non-guaranteed rates of return on cash values, current cost of insurance (mortality rates) and policy expenses, and the dividend portion of participating whole life policies.

Richard M. Weber and Christopher Hause adeptly and succinctly make the case for and describe the reasons for utilizing a proper acquisition and active management process for life insurance that includes the life insurance policy management statement, as well as illustrating the results from not following the proper acquisition and management process and purchasing the life insurance product "du jour" by relying on the constant assumption policy illustrations as follows:

> Active management ideally follows from a good acquisition strategy—flowing from the Life Insurance Policy Management Statement that establishes risk tolerance /needs / concerns / considerations of the client—and brings forward a policy or collection of policies (Efficient Choices) that lends itself to optimization and management over the life of the insured. It is important to understand what the client is trying to achieve: defining the ultimate death benefit and paying the appropriate premium for it over one's lifetime (taking into account the naturally depreciating value of the fixed, future payment due to inflation), or defining the resources available to support a policy—and optimizing the ultimate death benefit. This process is

---

128. For more information on the topic of the life insurance policy management statement and the delegation of policy management duties see Chapter 4, Process of Managing Life Insurance Policies.

a good deal more complex than "it used to be," and entails utilizing trained advisors who are skilled in balancing the assessment of current resources and ultimate uses/needs for insurance over the client's lifetime—and then matching those considerations with a policy or policies currently available in the marketplace. The most common error is to acquire the product "du jour"—illustrating the lowest premium for the highest death benefit—without any analysis or determination of the credibility of the "promise." When the promise doesn't occur, it's not uncommon for the client to be attracted to a replacement or "exchange" into the next "du jour" product offering that appears to offer a solution . . . and so continues the process until the client runs out of money or becomes uninsurable. The underlying products along the way weren't necessarily bad or wrong—but the expectations placed on those products through over-utilization of the policy illustration have caused enormous financial disruption of the long-term expectation.[129]

Finally, it is hoped that the above questions and guidelines prove helpful in the proper acquiring, maintaining, and management of life insurance policies, and in the creation of a life insurance policy management statement, so as to produce a successful life insurance program that fulfills policy owner expectations and avoids a life insurance policy crisis.

---

129. Weber and Hause, *supra* note 26, pages 77–78.

Chapter 7

Conclusion

The life insurance policy crisis was precipitated by the risk transfer paradigm shift. The risk transfer paradigm that was started in 1979 was caused by the introduction of life insurance policies where the pricing was no longer based upon long-term guarantees and fixed premium schedules but was based on current non-guaranteed assumptions and flexible premium payments. But this risk transfer required adaptation and a new support system of policy risk management and creditable policy evaluation that never materialized. In fact, this paradigm shift was almost completely ignored until policy owners discovered that their non-guaranteed policies either needed substantial remediation—in the form of either a substantial increase in premium or a reduction in death benefit—or the policy was insolvent due to a policy lapse.

In order to fully appreciate and understand the cause of the life insurance policy crisis, and to circumvent any future policy crisis, it is necessary to "go under the hood" a bit and discover the inner workings of the parts of the life insurance policy engine. After a basic understanding of how a life insurance policy engine works, the investigation switches to what can go wrong with the engine and the peculiar problems that can occur with each engine type. Finally, the attention is turned to a preventative maintenance schedule process, and a methodology to critically evaluate the condition of the engine on a routine basis.

Thus, Chapter 2 of this book started out with some life insurance basics by first looking at the detail of the building blocks of life insurance, followed by understanding mortality tables and life expectancy, and the mathematics behind term insurance and permanent types of insurance. The latter scrutinized the significant and critical differences between constant assumptions used in non-guaranteed product pricing and policy illustrations, and reality, and the lessons learned that one cannot rely on constant and continuous assumptions in predicting the performance of non-guaranteed life insurance policies.

Chapter 3 dealt with the risks of life insurance policies, starting with some background, history, and perspective on the risk transfer, and using trust-owned life insurance as a real example of risk transfer consequences. The next section of the chapter asked what is the definition of risk and what are life insurance policy expectations? This was followed by a detailed analysis of the risks of life insurance, including carrier solvency risk; purchasing power risk; risks by product types, which examined the seven main types of life insurance products issued today, what is guaranteed with each product type and what is not guaranteed, and what are the risks; product suitability risk; and diversification risk.

Chapter 4 explored the process of managing life insurance policies by first comparing traditional investment management versus life insurance management. Next, the importance of the life insurance policy statement was described, followed by the delegation of life insurance management duties, and an example from the fiduciary world of the best versus predatory practices in life insurance trust management. The last section of the chapter discussed in detail duration planning with universal life policies and using personalized life expectancy assessments.

Chapter 5 probed in depth the creditable evaluation of life insurance. This chapter started with the extreme disconnect between the most commonly used methods of policy evaluation today that the Society of Actuaries and Financial Industry Regulatory Authority (FINRA) regulations state is an improper method of policy evaluation. Next, improper policy evaluation methods were discussed, followed by a thorough description, examination, and an example of the use of Monte Carlo simulation and actuarially certified policy standards analysis—which is, in the author's opinion, the only creditable way to evaluate a flexible premium non-guaranteed life insurance policy. The chapter wrapped up with putting creditable evaluation of life insurance in perspective.

Applying the knowledge gained from the previous chapters to real-life planning issues connected with the acquisition and ongoing maintenance and management of a life insurance program was the focus of Chapter 6. This chapter entailed a series of practical questions and guidelines designed to assist policy owners in developing a well-thought-out plan for their life insurance program and implementing prudent systematic procedures for purchasing and managing their life insurance policy, or policy portfolio, to provide successful long-term outcomes tailored to their individual, unique goals, needs, and objectives.

The end of the book contains a series of Contributed Articles by nationally known authors and thought leaders within the areas and fields that encompass life insurance and the life insurance profession, such as the legal, actuarial, estate planning, financial advisory, and trust professions. The viewpoints and insights in these articles enhance, expand, and reinforce the concepts presented in this book. Most importantly, they provide different perspectives to the reader.

The risk transfer paradigm shift with life insurance has occurred and it appears there is no going back. Yet with knowledge of the risks involved, a support system that involves the process for risk managing life insurance policies, and creditably evaluating such policies using an actuarially certified evaluation process, the policy owner can now adapt to, and reap the benefits of, the new paradigm.

In summary, it is hoped that this book has explained the unexplainable by giving an understandable background on the pricing, mechanisms, and interrelated parts of permanent life insurance—both guaranteed and non-guaranteed; the risk transfer paradigm shift that precipitated a policy crisis, and the risks involved with life insurance policies; the process used to risk manage life insurance policies; and the proper and creditable way to evaluate flexible premium non-guaranteed life insurance policies.

About the Author

Gary L. Flotron, M.B.A., CLU®, ChFC®, AEP®, is principal of G.L. Flotron & Associates and specializes in the areas of trust-owned life insurance, estate and business planning, and executive and employee benefit plans. He is also the Associate Director Financial Planning Programs and an Adjunct Faculty member at the College of Business Administration, University of Missouri–St. Louis, where he teaches courses in estate and trust planning, planning for business owners and professionals, employee ben-
efits, and life insurance. In addition, he is a former Adjunct Professor with The American College of Financial Services of Bryn Mawr, Pennsylvania. An author and frequent national speaker, Gary has spoken to numerous professional associations and groups, including the Heckerling Institute on Estate Planning, the National Association of Estate Planners & Councils (NAEPC) Annual Conference, The Federal Tax Institute of New England, and the Society of Financial Service Professionals (FSP) Video Training Conference.

Mr. Flotron has been an active member in various professional associations. He is Chair Emeritus and a Member of the Executive Committee for the Synergy Summit, an organization and think tank composed of representatives from ten major national legal and financial services professional organizations involved in estate planning. Previously he has served as Chair of the Professional Education and Development Committee for the Synergy Summit. He is a Past President of the NAEPC and The NAEPC Education Foundation, as well as past Chair of The NAEPC Education Foundation Committee and past Chair of the Accredited Estate Planner® (AEP®) Designation Committee for NAEPC. A past Member of the National Board of Directors of the FSP, Mr. Flotron, in addition to having served on numerous national committees and task forces, is the current Editor of the *Estate Planning* quarterly publication for FSP. He is also a former member of the University of Missouri–St. Louis Planned Giving Advisory Committee.

A past President of the FSP Greater St. Louis Chapter, Gary is also a past President of the Estate Planning Council of St. Louis, and past President of the National Association of Insurance and Financial Advisors St. Louis Chapter. He is a past Member of the Board of Directors of the Foundation for Financial Service Professionals and a past Regional Chair for the National Council of The American College. Mr. Flotron has also served as a Member of the Chartered Financial Consultant (ChFC®) Curriculum Advisory Board for The American College of Financial Services.

An M.B.A. graduate of the Washington University John M. Olin Graduate School of Business Administration, where he was inducted into Beta Gamma Sigma, the National Business Honors Fraternity, Mr. Flotron completed his undergraduate work in engineering management with a concentration in electrical engineering (B.S.E. Mgt.) at the University of Missouri at Rolla (now Missouri University of Science and Technology). He received the Chartered Life Underwriter (CLU®) designation in 1984 and the Chartered Financial Consultant (ChFC®) designation in 1985, both granted by The American College of Financial Services. In 1995, he was awarded the Accredited Estate Planner® (AEP®) designation by NAEPC. Gary is the 1996 recipient of the Stan Towerman Excellence in Professional Education Award from the FSP Greater St. Louis Chapter, and a 1994 recipient of the Paul F. Mills Scholarship from the Foundation for Financial Service Professionals. He was inducted into the National Association of Insurance and Financial Advisors St. Louis Chapter Hall of Fame in 2003. The University of Missouri–St. Louis named Mr. Flotron as the recipient of the 2014–2015 Chancellor's Excellence Award for a Part-time Faculty Member.

Gary has two sons, Paul and John, a daughter-in-law Anna who is married to John, one grandson, Luke, and one granddaughter, Liliana. His hobbies include reading and learning, traveling, exercising, hiking, modern era architecture, photography, and walking/running his greyhound Jackson (at least in spirit and until he gets another greyhound). Gary's response when asked "what is something about you that is unique and most folks are unaware of?" is "I had a dinner party in my home for a man who subsequently led a coup d'état and is now the President/Dictator of an African country."

Contributed Articles

Introduction

As previously noted in the Acknowledgements section and elsewhere, the author is honored, delighted, and grateful that so many nationally renowned distinguished practitioners have graciously agreed to contribute articles that they authored—either alone or with co-authors—to this book. These articles definitely enhance this book by providing different insights, perspectives, thoughts, and viewpoints and by so doing significantly expand the topics and material in the book, as well as the publication itself.

It is noteworthy that among these eminent, notable, and renowned legal, financial, and life insurance professionals who are authors and co-authors of Contributed Articles to this book are six members of the National Association of Estate Planners & Councils Estate Planners Hall of Fame®, three nationally prominent estate planning attorneys with recognized expertise in life insurance, three esteemed financial planners, two of whom are also celebrated life insurance professionals as well, two extraordinary trust practitioners with administrative and fiduciary expertise with life insurance, and one incomparable and brilliant actuary who devised a unique method to come up with the creditable evaluation of flexible premium non-guaranteed life insurance.

Listed below are the names of these esteemed contributors along with their co-authors and the titles of their Contributed Articles.

Guy E. Baker, M.B.A., M.S.F.S., M.S.M., Ph.D., CLU®, ChFC®, CFP®, AEP® (Distinguished)
The BOX

Ben G. Baldwin, Jr., M.S.F.S., M.S.M., CLU®, ChFC®, CFP®, AEP® (Distinguished)
Between a Rock and a Hard Place: NAIC Regulators—Life Insurance Intermediaries—State and Federal Regulators

Jonathan G. Blattmachr, J.D., AEP® (Distinguished)
and Marc A. Pasquale, CPA
Buying Life Insurance to Fund Estate Taxes—Toward a More Objective Decision

Christopher Hause, FSA, MAAA, CLU®
The Miracle (and Disaster) of Compound Interest—Universal Life Edition

Donald O. Jansen, J.D., LL.M., AEP® (Distinguished)
TOLI Trustee Tread Tactfully

Michael E. Kitces, M.S.F.S., M.TAX, CFP®, CLU®, ChFC®, RHU®, REBC®, CASL®
Adopting a Two-Dimensional Risk Tolerance Assessment Process
The Sorry State of Risk Tolerance Questionnaires for Financial Advisors

Martin M. Shenkman, CPA, M.B.A., PFS, J.D., AEP® (Distinguished)
When to Hold Life Insurance in Trust; What Type of Trust

Charles M. "Mark" Whitelaw and E. Randolph Whitelaw, AEP® (Distinguished)
Was Your Client Sold the Most Expensive Policy on the Planet?
High Net Worth (HNW) Access to Institutionally-Priced Life Insurance for Personal Asset Diversification

E. Randolph Whitelaw, AEP® (Distinguished) and George P. Whitelaw
The Lapsing Life Insurance Policy Crisis—The Need for Dispute Defensible Advisor Practices and a Glidepath to Safety, Especially for Seniors

Again, the author is extremely humbled that this group of contributing authors so graciously has contributed articles for this book. The author tremendously appreciates the contributions and works of this group of top-notch professionals.

Format for the Contributed Articles

The Contributed Articles are presented in the alphabetical order of the names of the authors. Each Contributed Article will first feature Introductory Comments by the author of this book that summarizes information about the contributing author(s) and the Contributed Article and how that article relates to this book. This will be followed by an "about the contributing author(s)" section that contains bios and includes a photograph of the distinguished contributing author(s). Last, but certainly not least, will be the actual Contributed Article of the author(s).

The BOX

Guy E. Baker, M.B.A., M.S.F.S., Ph.D., CLU®, ChFC®, CFP®, AEP® (Distinguished)

Introductory Comments by Gary Flotron

Guy E. Baker, M.B.A., M.S.F.S., Ph.D., CLU®, ChFC®, CFP®, AEP® (Distinguished), is a true Renaissance man who is a financial planner and life insurance professional. A rare combination of a brilliant, successful, and accomplished practitioner, an erudite scholar of his profession, a skilled technician, a charismatic leader, and compassionate humanitarian, Dr. Baker has the unique ability to communicate complicated financial and estate planning concepts and techniques in plain, simple, understandable language. Besides all that, he is just a fabulous Guy!

When asked to provide a contributing article for this book, Guy graciously suggested and provided a short but concise book he wrote called *The BOX*. *The BOX* epitomizes Guy's talent in reducing the complexities of permanent life insurance to a very uncomplicated analogy that can be embraced by all who read this material. This book provides a refreshing perspective on the understanding of the basics of life insurance presented in Chapter 2. To paraphrase Dr. Baker, the choice of funding long-term life insurance needs is to either pay the curve or to put money into "The BOX." Explore and enjoy this elegant writing as you venture into *The BOX*!

About Guy E. Baker

Dr. Guy E. Baker is an experienced Wealth Coach, with extensive experience in financial planning, investments, and life insurance. With more than 50 years of experience, Guy has been featured on numerous talk shows and tele-video conferences, including speaking several times on the Million Dollar Round Table (MDRT) Main Platform. He was named by *Worth Magazine* as one of the USA's top 250 planners. *OC Metro* has consistently picked Guy as a 5-star adviser.

Guy helped found the National Association of Family Wealth Counselors dedicated to providing legacy and wealth planning to high net worth families. He has lectured at various estate planning council meetings, spoken at many Chartered Life Underwriter® (CLU®) Institutes, and was featured on six CLU® Conferences. A frequent writer and speaker, Guy has spoken to advisors in more than 40 countries.

A prolific writer, his most recent book, *The Great Wealth Erosion*, details the four factors investors need to manage to improve portfolio performance. Other books by Guy include *Manage Markets, Not Stocks* and *Investment Alchemy*; both are guides to understanding modern portfolio theory. He also wrote *Market Tune-Up*, *Why People Buy*, and *Baker's Dozen—13 Principles for Financial Success*, each with more than 50,000 copies in print. His bestselling booklet is *The BOX*, an easily understood guide to the mathematics of life insurance. He also wrote *Maximize the Red Zone*, a guide for business owners.

Dr. Baker's professional experience includes managing several entities developed to address the Three Circles of Wealth for High Net Worth Families. These include being the Co-Manager with Dean McCormick, CPA, of Insight Wealth Solutions, LP, a multi-disciplinary practice acting as a wealth coach for high net worth families and businesses; Managing Director of BTA Advisory Group, a risk management consulting firm specializing in life insurance and 401(k) plans; BMI Consulting, a national management consulting firm working with the problems facing closely held businesses—succession, executive compensation, and transition strategies; and Founder, Wealth Team Alliance, a registered investment advisory firm. Guy is internationally recognized as one of the world's top financial professionals. He has qualified for the Million Dollar Round Table 48 times and is one of only 15 to qualify more than 40 times for the Top of Table.

Guy received a B.S. in Economics in 1967 from Claremont McKenna College (CMC), an M.B.A. in Finance in 1968 from the University of Southern California, a Master of Science in Financial Services (M.S.F.S.), and a Master of Science in Management (M.S.M.) from The American College of Financial Services. In 2018, he finished his Doctorate in Financial and Retirement Planning (Ph.D.) from The American College of Financial Services. Additionally, Guy holds the following professional designations: Chartered Life Underwriter (CLU®) that was awarded in 1972, Chartered Financial Consultant® (ChFC®) that was awarded in 1981, Certified Financial Planner® (CFP®), Registered Health Underwriter® (RHU®), Certified Family Wealth Counselor, and Accredited Estate Planner® (AEP®) (Distinguished) from the National Association of Estate Planners & Councils (NAEPC). He is also a Registered Investment Advisor.

Some of the many professional affiliations, awards, and honors Guy has received include serving as the 84th President of the Million Dollar Round Table—the Premier Association of Financial Professionals® with more than 80,000 members in 80 countries; President, MDRT Foundation in 2000; Past Board Member, Advanced Association of Life Underwriters (AALU), working with Congress to formulate industry responsive legislations; serving two terms as president, National

Association of Family Wealth Counselors; recipient of Pacific Life's Preston Hotch-kis "Distinguished Achievement Award"; and election in 2005 to the NAEPC Estate Planning Hall of Fame®. Guy was the recipient of the 78th Annual John Newton Russell Memorial Award in 2019 from the National Association of Insurance and Financial Advisors (NAIFA). The award is the highest honor accorded by the insurance industry to a living individual who has rendered outstanding services to the institution of life insurance.

Dr. Baker is highly involved with his community. He is an Elder at Grace Church in Laguna Niguel, California, and a Founding Trustee for Grace Classical Academy, a private school for families seeking a Christian Classical education. He is also a Member of the President's Council of BIOLA University. Guy's previous involvement includes serving as Chairman of the Board of American Family Living; Past Regional Board Member of Link's International; Board member of the Mission Hospital Foundation; member of the Major Gifts Committee for the Orange County Center for Performing Arts; Fund Raising Committee for South Coast Repertory; Advisory Board member for the South Coast YMCA; Board member of Orange County Teen Challenge; and President of the Claremont McKenna Alumni Association and member of CMC's Board of Trustees.

The BOX
Guy E. Baker, Ph.D.

Most people think life insurance is very complex. Buyers are mystified by its structure, options and pricing. It is a fact, most people don't feel very comfortable discussing the entire subject of life insurance and death. That's why we're writing this booklet, to help readers understand the basics. We call it, *The Key to Understanding Life Insurance.*

Many financial writers and commentators have made their living commenting on the pros and cons of life insurance, especially term

But it's too important to the financial fabric of the family and business to be ignored.

insurance versus permanent insurance. But they rarely, accurately explain the fundamental principles of how insurance works. The jargon and vocabulary can stop people cold. What most buyers want to know is quite simple. Their questions are the same whether they are purchasing term insurance, universal life (UL) or some form of indexed or variable life or whole life. *What is the best policy for me? How much insurance should I buy? What will it cost? How long should I keep it?*

When these questions are not addressed, a mystique or confusion clouds the real value of the insurance product. It can often cause buyers to make a less productive purchase, or no purchase at all. With this booklet, we hope to clear up some basic confusion that surrounds insurance policy pricing and provide a simple foundation to answer your questions.

What Is Life Insurance?

Before we explain the key to understanding life insurance, let's define insurance and a few fundamental terms.

Insurance is a legal contract delivered to the buyer as a policy. It guarantees to pay a certain sum of money (death proceeds) to a specified person or entity (the beneficiary) when the insured dies. The policy coverage remains in force as long as the cost for the coverage (the premium) is paid according to the contractual provisions in the policy. These costs can be paid directly by the buyer or deducted from the values within the policy if any exist.

You can own the policy personally or have someone else own it instead. The owner has the legal right to name the beneficiary and may change the beneficiary at any time. The owner is responsible for any tax consequences related to the premium and the death benefits.

Most people don't think of life insurance this way, but it is risk sharing between members of a group with a common goal to provide cash for their beneficiaries when they die. Insurance is purchased because someone loves someone or something. Some of the reasons insurance is purchased are to:

- pay off a debt
- finance a tax due
- purchase an interest in a business
- buy a piece of property
- provide a guaranteed income and financial security for loved ones
- create supplemental retirement income

Life insurance can also be used by an entity to recover the cost of a promise made by the employer to an employee. For example, an employer may offer a retirement benefit for a selected individual. Life Insurance can recover the cost of that promised benefit. Practically, life insurance is often the ONLY way the beneficiary of the policy can provide money to meet financial needs. And, in most cases, it is the least expensive way to fund an obligation or liability.

Life insurance is based on the fundamental mathematical principle of probability. It is proven people die according to a predictable pattern. This pattern is referred to as a mortality table. It is built by accumulating historical data from census records.

life insurance is based on the fundamental mathematical principle of probability

Insurance companies cannot know "who" in the group will die or when, just "how many." This predictable pattern and the amount of coverage is then mathematically converted into a lump sum amount equivalent to the present value of the promised benefit. The company needs to know this lump sum amount in order to calculate the contractual annual payment required until death.

The contractual annual payments are impacted by a set of factors such as interest and expenses. By providing coverage to hundreds of thousands of people, insurance companies will offer coverage to each insured for a small payment each year compared to the sum insured. By each insured paying their proportionate share, the large lump sum is available to their family or business when death occurs. Life insurance is NOT a gamble as some suggest. It is a proven mathematical principle based on the measured probability of death and it is available to anyone who can qualify and wants agrees to pay the annual premium.

With this as background, let's look at why insurance works.

The Key to Understanding Life Insurance

As stated, life insurance is based on the predictable probability of one person dying among a group of insureds. The mortality table predicts the chances of a death occurring in any given year. Again, the actuaries (insurance company mathematicians) don't know who, just how many.

So suppose there are 1,000, 45-year-old healthy men, all non smokers. Insurance company mortality tables assume all will be dead prior to some age, typically 120. The mortality table shown in Table 1 predicts the chances of a person's death in any given year between ages 45 and 100.

Since life insurance is simply a group sharing the risk of funding a specified amount at death, the annual payment reflects their individual share. The first person in the group to die is paid for by those who remain. Those who die first, will benefit the most based on the ratio of their contribution to the proceeds. Those who die last will still receive the same proceeds, but they will have paid more to receive them.

Even if we factor in interest earnings, the last to die will always have to pay more into the fund than the first to die, but they will usually pay less than the full value of the expected death benefits.

Table 1. Age 45 Mortality Table

Age	Chance of death	Number living	Number of deaths
45	0.23%	1,000	2
46	0.26%	997	3
47	0.28%	995	3
48	0.29%	992	3
49	0.31%	989	3
50	0.33%	985	3
51	0.36%	982	4
52	0.40%	978	4
53	0.44%	974	4
54	0.49%	969	5
55	0.55%	964	5
56	0.61%	958	6
57	0.68%	951	7
58	0.74%	944	7
59	0.81%	936	8
60	0.89%	928	8
61	0.99%	919	9
62	1.11%	909	10
63	1.25%	897	11
64	1.40%	885	13
65	1.55%	871	14
66	1.70%	856	15
67	1.86%	840	16
68	2.03%	823	17
69	2.20%	805	18
70	2.41%	786	19
71	2.65%	765	21
72	2.96%	742	23
73	3.28%	718	24
74	3.63%	692	26
75	4.00%	664	28
76	4.41%	635	29
77	4.89%	604	31
78	5.45%	571	33
79	6.09%	536	35
80	6.79%	500	36

Age	Chance of death	Number living	Number of deaths
81	7.53%	462	38
82	8.41%	423	39
83	9.31%	384	39
84	10.30%	344	40
85	11.41%	305	39
86	12.63%	266	39
87	13.97%	229	37
88	15.41%	194	35
89	16.93%	161	33
90	18.51%	131	30
91	19.99%	105	26
92	21.54%	82	23
93	23.18%	63	19
94	24.91%	48	13
95	26.72%	35	13
96	28.38%	25	10
97	30.15%	17	8
98	32.04%	12	5
99	34.05%	8	4
100	36.21%	5	3

Source: CSO 2001 Male non smoker

Determining the Cost of Insurance

Staying with our group of 1,000 healthy 45-year-old males, let's follow what is likely to occur if they want $1,000,000 of insurance.

As we learned, the cost of life insurance is determined by the relative probability of death at various ages. If the people in this group die as predicted by the mortality table, we know two will die the first year. The group's cost will be $2,000,000. By spreading this cost over the entire group of 1,000 people ($2,000,000/1,000 people), the annual payment would be $2,000 per person. Notice there is no interest factored into this.

At age 50, the probability is that three of the original 1,000 will die this year. Three deaths times $1,000,000 of insurance divided by the remaining 985 people equates to $3,331 per person. At age 60, the cost is $9,000 per person, and at age 70 the cost is $24,695 per person, and so on.

Chart 1 is a graph of these outcomes. Notice the flat part of the curve at the beginning.

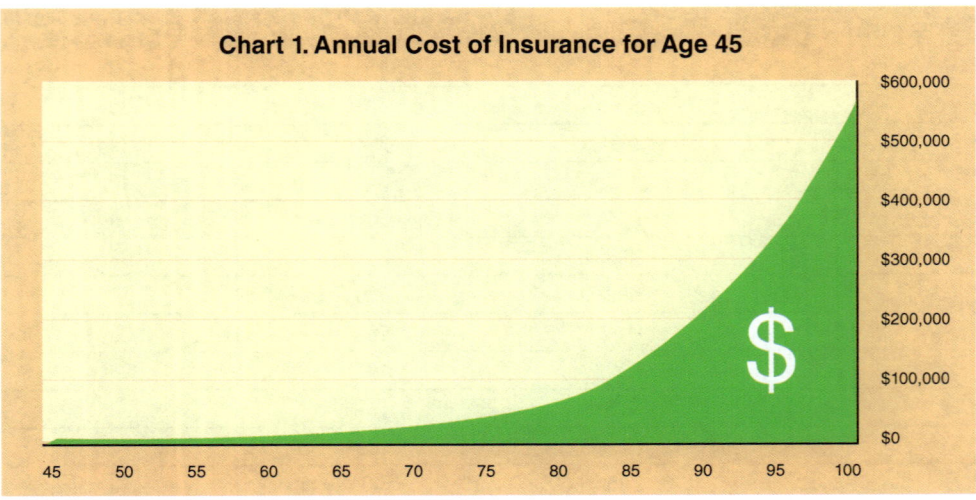

Obviously, this is when the group of insureds is very large and there are many sharing the risk. The coverage is very inexpensive early in the curve compared to the older ages. The real increase in the cost occurs when there are fewer and fewer in the group.

Where does the data come from to build a mortality table? Most large insurance companies have created their own data bank of death experience based on their years in business providing insurance coverage. In addition, the Federal government has calculated nationwide statistical measurements of mortality probabilities from the census information.

Each company's table is updated based on recent death claims. The national statistics are developed without the benefit of any physical examinations (called underwriting), but all the insurance company tables reflect actual quality underwriting information. The company medical underwriters receive full disclosure of all medical history plus a physical exam. This allows them to make an accurate assessment of the insured's health. For a person who has a known medical condition, cancer for instance, their probability of living a normal life expectancy is greatly reduced If, from the onset, a company can eliminate the people who are in poor health from their table of experience, the rates will be more reflective of the actual statistical probability of death for their insureds.

There are different methods of developing the mortality costs used by the insurance carrier. To determine pricing, insurance companies select the mortality table most appropriate for the risk they are willing to insure. If medical information is not readily available, the company uses the mortality table that best reflects that higher risk.

Without dwelling on the relative merits of these tables, it is important to understand that each measures the cost of dying for different groups of people. Chart 2 compares the difference between five commonly used methods for determining premiums.

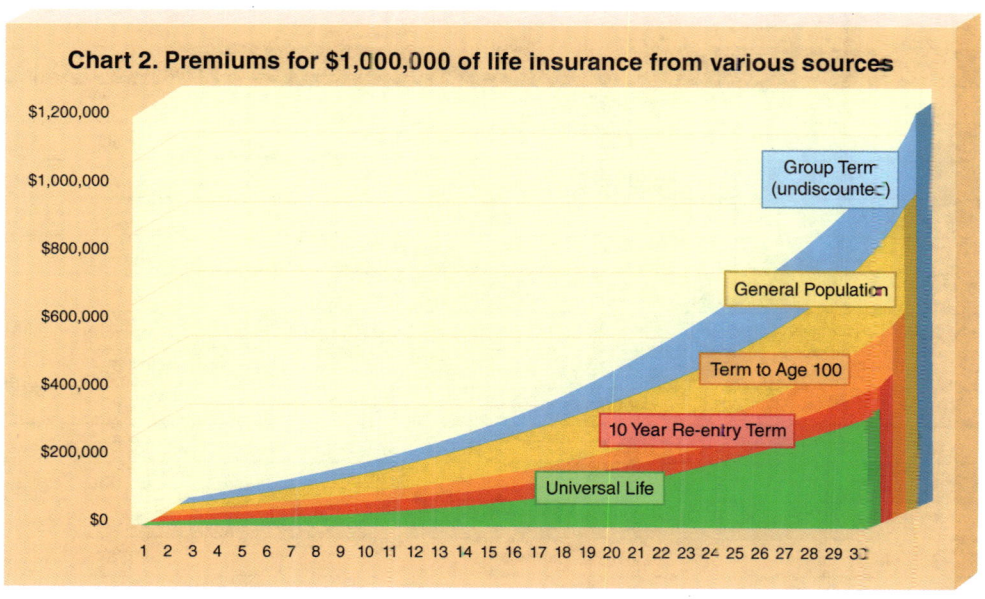

Chart 2. Premiums for $1,000,000 of life insurance from various sources

How Do You Determine The Cost of Life Insurance?

Is the cost the initial premium? Or is it the cumulative amount of premium you have paid to some age, say age 50? Age 60? Age 90?

Obviously, any specific age would be arbitrary. One logical age would be life expectancy. But most people don't understand the true meaning of life expectancy. They think this is when a person is supposed to die.

Not so!

When a newspaper announces that the Social Security Administration estimates the life expectancy of a male in the United States is 74.83 years and for females 79.96, it causes men to pause with trepidation. But, life expectancy is not the age a person is expected to die. Instead, life expectancy (LE) is the average age at which the people in the measured group will be dead. LE is different for each given age group at each point in time.

So, when the papers say that LE is 74.83 for males and 79.96 for females, they are referring to how long newborn babies are expected to live. The LE for a 65-year-old male nonsmoker from group is now 17.67 years. That means that the average age of death for all currently 45 year olds when they reach age 65 will be age 82.67. Approximately half of this group will be dead by age 82.67, but the balance will still be alive. In other words, you have about a 50/50 chance of living longer than LE. An 80-year-old male has a LE of 7.45. Even a 95 year old has a LE of 3 years. Table 2 shows life expectancies for various ages from our representative table.

Table 2. Life Expectancy

Current age	Age at life expectancy	Current age	Age at life expectancy
45	80.99	73	84.63
46	81.03	74	84.96
47	81.07	75	85.32
48	81.11	76	85.69
49	81.14	77	86.09
50	81.18	78	86.51
51	81.24	79	86.96
52	81.29	80	87.45
53	81.34	81	87.96
54	81.41	82	88.51
55	81.47	83	89.08
56	81.55	84	89.67
57	81.64	85	90.28
58	81.74	86	90.93
59	81.84	87	91.63
60	81.95	88	92.35
61	82.06	89	93.08
62	82.19	90	93.87
63	82.33	91	94.66
64	82.49	92	95.46
65	82.67	93	96.25
66	82.86	94	97.07
67	83.06	95	98.00
68	83.28	96	99.00
69	83.51	97	99.88
70	83.76	98	100.67
71	84.03	99	101.50
72	84.32	100	102.17

What Does Life Insurance Cost?

Most people focus on the initial premium when looking at the cost of life insurance, NOT the cost over their lifetime. But what happens when you add up the total cost of insurance (all the mortality costs) from today until life expectancy?

Chart 2 shows the results of this study. Assume you are part of our sample group of 45-year-old males. The sum of the mortality costs to LE is 70.8% of the face amount for a 45-year-old male. That means, if you wanted to own $1,000,000 of insurance starting today and you pay the annual mortality costs every year until life expectancy, you would need to pay $708,000.

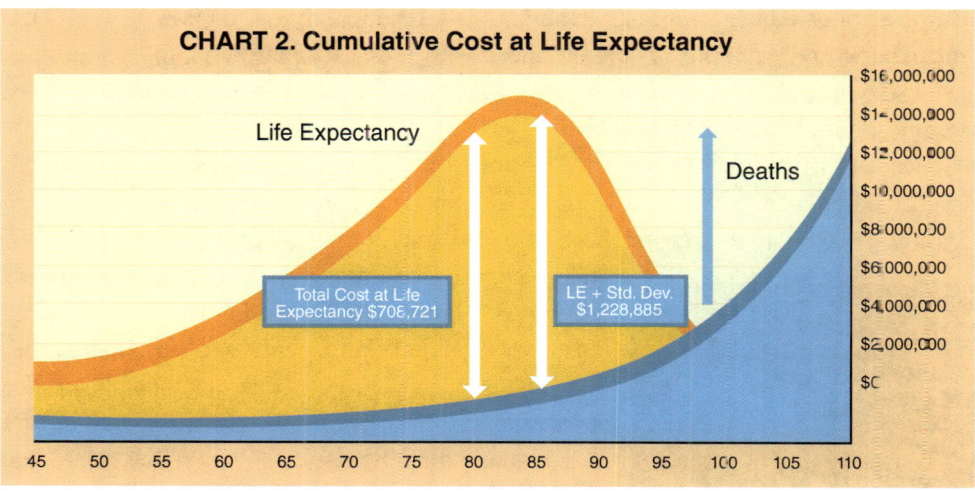

CHART 2. Cumulative Cost at Life Expectancy

We have measured this cost for over 20 major insurance companies, and the cumulative rates all come out within 1% of each other. Actuaries (the mathematicians) all work from the same base of statistics. Every insurance carrier must mathematically be near the same target, or they have violated the fundamental theory of risk sharing.

But only 50% of the group will be dead at LE. Fifty percent will still be living. What happens if you are "unfortunate" enough to live until two-thirds of the initial group is dead. (This is called the first standard deviation from the average.) The standard deviation is the next statistical breaking point from the average age of death (usually six to eight years later). If we add up all of the mortality costs for the same $1,000,000 of insurance to the first standard deviation, it equals 123% of the face amount. Yes, you would have paid $1,229,000 for $1,000,000 of coverage if you lived until the two-thirds of LE point.

But one third is still alive. If you should live until the second standard deviations (when 95% of the group is dead) the ratio of mortality costs ratio to benefits increases to about 298%. That means you have paid $2,975,000 for $1,000,000 of insurance. If you only pay mortality costs, no one could ever afford to keep their life insurance until death.

The Natural Consequences of Aging

Okay, so here's a test. What would you do if you were 82 years old and your insurance premium notice came in the mail telling you to pay $150,000 this year for your $1,000,000 policy? Most people would say they wouldn't pay it and throw the notice away. Wouldn't you?

They would let the policy cancel and laugh at the absurdity of paying $150,000 that year. But let's change the scenario. Suppose you just came back from your oncologist and knew you only had six months to live. Now what would you do?

Most of us have had enough experience with people dying to know it is only the fortunate who die quickly. There are those who linger for many months, sometimes years. If you got that premium notice in the mail, would you laugh and throw the premium notice away, or pay it? Most people say they would pay it.

The ability to choose whether or not to keep your policy based upon health conditions creates *"adverse selection."* The incentive to drop the policy if you are healthy or keep it if you are sick ruins the mathematical principle of probabil-ity. Insurance operates on statistical randomness to protect the integrity of the product. Healthy insureds must have an incentive to stay in the pool.

> *Insurance must have statistical randomness to protect the integrity of the product.*

It has been said actuaries calculate insurance premiums so the policy will lapse the day before the insured dies. Statistically, very few (less than 1%) mortality only insurance policies (called term insurance) ever pay a claim. People simply can't afford to pay the term insurance premiums at the older ages—the time they are most likely to die. As the mortality costs rise, if the only insureds who retain their policies are those who know their chances of claim are certain, the insurance carrier faces financial crisis.

Insurance history reveals an interesting footnote. In the early 1800's, only the people who were "near death" retained their insurance. The healthy people can-celed. And since there were no healthy insureds left to pay premiums, what do you think happened to all of the companies? If you guessed bankruptcy, you are correct. Research will show all of the old line insurance companies started in business after 1840. That's because many of the older companies went out of business or had to restructure due to *"adverse selection."*

So the companies called in the actuaries and told them to solve the problem. They went off with their abacuses and came back with a brilliant solution—***The BOX***.

Introducing The BOX

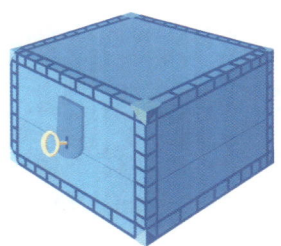

The obvious solution was to pre-fund the mortality costs from a reserve account—we call this account **The BOX**. By setting up this reserve account, insureds can pre-deposit future mortality costs and policy expenses.

As we have seen, if carriers only offered insurance premium plans on a "pay-as-you-go" basis, no one would ever be able to keep their insurance in old age.

Inside every permanent insurance contract is an individual account created to hold all premium payments. The premium payments include the current mortality costs PLUS an amortization of future mortality costs. From The BOX, the carrier deducts the annual cost of insurance (mortality costs) and policy expenses.

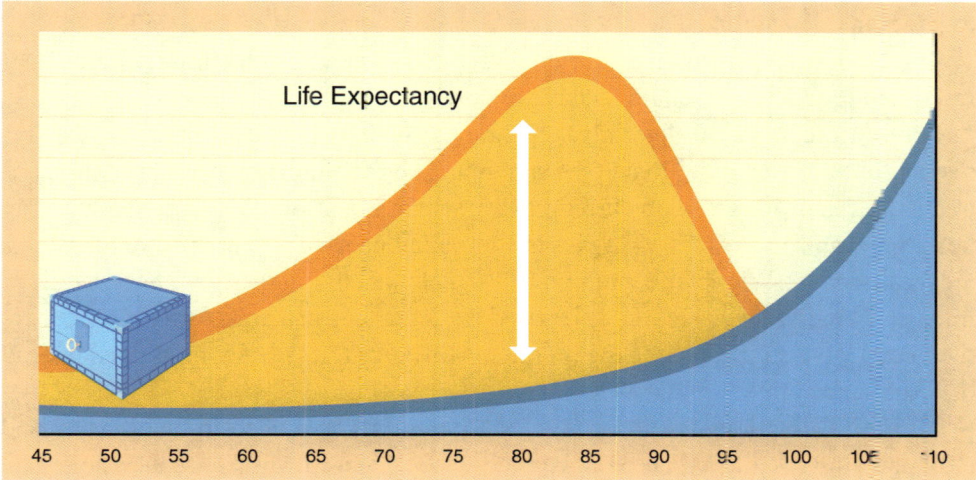

There is another element to The BOX, investment earnings. In order to offset the prohibitively expensive mortality costs, The BOX is credited with investment earnings to fund the future mortality costs and expenses. The investment element provides a powerful way to create additional funds in The BOX. The insurance company invests the premiums they receive (net of expenses), and then allocates earnings to The BOX after expenses and applicable management fees. The amount of earnings allocated varies according to the insurance contract.

In 1913, Congress passed the 16th amendment authorizing the collection of income taxes. The insurance industry sought regulatory relief to allow the money in The BOX to grow tax deferred for the policyholder. By allowing The BOX to grow tax deferred, the government is recognizing the contribution life insurance makes to the welfare of society.

Are There Different BOX Designs?

Once the concept of The BOX was introduced, insurance carriers began to design different payment configurations. Over the years, innovation allowed the policyowner to buy an insurance contract which required premiums for specific periods. So instead of a lump sum deposit, the premiums could be financed over 10 years, 20 years, until age 65, or for their whole life. Two basic funding strategies utilizing The BOX were developed—*Whole Life* (which offers a guaranteed premium) and *Universal Life* (which offers a flexible premium).

Whole Life guarantees the premium for the entire payment period. Any excess interest earnings, adjustments to mortality experience and expense loads are credited to The BOX as dividends. These dividends combine the earnings and costs together in one amount. This is often referred to as the *bundled* approach.

In 1980, several insurance carriers introduced a new architecture for permanent insurance products called Universal Life policy.

Policyholders could determine the amount of premium they paid and the frequency of payment for a given face amount. The premiums, instead of being contractually fixed, are based on current investment assumptions. These premiums may be lower than for a comparable whole life policy because the interest assumptions are prospective. Whole life premiums are calculated using a guaranteed rate of interest. The dividends are credited based on actual performance. This is retrospective. But Universal Life bases the premiums on current interest assumptions instead of a guaranteed rate.

If the assumptions are inaccurate, the premiums will need to be adjusted and although Universal Life can be illustrated to look more favorable than Whole Life (i.e., you pay a lower premium for the same coverage), it is important to remember The BOX still needs the same amount of money to pay the same death benefit at life expectancy.

There is no magic.

These differences can make understanding life insurance difficult.

So keep in mind, if all of the assumptions for Whole Life and Universal Life are the same (same mortality table, same expense loads, and same interest credit rate), the amount the insurance company will need to collect will actuarially be the same. Why? Life Insurance is a mathematical science.

The carrier is targeting a Lump Sum at each age. With a typical Universal Life policy, the premium to get to the lump sum is based on the current earnings assumptions projected over the lifetime of the policy contract. The premium for the lump sum with a Whole Life contract is based on a fairly low guaranteed rate, for example 3%. If the current rate for the Universal life is 5%, then the annual premium due would be projected to be lower for the Universal Life policy. Why? It is assumed the higher interest earned in The BOX would make up the difference in premium deposits. However, with Whole Life, there are earnings too. So when we factor in the dividend credits for the Whole Life policy, the performance of both policy types ultimately will end up being economically similar.

There are many reasons why advisors favor one type of insurance over the other. However, in the end, The BOX must have enough money to pay the mortality costs or you will be faced with paying them yourself.

The main difference between Whole Life and Universal Life is the flexibility the policyholder has to manage premium payments. With Whole Life, if they cannot pay the premium, the policy will borrow the money from The BOX. This loan will include interest payments that are payable annually. If the interest is not paid, the loan will increase. Universal Life is much simpler. The mortality costs and expenses are deducted from The BOX whether or not a premium is paid. No loans or interest payments required. However, this freedom from economic payments may ultimately jeopardize the goal of lifetime coverage if insufficient premiums are deposited in The BOX. This would defeat the entire purpose of using The BOX in the first place.

A Quick Summary

First, probability is the key to determining insurance premiums. People die according to a predictable pattern called a mortality table. The predictable pattern and the face amount of the policy are mathematically converted into a lump sum target that must be in The BOX in order to fund the contractual promise made by the policy. This lump sum can be financed by estimating the annual premium needed by The BOX in order to stay on target for the lump sum.

If the projected lump sum value of The BOX falls below the target, then the insurance carrier is unable to fulfill the terms of the contract. The policy will either be discontinued (lapse) or the annual funding amounts must be increased to get back on schedule for the lump sum. This is true for both Universal and Whole Life policies—although companies deal with the problem differently. If you have a Whole Life policy, you can end up with too little cash in The BOX if you borrow too much and fail to pay the interest on the policy loans or fail to pay your scheduled premiums. With Universal Life, you become underfunded by failing to have enough in The BOX to pay the annual costs (mortality, expenses, and others). Ultimately, the result is the same. The policy will be canceled for insufficient funds.

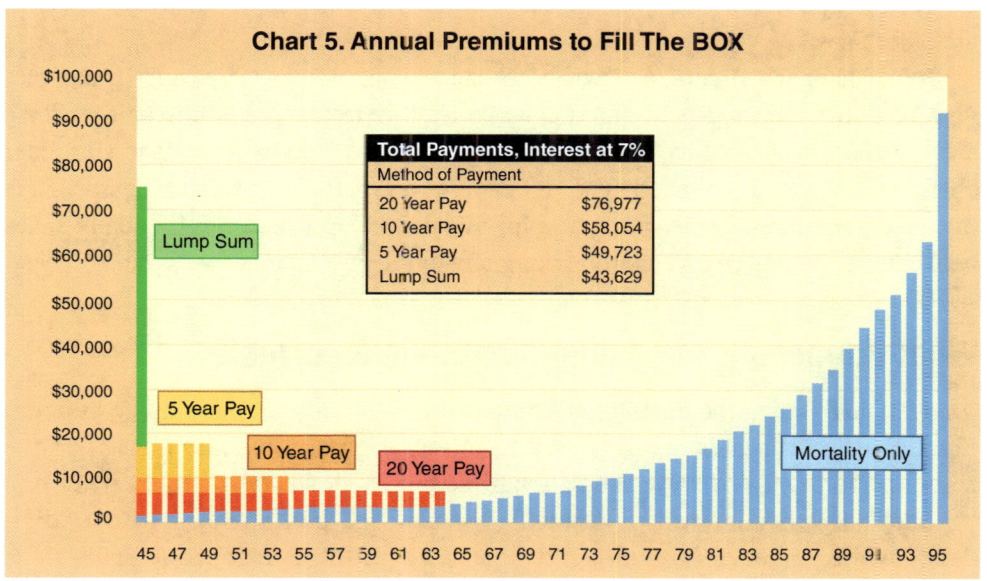

Chart 5. Annual Premiums to Fill The BOX

Total Payments, Interest at 7%	
Method of Payment	
20 Year Pay	$76,977
10 Year Pay	$58,054
5 Year Pay	$49,723
Lump Sum	$43,629

Earlier we discovered the total mortality costs at life expectancy are 74.7% of the projected death benefit. Chart 5 illustrates the total amount of payments required by a 45 year old to fund this 74.7% for a $1,000,000 policy using a 7% interest assumption. Notice the different amounts required at various funding periods. The single payment lump sum required in The BOX is only $43,629. However, if the insured elects to fund The BOX over five years, the total payments increase to $49,723 ($9,945 annually) and over a 20-year period to $76,977 ($3,849 annually).

The Factors That Impact Pricing

Let's explore the four specific factors which affect the amount you have to put into The BOX. These factors are:

1. The predictable pattern of death (mortality costs)
2. The cost of doing business (expense loads)
3. The amount of interest credited to The BOX each year
4. The number of people who actually keep their insurance policies (called persistency)

Your individual account (The BOX) holds your annual payments or your lump sum deposit as long as you retain the insurance contract. As long as all the original assumptions are achieved, the value of The BOX will grow to meet the projected lump sum targets according to the illustration provided by the insurance company.

Each year, The BOX must pay the annual cost of insurance (mortality costs) and the policy expenses. The BOX also receives the interest credited each year by the insurance company. The BOX allows pre-funding of the cost of insurance so if the policy performs according to the originally illustrated assumptions, premiums plus compound interest on The BOX will actually pay the higher insurance costs at the older ages.

What happens if someone wants to cancel their insurance early? In the first year or two there may be a significant shortfall between premiums paid and the cash surrender value of the policy. This is primarily due to expenses and surrender charges for early cancellation. The BOX must be assessed a surrender charge if the insurance company hasn't recovered all of its start-up expenses. It usually takes between five and fifteen years for a company to recover their costs.

What Happens If the Assumptions are Incorrect?

As we have seen, the insurance company projections are based on assumptions. So the actual results may vary from the original illustration based on the actual performance of these four pricing factors. With whole life, the carrier will "bundle" together interest, mortality, expenses and persistency into the "dividend" while universal life will "unbundle" each of these factors and apply them separately.

The BOX adjusts in size to reflect any changes in the actual performance of these factors. The BOX will either get bigger; become smaller depending upon the actual performance of the carrier.

So what if interest rates do decline (or expenses rise or people die faster than expected)? Conceptually, The BOX would need to have more money to reach the Lump Sum objective. So more money than originally illustrated needs to be paid as premium in order to deliver the results projected. With Whole Life this doesn't happen because the policy is guaranteed as long as the guaranteed premium is paid.

A drop in interest rates with a Whole Life policy will eventually cause the dividends to be reduced below the original illustration. Under an "abbreviated payment" approach (where dividend credits are used to pay premiums after a certain point), it is possible more premiums will have to be paid out-of-pocket than originally illustrated. With Universal Life, The BOX will require either a higher premium or, payments for a longer period if the policyowner was hoping to shorten the payment period.

But the opposite can also be true. If interest rates rise, expenses decline or people live longer, The BOX will not need as much money from as originally illustrated. The BOX can then become "smaller," reflecting the improved performance. With Whole Life, the dividends would be higher and could increase coverage or reduce the premiums sooner. With Universal Life, a "smaller" BOX would mean less out of pocket for the owner as the earnings would continue to pay mortality costs and expenses.

In the final analysis, The BOX must have enough accumulated to equal the mathematical lump sum targeted by the insurance company at any age. Otherwise, the company could not stay in business. If they have underfunded all of their contracts, the carrier would never have enough assets to meet their obligations.

A Closer Look at the Four Pricing Factors

Let's examine the four pricing factors mentioned previously to see how much impact future economic conditions can have on The BOX. Illustrations of The BOX will vary from company to company based on how they project these four factors. And if a carrier uses assumptions which are too aggressive, The BOX may not achieve the performance illustrated.

It is virtually impossible for most insurance buyers to know for certain how these factors will impact the specific product they purchased. But the surest way to protect yourself is by asking for a copy of the company IQ. This is the Illustration Questionnaire that all insurance companies have been asked to voluntarily provide. Questions about pricing assumptions for these four factors have been clearly stated. If the answers are unclear or the carrier has elected to not provide an IQ, ask why. This is comparable to "*taking the 5th*" in court.

> *purchasing a policy because one illustration shows better results than another may be a wrong conclusion*

Many insurance buyers believe that an illustration comparison between companies is a valid method for determining the best product to purchase. But purchasing a policy because one illustration shows better results than another may be a wrong conclusion.

The best illustration may contain very aggressive assumptions that make a direct comparison with an illustration from another company with more conservative assumptions impossible.

Let's look at some of the specific issues which impact the pricing structure of The BOX.

1. **MORTALITY COSTS**. As medical technology improves, people have been living longer. What happens to The BOX if the mortality experience for the insurance company is different than projected in your illustration? The company's actual mortality experience results from how long the people they choose to insure actually live. If their underwriting assessment was shoddy and inaccurate, the pool of insureds may die too soon. The company's financial reserves will be impaired. This will impact all of the other policies. The company will need to raise mortality costs which will drain money from your BOX faster than expected. This could increase the cost of your coverage.

   Unforeseen negative events can also cause problems for an insurance company. For instance, the AIDS epidemic could impact the overall mortality experience of the industry, or of a particular company. An outbreak of some unknown virus or other illness might adversely affect the statistics. Any of these occurrences could cause The BOX to be underfunded and unable to generate enough compound interest to pay the increased mortality costs in future years.

   Likewise, breakthroughs in medical care often reduce the company mortality costs. The BOX would grow faster because less costs are being deducted. But be careful! Some insurance companies are very aggressive and have already anticipated these improvements in mortality costs when they designed their illustrations. Check to make certain the carrier's IQ discloses any assumed mortality improvements. If they do, ask how these assumptions are made, and what impact these savings are projected to have on their product. If they haven't told you, then stay away from their BOX.

2. **EXPENSES**. Expenses associated with an insurance policy include administration, premium taxes, DAC taxes and sales commissions. Another cost factor is risk capital. Companies also have to measure the cost impact poor investment results might have on their products. Some companies will project expenses in their illustration including a factor for inflation. Most companies will illustrate expenses holding steady, assuming there will be no increases for the maintenance of their contracts over the next twenty or

thirty years. Again, the IQ should disclose how the carrier has priced their product to reflect their projected expense loads.

3. **INTEREST CREDITS.** Interest credits are the third factor in the pricing equation. Premiums (net of expenses) are invested by the company in a variety of bonds, stocks, mortgages and other investments. The returns credited to The BOX are based on this investment performance.

   In recent years, most insurance companies have failed to earn interest at the rate originally illustrated. The company illustrations showed The BOX growing much faster than their current performance could support. Carriers justified this because the interest rates were high and their investment portfolios were benefiting from the higher investment yields. But when interest rates declined, these same illustrations, which were originally based on higher rates, look substantially worse since they never achieved the original level of illustrated returns anticipated.

   The size of The BOX will expand or contract depending on how these four factors perform

4. **PERSISTENCY**. Persistency refers to the number of policies which stay in force from inception until death. We have already discussed how adverse selection can negatively impact the financial stability of a company. Persistency is directly tied to this same problem.

   An important aspect of persistency is the acquisition cost for each policy. It requires several years (often five to 15) before an insurance company can recover their costs. If a policy terminates before the company has recovered all of their costs, it could adversely impact other policyholders and the profitability of the company.

Persistency can also affect your policy through lapse supported pricing. Some companies assume an inordinate number of policies will actually terminate prior to the death of the insured. (By assuming lower death benefits will ever be paid, overall they can project insurance benefits for a lower premium cost.) But if these policies do not actually lapse, then the higher benefit payments will hurt the company's financial performance and impact your BOX.

The Dynamics of The BOX

The size of The BOX will expand or contract depending on how these four factors perform. (Remember, dividends are a composite of the four factors.) If mortality costs or expenses go up, or interest goes down, The BOX must get larger (more premiums required). Either premiums are paid for a longer period of time, if being paid under the Abbreviated Payment Plan (APP), or, as with Universal Life, the annual premiums must increase to reach the projected target. Likewise, if mortality costs improve, expenses stabilize or decline and/or interest rates increase, in order to reach target, The BOX can become smaller; this means fewer premiums are required if being paid under the APP or the premium may be reduced for a Universal Life policy.

So, The BOX isn't just static. The long term nature of the insurance obligation makes The BOX quite dynamic. The size of your BOX is impacted by the investment performance of the insurance company. It is also affected by the ultimate results achieved in their underwriting (mortality costs), expense control, and business retention (persistency). A conservative company is more likely to attain their original assumptions than an aggressive company which uses illustrations to attract new business.

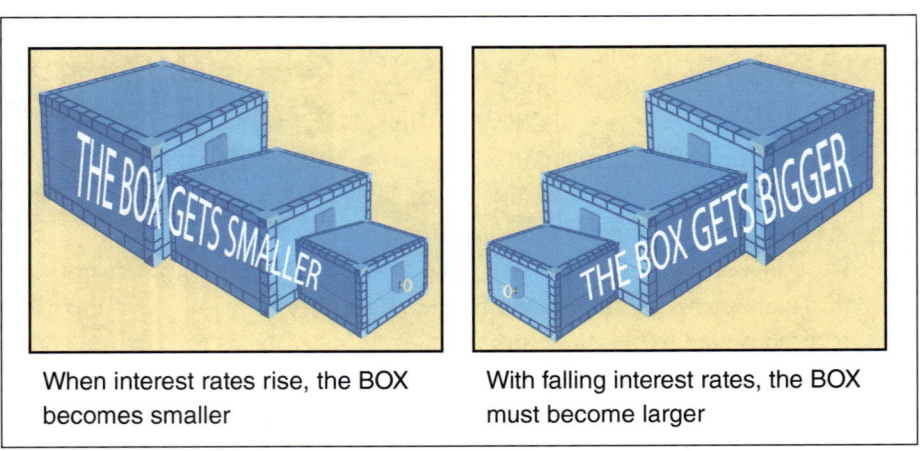

| When interest rates rise, the BOX becomes smaller | With falling interest rates, the BOX must become larger |

It would be wise for the fiscally prudent insurance buyer to consider overfunding The BOX to minimize the possible consequences of poor investment performance or the overstatement of pricing assumptions.

How Much Can You Put in The BOX?

So ask yourself this question! If you are purchasing life insurance for your entire life do you want to pay the mortality costs on a pay-as-you-go basis each year with your money or would you rather have The BOX pay them for you from the compound interest and tax benefits?

Before we answer this question, let's review The BOX is very flexible. When you start your BOX, you can select how you want to fund it. You can put premiums in The BOX as one lump sum; you can fund it over five years, 10 years, until age 65 or for life. In most cases, you can change your mind and raise or lower your contributions at any time. It is important to remember that the sooner you fill The BOX, the less you actually pay out of your own pocket.

When you select your BOX, the target is calculated on certain interest assumptions, mortality costs and expense assumptions. If interest rates decline, or mortality costs rise, The BOX will need more money. Likewise, if interest rates rise and/ or mortality costs drop, The BOX needs less money. The BOX should be evaluated every year to determine whether or not it is on target.

Interest earned by The BOX is tax deferred and potentially tax free if the policy is held until death. Tax is owed on withdrawals in excess of the amount you have deposited into The BOX. This can be a real economic advantage; so much so that in 1984 Congress instituted IRC § 7702. It defined life insurance and limits the amount of money you can put in The BOX. If you exceed that limit, then all of the earnings in The BOX become taxable. Your insurance carrier monitors this for you each year to make certain your plan does not exceed these guidelines.

The amount of contribution you can put into The BOX and still qualify as insurance ranges between pure cost of insurance and the maximum amount allowed under IRC § 7702.

The minimum amount needed to fund The BOX is just enough to pay a level contribution to fund the mortality costs until age 95. At this point, the policy would be canceled and you receive nothing back. However, you can elect to fund for amounts greater than the minimum. But whatever your targeted premium, it is an individual choice and based on your individual needs.

For instance, let's again assume you are 45 years old. Let's say you want to have your insurance fully paid by the time you retire. You want to design the premium to fill The BOX during the next 20 years. At that time, if the assumptions are accurate, the policy should stay fully funded for life.

Another option might be to fully pay The BOX in 10 years. In this instance, the premium would be calculated to fill The BOX in 10 equal installments. At the end of ten years, if the assumptions are accurate, The BOX would need no further payments.

It is still possible for company experience to be worse than assumed in making the original determination of the amount of premium required. If this happens, Whole Life dividends will be reduced, and Universal Life interest crediting rates may be reduced or mortality and expense charges increased. Under either policy, the result would be that you will have to pay more premium than originally contemplated or for a longer period. If company experience is better than originally assumed, you could reduce your level of premium payment. Generally it is better to keep paying the same premium, i.e., to be conservative and overfund The BOX than to play it too close and run the risk of having to increase your outlays at what might be a bad time for you.

There is one final consideration in determining the amount you can put into The BOX.

What is a MEC?

In 1989, Congress placed yet another limitation on the tax advantages of life insurance. IRC § 7702 already limited the size of The BOX; but Congress was concerned that life insurance taxation still offered too many income tax benefits when compared to other investments, especially annuities. So Congress enacted the Modified Endowment Contract (MEC) limitation to minimize the tax benefits. This is sometimes referred to as the seven pay test.

If The BOX becomes overfunded (less than the IRC § 7702 limits but more than the MEC limits), any distributions from The BOX will be treated for tax purposes first as income, and then as recovered cost (last in first out). If The BOX is not a MEC, then all premiums come out tax free before any of the gain is taxed (first in first out).

This diagram depicts the range of premiums you can put into The BOX.

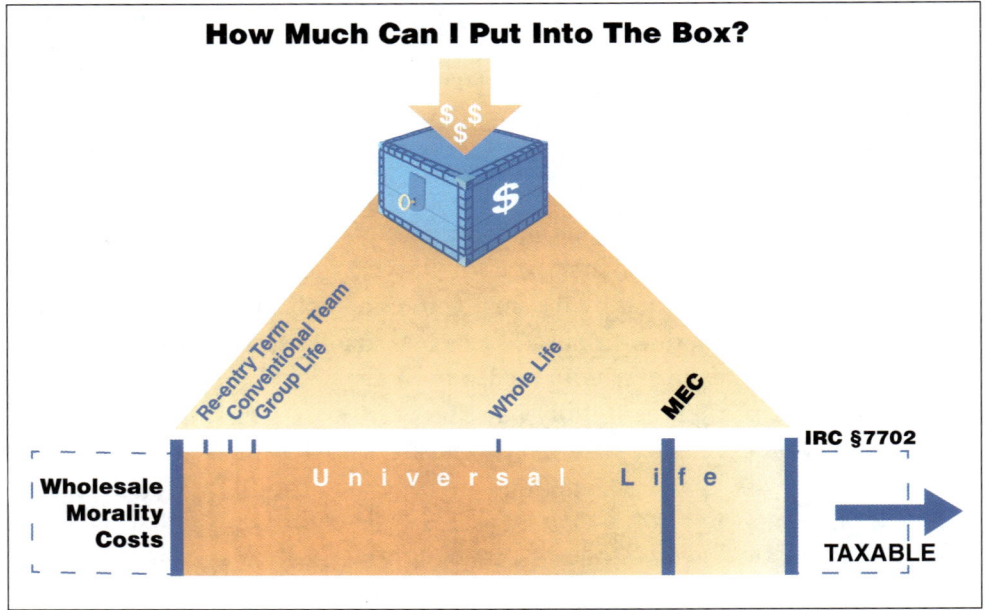

Notice that the range of premiums starts from the low end at the pure mortality costs. At the high end, the maximum you can put in The BOX is limited by the IRC § 7702. The MEC limit reduces even further the amount you can put in The BOX if you want the most advantageous tax treatment on withdrawals. If you are willing to keep the premiums in The BOX until death, the insurance benefits grow untaxed for your beneficiaries. This could be a significant advantage.

Retail Insurance Pricing

Carriers increase insurance premiums based on the amount of risk they feel they are going to assume in each specific situation. This risk is usually determined by asking the potential insured to provide evidence of health. However, some policies are issued with no evidence of health being required by the carrier. In this situation, the company usually adds a mortality surcharge to offset the possible risk they are accepting. These loads can increase the pure cost of insurance as much as 30%–50% or more.

Chart 2 illustrates the premiums carriers charge based on the amount of risk they feel they are being asked to accept. The base rate used for group life insurance products is referred to as "*New York Table Y*." Depending upon competitive pressures and the size of the group, carriers will often discount these costs to obtain new business. Sometimes these discounts run as much as 50%–70%. Annual Renewable Term to age 100 (ART 100) has a premium based on the risk associated with only one physical when the policy is first issued. After the beginning of the policy, the insurance company must continue to provide insurance coverage as long as the premiums are paid each year.

> *carriers will often discount these costs to obtain new business*

Re-entry Term requires the insured to submit new evidence of insurability before the policy will be renewed. The frequency of re-qualification depends on the contract. It can be every 5 years, 10 years, 15 years or 20 years. If you cannot re-qualify, you may still keep the policy, but at a significantly higher rate that will increase each year.

It is apparent that carriers set the premiums for their products based on the amount of risk they are contractually assuming and their ability to cancel the policy. If the company has a reasonable expectation of retaining the policy for the lifetime of the insured, it will set the mortality costs at or near their actual experience. The BOX is the only way the insured can benefit from these savings. In fact, most carriers offer mortality rates as low as or lower than the least expensive term rates to the policyholder who purchases The BOX.

Putting Money in The BOX

Once you start to put money (**premiums**) into The BOX, insurance companies will credit interest earnings to The BOX based on a mix of different investment strategies.

1. **DECLARED CREDIT RATE.** Most policy owners are content to accept the carrier's stated interest rate. This rate may change based on the overall performance of the underlying assets in the General Account of the carrier. Two types of underlying assets (investments) may be offered by carriers. A rate credited to a policy based on the overall assets of the carrier is called *portfolio yield*. A rate can be based on the return attributed to new money received by the company each year. This is called *new money rate*. Over time, the two rates blend together and achieve a similar return. But when rates are declining, the Portfolio rate holds up longer and shows a better

long term performance on the illustration. When rates are rising, the new money rate will respond quicker and look better on the illustrations.

In either case, the insurance carrier guarantees the principal in The BOX. Only the rate will vary annually.

2. **INDEXED CREDIT RATE.** This is one of the more recent innovations for crediting return to policies. Here, the carrier offers crediting rate tied to one or more selected market indices. Typically the S&P 500 is used. The BOX will be credited based on what the index did during a stated period of time. The typical approach is anniversary to anniversary. The BOX will receive a percentage of the performance (called participation rate) of the index up to a limit (called the cap). They will also provide a guaranteed (sometimes called a floor) rate. So it is impossible to have negative performance. This type of policy will usually allow some percentage of The BOX (from none to all) to be invested in this way, allowing the policy owner to determine how much market risk they are willing to take. The worst the policy can do is the floor rate.

3. **VARIABLE MARKET RATE.** The policyholder may wish to assume all the investment risk by selecting from a portfolio of mutual funds within The BOX. This is called a variable product and can be either a Whole Life or a UL. The range of investment options can be managed according to the risk tolerance of the policyholder. These selections include cash equivalents (money market, guaranteed government securities), fixed returns (bonds, high risk bonds) and equity (balance, index, international and growth). Funds may be shifted from fund to fund through telephone transfers as often as the policyholder desires.

Each fund is managed by experienced, professional investment managers who specialize in particular fields. One of the advantages is the tax free growth on premiums and cash value during the accumulation period. The policyholder assumes all the risk by selecting any combination of funds. There is the real possibility of losing principal. This risk is offset however, by the potential for gains far greater than the more conservative declared rate. If the plan fails to meet the basic growth assumptions of the funds, the values in The BOX could be much lower than projected. In this case, the death benefit might decrease or the policyholder would need to put more premiums into The BOX if they wanted to maintain the planned death benefits.

4. **HIDDEN RATE (No Lapse Guarantee).** This is the latest method used by carriers to credit returns to the BOX. For a premium higher than the amount illustrated to age 100, the carrier will offer to guarantee the death benefit until age 120. This specified age could be younger. The guarantee is independent of any cash available in the policy. The carrier does this by

calculating a premium based on an undisclosed crediting rate for what some call a "no lapse fund." These types of policies are valuable when the primary purpose of the insurance is a death benefit.

Conclusion

The application and selection of life insurance products for sophisticated tax and retirement solutions requires more than just a computer illustration.

"Mortality only" products (term insurance) offer an inexpensive solution to providing insurance coverage, but on a temporary basis. By paying the curve, you are guarantying you will have to cancel the policy. However, not everyone wants their insurance coverage to lapse when they need it most, at death. They want the coverage to last as long as they do.

The BOX offers a unique way to utilize compound growth in a tax advantageous way. The net result, is that you pay significantly less "out of pocket" for the mortality charges. The mortality costs are the same, but tax free investment returns help you pay the cost. But you have to fill The BOX to achieve this objective.

Either way, whether you pay the curve or fill The BOX, insurance provides a unique product which can deliver large amounts of capital for a fraction of the cost. Over time the cost of coverage must reflect your older age. So, if coverage is still desired when you are in your older years, The BOX provides the only economically acceptable, long term solution to pay those mortality costs.

In the final analysis, when you buy life insurance, you always buy term insurance. The only question is whether you pay the increasing mortality costs out of your pocket or you fund for it and pay it with investment returns. You either pay the curve or you fill The BOX.

Between a Rock and a Hard Place: NAIC Regulators—Life Insurance Intermediaries—State and Federal Regulators

Ben G. Baldwin, Jr., M.S.F.S., M.S.M., CLU®, ChFC®, CFP®, AEP® (Distinguished)

Introductory Comments by Gary Flotron

Ben G. Baldwin, Jr., M.S.F.S., M.S.M., CLU®, ChFC®, CFP®, AEP® (Distinguished), is a humble, gentle, quiet-spoken man who in this author's opinion is the quintessential financial planner. A superb teacher, writer, and speaker, Ben has published at least three books, written numerous articles, and has done countless educational seminars and programs for professionals throughout the country. Financial practitioners have been enriched by his thoughtfulness, wisdom, and insights over the years, as have his clients. A natural leader, he is one of only two individuals to have served both as a member of the Certified Financial Planners Board of Standards Board of Directors and the Society of Financial Service Professionals (FSP) National Board of Directors.

Mr. Baldwin has been awarded three major national professional awards, all of which recognize his lifetime achievements. For his exemplative qualities of leadership and unfettering commitment to education, ethics and professional, and client relationships, Ben was in 2006—the first year the award was given—a recipient of the FSP's esteemed Kenneth Black, Jr. Leadership Award. He is the first recipient of the prestigious Loren Dunton Award (named after the founder of the financial planning profession) presented by the National Association of Insurance and Financial Advisors (NAIFA) in recognition of his significant contributions as an agent, author, leader, educator, and financial planner to the financial services profession and the public. In 2004, Mr. Baldwin was a member of the chartered class of inductees into the National Association of Estate Planners & Councils (NAEPC) Estate Planning Hall of Fame® and simultaneously awarded by NAEPC the Accredited Estate Planner® Distinguished (AEP® (Distinguished)) designation. This is certainly quite a "hat trick" in anyone's book.

In April 2018, Ben wrote an extraordinary article titled "Between a Rock and a Hard Place: NAIC Regulators—Life Insurance Intermediaries—State and Federal

Regulators" in his "Insurance Planning" section of *Estate Planning Review—The Journal* that is published by CCH, a part of Wolters Kluwer. The article describes the disconnect of the National Association of Insurance Commissioners (NAIC) Life Insurance Model Regulation (Model # 582), adopted by almost all states, that mandates the requirement that at the point of life insurance policy delivery the policy owner must be provided with a voluminous, linear, constant assumption policy illustration that for the non-guaranteed elements of the policy is flagrantly misleading. Clearly, the NAIC Model Regulation for illustrations is in conflict with the goals of protecting the consumer, and, in fact, could be deemed harmful to the consumer. The article is a call to action among various regulators and the life insurance industry to solve this dilemma.

After reading the article it was a no-brainer for the author to request permission from Ben Baldwin and CCH the publisher to reproduce the article as a contributed article for this book. Both Mr. Baldwin and CCH graciously granted that permission. Part of the lessons from Chapter 2 of this book is that for non-guaranteed life insurance products we cannot rely on the use of constant and continuing assumptions as depicted in traditional policy illustrations in predicting the performance of the life insurance policy. These illustrations are completely misleading. Ben's refreshing article is suggesting how to approach the NAIC regulatory problem and end this catastrophic situation before it is too late for the life insurance industry.

About Ben G. Baldwin, Jr.

Ben G. Baldwin, Jr., M.S.F.S., M.S.M., CLU®, ChFC®, CFP®, AEP® (Distinguished), is Director Emeritus of Baldwin Financial Advisors, LLC of Arlington Heights, Illinois, a registered investment advisory firm owned and managed by his daughter, Kathleen Baldwin Leipprandt, CLU®, ChFC®, CFP®, specializing in financial education and consulting for corporate and individual clients.

An English major from the University of Rochester and an ex-Navy pilot, Baldwin's professional education started at The American College in 1965. He attained the Chartered Life Underwriter® (CLU®) designation in 1970, followed by the Master of Science in Financial Services (M.S.F.S.) degree in 1979, the Certified Financial Planner® (CFP®) in 1981, the Chartered Financial Consultant® (ChFC®) in 1982, and the Master of Science in Management (M.S.M.) in 1986. He is the author of *The Complete Book of Insurance* (Irwin Professional Publishing 1996), *The New Life Insurance Investment Advisor* (Probus 1988, McGraw-Hill 1994; Second Edition 2002), and *The Lawyer's Guide to Insurance* (American Bar Association, Senior Lawyers Division 1999).

Baldwin's recent career activities have included serving on the CCH Financial and Estate Planning Advisory Board; columnist for Wolters Kluwer CCH *Estate*

Planning Review—The Journal; article reviewer for The *Journal of Financial Service Professionals*; speaking, teaching, and writing; and serving as an expert witness in U.S. Securities and Exchange Commission (SEC) and Financial Industry Regulatory Authority (FINRA) cases involving life insurance and annuities.

Between a Rock and a Hard Place: NAIC Regulators—Life Insurance Intermediaries—State and Federal Regulators
Ben G. Baldwin, Jr.

NAIC Regulators Mandate Linear Paper Illustrations Be Used in the Sale of Life Insurance

The National Association of Insurance Commissioners (NAIC) Life Insurance Model Regulation (Model # 582) states in part in Section 9:

> . . . *in the case of an illustration provided at time of delivery, as required in this regulation.*
>
> > *(1) A statement to be signed and dated by the applicant or policy owner reading as follows: "I have received a copy of this illustration and understand that any non-guaranteed elements illustrated are subject to change and could be either higher or lower. The agent has told me they are not guaranteed.'*
> > *(2) A statement to be signed and dated by the insurance producer or other authorized representative of the insurer reading as follows: "I certify that this illustration has been presented to the applicant and that I have explained that any non-guaranteed elements illustrated are subject to change. I have made no statements that are inconsistent with the illustration."*[1]

It goes on to state in Section 12. Penalties:

> *In addition to any other penalties provided by the laws of this state, an insurer or producer that violates a requirement of this regulation shall be guilty of a violation of Section [cite state's unfair trade practices act].*[2]

This Model Regulation has been adopted by most of the states and is adhered to by all multi-state life insurance sales organizations. Life insurance intermediaries take these illustration requirements, and threat of **penalties**, seriously.

---

1. NAIC Life Insurance Model Regulation (Model #582), Section 9, para D (1) and (2)
2. Ibid. Section 12.

Regulated life insurance illustrations display to consumers, in a voluminous number of pages of paper, the annual values from the date of policy delivery to the insured's age 100 and often until age 120. These values are based upon a fixed linear assumed rate of return, assumed expenses and assumed mortality rate to the nearest $1.00, including non-guaranteed elements, for the duration of the illustration. The life insurance industry has endured a flood of litigation the last three years because of the changes the life insurance companies have been attempting to make in the non-guaranteed elements of cost of insurance (COI) and expenses. The amount of litigation is clear evidence that illustrations mislead. The cost of that litigation will be passed on to the consumer within the cost of future life insurance.

How You Ask for an Illustration for UL and VUL Policies Is Very Important

When an advisor or consumer asks: Please **send me an illustration** on a specific policy, what they will often get is only the "Regulator Required" Illustration as described above. Multiple pages of numbers under a fixed set of assumptions. An advisor needs more than just the regulator required illustration. To get the most valuable information when asking for an illustration ask in the following fashion: **Please provide an illustration including the following supplement reports:**

1. **The Input Summary or Output Design Page.** This page will show the static inputs that went into the illustration allowing you to discuss with your client how these inputs might change and allow you to design more meaningful inputs for the client situation.
2. **The Cost Detail or Annual Policy Charges Page.** This shows what the Cost-of-Insurance (COI) and expenses being deducted or required to be paid, each year to keep the policy in force which allows you to counsel with the client the ongoing need for the amount at risk and its affordability going forward.
3. **The Tax Detail Report or Tax Information Page.** This report shows the tax/premium limitations regime under which the policy is measured to make sure it remains a life insurance policy and retains all the tax benefits of life insurance. It will indicate the Cash Value Accumulation Test (CVAT) or the Guideline Premium Test (GPT) and the limitations on the amount of premium that may be put into the policy without jeopardizing its Tax Status. Tax status is covered in greater detail in a previous Estate Planning Review.[3]

---

3. *Flexible Life Insurance: GPT v. CVAT—An Important Choice*, Estate Planning Review—the Journal, August 20, 2013, pages 143–149.

Guideline Premium Test or Cash Value Accumulation Test: Which Choice Is in the Best Interests of the Policyowner? Journal of Financial Service Professionals, July 2014, Vol. 68, No. 4, pages 42–47.

Life Insurance Litigation Creates Pressure for New Regulation

Now that we have experienced the incredible cost of this ongoing litigation, regulators have determined that it is time to create a "Model Law" that could be adopted by the various state insurance commissioners. The first to establish such a law is New York state. The law is to be effective March 19, 2018, Part 48 of Title 11 of the Official Compilation of Codes, Rules and Regulations of the state of New York (Insurance Regulation 210).[4]

It is important to note that the purpose of the now effective NYS insurance Regulation 210 is *to ensure that policy forms do not contain provisions that may mislead policy owners . . . or contain provisions that are unjust, unfair or inequitable.*[5] The NYS regulators apparently believe that transgressions exist in the life insurance industry necessitating regulation to correct the situation. The National Association of Insurance Regulators (NCOIL) is in discussions to determine if the NYS Regulation 210 can be adapted to provide a basis for a Model Law that could be considered by all state insurance commissioners.

Credible Life Insurance Advisors Agree—Today's Regulated Illustrations Mislead

Many of the best life insurance minds available have bemoaned the misleading nature of illustrations. The required paper illustrations have been disparaged as . . .

- Affirmatively misleading minutiae
- All they prove is that ink sticks to paper
- "Artificial" Intelligence.

The renowned Joseph M. Belth, Ph.D., considered by many of us to be the dean of the life insurance industry, is professor emeritus of insurance in the Kelley School of Business at Indiana University. He is the author of *Life Insurance: A Consumer's Handbook* as well as of several other books and numerous journal articles. His blog on the insurance industry is available at (www.josephmbelth.com). Professor Belth founded *The Insurance Forum*, an independent monthly periodical, and was its editor for its entire 40 years—from January 1974 through December 2013. He has been known to say that the paper life insurance illustrations are *out of control.*

Richard M. Weber, MBA, CLU AEP (Distinguished) founder of The Ethical Edge, Inc., a consulting firm providing professional life insurance assessment and management services to businesses, family offices, and financial advisors. Dick

---

4. New York State, Department of Financial Services, 11 NYCRR 48, Insurance Regulation 210, Life Insurance and Annuity Non-Guaranteed Elements

5. Ibid, Section 48.0 Purpose, scope, and unfair trade practice.

is an active contributor to the Society of Financial Service Professionals, a past President of the Society and served six years as Chair of the Society's Illustration Task Force. During those years the Task Force produced three tools to help agents deal with illustrations, The Illustration Questionnaire (IQ), four pages of questions, the Replacement Questionnaire (RQ), four pages of questions, and the Variable Insurance Questionnaire (VIQ), three pages of questions. All these questions were designed to help agents understand the fragile nature of NAIC required illustrations that are not clear in the illustration otherwise. You cannot find anyone who has greater expertise about life insurance policy paper illustrations than Richard Weber. Weber stated in his 2005 book *Revealing Life Insurance Secrets* that *"today's regulated policy illustrations are simply incapable of accomplishing the NAIC objectives"*[6] of helping consumers understand life insurance and be able to handle its ongoing management prudently.

In a legal action initiated by the SEC against five life insurance agents, in which I acted as an expert witness on behalf of the agents, the lawyer for the SEC attacked me during my deposition because the agents had used illustrations for variable universal life policies using a constant linear interest rate out to the insureds' age 100. The lawyer ranted that that was impossible, can't happen, misleading to the extent of fraud! I explained that it was not my fault nor the fault of these agents. Those illustrations were mandated by our regulators, the National Association of Insurance Commissioners (NAIC). That did get us beyond the issue temporarily, but, the SEC lawyer continued to insist that *assuming interest rate return constant in linear paper life insurances illustrations showing pages and pages of numbers for each year down to one dollar to and beyond age 100* defies logic!

We have the insurance companies and their legions of sales managers and agents who choose to believe these impossibilities and who project them out to ages even beyond age 100. Flagrantly misleading illustrations for policies are presented to consumers as retirement vehicles. They show the policies accumulating cash value up to age 65 and then illustrating a steady stream of policy loans, as income tax-free retirement income, coming out. The consumer who believes the illustration and buys into such a plan may believe they have solved their retirement security issues only to learn later that this plan doesn't work! The insurance company may have increased the interior cost of insurance and expenses and, although the company is in litigation as a result of these changes, the consumer's retirement dreams are devastated. The problem is that insurance regulators mandate illustrations and so salespeople manipulate them. The insurance companies and marketing organizations have legions of sales managers dependent on agent sales for their bonuses. Sales organizations provide back room "Advanced Sales Departments" to

---

6. Revealing Life Insurance Secrets, Richard M. Weber MBA, CLU, Market Place Books Columbia Maryland 2005.

devise illustrations to create attractive scenarios to entice consumers and effectively sell insurance. They then promote the illustrations throughout the company . . . to generate more sales.

All this in an environment of constant life insurance litigation by irate consumers complaining that companies have lied to them and misled them.

In this age of computing power and visual presentation, there must be a better way to protect consumers and to foster consumer education. A system to ensure that illustrations do not mislead purchasers of life insurance and to make the inner workings of investment-related life insurance more understandable, without the fictions presented in linear paper illustrations. The idea of an interactive I-Pad dynamic life insurance illustration system was extensively covered in a 2013 Estate Planning Review.[7]

On June 18, 2015 the NAIC started in the right direction by adopting Actuarial Guideline XLIX (AG49) for Indexed Universal Life illustrations. AG49 constrains the crediting rates in Indexed Universal Life (IUL) illustrations to that which the Life Actuarial Task Force deem realistic.[8] The NAIC should work with the life insurance industry in building generic illustrations with agreed upon realistic constraints. Let prospective purchasers vary all the inputs while watching the impact of varying inputs on the I-Pad showing the visual impact of their choices dynamically.

NAIC Life Insurance Illustrations Model Regulation, Section 1

The purpose of Section 1 is to protect consumers, foster consumer education, ensure that illustrations do not mislead and make the inner workings of investment-related life insurance more understandable. As Mr. Weber states above; *"today's regulated policy illustrations are simply incapable of accomplishing the NAIC objectives"*[9] [10]

In a speech on February 23, 2018 to the Practicing Law Institute's SEC Speaks program in Washington, DC, the Chairman of the Securities and Exchange Commission (SEC), Jay Clayton, used an example to outline the SEC's Fiduciary Goals.[11] The example was the portfolio of an investor (and the intermediary(s) who had created it on behalf of the client) with a 401(k), an annuity and a brokerage account. That portfolio would be regulated by state insurance commissioners, state securities regulators, the Financial Industry Regulatory Authority, Inc. (FINRA),

7. Linear Life Insurance Illustrations; Are They Deceptive? Ben G Baldwin, Estate Planning Review—The Journal, April 18, 2013, pages 61–65.

8. naic.org, NAIC News Release of June 18, 2015, NAIC MEMBERSHIP ADVANCES REGULATORY PRIORITIES.

9. Revealing Life Insurance Secrets, Richard M. Weber MBA, CLU, Market Place Books Columbia Maryland 2005.

10. Revealing Life Insurance Secrets, Richard M. Weber MBA, CLU, Market Place Books Columbia Maryland 2005.

11. Investment News, February 28. 2018, Fiduciary Future, *Clayton outlines SEC Fiduciary goals* by Mark Schoeff Jr., page 22.

the SEC, the Department of Labor (DOL) and, we would add, by the Certified Financial Planners (CFP), the CFP Board and the Codes of Ethics of the various professional associations to which they choose to belong. **All demand fidelity to the consumer**.

State & Federal Regulators and the Courts Can Impose Severe Penalties for Using NAIC Regulated LI Illustrations

One can safely conclude that, as all these regulators work on their fiduciary definitions, regulatory requirements and enforcement penalties, none of them will look favorably on one of their own, the National Association of Insurance Commissioners (NAIC) mandating the use with consumers of tools that are . . .

- Misleading.
- Give a false sense of authority, by process, by volume and by specificity down to a single dollar.
- That are deemed to be out of control by credible life insurance authorities.
- That are simply incapable of attaining NAIC objectives.
- That defy logic.

Life Insurance Intermediaries Are Between Regulatory Rocks

How will this play out? Will the NAIC man-up? Will the industry understand the impossibility of using linear life insurance illustrations in a fiduciary-enthusiastic environment in which the SEC seeks to bring clarity and harmony to investment advisor and broker-dealer standards of conduct? Will the life insurance industry pay the ongoing price of business as usual? or . . .

Will it establish a life insurance industry task force to address the obsolescence of today's illustrations? Can the industry come together with the regulators to come up with a credible way to help consumers understand the impact of even small changes in the non-guaranteed elements of life insurance policies? They need to develop an illustration system designed to manage consumer expectations, to project the implications of their behavior and the impact of insurance company changes as they manage their life insurance contract over a lifetime. If the NAIC says such an expense is not in their budget, why not ask the life insurance manufacturers to each contribute just one-tenth of what they are paying out in COI litigation to the NAIC-led effort with the objective of diminishing COI litigation and making it less profitable for lawyers in the future.

Or will it take an injured life insurance intermediary who sues the NAIC because using the NAIC-mandated illustration was deemed harmful to a consumer? The consumer sued the intermediary and won in the state courts causing significant loss to the intermediary?

Or will the SEC, the DOL, FINRA, the various states attorneys general sue the NAIC for imposing misleading sales material (illustrations) on their un-protected consumers?

All of us who work with and guide consumers on their purchase and management of life insurance have a stake in this, so it is appropriate that we also act. To the extent that you agree with the arguments put forth here please obtain copies of this column and send it to all the appropriate regulators you can. Let's start a dialogue and really create a system that will protect and educate as opposed to a system, proven by its results, to mismanage consumer expectations, mislead and create ill-will against the life insurance industry, insurance companies and life insurance intermediaries. This ill-will exacerbates the difficulty of helping consumers purchase, maintain and use insurance products properly to build their own personally-provided family financial security, and to eliminate their dependence on other family members, on handouts, on charity or on the government. Inaction is costly to all.

Buying Life Insurance to Fund Estate Taxes: Toward a More Objective Decision

Jonathan G. Blattmachr, J.D., AEP® (Distinguished) and Marc A. Pasquale, CPA

Introductory Comments by Gary Flotron

Jonathan G. Blattmachr, J.D., AEP® (Distinguished), is one of the most brilliant, intriguing, creative, and innovative estate planning attorneys in the country. Among Jonathan's prolific and amazing accomplishments are the development of the concepts of trust "decanting," family split-dollar insurance arrangements, installment sales to a grantor trust, and the list goes on and on. (See "About Jonathan G. Blattmachr" for a more complete list of his accomplishments.) However, Jonathan considers his most important contribution to the profession was the development of the automatic drafting system now known as Interactive Legal.

While now a retired partner of the New York Law firm of Milbank, Tweed, Hadley & McCloy, LLC, Jonathan still wears many hats as he is Principal of Pioneer Wealth Partners, LLC, a boutique wealth advisory firm in Manhattan, and the Director of Estate Planning for Peak Trust Company (formerly Alaska Trust Company). Mr. Blattmachr is a true Renaissance man as he is also an instrument rated land and seaplane pilot and is a licensed hunting and fishing guide in the town of Southampton, New York.

When asked to provide a contributing article for this book, Jonathan graciously thought of three articles but it was felt an article written with co-author **Marc A. Pasquale, CPA**, would be the most relevant and appropriate.

One of the messages of the book, particularly from Chapter 6, is to select life insurance policies first based on realistic duration of needs, second based on risk tolerance, and third based on a preference for either minimum premium outlay or the ability to develop increasing cash values and death benefit amounts. However, because of varying rates of return and possible changes in current cost of insurance (COI) for non-guaranteed flexible premium life insurance policies, a minimally funded policy (i.e., one with the maximum death benefit relative to premium) has a very low probability of sustaining itself to life expectancy or longer based on actuarial evaluation as discussed in Chapter 5. Thus, higher premium-funded policies relative to initial death benefit not only have a greater chance of sustainability for non-guaranteed flexible premium products to life expectancy and beyond based on actuarial evaluation but result in significantly higher growing cash values and death benefits.

In their contributed article, "Buying Life Insurance to Fund Estate Taxes— Toward a More Objective Decision," Jonathan Blattmachr and Marc Pasquale advocate for purchasing a policy with a higher premium, low initial death benefit, and higher cash values. This is because of overall cost efficiency, continued death benefit increases, particularly at life expectancy and beyond, flexibility accorded due to the need to change or cancel the policy, and other reasons as discussed in the article. Although the analysis in the article was illustrated with constant assumption illustrations, this author fully concurs with the conclusions of the article.

While the contributed article was done with reference to purchasing life insurance to fund estate taxes, the principles enumerated in the article apply equally as well to other purposes and needs to purchase life insurance policies. Also, the article was originally published in *Trusts & Estates* in July 2012. Although since that time the estate tax exemption and tax rates have changed, the principles and techniques discussed are still applicable and appropriate today.

What is particularly relevant and refreshing about the article is that Messrs. Blattmachr and Pasquale approach and evaluate the purchase of a life insurance policy from the combined perspectives of an extremely sophisticated and knowledgeable estate planning attorney and an accountant. The resulting synergistic, thoughtful analysis provides additional insights and dimensions to the material contained in the book. Be prepared to be enriched by the wisdom of these two advisers!

About Jonathan G. Blattmachr

Jonathan G. Blattmachr, J.D., AEP® (Distinguished), is a Principal with Pioneer Wealth Partners, LLC, a boutique wealth advisory firm in Manhattan, the Director of Estate Planning for Peak Trust Company (formerly Alaska Trust Company), and a retired member of the New York law firm of Milbank, Tweed, Hadley & McCloy, LLC and of the Alaska, California, and New York bars. He served as an adjunct professor of law at New York University School of Law and as a lecturer in law at the Columbia University School of Law, from which he graduated cum laude.

He has been involved with many of the most important developments in recent times in estate planning and administration. Among his prolific accomplishments include that he was the developer and drafter of legislation, adopted by all states, that allowed fiduciaries, such as executors (personal representatives) and trustees, to be able to distribute property otherwise to be received by a minor to a custodian under the Uniform Gifts to Minors Act (now the Uniform Transfers to Minors Act). He also drafted the legislation that expanded the type of property a custodian may lawfully hold in such an account.

Jonathan pioneered, in the early 1970s, granting trustees the power to invade a trust by paying its assets to another trust, known as "decanting." He wrote the first two decanting statutes in the country (for New York and Alaska). He developed the concept of and wrote the first article explaining an installment sale to a grantor trust. (See Blattmachr, "Adventures in Partial Interest Transfers: Avoiding the Zero Valuation Legacy of Section 2702," *USC Law Center Institute*, para. 1305.5(G) (1992)).

Mr. Blattmachr developed the concept of "rolling" GRATs (grantor retained annuity trusts) and "asset splitting" GRATS. He helped draft a number of provisions in the Internal Revenue Code including section 2055(e)(3), which permits the reformation of charitable remainder trusts and charitable lead trusts to be in qualifying form. Additionally, he developed and obtained the first private letter ruling under which a charitable remainder trust could mimic a retirement plan—both the Chase Manhattan Bank and JP Morgan offered commercial products using the concept respectively called the private retirement trust and the charitable deferred income trust.

Jonathan developed and wrote the first legislation in the United States allowing asset protection (self-settled) trusts. He developed and obtained the first private letter ruling for private (family) split-dollar insurance arrangements (PLR 96-36-003). He developed and wrote the first legislation in many areas of trust and estate administration in many states including New York, Delaware, and Alaska. He also developed and wrote the Alaska Community Property Act, which is the only form of "opt in" community property in the country, including the concept of a community property trust, which allows non-Alaskan married couples to create community property.

He is co-developer of Wealth Transfer Planning, a computerized system for lawyers that automatically generates estate planning documents, such as wills and trusts, and provides specific client advice using a form of artificial intelligence.

He is the author or co-author of nine books and more than 500 articles on tax and estate planning matters. In 2004, Mr. Blattmachr was a member of the Chartered Class of inductees into the National Association of Estate Planners &Councils (NAEPC) Estate Planning Hall of Fame® and simultaneously awarded by NAEPC the Accredited Estate Planner® Distinguished (AEP® (Distinguished)) designation. In 2017, NAEPC awarded Jonathan the Hartman Axley Lifetime Service Award for his contributions both to the estate planning community and to the crucial development of the Association. He was also awarded the Lifetime Achievement Award by the Orange County Society of Trusts and Estate Practitioners.

He is a former chairperson of the Trusts and Estates Law Section of the New York State Bar Association and of several committees of the American Bar Association. Jonathan is a Fellow and a former Regent of the American College of Trust and Estate Counsel and past chair of its Estate and Gift Tax Committee. Among professional activities, which are too numerous to list, Jonathan has served as an advisor on the American Law Institute, Restatement of the Law, Trusts 3rd, and as a Fellow and Director of The New York Bar Foundation and as a Fellow of the American Bar Foundation.

Jonathan graduated from Columbia University School of Law cum laude, where he was recognized as a Harlan Fiske Stone Scholar, and received his A.B. degree from Bucknell University, majoring in mathematics.

Jonathan served in the U.S. Army from 1970 to 1972, reaching the rank of captain, and was awarded the Army Commendation Medal. He is also an instrument rated land and seaplane pilot and is a licensed hunting and fishing guide in the Town of Southampton, New York.

About Marc A. Pasquale

Marc A. Pasquale, CPA, is a Principal in Pioneer Wealth Partners, LLC estate planning advisory and risk management groups. Marc brings more than 15 years of experience in accounting, tax, insurance, and financial planning. He began his career in the audit and tax department of Ernst and Young LLP. He then moved to Sagemark Consulting where he was a financial planner focused on the structuring and implementation of sophisticated wealth preservation transactions. Marc went on to found Oak Venture Advisors, LLC, which specialized in insurance and estate planning transactions for a high net worth client base. Marc holds a B.S. degree in accounting from the University of Notre Dame. He is also a registered Certified Public Accountant.

Buying Life Insurance to Fund Estate Taxes: Toward a More Objective Decision
Jonathan G. Blattmachr & Marc A. Pasquale

Trusts & Estates/Wealthmanagement.com—July 2012

One may consider an alternative approach when acquiring life insurance to fund estate taxes. This approach may initially seem to be counter intuitive to the traditional or common practice of purchasing the maximum initial death benefit based upon premiums paid.

Why Large Policies?

Many purchases of large death benefit life insurance policies occur because a property owner perceives that her surviving family members will suffer an unacceptable erosion of wealth upon the owner's death on account of the imposition of estate tax. The solution is the acquisition of an insurance policy on the property owner's life. That solution is seldom perfect and, in fact, often will prove more costly than if the insurance hadn't been acquired and alternative action (traditional estate tax planning) was taken or if an alternative lower death benefit, higher cash value policy had been purchased.

Typically, the death benefit under the policy is selected by running numbers that indicate how much estate tax will be due when a property owner dies. One assumption that a property owner and her advisors must make is what the effective rate of estate tax likely will be when she dies. If the property owner is married, she can postpone the estate tax until her spouse dies, by transferring property to the surviving spouse under the protection of the marital deduction.[1] This rate has varied over the past several years from a high of 60 percent to a low of 35 percent.[2] About a third of the states currently impose an additional estate tax of 10.4 percent.[3] The United States now imposes a rate of 35 percent, but that rate is scheduled to increase after 2012 to 55 percent.[4]

History indicates that forecasting what the effective rate of estate tax will be on death is difficult, because it's a political matter. Virtually every Republican presidential candidate has vowed to repeal the estate tax.[5] Whether a Republican becomes the next president of the United States, it's uncertain if the estate tax will be repealed or reduced.[6] Years ago, then-president-elect George W. Bush stated that his number one domestic political agenda was the repeal of the estate tax. Repeal didn't occur until after Bush's second term ended, and it lasted (by affirmative election) for only one year. In any case, buying life insurance to pay for estate tax often will be perceived as a wasteful decision if there's no such tax in effect when the insured dies.

Timing of Death

Even if no estate tax is in effect when the insured dies, the purchase of life insurance policy likely will be viewed as a financially efficient decision if the insured dies

---

1. *See* Internal Revenue Code Section 2056(a).
2. *See* IRC Section 2001(c).
3. Under IRC Section 2058, an estate tax deduction is allowed for state death tax imposed. Most states impose 16 percent as their highest death tax rate. Because the current highest federal estate tax rate is 35 percent, the effective state death tax rate is .65 x .16 or 10.4 percent. See www.actec.org/private/freeform/page.asp?PageID=155, prepared by attorney Charles Fox. Under current law, the federal estate tax rate will increase back to 55 percent, as it was before 2001. In addition, Section 2058 will be eliminated, and the credit for state death tax under Section 2011 will be restored.
4. *See* IRC Section 2001(c).
5. *See* The Tax Foundation, Election 2012: Presidential Candidate Tax Plan Comparison.
6. Hani Sarji, "Estate of Confusion: Estate Tax Bills In Front of 112th Congress," http://blogs.forbes.com/hanisarji/estate-tax-bills/.

earlier than the insurance company had forecast.[7] One of the key factors in determining the cost of life insurance is predicting when someone of the insured's age, gender and health probably will die.[8] Although it's impossible to discern accurately when a particular individual will die (unless death is imminent),[9] it's generally possible to ascertain the average time when a large group of individuals of the same age, gender and health will die. For example, an insurance company may forecast that a healthy 60-year-old male insured will die, on average, in 26 years and will price the premiums accordingly.[10] On average, insurance policies have an approximate 6 percent return compounded annually if the insured dies at her actuarial life expectancy, as estimated by the insurer.[11] If a particular insured dies earlier, the return will be greater; if she dies later, the return will be smaller.[12] Nevertheless, few large death benefit policies acquired to pay estate tax would have been purchased if the insured knew there would be no estate tax: The 6 percent average return, coupled with the uncertainty of that return (which as the insured ages will diminish), because the time of death for a specific individual can't be accurately predicted, means that the property owner likely would decline to buy the policy.

Other Factors

Additional factors should be, but rarely are, considered by property owners when deciding whether to buy life insurance to pay for estate tax. One is that the majority of policies are cancelled before the insured dies.[13] One reason for this is that most life insurance policies become less efficient over time.

A policy's decreasing efficiency may be due to the fact that the longevity of every age class in the United States has been consistently increased over the past 100 years.[14] As average human longevity increases, the cost or level of the insurance premiums (on newly issued policies) for each age decreases.[15] Hence, a policy that's been in effect

---

7. For example, assume an initial premium of $10,000 is paid for a policy with a $1 million death benefit. If the insured dies at the end of the year, the return on the premium is over 9500 percent, using a 5 percent discount rate.

8. Almost universally, insurance carriers charge different premiums for females.

9. Cf. Treasury Regulations Section 25.7520-3(b)(3), which doesn't permit the use of standard mortality tables if "an individual who is known to have an incurable illness or other deteriorating physical condition is considered terminally ill if there is at least a 50 percent probability that the individual will die within 1 year."

10. Calculation made from the 2008 Select and Ultimate VBT Tables for Male Non-Smokers.

11. Returns calculated for an insured age 60 paying the level premium until life expectancy. Returns vary with the age at issue and sex of the insured.

12. There are two reasons for that. The sooner the insured dies, the smaller the total premiums paid (keeping in mind that even if the premiums have been paid up, there will be term insurance charges against the cash value inside the policy). Also, the longer the time until the death benefit is paid, the lower the return on a present value basis. In other words, if the death benefit, for example, is $1 million and is paid five years after the policy is issued, the annualized return is much higher than if it's paid 20 years after the policy is issued.

13. Timothy C. Pfeifer, F.S.A., Milliman USA (Feb. 19, 2004).

14. U.S. Vital Statistics 2007.

15. "[T]he actual cost of product has come down when it comes to life products, which is something that the industry has done a lousy job of advertising. A term policy is somewhere between 30 and 50 percent cheaper than

for a considerable period of time will be more costly than a new policy, all other things being equal. Another reason most policies prove to be inefficient is that the particular insured lives too long.[16] Once the insured reaches an advanced age, the cost of the insurance increases significantly because the probability of dying each year increases with age. This makes it appear that the efficiency of the policy worsens over time.

Some policy illustrations indicate that there's no or minimal cost for life insurance once the individual reaches an advanced age. But, the illustrations may be misunderstood. What's probably happening is that the amount of real insurance is significantly less than the stated amount of death benefit. Rather, the amount that will be paid at death will consist in large measure of cash value, which is the investment component inside the policy, similar to a brokerage account. This frequently occurs with whole life policies, because they're structured so the cash value will equal the death benefit at an advanced age (for example, age 100). The cash value is already owned by the policy owner and can be accessed at any time. Often, the amount of real insurance (that is, the amount the insurance company must pay, which is sometimes called the "net amount at risk") will decline to nothing or almost nothing.

Buy Term Insurance Instead?

An alternative is to buy what's called "term" or "pure" insurance. Most insurance (not just life insurance) is term insurance. Car insurance, household insurance, fire insurance and malpractice insurance are simply term policies. The insured pays a premium for the insurance coverage for a fixed period of time (typically one year). If the event that the insured doesn't want to happen (such as a fire destroying the insured's home) occurs, the insurance company pays for the loss out of the company's own resources. If the event doesn't occur, the insurance company keeps the premiums and the insured gets nothing (except, perhaps, the peace of mind of knowing that if the adverse event had occurred, the insurance company would have had to pay for the loss).

Life insurance works in a similar manner, although cash value policies couple declining term or pure insurance with an investment or cash value account.[17] Almost always, if the policy is in effect when the insured dies, a term policy will have been much more efficient than a cash value policy. One reason is that with most cash

---

it was 10 years ago. Cheaper!" See "American College Chief: Insurance Industry Must Fight for Relevance," Insurancenewsnet.com, Larry Barton (President of the American College).

16. Another factor is that once a premium is paid and the insured doesn't die before the next premium is due, the premium previously paid has been "wasted." However, it's generally impossible to forecast whether that will occur. Hence, it doesn't appear to be a reasonable factor to consider in determining whether an existing policy is more efficient than a newly issued one.

17. Some cash value policies (commonly called "universal life" policies) permit the amount of the term insurance component to be maintained at a fixed level and even beyond age 80 (at which point most companies will not provide pure term insurance protection), but the annual cost of the term insurance will increase dramatically at older ages. ACLI Life Insurer's Fact Book 2011, p. 64.

value policies, each year the insurance company's own risk declines, because cash value increases and replaces part of the term or pure insurance component under the policy—hence, there's less term insurance each year, meaning the shift of potential resources from the insurance company to the insured (or the insured's beneficiary) diminishes each year.

Other Limitations

One limitation of term life policies, however, is that if the insured lives to an advanced age, the cost of the insurance becomes extremely high—so high, in fact, that, unless the death of the insured is imminent, the policy almost certainly will be cancelled. Also, very few companies offer term insurance above age 80—hence, the market is very restricted (and the cost or premium climbs very steeply at such ages).[18] Although many term policies permit a conversion to a cash value policy when the term policy expires, the cost of such a converted cash value policy is very high and, again, unless death is imminent, probably will be cost-inefficient.[19]

Funding Estate Taxes

In essence, a life insurance policy is nothing other than a sinking fund: If the insured lives to her estimated normal life expectancy, it will return the premiums paid with about a 6 percent return compounded annually, unless the policy is cancelled before death, which, usually, is what occurs. Even if the policy is held until death, it likely will be insufficient to cover the estate tax if such a tax is in effect at death. That's because the property owner's wealth likely will increase over time. Inflation coupled with reasonable investment performance is likely to push the value of the property owner's wealth to a significantly greater level, and that will mean the insurance covers only a portion, and often only a small portion, of the estate tax due.[20]

---

18. At www.thepg.com/term-quotes, only Protective Life and Transamerica sell term insurance for individuals over age 80, and there were no companies that sold term insurance when the insured reaches age 89.

19. One reason the premiums on such a converted policy are so high (on a relative basis) is the rule of adverse selection. Those whose health has diminished while the term insurance is owned are more likely to convert than those whose health hasn't declined, as the latter can shop for less expensive (lower premium) policies.

20. For example, say a 50-year-old, who's already used her wealth transfer tax exemption, has $50 million in wealth, and her advisors estimate that the effective estate tax rate at her death will be 50 percent. She, therefore, acquires a $25 million death benefit policy and arranges for the proceeds, which will be used to fund the estimated $25 million of estate tax, to be excluded from her gross estate for federal estate tax purposes. However, she lives for 30 years, and her wealth grows at 7 percent a year compounded. At the time of her death, her wealth will have grown to $200 million. If the advisors were correct that the effective tax rate would be 50 percent, her estate would owe $100 million in estate tax, of which the $25 million of insurance proceeds will provide only one quarter of the amount needed to pay the estate tax. Of course, she could acquire additional life insurance as her wealth grows. However, as she ages, the insurance will be more costly, the ability to avoid gift tax to prevent having the proceeds themselves being subject to estate tax will become more difficult (and likely impossible as a practical matter) and her health may decline making the premiums on a new policy cost prohibitive.

Role of Insurance

Does that mean that it's unwise to consider acquiring life insurance as part of a well-balanced estate tax plan?[21] No. But it does mean that a balanced plan must take into account several additional factors. Foremost, perhaps, is that the property owner should consider taking steps to stabilize or reduce the tax value of her estate. Several arrangements, including grantor retained annuity trusts (GRATs), installment sales to grantor trusts, qualified personal residence trusts, family partnerships and the use, year-in and year-out, of the gift tax annual exclusion, should be considered.[22] Such steps, over time, will reduce the growth in wealth, if not the level of wealth. And the key benefit of such action is that the lower the value of wealth, the smaller the estate tax.

Many estate-planning arrangements won't achieve their goals if death occurs early. For example, all or a portion of a GRAT will be included in the estate of the property owner if she dies while the trust is making annuity payments to her.[23] Life insurance can be used to hedge against an early death: Although the GRAT likely may have failed to achieve its goal of removing property from the property owner's gross estate, the insurance will provide, in effect, an economic windfall for the property owner's family, providing liquidity to pay estate taxes on the property in the GRAT and, perhaps, much more.

Type of Policy

This leads to the question of what type of policy should be purchased to fund estate tax. Due to the ever increasing cost of term (or pure) life insurance, which is an essential component even of cash value policies, the possibility of estate tax repeal and the prospect of the insured living much longer than the insurance company forecasts (making any policy less efficient), clients should consider acquiring a policy that will not only return the premiums paid, even if the policy is cancelled well before death, but also provide a profit over time. Several life insurance carriers offer such policies.

---

21. There are many reasons to acquire life insurance other than to fund estate tax that may arise on death. The most common reason is to replace lost earnings when a breadwinner dies and her salary or wages are lost. Of course, that may also occur when the breadwinner retires. In fact, many insureds who have acquired policies to replace lost earnings at death cancel their life insurance policies soon after retirement. *See* CNN Money, "How Long a Term for Term Life Insurance?" http://money.cnn.com/magazines/moneymag/money101/lesson20/index.htm.

22. The Obama Administration has proposed several changes to the federal wealth transfer tax system that would reduce the wealth transfer tax efficiency of arrangements commonly used to reduce estate and similar taxes. *See generally* Jonathan G. Blattmachr, Michael L. Graham and Douglas J. Blattmachr, "A Look at the Obama Estate Tax Proposals: What They Mean for Planners and Clients," *Alaska Trust Company Newsletter* (March 2012), www .alaskatrust.com/assets/files/newsletters/Newsletter-2012-03.pdf.

23. Treas. Regs. Section 20.2036-1(b).

Certain policies are structured so the cash value growth over time is as important a component as the initial death benefit. This is accomplished by purchasing a lower initial death benefit (see Policy A in "Consider the Alternatives," below) than could otherwise be acquired for the same premium. The result of this lower initial death benefit is that it often provides a small profit (that is, cash surrender value above premiums paid) within the first five years and even higher returns over longer periods of time.[24] Although the initial death benefit of such policies is often considerably lower than if the policy provided a maximum death benefit (see Policy B in "Consider the Alternatives," this page), the cash value of these high death benefit policies erodes over time. And, as indicated, in many cases, policies are cancelled before death, meaning the amounts paid for the additional death benefit have been wasted.

Consider the Alternatives

If the cash value of high death benefit policies erodes over time as compared with other policies with lower initial death benefits*

Age	Year	Policy A		Policy B		Policy C	
		Current Cash Surrender Value	Minimum Death Benefit	Current Cash Surrender Value	Maximum Death Benefit	Current Cash Surrender Value	Maximum Guaranteed Death Benefit
51	1	4,540,525	14,615,640	4,249,500	22,610,000	3,782,753	25,609,897
55	5	5,667,847	15,541,063	5,344,487	22,610,000	4,299,462	25,609,897
60	10	7,393,223	16,724,133	6,971,579	22,610,000	4,958,611	25,609,897
80	30	17,570,340	23,713,634	14,534,208	22,610,000	447,378	25,609,897
85	35	20,971,721	26,063,864	16,492,859	22,610,000	—	25,609,897
90	40	24,333,718	28,432,247	17,926,001	22,610,000	—	25,609,897
95	45	27,771,092	31,133,338	18,914,483	22,610,000	—	25,609,897
100	50	31,666,640	34,491,304	19,725,975	22,610,000	—	25,609,897

*Assume a $5 million single premium universal life policy for a male age 50 standard risk.

Johnathan G. Blattmachr

To attempt to achieve higher (or adequate) cash value growth, some choose so-called "variable" policies, under which the policy owner may decide to invest the cash value component in the market (essentially, through a selection of mutual funds). However, whenever one chooses to invest in the market, there's a risk of performance. That is, the returns may be lower than what's needed to maintain the policy and lower than what the insurance company would credit to the cash value account in a non-variable policy. If the variable product doesn't produce adequate growth, additional premiums will have to be paid to maintain the desired death

---

24. That's based upon current earnings crediting rates and current charges for the term insurance provided under the policy. Each policy provides a minimum earnings crediting rate (against which the insurance company charges expenses and cost of insurance charges (COI)) and a maximum COI charge.

benefit, the level of death benefit will have to be reduced or the policy will most likely be cancelled.

Hence, a high cash value policy should be considered.[25] Nevertheless, in all events, additional estate tax planning should be implemented. In some cases, the lifetime estate-planning steps will be so successful that the need for life insurance to fund estate taxes will be minimized and, in some circumstances, eliminated.

Policy Comparisons

"Consider the Alternatives" illustrates various types of cash value products and the ways they can be funded. The three polices are all traditional cash value universal life funded with a single $5 million premium. Policy B has the maximum initial death benefit that's effectively maintained throughout the life of the insured. Policy A has a minimum initial death benefit at inception. By the time the insured reaches age 80, Policy A results in more death benefit than Policy B through any age thereafter. In addition, Policy A consistently has more cash surrender value than Policy B. Hence, there appears to be a mismatch with respect to Policy B: The death benefit is greater than Policy A when the insured is less likely to die and lower than Policy A when the insured is more likely to die. Policy C has a guaranteed death benefit (in which the death benefit is constant regardless of when the insured dies).

Under Policy C, there's a high death benefit, which is maintained throughout the insured's lifetime, but cash value is rapidly eroded and disappears shortly after the insured turns 80. That means there's limited flexibility if it's determined that the resources dedicated to acquire and maintain the policy would be better applied elsewhere (such as when a decision is made that the insured will live a very long time or the estate tax is repealed or other means have been or could be taken to reduce the size of the taxable estate). Also, Policy A (the low initial death benefit) not only will produce a higher death benefit by age 80 than Policy B (the maximum initial death benefit) as well as Policy C (the maximum initial guaranteed death benefit) by age 85, but also, it will have more cash surrender value in all instances.

Weighing the Options

Life insurance often is used as a tool to fund estate taxes that will be due when the property owner dies. Term insurance, initially, will be much less expensive than a cash value policy. However, term policies end typically when the insured turns 80 and, as a result, such policies provide no help in funding estate tax if the insured

---

25. Note that the IRC requires a minimum amount of death benefit for each dollar of premium paid based upon the age (or deemed age on account of health profile) and gender of the insured for the contract to constitute a life insurance policy under the IRC. The amount of death benefit necessary to constitute a life insurance policy decreases with age (or deemed age). See IRC Section 7702(a).

lives beyond that age. In addition, the cost of annual term premiums becomes very high as the insured reaches advanced ages. Approximately 85 percent of term policies are cancelled before the insured dies.[26]

Cash value policies may last until the insured dies, no matter how old she may then be. Cash value policies are structured in many ways. The most efficient cash value policy, if there's a significant chance that the insured will live to or beyond her actuarial life expectancy, is one that provides the minimum initial death benefit, but maximum cash value.[27] Although the initial death benefit obviously will be lower with such a maximum cash value policy, it ultimately will provide a greater death benefit at older ages and almost always will provide greater cash value if the policy is cancelled before death. Regardless of what type of insurance is acquired to fund estate taxes, additional planning steps to retard or reduce the value of what will be included in the insured gross estate for federal estate tax purpose are an essential ingredient of any sensible estate tax plan.

Source URL: http://wealthmanagement.com/insurance/buying-life-insurance-fund-estate-taxes

---

26. Letter dated Feb. 19, 2004 from Timothy C. Pfeifer, F.S.A., Milliman USA to Coventry First. It should be noted that often a new term policy is acquired when a currently owned term policy is cancelled or lapses.

27. As indicated above, for a contract to constitute a life insurance policy, it must provide for a minimum death benefit. See IRC Section 7702(a).

The Miracle (and Disaster) of Compound Interest—Universal Life Insurance Edition

Christopher H. Hause, FSA, MAAA, CLU®

Introductory Comments by Gary Flotron

Christopher H. Hause, FSA, MAAA, CLU®, is a pure actuarial genius! He is the codeveloper and coinventor (along with Richard M. Weber, M.B.A., CLU®, AEP® (Distinguished)) of a software system originally called the Dynamic Illustration System (DIS). This system uses actuarially certified policy benchmark standards for cost of insurance (mortality rates) and policy expenses combined with Monte Carlo simulation with regard to non-guaranteed policy earnings to arrive at a statistical probability that a policy-planned funding premium will successfully sustain a policy to a desired duration such as life expectancy or policy maturity. In other words, this system accounts for the volatility of non-guaranteed policy earnings that a constant assumption policy illustration is thoroughly incapable of accomplishing. This policy evaluation system is described in Chapter 5 of this book.

Chris is the President and founder of Hause Actuarial Solutions, Inc. based in Overland Park, Kansas. This firm, formed in 2001, is a full-service actuarial consulting firm that is ranked by A.M. Best as a Top 20 Ranked Life Actuarial Firm in the United States. Chris is very active both nationally and locally with the Society of Actuaries and has served as Chair of many prominent committees, as well as being Past President of the Kansas City Actuarial Club.

In his contributed article, "The Miracle (and Disaster) of Compound Interest—Universal Life Edition," Chris tells the saga and experiences of Mr. Paul C. Holder, a 45-year-old who purchases a universal life insurance policy in 1985. Naturally and unfortunately, the agent who sold the policy, Mr. Rich N. Sales (don't you love Chris's humor with the names?), suggested a planned funding premium for the policy based on a constant assumption policy illustration and a 10 percent constant rate of return. Of course, as we follow the history of this policy sold in 1985, interest rates declined. Mr. Holder had to increase his planned funding premiums along the way a couple of times and each time Mr. Holder was shocked and amazed at the increase.

All of this goes back to the "very delicate relationship" mentioned first in Chapter 2 of this book between rates of return and the net amount at risk. Chris very beautifully describes this phenomenon in his "Actuarial Asides" and in more detail in his short explanation appendix to his article as being "on the curve." Additionally,

Chris elegantly, understandably, and simply explains the concept of "COI Leveraging" in a second short appendix to his article. All of this reverts back to the theme of his article, "The Miracle (and Disaster) of Compound Interest." For it is compound interest that is at the core of this situation.

Chris notes at the end of paragraph one of his article "that neither the agent nor the policyholder fully appreciates the magnitude of the premium sufficiency risk assumed by the policyholder in universal life products." He further notes in a latter paragraph "[w]hat many policyholders and agents failed to appreciate was the magnitude of the effect of declining interest rates on a Universal Life policy, even a well-managed one." This, of course, reflects part of the theme of this book being "the Risk Transfer Paradigm Shift that Precipitated a Policy Crisis," which was discussed in Chapters 1, 2, and 3.

Another interesting issue Chris addresses before the end of his article is given Mr. Holder's experience with his Universal Life policy, in hindsight would he have purchased another type of life insurance policy, and what type of experience and results would have occurred? Read the contributed article for the answer to these questions.

While the saga of Mr. Holder is a sad one, it is an enlightening one and there are many lessons to be learned from this wonderfully told but horrific tale and very well-written, informative article!

About Christopher H. Hause

Chris is President of Hause Actuarial Solutions in Overland Park, Kansas. Hause Actuarial Solutions specializes in financial reporting and analysis, product management, policy development, and Credit Insurance. Chris recently assisted in performing nationwide studies on credit morbidity and credit mortality primarily for the purpose of establishing consistent and appropriate statutory reserving standards for credit disability and life insurance.

Prior to forming Hause Actuarial Solutions, Chris was Managing Partner of William M. Buchanan & Associates and has worked in the insurance industry for more than 30 years.

Chris's past work experience includes exposure to a broad range of products and distribution systems. Prior to being the Chief Actuary at IAC, Chris worked at The Pyramid Life Insurance Company in Mission, Kansas; Allianz Life (formerly North American Life and Casualty); and ITT Life Insurance Company in Minneapolis.

Chris received his Bachelor's degree in Mathematics from the University of Wyoming in 1975. He is a Fellow of the Society of Actuaries, a Member of the American Academy of Actuaries, and a Chartered Life Underwriter.

Chris is a member of several special interest sections of the Society of Actuaries and is the former Chair of the Non-Traditional Marketing Section Council, as well as the Smaller Insurance Company Section, and is the current Chair of the Credit Insurance Experience Committee. He is also a past president of the Kansas City Actuaries Club.

Chris has been a frequent speaker on the topics of Bank Distribution of Insurance, Credit insurance, and Debt Cancellation, and has written several articles and white papers regarding risk and funding considerations of flexible premium insurance products.

The Miracle (and Disaster) of Compound Interest—Universal Life Insurance Edition
Christopher H. Hause, FSA, MAAA, CLU®

Please forgive the provocative title, as we actuaries are not generally given over to hyperbole. However, as pointed out several times in this timely book by Gary Flotron, the miracle of compound interest plays a crucial role in the risk of premium sufficiency that has been transferred from the insurance company to the policyholder. The miracle of compound interest is in the power of compounding; the potential disaster of compound interest is in the poorly understood risks arising from changing interest rates. We believe that neither the insurance agent nor the policyholder fully appreciates the magnitude of the premium sufficiency risk assumed by the policyholder in universal life products.

Prior to the introduction of Universal Life, a premium was a premium. The premium did not change, or at least did not increase. Even though policyholders were generally aware that the dividends in a participating whole life were not guaranteed and could be subject to fluctuations, there was an assurance that the policy would still stay in force if required premiums were paid when due.

Perhaps it was an oversight to continue to call these suggested deposits into Universal Life policies "premiums" because the fact is that these so-called "premiums," even when paid as due, could not have reasonably been expected to continue a policy in force. Interest rates were not likely to stay at the level of 10% (a common credited interest rate in the mid-1980's) forever. What many policyholders and agents failed to appreciate was the magnitude of the effect of declining interest rates on a Universal Life policy, even a well-managed one.

With the advantage of 20/20 hindsight, we will consider an example of a well-managed Universal Life policy, sold in 1985, as it would have unfolded over the following years.

To do this, we have constructed a middling Universal Life policy. The specifications are listed as an appendix, to save all but the curious actuaries in the crowd the trouble of skipping over them in the body of this article.

However, we feel compelled to share with you the annual credited interest rates we used, which are listed below. These interest rates were taken from a report by the TOLI Center and reflect average interest rates credited on fixed Universal Life policies from 1985–2008.

Year	Credited Rate	Year	Credited Rate	Year	Credited Rate
1985	10.00%	1993	7.75%	2001	6.00%
1986	10.00%	1994	7.50%	2002	6.00%
1987	10.00%	1995	7.25%	2003	5.50%
1988	9.50%	1996	7.00%	2004	5.00%
1989	9.00%	1997	6.50%	2005	5.00%
1990	8.50%	1998	6.25%	2006	4.75%
1991	8.25%	1999	6.00%	2007	4.75%
1992	8.00%	2000	6.00%	2008	4.50%

In our story, we follow a gentleman nonsmoker (a Mr. Paul C. Holder), who, having turned 45 and feeling the need for $100,000 of additional life insurance, contacted his local agent (Mr. Rich N. Sales) and asked what kind of life insurance he should buy. Knowing that his client's insurance need was a long-term one, he recommended a permanent plan, and since the client had a reasonable risk profile, recommended a Universal Life policy. The agent used his fancy new IBM Personal Computer XT and printed out on his dot matrix printer (look it up, millennials) an illustration that neatly matured the policy for exactly $100,000 at the maturity age of 95.

The annual "premium" was a very affordable at $863.59 per year, which was 45% lower than the $1,520.00 premium the local mutual company's agent had proposed for a whole life plan.

Things went along swimmingly for a few years, with Mr. Holder receiving his Annual Reports showing the insurance company continuing to credit 10% to his policy account value, and his Account Value growing just like it showed on the illustration.

However, like most good things, the days of 10% interest came to an end. Pretty soon, Mr. Holder noticed that the credited interest rates were not staying at 10% and he asked Mr. Sales about that. To which Mr. Sales replied that fluctuations in interest rates were to be expected, and if interest rates stay "low" that they should review the policy in a few years to see what should be done.

So, in about 1992, when the credited interest rate hit 8%, the policy's Account Value—instead of the projected $5,452.90, which was on his original illustration (of course he kept it handy)—Mr. Holder only had an Account Value of $5,235.17. While he was not all that concerned about the $217.73 shortage in Account Value, he was justifiably concerned that the policy would not mature for $100,000 if this continued.

So, he asked Mr. Sales to run a new illustration, based on his current Account Value and the current 8% credited interest rate, to see what the maturity value of the contract would be now that the credited interest rate had slipped. The answer surprised them both, because not only was there no maturity value at all, but the policy was now projected to lapse at age 78, in the year 2018!

But, he still really wanted to restore his plan to mature his policy, and so he asked Mr. Sales to run a new illustration, based on his current Account Value and the current 8% credited interest rate, to see what the new "premium" was that would mature his policy—and the answer was once again surprising. It was $1,224.78!

Well, this could not be . . . that is a 42% increase! All because interest rates went down from 10% to 8%? After checking the figures with the insurance company and verifying that—yes—nothing else had changed with the policy, he decided to retain the policy and immediately increased his "premium." All was well with the world, and his policy was back on track.

[Actuarial Aside] through mathematical wizardry, we were able to split this "premium" increase into two distinct factors. The first part was easy to figure out by calculating the 8% "premium" from issue. That turned out to be $1,068.88—which is quite a jump from the $863.59—but still far short of $1,224.78. The reason the required funding level jumped another $155.90 is that, in order to be "on the curve" (see explanation below) at an 8% interest rate, an account value of $6,895.32 was required. This difference between his actual Account Value and the 8% target Account Value is $1,660.15—which now must be made up over the remaining "premium" payments.

Although somewhat disgruntled, Mr. Holder paid the new "premium" for another several years until 1999, when the Annual Report announced that the new credited interest rate was declared at 6%. Knowing that his original and revised illustrations were now useless, he went straight to Mr. Sales (who was now considering retirement, but very willing to help) and asked what he needed to do to get his policy back to where it would achieve his original aim of maturing for $100,000. This time, though, he was ready for a shock. What came was a "premium" of $1,896.92, another 55% increase; and much to his dismay this was even higher than what he thought was a preposterous amount back in 1985 (remember $1,520.00?)!

[Actuarial Aside] Same basic story, but now there are even fewer years to try to make up the difference of not being "on the curve."

Undeterred, Mr. Holder increased his "premium" to the $1,896.92 until 2008, when he was informed that the credited interest rate had now hit rock bottom and was at the 4.5% minimum guaranteed in the policy. Figuring this was all the bad news he could possibly get, he called Mr. Sales's office and was informed that Mr. Sales had retired to Florida and the agency no longer represented that company. And, that the company had gone out of the Universal Life business. And, they had a different company handling the policy administration. Fortunately, Mr. Sales's former secretary had the number for policyholder service at that company—which matched the number on Mr. Holder's Annual Report. So, he gave it a try.

He got hold of a very nice and knowledgeable policyholder service representative, who understood his situation and was "more than happy" to run an inforce illustration and figure out the new "premium" required to fulfill his original intent to mature the policy at age 95. The new "premium" was $2,769.21, which was 320% of his original "premium." Ouch!

The reason I go through all of this, dear reader, is this is a story of a person who paid his "premiums" as they came due, managed his policy reasonably effectively by most measures, had reasonably good information and support, and is now justifiably disappointed by the original "promises" made when he bought the policy.

I dare to say two things about this story. One is though he realized that the policy might need him to pay higher "premiums" if interest rates were to go down, he had very little idea of the magnitude of the increase needed for a relatively small (and easily foreseen) decrease in credited interest rates.

The other thing that might be said is that if this story had been told at the beginning of the process, in 1985, he probably would have paid higher "premiums" or chosen a different type of policy. To that end, we went back to our original 1985 illustration to see how his Universal Life policy would have performed had it been funded at the Participating Whole Life premium level of $1,520.00, and using the same historical credited interest rate pattern. Not only does the policy mature, the cash value accumulation would have pushed the death benefit over $100,000 at attained age 81, and the policy would currently be projected to endow for $188,000 at age 95.

Another fun fact is that the increasing pattern of premiums actually paid to age 95 in this story totals $106,459.51 and matures the policy for $100,000 at age 95. Had Mr. Holder funded the policy at $1,520.00 for fifty years, the total of the premiums paid would be $76,000.00. And that reveals the magic of compound interest (and the "COI leveraging" effect in a Universal Life policy).

If there is good news, Mr. Holder has now enjoyed ten years of interest credits—at 4.5%—that are better than what he could get on comparable newly issued policies, and his Annual Reports are showing he is finally on track (for good) since the insurance company cannot lower his credited interest rate any more.

And then he got a letter saying his cost of insurance rates are increasing. . .

Explanation of "On the Curve"

When we use this term in the article, we are considering the curve toward ultimate maturity of a level-funded Universal Life plan. As explained in the Actuarial Aside, part of the additional required funding from the point of an interest rate decrease forward is the deficiency between being "on the curve" at the previous interest rate and "on the curve" at the new interest rate.

Consider the chart below:

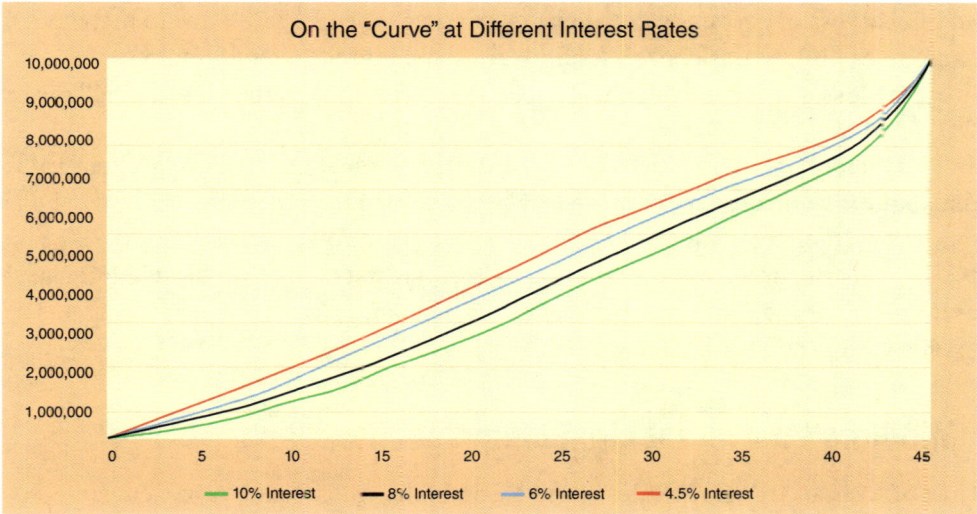

While there does not visually appear to be much difference between these lines, appearances can be deceiving. At policy year 30, being "on the curve" at 10% requires an Account Value of only $42,760. At 4.5%, it requires $56,781. Catching up that $14,021 deficiency over the remaining 20 policy years adds significantly to the required funding difference.

Explanation of "COI Leveraging"

When we used the term "COI leveraging" in this article, we are considering the degradation of policy value caused by underperformance of the investments supporting the account value, coupled with the increase in net amount at risk, which increases the Cost of Insurance charge.

Although Variable Universal Life is not the topic of this article, it is a convenient vehicle to demonstrate the effect of COI Leveraging. And to be honest, it was in studying the volatility of returns in a VUL environment where we first noticed the potentially dramatic effect this can have on policy values.

Consider a VUL policy issued at age 45 that is "on the curve" at attained age 80 at an 8% assumed rate of return. The account value is $57,429.84 at that point. Now, let us assume that the market suffers a 20% downward "correction" in the first policy month after the policyholder attains age 80. While the account value decreases by 20% (to $45,943.87), the net amount at risk increases by about 27%—from $42,570.16 to $54,056.13. The annual cost of insurance in our middling policy is 0.08211, so (assuming there is not an immediate offsetting gain to the "correction") instead of an annual COI charge of $3,405.61, the charge is now $4,438.55.

So, on top of the market loss to the account value of $11,485.97, there is an additional loss of account value in the ensuing year of $1,032.94 due to higher COI charges. So, if we consider this additional charge into the overall return on the contract, the loss of account value is 21.8%—not 20%—due to the "leveraging" of the COI charges.

It is important to note that the opposite is true—that increases in account value due to positive investment performance will leverage the account value upward due to lower COI charges assessed against the policy's account value.

NOTE: It is important to note that, for ease of understanding, we have ignored several aspects of the inner calculations of the account value in this explanation. The explanation is no less valid despite this omission.

"Middling" Universal Life Policy Specifications

Cost of Insurance Annual Rates: 1980 Basic Male, Nonsmoker, Age Nearest Birthday
Monthly Cost of Insurance Rates: Calculated Using
$ROUND(1000*(1-(1-AnnualRate)^{(1/12)}),5)$
Monthly per Policy Expense Charge: $5.00, Current = Guaranteed
Percent of Premium Load: 5%
Guaranteed Credited Interest Rate: 4.5%
Maturity Age: 95
Death Benefit Option: Level Death Benefit
Premium Frequency: Annually on the Policy Anniversary
Corridor Factors: DEFRA

TOLI Trustee Tread Tactfully

Donald O. Jansen, J.D., LL.M., AEP® (Distinguished)

Introductory Comments by Gary Flotron

Donald O. Jansen, J.D., LL.M., AEP® (Distinguished), is a steadfast, extremely admirable estate planning attorney who is one of the pillars of the profession. An estate planner's estate planner, Don is particularly knowledgeable with regard to the irrevocable life insurance trust (ILIT) and uses of life insurance in sophisticated estate planning. In 2017, he co-authored (along with Lawrence Brody) an excellent and authoritative book titled *Leveraging Life Insurance Premium Payments: Using Split-Dollar and Related Party Premium Financing Techniques* that was published by the American Bar Association Section on Real Property, Trust, and Estate Law. This book is destined to become the standard on the topic.

An unbelievably gracious and accomplished man, Don epitomizes the virtues of trustworthiness, thoughtfulness, reliability, thoroughness, and expertise in his craft. In many ways he is the perfect Boy Scout, and he is, indeed, an Eagle Scout. In fact, in 2014 he was the recipient of the Outstanding Eagle Scout Award presented by the National Association of Eagle Scouts. The author had the honor and privilege of nominating Mr. Jansen for the National Association of Estate Planners & Councils (NAEPC) Estate Planning Hall of Fame® in which he was inducted in 2017 and simultaneously awarded the Accredited Estate Planner® Distinguished (AEP® (Distinguished)) designation.

Don's original contributed article provides a much-needed dimension to this book; that is, Mr. Jansen provides the perspective of a learned estate planning attorney who has worked with many clients that need and require life insurance as part of their estate plan. Quite frequently, this life insurance needs to be owned by an irrevocable life insurance trust (ILIT), and properly selected, acquired, monitored, and managed by the trustee of this trust created by the insured clients of Don. The trustee of these trusts—that often before the death of the insured(s) only contain the life insurance policy(ies)—has an awesome responsibility that has become more acute because of two major developments: the advent of universal and variable life policies, and the enactment in 1994 of the Uniform Prudent Investor Act (UPIA).

These changes have challenged and complicated the duties of managing trust-owned life insurance (TOLI) for the trustee, who quite frequently is not a professional trustee and serves the post as an accommodation to the trust settlor. Hence, the title for Don's contributed article, "TOLI Trustee Tread Tactfully," is quite fitting and appropriate. (Besides, who cannot love the alliteration in the title?)

This article gives an estate planning attorney's perspective to the life insurance risk shifting brought about by the introduction of non-guaranteed flexible premium policies. It further discusses the evolution of life insurance products and the nature (and risks) of each product type. More importantly, the article emphasizes the requirements of the UPIA with respect to the trustee duties to prudently select, acquire, monitor, and risk manage the life insurance contained within the ILIT. Mr. Jansen gives some very good rules of thumb in the execution of these trustee duties with respect to life insurance.

But the biggest surprise and delight to this author about Don's article were the unexpected compliments contained in his article for this book. Among these very gracious and kind comments were that the book "performs a much needed service for the estate and trust planning community in highlighting the monitoring responsibilities for ILITs and in setting out guidelines to do so." For this the author is very humbled and grateful.

So, tread thoughtfully and thoroughly as you read "TOLI Trustee Tread Tactfully."

About Donald O. Jansen

Donald O. Jansen is Assistant General Counsel, University of Texas System Office of General Counsel. He is a retired senior partner of Fulbright & Jaworski L.L.P. (now Norton Rose Fulbright). He is a Fellow of the American College of Trust and Estate Counsel and a Fellow of the American College of Tax Counsel. Mr. Jansen is a past Chairman of the Committee of Significant Current Literature and Vice-Chair of the Insurance Committee, Probate and Trust Division, Real Property, Probate, and Trust Law Section of the American Bar Association. Mr. Jansen is a specialist in Estate Planning and Probate Law certified by the Texas Board  of Legal Specialization and is the past Probate Editor of the Newsletter of the Real Estate, Probate, and Trust Law Section of the State Bar of Texas. He has been designated by his peers as a Texas Super Lawyer in estate planning in 2003, 2004, and 2005. He is a 2014 recipient of the Outstanding Eagle Scout Award presented by the National Association of Eagle Scouts. He is a past member of the Federal Bar Association National Council and a past president of the Southern District of Texas Chapter. Don was inducted into the Estate Planning Hall of Fame® in 2017 by the National Association of Estate Planners & Councils (NAEPC). He is an Accredited Estate Planner (AEP® (Distinguished)). Mr. Jansen is a member of the Advisory Committee, Heckerling Institute on Estate Planning, University of Miami School of Law.

TOLI Trustee Tread Tactfully
Donald O. Jansen, J.D., LL.M., AEP® (Distinguished)

I was very pleased and honored when Gary Flotron asked me to prepare a contributing article for his new book "Understanding Life Insurance and Rethinking Policy Management and Evaluation: Explaining the Unexplainable." Gary's book is most timely. We both lived through the times that led to life insurance risk shifting and the current crisis for trustees concerning trust owned life insurance (TOLI). Gary's involvement is on the life insurance policy side and my involvement is as an attorney in estate planning.

When your author began his legal practice many years ago, irrevocable life insurance trusts (ILITs) were important items in the estate planner's tool kit, as they still are today. They were the source of funds free from the insured's and the beneficiary's creditors and the taxman which could provide liquidity to pay death taxes and other outstanding obligations and, if desired, provide for the support of future family generations. Because of the current high exemptions from estate/gift taxes, the vast majority of families do not have to worry about estate/gift taxes, at least at the Federal level. But the non-tax reasons for ILITs of providing cash at the death of the insured remain. In fact, ILITs (and other trusts) now can be used for the family purposes as originally intended by estate planning without undue influence of transfer taxes.

The Days of Unmonitored ILIT Policies

In the days before the 1980s, we thought we lived in simpler times with regard to creation and management of ILITs. Most of our clients created an ILIT which was dry of assets except for a single policy on the life of the grantor. These were essentially passive trusts designed just to hold the policy until the death of the insured. At that time, the action would begin when the trust collected the death proceeds. Normally, a family member of the insured served as "nominal" trustee (sometimes the insured's bank would serve as trustee as an accommodation charging a minimal fee). The trust policy was placed in a drawer without much further thought until it was dusted off when the insured died.

The ILIT trustee's duties were perceived to be minimal before the insured died—see that the premiums were paid and Crummey notice letters delivered. In fact, the grantor fought against any significant trustee fees or management expenses which the grantor would have to contribute to the trust for payment. If a professional trustee was not already serving as the accommodation trustee, many times a professional replaced the family member as trustee at the death of the insured if the trust was to continue for many more years. After all, when the cash was received, it was perceived that this was the time that investment and management experience was needed.

Before 1980, the only cash value policy was the whole life policy. This policy did (and still does) offer many guarantees with the insurance carrier (and not the trustee) bearing most of the risk. The premium and death benefit are guaranteed for the life of the insured—the latter if the fixed premium is paid. A minimum cash value is guaranteed. Consequently, the insurance carrier assumed the risk of changes in the cost of insurance (mortality charges), investment return supporting the guaranteed cash value, policy expenses and policy lapse rates. Under the "Prudent Man Rule" of the Restatement (Second) of Trusts, section 228 (1959) most of the investment risk responsibilities of the trustee were assumed by the insurance carrier. But even in those halcyon days of whole life policies, ILIT trustees commonly ignored other Prudent Man Rule obligations—selection and continued monitoring of the carrier as to solvency, expenses, cost of insurance. Although it was common to check out the carrier when the policy was issued choosing one with high ratings from A.M. Best, Fitch, Moody's and S&P, trustees often failed to continue to monitor ratings for the insurance carrier after the policy was purchased.

The danger to the trustee in holding an unmonitored policy in an ILIT increased significantly because of two events—the advent of universal and variable life policies and the enactment by most states of the Uniform Prudent Investor Act to replace the Prudent Man Rule.

Advent of Universal and Variable Life Policies

The first universal life policies were issued in 1979 by E.F. Hutton & Co. Today the vast majority of issued policies with cash value are universal life and variable life policies.

The key to these policies is that they are cheaper than whole life and are more flexible but in exchange there are far less guarantees. Much of the risk is shifted to the policyholder.

A universal life policy has a guaranteed death benefit as long as there is sufficient cash value to support the premium payment. The cash value is not guaranteed although the carrier may guarantee a minimum interest credit to the cash value. Except for the first year, premiums are not fixed—they can be increased, decreased or skipped. The premiums and current interest credited by the carrier are added to the cash value and the cost of insurance (COI) and expenses (up to a contract maximum) are subtracted. None of this is guaranteed and the policy will lapse when the cash value can no longer cover the current COI and expenses. Constant monitoring is required to make sure current premiums plus income are adequate to sustain the policy.

A variable universal life policy is a universal life policy but the cash value is invested in investment funds chosen by the trustee which funds are made available by the carrier. There is no guaranteed minimum interest credited by the carrier to cash value. Like any mutual fund investment, the trustee will have to monitor to make sure the funds are adequate to sustain the policy.

An indexed universal life policy falls between traditional universal life and variable universal life since it has some market investment exposure. The cash value will rise and fall based upon an established market index (e.g. S&P 500). There is a floor and a ceiling to the losses and gains are shared at various participation rates with the carrier up to the ceiling. There is no guaranteed minimum interest paid by the carriers to the cash value.

Secondary guarantee (also known as no lapse guarantee) policies are still universal life policies but they have some of the guarantees found in whole life policies. A level premium and a death benefit are guaranteed if the annual premium is timely paid. The cash value is small or non-existent. If the premiums are timely paid (some policies have a grace period for payment), the carrier assumes risk of COI, expenses and investment return. If the premiums are not timely paid, the guarantees are lost. The trustee must be very diligent in making sure the premium is timely paid.

To meet the competition, there are some variations of whole life policies that are available which the trustee would need to evaluate—variable whole life policies and current assumption whole life policies.

With the advent of the above policies, the ILIT trustee can no longer leave the policy unmonitored. It is no longer just a decision which carrier to select and the subsequent monitoring of the carrier, but now the selection of the type of policy and the monitoring of the performance of that policy.

Enactment of UPIA

In 1994 the National Conference of Commissioners of Uniform State Laws proposed the Uniform Prudent Investor Act (UPIA). It has been adopted by 43 states. This was a revolution in trustee management of trust investments. The Prudent Man Rule was replaced by the Modern Portfolio Theory. UPIA required diversification, comparison of risk taken to performance, reasonable and minimized fees and costs, balancing income production with maintenance of principal and delegation of investment management responsibilities when needed. UPIA Sections 2, 3, 7 and 9.

Thus under UPIA, particularly for universal life policies, the trustee must exercise care in selecting a carrier (the author's rule of thumb is a carrier should be in the top 20 of the combined ratings), diversify the number of carriers to hedge against risk of insolvency (author's rule of thumb is that multiple carriers be considered if there is over $3 million of coverage), diversify the types of policies (e.g., guaranteed whole life, universal life, variable life, etc.) unless diversity comes from combining the ILIT investments with all other assets of the grantor, monitor policy for underperformance which might require added premiums or alternative investments and the list goes on. If the trustee does not have experience in one or more of these areas, the trustee has an obligation to delegate these duties to experts and to continue to monitor the performance of the experts. In In Re Stuart Cochran Irrevocable Trust v. KeyBank, 901 N.E.2d 1128 (Ind. Ct. App. 2009), the trustee barely did adequate due diligence under UPIA. This case shows what due diligence should be performed by the trustee.

As discussed by Gary Flotron and many others in this field, it is essential to have a written Life Insurance Management Statement setting the grantor's goals, assigning duties to various persons, establishing risk tolerance, specifying diversity and setting policy management guidelines.

How do the trustee and the delegated experts exercise reasonable care? It must be done by comparing the existing policies with some sort of ILIT benchmark. That is the discussion in chapter 5 of Gary Flotron's "Understanding Life Insurance and Rethinking Policy Management and Evaluation: Explaining the Unexplainable." Also see the discussion in Ballsun, Collins & Jurkat, "Evidencing Care, Skill and Caution in the Management of ILITs," part 3 of 4, 32 ACTEC Journal, pp. 145–158 (2006).

Conclusion

Even before 1980, there were management responsibilities for the ILIT trustee but, with the advent of universal life policies and the UPIA, ILIT trustees, whether family members or professionals, have serious obligations. The grantor must understand that there is no easy way to manage an ILIT on the cheap. The costs of monitoring ILIT performance must be incurred not only for the protection of the trustee but for the achievement of the grantor's plan in establishing the ILIT in the first place.

"Understanding Life Insurance and Rethinking Policy Management and Evaluation" performs a much needed service for the estate planning and trust community in highlighting the monitoring responsibilities for ILITs and in setting out guidelines to do so.

Disclosures

This article is not intended to be tax advice. A taxpayer should seek advice based on the taxpayer's particular circumstances from an independent tax advisor.

The views expressed in this outline are those of the author and do not necessarily reflect the position of The University of Texas System.

Adopting A Two-Dimensional Risk Tolerance Assessment Process

The Sorry State Of Risk Tolerance Questionnaires For Financial Advisors

Michael E. Kitces, M.S.F.S., M.TAX, CFP®, CLU®, ChFC®, RHU®, REBC®, CASL®

Introductory Comments by Gary Flotron

Michael E. Kitces, M.S.F.S., M.TAX, CFP®, CLU®, ChFC®, RHU®, REBC®, CASL®, is an amazing, erudite gentleman who at the tender age of 42 is a super-star in the financial planning world. Michael describes himself as "a lifelong learner with a passion for sharing what I've learned with others."

Mr. Kitces started out as a financial adviser the first business day after college as a life insurance agent. He quickly discovered financial planning and that there was a broad range of financial planning topics to learn. He quickly dove into the educational process full steam, ultimately racking up two Master's degrees (one in Financial Services and one in Taxation), along with the Certified Financial Planner/ (CFP®) mark and a slew of other designations as well. Thus, he spent the decade of his 20s working as a full-time financial planner and part-time student on the side, learning as much as he could and sharing those ideas, concepts, and solutions with his clients. It is this background of professional experience and his passion for learning his craft that has resulted in Michael becoming one of the most knowl-edgeable, sought after consultants, educators, writers, and speakers in the financial planning profession. If there is anyone who is the paragon of virtues for the finan-cial planning profession it is Michael Kitces.

Chapter 3 of the book discusses the risks of life insurance policies, but vaguely, at the end of the chapter, mentions risk tolerance as a selection criterion for a product type or a portfolio of product types. Similarly, Chapter 4 mentions that life insurance policy management statements need to specify risk tolerance pursuant to the objec-tives of the insured, policy owner, or trust grantor, and that risk tolerance plays a very important part with duration planning for universal life policies. The very essence of actuarial evaluation of life insurance policies, discussed in Chapter 5, using actuarially certified policy benchmark standards and Monte Carlo simulation requires the speci-fication of a statistical probability of confidence that in itself is a measurement of risk tolerance. Practical guidelines are given in Chapter 6 in selecting the appropriate per-manent life insurance product type or types based on determining the risk tolerance of the policy owner. However, like many other financial planning and advice treatises and publications, this book falls short in addressing the process of how to determine and assess risk tolerance. To compensate for this shortfall the author felt whom bet-ter to ask to write a contributing article on the topic of determining and assessing risk tolerance than a leading "Deep Thinker," top-notch financial planner who has an undergraduate degree with a psychology major—namely, Michael Kitces.

Michael suggested the use of either of two articles he wrote on risk tolerance assessment from his excellent blog *Nerd's Eye View* at www.Kitces.com. The author felt that both articles were fantastic and germane and contained different aspects of the topic, and that it was impossible to choose between the two. Fortunately, Michael graciously agreed to allow the publication of both as contributed articles to this book.

The assessment of risk tolerance traditionally consists of two factors: the will-ingness to take risks and the capacity to take risks. Generally, this is accomplished through the use of a risk tolerance questionnaire that attempts to ask questions about both of the risk tolerance components and, all too often, comes up with a single composite "risk score" that is used to determine a recommended portfolio. However, this one-dimensional approach of averaging together the scores from the willingness to take risks and the capacity to take risks, where either clients have an extremely low score for tolerance to take risks or a low score for the capacity to take risks, can result in a false risk profile that causes the adviser to make invest-ment recommendations that are more aggressive than is actually suitable for the client. In "Adopting A Two-Dimensional Risk Tolerance Assessment Process," Mr. Kitces advocates that willingness to take risks and risk capacity should be measured separately and scored on a two-dimensional scale. This procedure then properly recognizes the significant restraint of either a low risk tolerance or risk capacity on investment recommendations that is blurred by a single number that is the result of averaging the sum of the two risk components.

If a picture is worth a thousand words then Michael's outstanding graphics and illustrations in this article—and the subsequent article discussed below—dramati-cally demonstrate the concepts espoused in the article. What is of particular rel-evance is the illustration of comparison of investment portfolios resulting from the one-dimensional versus the two-dimensional risk tolerance assessments.

But determining a client's willingness to take risks and risk capacity, and the process to do such, are just part of composing a client's risk profile and the ultimate product solution(s) to achieve the goal(s) of the client. Thus, this first contributed article from Michael leads into his second contributed article that explains in more detail, and breaks apart, the three core constructs of the consumer behaviors around risks and how these behaviors influence investment decisions.

All investment regulators make it a requirement of financial advisors to "Know Your Client." This, of course, includes the client's tolerance for taking risks. However, none of the regulators provide guidance or standards as to how to correctly do such task. In fact, as Michael points out, "the problem stems from the reality that neither regulators, academics, nor advisors themselves, even have agreement on exactly what key factors of a client's 'risk profile' should be evaluated in the first place." While academic research is beginning to articulate a clear risk profiling framework—as discussed succinctly by Mr. Kitces in the section of the article titled "Breaking Apart the Risk Profile—Tolerance, Capacity and Risk Perception" (the three core constructs)—measuring these factors and traits is a daunting task. Quite frequently, various risk tolerance questionnaires are employed to make these assessments. Unfortunately, a recent survey of the global landscape for best practices in risk profiling by a Canadian financial planning software provider—PlanPlus—revealed a disturbing lack of quality risk tolerance questionnaires and support tools for financial planners. While Michael's second contributed article, titled "The Sorry State of Risk Tolerance Questionnaires for Financial Advisors," certainly addresses this dilemma and frustration, the real extraordinary value of this article lies in the discussion of the risk profile factors mentioned above and the arduous challenges of designing effective risk profiling tools that can accurately assess what they are purported to measure. Mr. Kitces goes on to consider the future of assessments of risk tolerance and a better world for such. Of course, the role and need for a good financial advisor must never be underestimated. The experience and judgment of a good professional advisor is always needed because there are always clients with unusual personal circumstances that just do not fit the "normal" mold. The role of the advisor is to recognize these situations and act accordingly in the best interest of the client.

Initially, the author was reluctant to use "The Sorry State of Risk Tolerance Questionnaires for Financial Advisors" as a contributed article primarily because of the negative connotation of the title and the feeling that the article was, perhaps, concentrating too much on the risk questionnaires rather than the techniques of determining the risk tolerance and risk profile of the client. In fact, while the first contributed article by Michael Kitces, "Adopting A Two-Dimensional Risk Tolerance Assessment Process," really comprises a topic that is just a subset of the broader topic of risk profiling, covered in the second contributed article, the author felt that that particular excellent article set the stage for the second contributed article and the title had a positive connotation. However, despite the title of the second contributed article, the bigger picture is that the article itself does an unbelievable job of explaining and analyzing the factors composing risk tolerance assessment to derive a client risk profile, the difficulties and challenges of measuring and weighting such factors, the academic research and lack of agreement on terminology for the factors and the relevance for the various factors, and the current "state of the art" for assessments of risk tolerance. In other words, this article is an extraordinary glimpse into the entire topic of risk tolerance assessment and risk profiling, and the traits and factors influencing a client risk profile. The author truly feels that this is one of the best articles out there on the topic and that every professional advisor needs to know and understand the material contained in this article.

About Michael E. Kitces

Michael E. Kitces, M.S.F.S., M.TAX, CFP®, CLU®, ChFC®, RHU®, REBC®, CASL®, is a partner and the Director of Wealth Management for Pinnacle Advisory Group, a private wealth management firm located in Columbia, Maryland, that oversees approximately $1.8 billion of client assets. In addition, he is a co-founder of the XY Planning Network, AdvicePay, and New Planner Recruiting, the former Practitioner Editor of the *Journal of Financial Planning*, the host of the *Financial Advisor Success* podcast, and the publisher of the popular financial planning continuing education blog *Nerd's Eye View* through his website www.Kitces.com, all dedicated to advancing knowledge in financial planning.

Beyond his website, Michael is an active writer and editor across the industry and has been featured in publications including *Financial Planning*, the *Journal of Financial Planning*, *Journal of Retirement Planning*, *Practical Tax Strategies*, and *Leimberg Information Services*, as well as the *Wall Street Journal*, *BusinessWeek*, *CNBC PowerLunch*, *NBC Nightly News*, and more. In addition, Michael has co-authored numerous books, including *The Annuity Advisor* with John Olsen (now in 3rd edition), the first balanced and objective book on annuities written for attorneys, accountants, and financial planners, and *Tools & Techniques of Retirement Income Planning* with Steve Leimberg and others.

Michael is one of the 2010 recipients of the Financial Planning Association's "Heart of Financial Planning" awards for his dedication to advancing the financial planning profession. In addition, he has variously been recognized as financial planning's "Deep Thinker," a "Legacy Builder," an "Influencer," a "Mover & Shaker," part of the "Power 20," and a "Rising Star in Wealth Management" by industry publications. These awards were presented to honor Michael's active work in the financial planning community, which currently includes serving as a member of the Editorial Review Board for the *Journal of Financial Planning*, national chair of the Financial Planning Section for the Society of Financial Service Professionals, and numerous other boards and committees for the Financial Planning Association and the Society of Financial Service Professionals at the local and national levels. Michael is also a co-founder of NexGen, a community of the next generation of financial planners that aims to ensure the transference of wisdom, tradition, and integrity, from the pioneers of financial planning to the next generation of the profession.

Adopting A Two-Dimensional Risk Tolerance Assessment Process

Michael E. Kitces, M.S.F.S., M.TAX, CFP®, CLU®, ChFC®, RHU®, REBC®, CASL®

January 25, 2017

Executive Summary

The process of assessing an investor's risk tolerance is all about determining his/her willingness to take investment risk, and financial capacity to bear risk, and blending it together to match to an appropriate investment portfolio. Most commonly, this is done with a risk tolerance questionnaire that posits a series of questions about time horizon and need for income, and attitudes about risk and market volatility, to calculate a "risk score" and determine the portfolio that goes with it.

The caveat to this one-dimensional approach, however, is that by averaging together risk tolerance and risk capacity scores, the advisor can unwittingly end up in situations where clients with extremely low risk tolerance (or risk capacity) end up with portfolios that are far too risky for their situation. In other words, the low risk tolerance (or capacity) should have acted as a constraint to the investment policy statement, but didn't.

So what's the alternative? Simply put—risk tolerance and risk capacity should be measured *separately*, and then scored on a two-dimensional scale that considers the contributing role (and limiting nature) of each (rather than a single continuum that merely averages the two together).

Fortunately, there are numerous risk tolerance software solutions specifically designed to assess "pure" risk tolerance on a standalone basis, including FinaMetrica and Riskalyze. And for comprehensive financial planners, the reality is that the financial plan itself *is* a measure of risk capacity, as reflected in the Monte Carlo probabilities of success and failure.

For those who don't do full retirement planning projections for every client, a recent alternative software solution is Tolerisk, which is designed to perform a two-dimensional risk tolerance assessment by separately gathering information about the client's risk attitudes and their basic financial goals.

The bottom line, though, is simply to recognize that risk tolerance and risk capacity are two different dimensions of the client's overall risk profile, and must be assessed and "scored" separately to properly recognize the constraining role that each have on the appropriate investment policy statement!

Separating Risk Tolerance From Risk Capacity

The standard approach to determining risk tolerance is to ask investors a series of questions. This might include assessing their time horizon, available assets, and need for income, along with their willingness to sustain market volatility and comfort level staying invested through a market decline.

These risk tolerance questions can be grouped into two categories. The former are questions about "risk capacity"—the investor's financial ability to have "something bad" happen in the portfolio and not ruin his/her goals (i.e., and still have time to recover). The latter, regarding willingness to take on market volatility and stay invested, assess the investor's attitudes about risk—in essence, their true "tolerance" for market risk.

Classically, the scores from these risk capacity and tolerance questions would then be merged together into a single "score" of risk tolerance, where the investor gets a lot of "points" for a long time horizon and a willingness to tolerate a lot of market volatility, but no points if he/she isn't willing to stay invested in a down market or has an unusually high withdrawal spending need (such that the goal would be ruined by an ill-timed bear market).

The combined final score can then be mapped to an "appropriate" portfolio and associated investment policy statement—with high scores tied to an aggressive portfolio, moderate scores tied to a moderate growth portfolio, and a low score tied to a conservative portfolio.

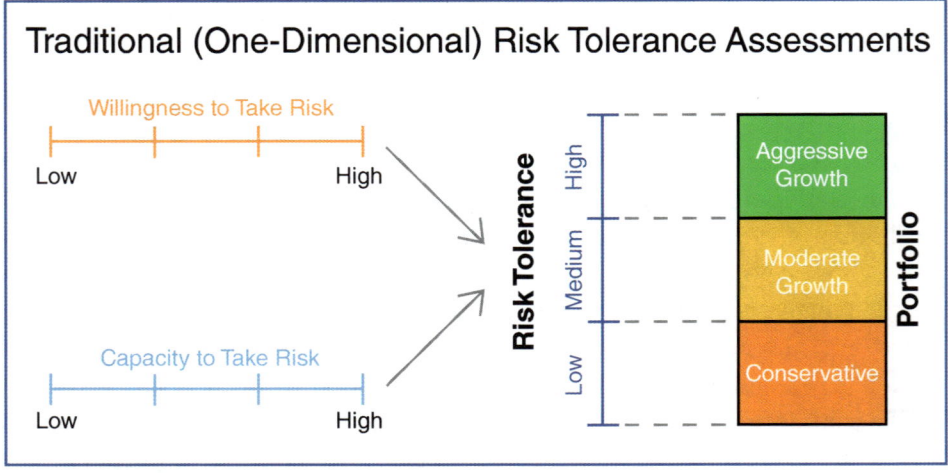

© Michael Kitces, www.kitces.com

Unfortunately, though, there's <u>a fundamental problem with this risk tolerance questionnaire approach</u>. The issue is that while it's called a "risk tolerance" score, it's really the combination of risk tolerance <u>and</u> risk capacity. Which both impact the appropriate investment portfolio . . . but blending them together into a single score ignores the <u>unique</u> contribution that each brings!

<u>Traditional risk tolerance assessments ignore unique contributions of risk tolerance and capacity!</u>

In particular, the "gap" that is created by the combined-tolerance-and-capacity risk score is that <u>just because an investor can afford to take risk doesn't necessarily mean he/she wants to or needs to</u>. After all, having a lot of wealth or a long time horizon means the investor <u>could</u> take risk (and still have enough time/assets to recover), but also means he/she might not <u>need</u> any risk to achieve the desired goals! Similarly, an investor who has a high tolerance for risk but limited wealth might be <u>willing</u> to take risks, but won't be able to achieve his/her goals if the risk event actually happens.

Unfortunately, though, when risk tolerance and capacity scores are merged together, there's no way to spot these discrepancies!

Aligning Two-Dimensional Risk Tolerance And Risk Capacity

So given these dynamics, what's the alternative? Simply put, it's not to add risk tolerance and capacity scores together to a single item, but instead, to evaluate (and score) them separately.

The end result is that instead of a one-dimensional "risk tolerance" score from conservative to aggressive, the advisor ends up with a two-dimensional perspective on how to assess the appropriate portfolio.

Of course, clients who have <u>both</u> a high tolerance and high capacity for risk will still get an aggressive portfolio, and those who have no tolerance nor capacity for risk will be conservative (or outright in cash).

The distinction, however, is that when investors score high on one measure but <u>low</u> on the other, the "classic" single-score approach adds the scores (which tends to skew them to at least moderate growth portfolios), while the separate approach properly recognizes low risk tolerance (or low risk capacity) as a constraint.

In other words, if an investor has a very long time horizon but no tolerance for risk—i.e., an ultra-conservative young investor—the traditional approach would drive them into a moderate growth portfolio they can't tolerate (just because they can "afford" to lose money and wait for it to recover), while this approach will recognize that tolerance for risk should <u>always</u> be a constraint. Putting a young investor into a volatile portfolio he/she truly can't tolerate is just an inevitable lawsuit waiting to happen in the next market downturn.

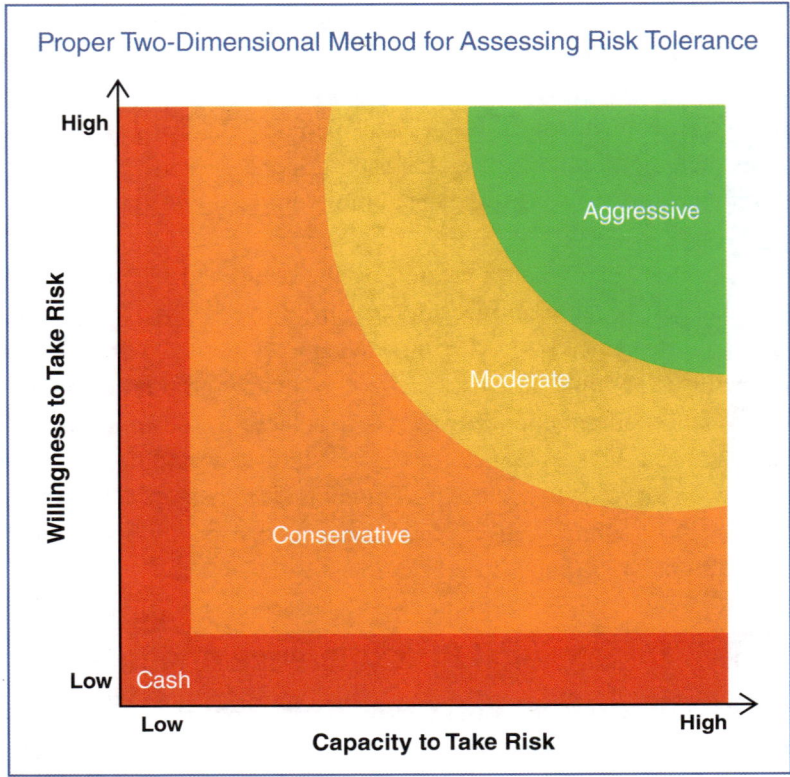

Proper Two-Dimensional Method for Assessing Risk Tolerance

© Michael Kitces, www.kitces.com

Similarly, an ultra-risk-inclined investor who has <u>no</u> emergency savings and a near-term time horizon might get a "moderate growth" portfolio with a blended score (since he/she <u>is</u> very tolerant of risk), but the separate approach will properly recognize that the investor simply can't afford to <u>take</u> that risk.

In essence, having a low willingness to take risk, and/or limited capacity to afford risk, should be viewed not just as a component of the risk score, but a <u>constraint</u> to the proper portfolio the investor agrees to in an Investment Policy Statement. Which means investors who have low tolerance <u>or</u> low capacity should remain in conservative portfolios and, similarly, investors with "just" moderate tolerance or capacity should stay in moderate portfolios, and not drift up to aggressive just because their <u>other</u> score is high.

Assessing Two-Dimensional Risk Tolerance And Risk Capacity (Separately)

Ultimately, the <u>key problem of most risk tolerance questionnaires today</u> is not that they seek to assess both risk tolerance <u>and</u> risk capacity; it's simply that they evaluate the <u>results</u> together in a single score, rather than using each <u>separately</u> to

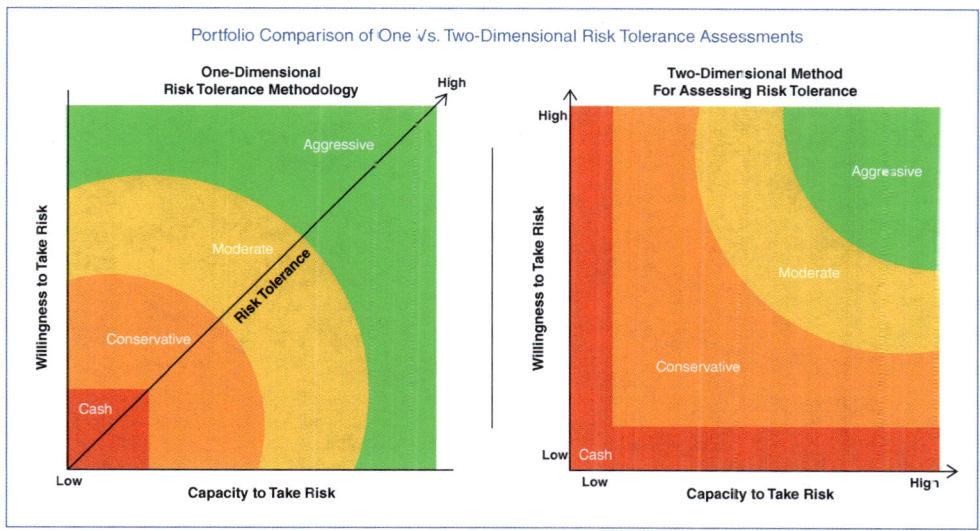

Portfolio Comparison of One Vs. Two-Dimensional Risk Tolerance Assessments

determine an appropriate portfolio. Unfortunately, though, so many risk tolerance assessment tools are <u>built</u> this way from the start—including those produced by many compliance departments—which means in practice, "unbundling" the two may be necessary.

The good news, however, is that there actually <u>are</u> a number of standalone risk tolerance assessment tools out there that do look <u>only</u> at measuring risk attitudes and the pure "willingness" to take risk.

The longest standing pure risk tolerance assessment tool is <u>FinaMetrica</u>, which has a robust psychometrically designed risk tolerance questionnaire. A more recent alternative would be <u>Riskalyze</u>, which similarly asks investors a series of questions to understand their willingness to engage in various levels of risky investment trade-offs.

Of course, if the advisor is going to assess pure risk tolerance on a standalone basis—without mixing in risk capacity questions regarding goals and time horizons—it's still necessary to separately evaluate risk capacity, too. On the plus side, the reality is that for those who do financial planning, the financial plan itself <u>is</u> a measurement of risk capacity!

<u>A holistic risk assessment is the combination of tolerance AND a financial plan!</u>

For instance, if the client's Monte Carlo probability of success for the retirement plan is at 95%+, the client has a high capacity for risk (because even a substantial market decline wouldn't <u>necessitate a very large adjustment to keep the goal on track</u>). However, if the Monte Carlo results are only 80% to 95%, the plan has only a moderate capacity for risk. And if the Monte Carlo probability of success is 79% or lower, there's a material risk that an adverse market event could impair the client's goal, so this would be viewed as a "low" capacity for risk.

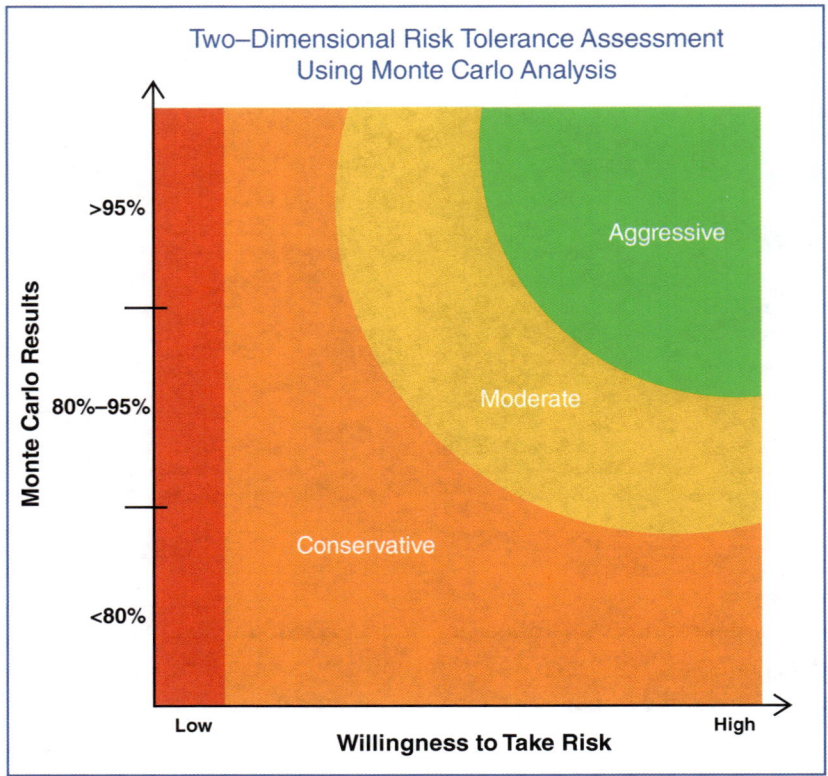

© Michael Kitces, www.kitces.com

Notably, for advisors who <u>don't</u> do a full financial plan for every client, it's clearly still necessary to have <u>some</u> assessment process for risk capacity.

The starting point could simply be to use the "traditional" risk tolerance questionnaires—with questions on both risk tolerance, and risk capacity—and just recognize that they need to be scored separately. In other words, don't score the questions and add them up to a <u>single</u> result. Instead, score them separately, and put the results on a grid (similar to the one above) with the low/medium/high scores for <u>each</u>, to ensure the actual portfolio the client gets is matched appropriately.

Fortunately, new risk assessment tools are beginning to emerge that help to accomplish this. For instance, <u>Tolerisk</u> measures the client's willingness to take risk with a "standard" kind of risk tolerance questionnaire. But the software <u>also</u> separately assesses the client's financial ability to take risk, by gathering "basic" financial planning information to project the client's anticipated withdrawal/spending needs over the next 20 years, and then using a proprietary algorithm to "score"

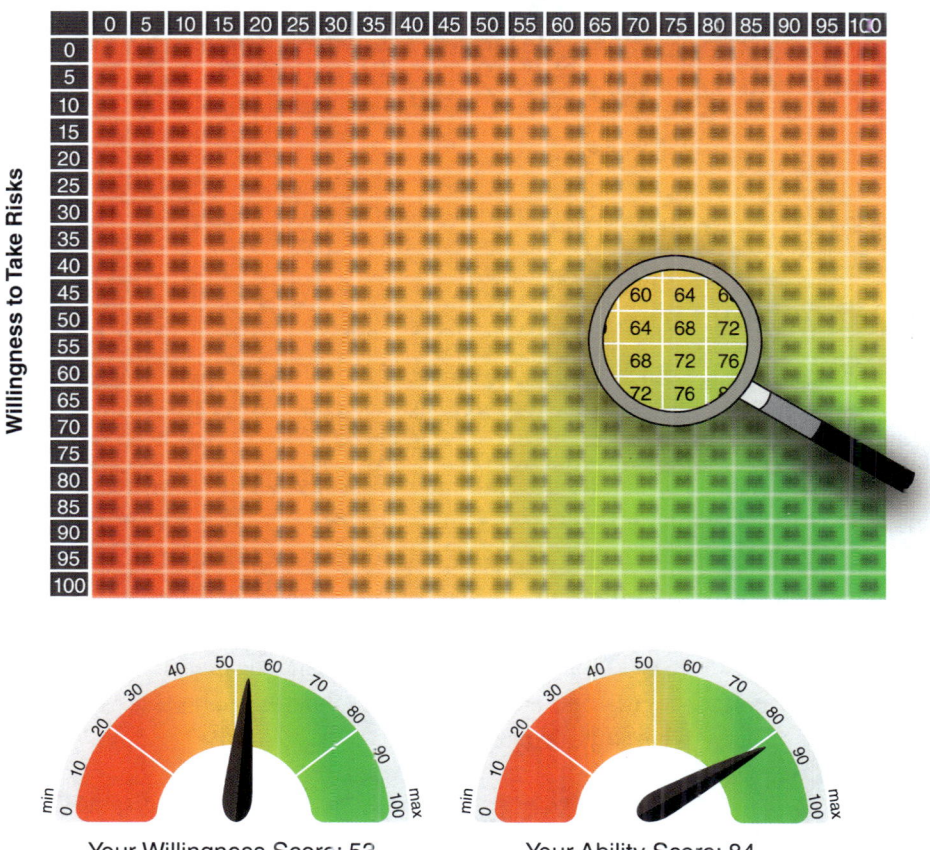

Your Tolerisk® Score: 70
Ability to Take Risks

Your Willingness Score: 53   Your Ability Score: 84

those withdrawal/spending goals as a form of risk capacity. The end result of the software is a matrix of recommended portfolios at the intersection of willingness (tolerance) and ability (capacity) to take risk.

The bottom line, though, is simply this: beware using risk tolerance assessment tools that blend together the results of measuring risk tolerance and risk capacity into a single score/result. Instead, the two need to be measured separately and only then blended back together in a two-dimensional assessment where they operate as <u>constraints</u> to a portfolio—not a cumulative score to invest as aggressively as possible (a <u>challenging bias of investment-management-based financial advisors</u>)!

The Sorry State Of Risk Tolerance Questionnaires For Financial Advisors

Michael E. Kitces, M.S.F.S., M.TAX, CFP®, CLU®, ChFC®, RHU®, REBC®, CASL®

September 14, 2016

Executive Summary

The requirement that a financial advisor must "Know Your Client," including his/her tolerance for taking risks, is a universal requirement amongst investment regulators around the world.

Yet a recent survey of the global landscape for best practices in risk profiling by Canadian financial planning software provider PlanPlus reveals a disturbing lack of quality risk tolerance questionnaires (RTQ) and support tools for financial advisors. In part, this appears to be driven by the fact that regulators articulate the principle of "know your client's risk tolerance" but provide little guidance on how it should be done to ensure that it's right. And to a large extent, the problem stems from the reality that neither regulators, academics, nor advisors themselves, even have agreement on exactly what key factors of a client's "risk profile" should be evaluated in the first place.

Nonetheless, a growing base of academic research is beginning to articulate a clear risk profiling framework, from recognizing the separation of risk tolerance from risk capacity, the role of risk perception (and misperceptions) on client behavior, and how "risk composure" (the stability of a client's perceptions of risk) itself can vary from one client to the next. Of course, just because these factors can be identified doesn't make them easy to measure with a questionnaire, especially when it comes to "subjective" abstract traits like risk tolerance. On the other hand, the research suggests that financial advisors just trying to interview clients about risk may not be doing a better job, either.

In the end, the optimal approach may eventually be a combination of both, where psychometrically designed risk tolerance questionnaires assess a client's willingness to pursue risky trade-offs, and the financial advisor can then assess the client's risk capacity, financial goals, and ability to achieve their objectives given the constraint of their tolerance. And ultimately, an effective risk tolerance questionnaire may not only make it easier to properly match investment solutions to a client's needs, but also make it easier to manage client risk perceptions and

226

investment expectations on an ongoing basis. Or at least identify which clients are most likely to be challenged when the next bear market comes along!

PlanPlus Searches For Global Best Practices In Investment Risk Profiling

Assessing a client's risk tolerance, as a part of providing investment management advice or investment product recommendations, is universally recognized as essential by regulators around the globe.

Notably, though, there's a wide range of perspectives amongst regulators about what, exactly, "risk tolerance" actually is, <u>how</u> it should be measured, what factors are and are not relevant, and how those factors should be weighted when evaluating if an investment recommendation was appropriate or not.

To understand the landscape, the Ontario Securities Commission of Canada engaged <u>PlanPlus</u> (a leading financial planning software provider in Canada that has a global footprint, albeit little presence in the US) to assemble a research team that would compare Canadian practices on risk tolerance assessments to the best practices globally.

Unfortunately, though, what the researchers found was that most regulators around the world are "principles-based" in requiring that advisors understand and assess the client's risk profile—an essential step to fulfill any advisor's "Know Your Client" (KYC) obligations—yet provide little guidance about how, exactly, that should be done.

Of course, if there was a clear and universally accepted academic framework for evaluating risk tolerance, this might not necessarily be an issue. For instance, in the U.S., <u>an investment fiduciary has an obligation to provide the advice that a prudent expert would have given</u> a similar client in similar circumstances. And although this principles-based "prudent expert" standard isn't explicitly defined, the courts have recognized it to mean that the expert should have followed the principles of the academic Modern Portfolio Theory framework. Yet when it comes to risk tolerance, regulators have provided a principles-based expectation and obligation on advisors to make an assessment, but without any acknowledgement of the missing academic framework that would/should clarify how advisors <u>actually</u> do it.

In fact, the researchers found that there's a surprising paucity of any academic research to validate most key concepts associated with a client risk profile. The situation is further complicated by the fact that there isn't even clear agreement about what all the relevant factors are that <u>should</u> be considered, not to mention how they should be incorporated together to make a recommendation. And what little research has been done is difficult to bring together, because there isn't even a consistent usage of terms regarding risk tolerance and a client's overall risk profile!

Breaking Apart The Risk Profile—Tolerance, Capacity, and Risk Perception

From the academic perspective, those who study consumer behaviors around risk and how it influences investment decisions are converging on three core constructs.

The first is risk tolerance itself. In the academic context, risk tolerance very narrowly and specifically refers to a client's willingness to take on risk—i.e., to pursue an uncertain positive outcome, with the potential that a negative outcome could result instead. Those who have greater risk tolerance are more willing to engage in larger "risky trade-off" scenarios, while those with less risk tolerance tend to avoid them. Notably, some research in this regard focuses on risk <u>aversion,</u> or the dislike a client has towards risk or falling below a certain income/wealth threshold. Ultimately, though, risk aversion can be viewed as the opposite side of the same coin (e.g., an unwillingness to take risks—low risk tolerance—is akin to having a high risk aversion).

The second construct is risk capacity, or the client's <u>financial</u> ability (in dollars and cents terms) to endure a potential financial loss, and still be able to achieve his/her goals. Of course, whether goals can be achieved in the event of a risky/ bad outcome depends on what the goal is in the first place. And some goals are so aggressive that they may actually necessitate taking greater risk just to be achievable (which means <u>the goal itself is risky</u>, and has a higher "risk need" associated with it). Notably, though, <u>risk capacity and the associated risk need to achieve a goal exist independently of the client's risk</u> tolerance. The mere fact that a client can <u>afford</u> to take risk, or <u>needs</u> to take risk, doesn't mean he/she <u>wants</u> to or is <u>willing</u> to take risk (though of course, a risky goal for a low-risk-tolerance client implies that it might be time to find a new goal!).

The third construct is to recognize that <u>different clients have different risk</u> perceptions—how risky they <u>think</u> markets (or rather, their investments) are in the first place. The key point is that if perceptions are (or become) misaligned with reality, investors may engage in "surprising" behavior that seems inconsistent with their risk tolerance. For instance, an individual who is highly risk tolerant, but has the (mis-)perception that a calamitous economic event will cause the market to crash to <u>zero</u>, might still want to sell everything and go to cash. Even though he/she is tolerant of risk, no one wants to own an investment going to zero! In addition, the research suggests that some people may have better risk <u>composure</u> than others; in other words, some investors can keep their composure and maintain a consistent perception of the potential risks around them, while others have risk perceptions that are more likely to move wildly. And of course, perceptions of risk themselves also vary by the information that the individual has available to them—poor financial literacy and education can increase the likelihood of risk misperception, as can media coverage of scary/risky events (triggering <u>the availability bias</u>).

Notably, in this context, risk capacity is an objective measure (the dollars-and-cents mathematical analysis of the consequences of risky events), while risk tolerance

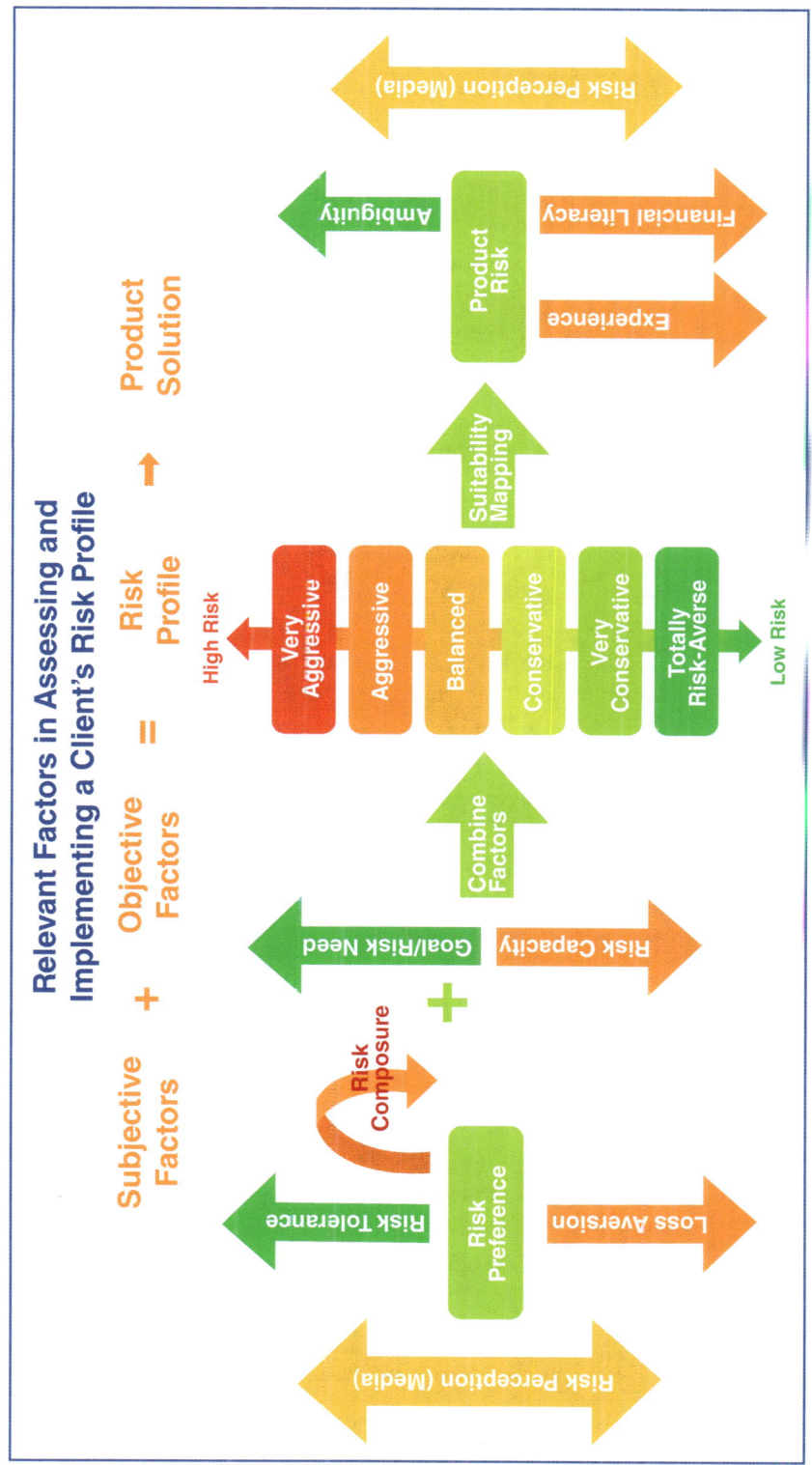

Source: Figure 1. Visual Summary of Risk Concepts Reprinted from "Current Practices for Risk Profiling in Canada and Review of Global Best Practices," by S. Brayman, M. Finke, E. Bessner, P. Griffin, and R. Clement, November 2013. © Michael Kitces, www.kitces.com

(and risk perception) remains more subjective (an assessment of an abstract psychological trait). And it's the combination of all of those subjective and objective factors that characterize the client's entire "risk profile," which in turn will lead to investment recommendations that may vary from very-aggressive to very-conservative.

Of course, even after evaluating the objective and subjective domains of the risk profile, it's <u>still</u> necessary to actually map the results of the risk assessment to actual investment solutions . . . which again entails understanding both the objective risk of the investment product, how it fits into the client's risk capacity and needs and goals, and also the subjective <u>perceived</u> riskiness of the investment (as even an objectively appropriate investment may <u>subjectively</u> seem overly risky if the client misperceives/misjudges the risk of the solution).

The Challenge Of Designing Good Risk Profiling Tools And Assessments

The good news of our increasingly robust understanding of all the different dimensions of a client's risk profile is that it allows us to better match investment solutions to client goals while also being consistent with their tolerance for risk. The bad news, however, is that when there are so many factors involved—and "subfactors" that are relevant as well (e.g., tolerance for risk based on upside potential may not be a mirror image of downside risk aversion, as <u>prospect theory</u> has shown)—it's difficult to figure out how to blend them all together for an appropriate recommended solution.

In addition, the reality is that it's difficult to measure the subjective aspects of risk tolerance itself, simply because it's the representation of an abstract psychological trait in the first place. In other words, we can't just objectively look into someone's brain and figure out what their risk tolerance is. Instead, we have to ask questions, evaluate the responses, and try to figure out how clients feel about their willingness to take risky trade-offs, and how they perceive the risks around them.

Unfortunately, though, <u>many risk tolerance questionnaires (RTQs) don't actually do a very good job of helping to predict a client's actual investment behavior during volatile markets,</u> particularly when they ask about how the investor believes he/she would behave in the event of a significant financial loss. In part, this appears to be due to differences from one investor to the next as to what constitutes a "risky" and undesirable loss in the first place, which can be based on sometimes-arbitrary reference points. An investor whose portfolio recently ran up from $1M to $1.2M may not stress about a subsequent $200,000 loss (because they've still got their $1M, and the lost gains were just "house money" to them), while someone who just inherited $2M (and uses the full $2M as a reference point) may be far more stressed about the same dollar amount decline (even though it's actually a smaller percentage loss). So an RTQ that asks about the consequences of a $200,000 loss would get somewhat counterintuitive responses (where the wealthier client is more averse simply because of a different reference point for "losses").

The situation is further complicated by the fact that when we take RTQs, we tend to answer the questions calmly and rationally, but when risky events occur, we may respond emotionally (literally using a different part of our brain). Known as the "dual self" or "dual process" theory, this disconnect between how we react to risky events in real time, and our (rational) expectation of how we will react, makes it challenging to simply ask consumers (in the hopes of getting a good answer) about their tolerance for taking future risks.

Fortunately, though, while questions like "how would you react if the markets declined by X%" aren't very effective at evaluating our likely tolerance for risk in real time, it does appear feasible to get at least some understanding of how a particular investor will likely behave in the face of a risky event. The challenge is greater for younger investors, along with those who have poor financial literacy, because they're even less capable of making financial self-assessments (due to the lack of experience, knowledge, or both). Nonetheless, one study found that when we're simply asked whether we're more concerned about possible losses or potential gains, we can reasonably self-assess our preference (which at least partially reflects risk tolerance). For instance, an investor's risk tolerance (and their likelihood of going to cash in a financial crisis) can be at least partially predicted by their willingness to engage in risky income trade-offs (e.g., "would you prefer a job with smaller pay increases and more job security, or one with bigger pay increases but less job security?").

In combination, the research suggests that it really *is* feasible to get some good perspective on an investor's risk tolerance, and how it may vary from one person to the next. In fact, there is an entire science of "psychometrics"—the process for making good tools to measure abstract psychological traits—that can be applied to formulate an effective risk tolerance questionnaire.

Finding a balance is still challenging, though, as neither clients nor advisors seem willing to use questionnaires that have "too many" questions (although Guillemette, Finke, and Gilliam found that a small number of high quality subjective risk tolerance questions can still be reliable). Still, though, the impact of a good risk tolerance questionnaire is striking—one study found that advisors trying to assess client risk tolerance with a conversational interview had only a 0.4 correlation to the client's actual psychometrically-measured risk tolerance. In other words, a well-designed RTQ is actually far more effective than an advisor's professional (but highly subjective and potentially-business-model-biased) judgment.

The Sorry State Of Current Risk Tolerance Questionnaires (RTQs) And Risk Profiling Tools

When looking across the globe, the PlanPlus research team found that there are still surprisingly few risk tolerance and risk profiling solutions available for advisors, with only about 10 solution providers of any broad reach. And amongst those providers, only 30% were able to document any form of psychometric validity to their risk tolerance questions and process itself, and few were even clear about defining their terminology and focus on what exactly they purported to measure (or not) in the first place (e.g., just tolerance, or also capacity, or also perception, etc.).

Amongst the available providers, the researchers characterized them into one of three categories: a) Comprehensive Risk Profiling tools, which used psychometrically designed questions that were adapted for (and mapped to) the company's specific products and services; b) Risk-Tolerance-Only questionnaires, which focused solely on effectively measuring subjective risk tolerance (with the idea that it was the advisor's job to fit the risk tolerance results into the rest of the picture, including risk capacity and financial goals, to make appropriate recommendations; and c) Asset Allocation Calculators that tended to combine the subjective aspects (risk tolerance) and the objective ones (risk capacity and time horizon) to formulate an asset allocation recommendation.

While arguably any of these can be reasonable approaches, when used appropriately, unfortunately few of the solutions were clear to even distinguish their limitations. All three types held themselves out similarly as "risk tolerance" or "risk profiling" solutions, despite their substantively different approaches, varying degrees of actual psychometric validation of the methodology, and thoroughness of their solution (e.g., "just" for asset allocation, or a more holistic risk tolerance

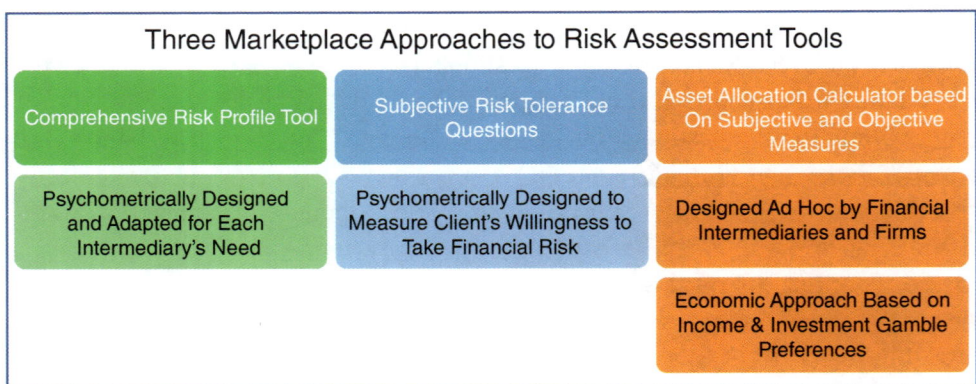

Source: Figure 10. Three Marketplace Approaches. Reprinted from "Current Practices for Risk Profiling in Canada and Review of Global Best Practices," by S. Brayman, M. Finke, E. Bessner, P. Griffin, and R. Clement, November 2013. © Michael Kitces, www.kitces.com

analysis). For instance, here in the U.S., <u>FinaMetrica</u> would fit into the "Subjective Risk Tolerance Questions" category, while <u>Riskalyze</u> better fits as a tool to determine asset allocation based on gamble preferences; yet both frame themselves as "risk tolerance" or "risk profiling" tools without a clear distinction between them.

Furthermore, in Canada (where the analysis was based), only 10% of the risk tolerance solution providers have been validated in any way, and only 16% were even "fit for purpose" (with the rest either using poorly constructed questions, hopelessly conflated different factors, grossly overweighting a particular factor, or simply had no mechanism to actually identify highly risk averse consumers). And it's not clear that an evaluation of most risk tolerance questionnaires would fare any better here in the U.S., either.

The Future Of (Better) Assessments Of Risk Tolerance

The poor state of affairs in risk tolerance questionnaires—both in Canada, and around the world—suggests that there is ample room for improvement.

However, the PlanPlus researchers suggest that there will be little progress until we first get agreement on a common set of terminology and the associated definitions for key terms pertaining to risk profiling (e.g., for risk tolerance and risk capacity, the difference between those and risk perception, etc.). And realistically, this change may have to be driven <u>by</u> regulators, given that regulators universally seem to require <u>some</u> kind of risk tolerance assessment process as a part of the advisor's Know Your Client obligations, and if regulators aren't clear about the terminology when writing the KYC requirements, advisors (and the solutions for them) aren't likely to fill the void.

And ironically, the challenge of getting clearer about the nuances of risk profiling is that as more factors are introduced, it becomes both more difficult to measure them, and more complex to figure out how to fit them <u>back</u> together in order to craft an appropriate recommendation. Even relatively "simple" conceptual adjustments—like separating risk capacity from risk tolerance—have profound consequences relative to the "traditional" approach in risk profiling. For instance, when analyzed separately, <u>younger clients with long time horizons would</u> not always have aggressive portfolios (because even if they have the risk capacity for it, they may not have the tolerance).

Perhaps the greatest challenge in improving the assessment of risk tolerance, though, is simply figuring out what the role of a questionnaire should or should not be in the first place. Ironically, many of today's risk tolerance questionnaires are so badly designed, they may actually be worse than using no questionnaire at all, and/or simply allowing financial advisors to make their own professional-albeit-subjective assessment. Yet the potential remains that if advisors begin to actually insist on risk tolerance questionnaires that are actually psychometrically validated as such—and/or regulators require it on their behalf—that there may be a breakthrough in the adoption (and actual usefulness) of risk tolerance questionnaires.

Many risk tolerance questionnaires are bad, but that just means we need better ones!

Fortunately, finally getting a "good" risk tolerance questionnaire doesn't obviate the need for a good financial advisor. The PlanPlus authors suggest that the best balance may be to have RTQs focus on just risk tolerance, and allow the financial advisor as a professional to determine the optimal investment/portfolio solution that incorporates that risk tolerance, along with the client's risk capacity and financial goals. And because at least some clients may have unusual personal circumstances that don't fit the "normal" risk tolerance questionnaire, there can always be a role for the professional advisor to identify situations where it's necessary to "override" the risk tolerance questionnaire based on additional factors or nuances. In fact, regulators around the world—including here in the US—have raised concerns that a purely automated (e.g., "robo") risk tolerance questionnaire process could miss out on key client information (that the questionnaire didn't know to ask in advance), and that a financial advisor should be involved at least to affirm the appropriateness of the questionnaire's results.

In the long run, though, the greatest opportunity of improving risk tolerance questionnaires and overall risk profiling may be the way it helps financial advisors to better manage ongoing client relationships. After all, the clearer we are about a client's "true" risk tolerance, the easier it is to identify clients who may have risk misperceptions (e.g., the client who really is risk tolerant, but is acting risk averse, and therefore may be over-estimating their actual risk). And the potential to someday determine how to measure risk composure introduces the possibility of actual knowing, in advance, which clients are most likely to panic during turbulent markets, and therefore who might need extra education, guidance, or hand-holding when the next bear market comes.

But at a minimum, the PlanPlus study reveals that while many advisors may be frustrated that traditional risk tolerance questionnaires seem to do a poor job of predicting actual client investor behavior in times of risk, that may not be a failure of the approach of trying to assess risk tolerance, but simply a recognition that there's still a lot of room for improvement to do it better in the first place.

When to Hold Life Insurance in Trust; What Type of Trust

*Martin M. Shenkman, CPA, M.B.A., PFS, J.D., AEP®
(Distinguished)*

Introductory Comments by Gary Flotron

Martin M. Shenkman, CPA, M.B.A., PFS, J.D., AEP® (Distinguished), is an icon in the estate planning community. A prolific writer, he has authored 42 books and more than 1,200 articles, and has served on the editorial board of numerous, prestigious tax, estate, and real estate publications. Mr. Shenkman annually attends the major estate planning conferences—such as the Heckerling Institute on Estate Planning and the Notre Dame Tax and Estate Planning Institute—and publishes his detailed, invaluable notes that he takes at those conferences that are a must-read for every estate planning practitioner whether or not they also attended those conferences. He is also a popular and frequent speaker at many national professional continuing education events.

Marty is an extremely gracious, conscientious, compassionate, and caring man. Each summer he travels the country in his RV giving pro bono talks to professional advisers, charitable groups, and members of families that have a loved one with a chronic illness such as multiple sclerosis. In fact, he is the founder of ChronicIllness-Planning.org, which educates professional advisers on planning for clients with chronic illnesses and disability. He has also written books for the Michael J. Fox Foundation for Parkinson's Research, the National Multiple Sclerosis Society, and the COPD Foundation on the topic of planning for those with chronic illnesses and disabilities.

Mr. Shenkman has been honored with numerous professional awards including being inducted in 2013 into the National Association of Estate Planners & Councils (NAEPC) Estate Planning Hall of Fame® and simultaneously awarded by NAEPC the Accredited Estate Planner® Distinguished (AEP® (Distinguished)) designation. In 2012, he was selected as the Pro-Bono Financial Planner of the Year for his efforts on behalf of those living with chronic illness and disability, and the American Cancer Society in 2016 selected Marty as the Professional Advisor of the Year.

To paraphrase the great county singer Kenny Rogers, "you've got to know when to hold 'em." Marty Shenkman answers that statement for life insurance in his contributed article "When to Hold Life Insurance in Trust; What Type of Trust."

Marty advocates holding life insurance in an irrevocable life insurance trust (ILIT) and points out many of the non-federal estate tax reasons and advantages connected with such policy ownership.

But there are two categories of ILITs for income tax purposes, referred to as the grantor trust and the non-grantor trust. The difference is that with the grantor trust for income tax purposes the creator/settler/grantor of the trust is treated as owning the assets of the trust and, hence, pays income tax on the income of the trust and also receives the income tax deductions attributed to trust assets; whereas the non-grantor trust is a separate income tax entity. With a non-grantor trust, income earned during the year and distributed (or deemed distributed) to the beneficiary or beneficiaries of the trust is taxable to the beneficiary(ies). Income of the trust during the year that is retained inside the trust is taxable to the trust itself at the very compressed tax rates for estates and trusts. The provisions of the trust that require grantor trust status are spelled out in sections 671 to 679 of the Internal Revenue Code.

Mr. Shenkman describes the many advantages of grantor trust status and points out that "it may be difficult or impossible for a trust to own life insurance and not be characterized as a grantor trust." However, he also examines the important reasons life insurance should be held in a grantor trust.

After the 2017 Tax Act, the use of non-grantor trusts has grown in popularity for the reason cited by Marty in the article. While life insurance should still remain in a grantor trust, if the taxpayer can benefit from the tax advantages mentioned in the article from a non-grantor trust then a new non-grantor trust should be created. In fact, as the non-insurance assets grow within the non-grantor trust, the non-grantor trust can be used to fund the life insurance premiums by loaning money to the grantor trust ILIT via a loan regime split-dollar arrangement.

This short, concise, thoughtful, and extremely informative article is well worth reading and demonstrates why Marty Shenkman is so respected by estate planning practitioners!

About Martin M. Shenkman

Martin M. Shenkman, CPA, M.B.A., PFS, J.D., AEP® (Distinguished), is an attorney in private practice in Fort Lee, New Jersey, and New York City, New York, with Shenkman Law. His practice is concentrated in estate and tax planning, planning for closely held businesses, and estate administration. Mr. Shenkman is the author of 42 books and more than 1,200 articles. He is an editorial Board Member for *Trusts & Estates Magazine*, CCH (Wolters Kluwer), where he serves as Co-Chair of the Professional Advisory Board, *CPA Journal*, and the *Matrimonial Strategist* (through 2018). He has previously served on the editorial board of many other tax, estate, and real estate publications. Mr. Shenkman is also a frequent source for numerous national publications, and guest expert appearances on major financial and other television and radio shows.

Some of Marty's many awards and recognitions include the 1994 Probate and Property Excellence in Writing Award; the Alfred C. Clapp Award presented in 2007 by the New Jersey Bar Association and the Institute for Continuing Legal Education for excellence in continuing legal education; *Worth Magazine*'s Top 100 Attorneys (2008); *CPA Magazine* Top 50 IRS Tax Practitioners (April/May 2008); his article "Estate Planning for Clients with Parkinson's" received the "Editors' Choice Award" in 2008 from *Practical Estate Planning Magazine*; his article "Integrating Religious Considerations into Estate and Real Estate Planning" was awarded in 2008 "The Best Articles Published by the ABA"; New Jersey Super Lawyers (2010–16); his book *Estate Planning for People with a Chronic Condition or Disability* was nominated for the 2009 *Foreword Magazine* Book of the Year Award; the 2012 recipient of the AICPA Sidney Kess Award for Excellence in Continuing Education for CPAs; inducted in 2013 into the National Association of Estate Planners & Councils (NAEPC) Estate Planning Hall of Fame® and simultaneously awarded by NAEPC the Accredited Estate Planner (AEP® (Distinguished)) designation; *Financial Planning Magazine* 2012 Pro-Bono Financial Planner of the Year for efforts on behalf of those living with chronic illness and disability; featured on *Investment Adviser Magazine* cover of its April 2013 issue as the lead of their "all-star lineup of tax experts"; in June 2015 he delivered the Hess Memorial Lecture for the New York City Bar Association; and the American Cancer Society, 2016 Professional Advisor of the Year award.

Marty has been extremely active in many charitable and community causes and organizations. Some of these activities include being the founder of ChronicIllnessPlanning.org, which educates professional advisers on planning for clients with chronic illness and disability and which has been the subject of more than a score of articles; writing books for the Michael J. Fox Foundation for Parkinson's Research, the National Multiple Sclerosis Society, and the COPD Foundation; presenting more than 60 lectures around the country on the topic of chronic illness and disability for professional organizations, charities, and others; more than 50 of the articles he has published have addressed planning for those facing the challenges of chronic illness and disability; and serving on the American Brain Foundation Board of Directors, Strategic Planning Committee, and Investment Committee.

Marty received his Bachelor of Science degree from the Wharton School, University of Pennsylvania with a concentration in accounting and economics. He earned his M.B.A. from the University of Michigan, with a concentration in tax and finance, and a law degree from Fordham University School of Law. Mr. Shenkman has been admitted to the bar in New York, New Jersey, and Washington, D.C., and he has a CPA license in New Jersey, Michigan, and New York. He is also a Registered Investment Adviser in New York and New Jersey.

When to hold Life Insurance in Trust; What Type of Trust

Martin M. Shenkman, Esq.

Introduction

The 2017 Tax Act has had dramatic impact on life insurance planning. Many life insurance plans may no longer be relevant and should be reviewed to determine their continued relevance and what if anything might be done with the coverage involved. New insurance coverage will no doubt continue to be sold for a wide range of purposes after the 2017 Tax Act.

Trusts Should Still Own Life Insurance

In most cases life insurance should continue to be held in trust even after the 2017 Tax Act. Many clients might resist using trusts because they might perceive the need for trusts as irrelevant if the approximately $22 million+ exemption per couple makes the estate tax irrelevant to them. While a significant incentive to use trusts had been to assure that the insurance proceeds were not included in the estate of the insured for many this reason might now seem irrelevant. However, insurance professionals should not be seduced by the simplicity of an insurance sale without the need for a trust, when a trust is still the better option. Further, insurance professionals will have the task of educating clients as to the reasons trusts remain important, and which types of trusts should own the insureds life insurance in the current planning environment.

Life insurance should continue to be held in trusts for a myriad of reasons, including some of the following:

- The current high exemptions are scheduled to be cut in half in 2026 (from $10 million per taxpayer to $5 million inflation adjusted).
- There is no assurance that a future administration in Washington may not reduce exemptions at an earlier date, and even to a lower level.
- A number of states still have estate tax systems that are decoupled from the federal estate tax system.
- Life insurance has no basis step up issues. In the past common estate tax minimization planning for many clients was to shift discountable business and real estate interests to irrevocable trusts to lock in discounts, and to shift future growth out of their estates. Under the current high exemptions some client families may be better off by retaining the business and real estate

interests in the estate to garner a step up in income tax basis on death and using a robust insurance plan held in a trust to address any risks of liquidity, future estate taxes, etc.

- States might reinstate state estate tax systems or make existing systems harsher.
- Asset protection benefits of insurance trusts are independent of tax benefits and remain relevant to a large number of clients.
- Divorce protection (spouse remarries, heirs who are beneficiaries of the insurance divorce), etc. remains vitally important to most clients. Regardless of the changes made or to be made to the estate tax system this benefit will motivate many if not most clients with policies of a substantial size to have those policies held in trust.
- Professional management of insurance proceeds is vital to the future security of many client families. Holding the life insurance in trust can assure that the proceeds will be professional managed as the trust provides.

Thus, regardless of the changes in the tax laws, the use of irrevocable trusts to hold life insurance will continue to be advantageous for many if not most clients. The question remains what type of trust should hold that insurance?

Use of Grantor Trusts

Prior to the 2017 Tax Act, most irrevocable trusts were structured as "grantor" trusts for income tax purposes. There were several reasons for this:

- As a grantor trust the settlor bears the income tax cost of the income earned by the trust. This so-called grantor trust "tax burn" (of the settlor paying income taxes on income earned by and retained in the trust) further reduces the size of the settlor's estate.
- The settlor could retain the power to swap or substitute trust assets for personal assets and use it to shift appreciated assets from the trust into his or her estate to gain a basis step up on death.
- Appreciated assets could be sold to the trust to lock in discounts and shift future appreciation outside the estate without triggering capital gains.

For some clients the continued use of grantor trusts will remain optimal, at least for some of their trusts:

- Existing trusts to which note sales were made of appreciated assets may not be able to convert to non-grantor trusts without triggering tax costs.
- For very high net worth clients the ability to sell assets to a grantor trust might justify retaining or creating a grantor trust.
- Life insurance, as discussed below, will be held by grantor trusts.

Life Insurance and Grantor Trusts

Likely, a trust holding life insurance may be characterized as a grantor trust. If trust income can be used, directly or indirectly, to benefit the grantor, the grantor will be treated as the owner of the trust. IRC Sec. 677. This includes the application of income to pay premiums on life insurance policies insuring the life of the grantor or the grantor's spouse. IRC Sec. 677(a); Treas. Reg. Sec. 1.677(a)-1. Specifically, the grantor is deemed the owner of any portion of the trust or the trust income which can be used (without the consent of an adverse party) to pay premiums on life insurance policies. IRC Sec. 677(a)(3). Prior cases, under a predecessor statute, held that the grantor was only taxable on trust income actually used to pay premiums. Rand v. Comr., 40 B.T.A. 233 (1939), acq., 1939-2 C.B. 30, aff'd, 116 F.2d 929 (8th Cir. 1941), cert. denied, 313 U.S. 594 (1941). The IRS has held that if trust income is used to purchase life insurance even in contradiction of the terms of the trust, the trust will still be characterized as a grantor trust. PLR 8839008.

Thus, it may be difficult or impossible for a trust to own life insurance and not be characterized as a grantor trust.

Life insurance will continue to be held in grantor trusts for several reasons.

- If two trusts are grantor trusts as to the settlor/insured, the transfer of insurance between trusts cannot create a taxable event. There can be no transfer of the policy between trusts that are both disregarded. IRC Sec. 101(a)(2).
- Transfers of a policy between two grantor trusts (e.g., in a decanting from an old trust to a better crafted new trust) should also qualify for an exception to the transfer-for-value rule, as a transfer to the grantor/insured. Similarly, a sale of a policy from a grantor trust to another grantor trust will not trigger the transfer for value rules. PLR 200518061 and 200514001; Rev. Rul. 2007-13, IRB 2007-11, 684.

Burgeoning Use of Non-Grantor Trusts

After the 2017 Tax Act the use of non-grantor trusts has grown substantially in popularity. In many instances non-grantor trusts will be used to endeavor to secure income tax benefits including:

- Property tax deduction in light of the $10,000 limitation on state and local tax ("SALT") limitations.
- To hold investment assets in a low tax state to endeavor to minimize income tax on passive assets that would otherwise be assessed by a high tax state.
- Maximizing 199A deductions by fractionalizing ownership of pass through entity interests in non-grantor trusts to avoid the taxable income limitation.
- Salvaging charitable contribution deductions from the new higher standard deduction.

As a result of these benefits, many taxpayers are creating new non-grantor trusts or converting old existing trusts into non-grantor trusts. If the taxpayer has life insurance coverage, the existing grantor trust should be retained and should not, based on the discussion above, be converted to a non-grantor trust. Instead, if the taxpayer can benefit from a non-grantor trust a new non-grantor trust should be formed.

The Insurance Planning Complexity Scale

There are several layers of increasing complexity which can be used in life insurance trust planning, including the following:

- Traditional ILIT—this can be a relatively simple home state trust naming a family member as a trustee and holding a bank account and insurance policy. This trust will likely be characterized as a grantor trust but since there is so little income the only relevance of that will be that the trust can avoid the transfer for value rules and provide flexibility if the insurance plan is restructured.
- Robust ILIT-SLAT—A spousal lifetime access trust or "SLAT" is often created to hold significant gift assets to grow assets outside the taxpayer's estate and provide asset protection benefit. SLATs can be structured along a spectrum from simpler and lower cost home-state trusts to more robust, costly and complicated trusts formed as directed trusts in a trust friendly jurisdiction. These trusts can be designed to hold life insurance or decanted or otherwise modified to do so.
- As more assets grow post 2017 Tax Act in non-grantor trusts because of the income tax benefits these provide, those non-grantor trusts may loan money to a grantor trust pursuant to a split-dollar arrangement to fund the cost of insurance and avoid the issues of the insurance recharacterizing the non-grantor trust as a grantor trust.

Conclusion

After the 2017 Tax Act life insurance planning will continue and policies in many cases should still be held by irrevocable trusts. However, the decision as to which trusts will be more complex considering the more common use of non-grantor and grantor trusts.

Was Your Client Sold the Most Expensive Life Insurance Policy on the Planet?

High Net Worth (HNW) Access to Institutionally-Priced Life Insurance for Personal Asset Diversification

Charles M. "Mark" Whitelaw and E. Randolph Whitelaw, AEP® (Distinguished)

Introductory Comments by Gary Flotron

This Contributed Articles section and the following Contributed Articles section contain articles co-authored by the Whitelaw brothers. This Contributed Articles section features two articles written by Charles M. "Mark" Whitelaw and E. Randolph Whitelaw, AEP® (Distinguished), and the next Contributed Articles section has one article authored by E. Randolph Whitelaw, AEP® (Distinguished), and George P. Whitelaw.

The Whitelaw brothers are pioneers and innovators in highly sophisticated life insurance planning, fiduciary, and administrative management for corporations, banks, trust companies, and high net worth individuals, as well as the advisor community. They each are life insurance geniuses with regard to specific aspects and expertise within the profession! For more than 30-plus years the brothers have either worked together within the same family firm, separately with various related entities, or separately with various other ventures connected with sophisticated life insurance planning and fiduciary and administrative management, but always collectively.

Mark Whitelaw has unique expertise in the investment analytics and administration of life insurance-funded executive benefits, trust-owned life insurance (TOLI), and individually owned institutional life insurance (ILI) plans. In fact, for more than 35 years he has been managing the design, funding, communication, implementation, and administration of non-qualified benefit plans funded with specially designed life insurance policies. His specialized knowledge is readily apparent in the two contributed articles. Mark is currently Head of Design for Winged Foot Partners (WFP) and is a Registered Representative with World Equity Group, Inc.

WFP provides institutionally priced life insurance access, analytics, and administrative services to accredited investors, the financial services sector, and trustees.

E. Randolph Whitelaw, known as Randy, is the managing director of Trust Asset Consultants, LLC (TAC). TAC is a fee-based life insurance consulting firm to family groups, businesses, trustees, and attorneys. TAC specializes in formalizing each client's life insurance planning objectives and implementing the plan and policy administration, risk management, and participant communication. Further, TAC specializes with impaired risk underwriting, life insurance portfolio management, viatical and life settlements, and family meetings. Randy is also the co-founder and co-managing director of The TOLI Center, LLC (TTC) a fee-based, independent third-party life insurance policy evaluation, administration, and risk management firm that provides services for professional and personal trustees, advisors, and policy owners. The TTC clientele includes many national trust companies, affluent family groups, businesses, attorneys, and other advisors. TAC and TTC work hand in hand as "big picture" issues are addressed by TAC and life insurance policy management is addressed by TTC.

Mark and Randy's first article, titled "Was Your Client Sold the Most Expensive Life Insurance Policy on the Planet?," deals with indexed universal life products. Chapter 3 of this book covered the risks by product types of life insurance including a subsection on indexed universal life. The coverage of the risks of the various life insurance products was intended to be factual but neutral in nature. However, it was pointed out the non-guaranteed elements of indexed universal life insurance constituted risks to the policy owner and included the fact that the participation rate and caps on the maximum credited rates of increase could change with each measuring period for the index or indices. It was also noted that the current cost of insurance (mortality rates) and current policy expenses could be increased to the maximums specified in the policy, and there is a lot of wiggle room in this area. Chapter 2 of this book discussed transparency, or lack thereof, of the "actual" costs and earnings elements, and the noncomparability of such among universal life policies, and succinctly pointed out that life insurance pricing and costs must be viewed as a whole and not separately. What the Whitelaw brothers' first article prominently demonstrates is that there is no life insurance product where the abovementioned topics from Chapters 2 and 3 of this book are more relevant than with indexed universal life insurance products today.

As pointed out in their article, the "win the illustration game" still exists with indexed universal life marketing. Unfortunately, in this author's opinion, there are a lot of "gimmicks" associated with the indexed universal life product such as higher cost of insurance (mortality rates) and policy expense charges used to pay for higher caps or participation rates, and/or fixed or formula bonus credits and other return enhancements based on future selected index account returns, which may be completely illusionary. Remember that despite having a small percentage of put and call options in the general asset accounts backing the indexed universal life policies, the bulk of the investments underlying the policies are primarily in high-grade fixed-income securities, mostly corporate or government bonds. So, in order to illustrate greater returns, the insurers increased the cost of insurance (mortality rates) and other policy expenses. Is this not a "shell game" that demonstrates that life insurance pricing and costs need to be viewed as a whole and not separately?

The Whitelaw brothers did a study with a number of major insurers comparing indexed universal life policy cost of insurance (mortality rates) and other policy expenses with the costs associated with regular universal life and variable universal life products of the same carrier. What they discovered was that the costs with the indexed universal life products were 1,500 percent to 3,000 percent greater than the costs associated with either a universal life product or variable universal life product illustrated in a consistent policy management manner with the same carrier. In fact, their conclusion to their article ends with the question to agents, advisors, and trustees on a ratio basis cost comparison of a indexed universal life policy compared to a variable life policy, "can you explain why you considered a $30,000 cost of insurance, rather than a $1,000 cost of insurance, was in the client's best interest?"

One other fascinating and very useful aspect of Mark and Randy's article was the Financial Industry Regulatory Authority (FINRA)-compliant comparison over the past 25 years, by year, of the minimum, maximum, and average returns of the Standard & Poor's (S&P) 500 total returns versus sample indexed return alternatives that include variable universal life insurance, indexed universal life insurance, plus taxable funds. The conclusion from the table of the data is that the indexed universal life policy may be the worst choice, but that is up to the reader to decide.

The Whitelaw brothers' article is a refreshing and needed exposé on indexed universal life insurance policies. The indexed universal life insurance policy is, by far, the most complex and complicated insurance product available. As noted in their article, the product has "evolved into a level of complexity that is *extremely* difficult for consumers and professional advisors to separate financial 'sizzle' from financial 'steak.'"

For their second article, titled "High Net Worth (HNW) Access to Institutionally-Priced Life Insurance for Personal Asset Diversification," Mark and Randy discuss and analyze a unique niche and specialized life insurance product known as "institutional life insurance." The focus of this book was predominantly on life insurance products designed primarily to provide death benefit protection, but that could also be additionally designed to provide high cash values and increasing death benefit protection for either retirement income purposes or to protect the purchasing power of the death benefit. These products are available to the general public and businesses from what is commonly referred to as the retail distribution and marketing channels. There are two other life insurance product distribution and marketing channels: the ILI channel and the private placement life insurance channel. Both of these channels contain extremely sophisticated specialized products catering to niche markets that mostly consist of corporations, banks, and HNW and ultra-HNW clientele. Both of these channels use the variable universal life insurance "chassis" as the platform for the insurance product and utilize the tax advantages of the insurance "wrapper."

ILI had its genesis in the mid-1980s and was used by corporations primarily to "informally" fund supplemental executive retirement plans (SERPs) and other non-qualified deferred compensation plans. At that same time, it was acquired by banks to satisfy Tier I capital requirements for bank regulators. The banks discovered that it was more economical to pay the mortality and other charges associated with the ILI than the capital gains and ordinary income taxes associated with maintaining security portfolios.

While it is beyond the scope of both this book and the Whitelaw brothers' article, suffice it to say that private placement life insurance is only available to accredited investors (an investor with at least $1,000,000 in net worth in investment assets and a continued income of $200,000 or more) and qualified purchasers (individuals or family businesses with more than $5,000,000 in investments), and such individuals are required to contribute, generally, a minimum of $2,000,000 in order to set the policy up. The policies are, generally, negotiated and set up with offshore insurers and are frequently owned by irrevocable trusts. Since the policies are "customizable" they frequently feature hedge fund-type investment choices. The private placement life insurance arrangement can have tremendous advantages for super-wealthy families willing to engage in this type of multi-generational estate planning.

The basic premise of ILI is fairly simple. It is a defined contribution corporate variable universal life product, where the contribution funds the policy to the maximum allowed by the section 7702 guideline premium test, such that the policy qualifies as life insurance and is not a modified endowment contract (MEC). The death benefit is a secondary consideration. The policy features a large variety choice of quality sub-accounts with low institutional fund and management fees, plus minimal or no expense loading for commissions and other administrative expenses. The current mortality charges are based on the current mortality experience of high-income white-collar executives (the only group of insureds that qualify for the ILI policy) that as a group experience very, very favorable mortality. With the extremely low policy costs, this product serves as an alternative to taxable investing in portfolios of securities. Basically, the mortality and other policy costs are far less than those of the capital gains and ordinary income taxes that would have to be paid with taxable investment alternatives. Thus, the tax advantages of the life insurance "wrapper"; it provides for tax-deferred growth of the cash values, at a very minimum, and in most cases provides completely tax-deferred growth and tax-free access to the cash values, plus income tax-free death benefits—and, if contained in an irrevocable trust or owned by a third party, estate tax-free death benefits.

Interestingly, since the ILI policy is maximumly funded, there is no need for actuarial evaluation, as discussed in Chapter 5, for purposes of determining policy sustainability to any duration testing point, the correcting premium required to reach the selected duration testing point with the statistical confidence specified by the policy owner, or earliest lapse or five-year range of most lapses. However, actuarial evaluation could be used to determine the relative pricing deviation of cost of insurance and other policy expenses from an actuarially certified policy standards database of ILI policies; plus, utilizing Monte Carlo simulation, an expectation of policy results within statistical degrees of confidence.

Mark and Randy do a superb job of providing a background on the derivation and development of ILI. Two of the most recent exciting developments for this product were the availability of this product to investment advisors and agents through the life insurance industry broker general agency system, and, more recently, a non-commissionable product version with compensation strictly assets under management (AUM) for the registered investment advisor (RIA) and other financial planners and fiduciaries. The article contains an excellent analysis of the advantages of the ILI alternative, pointing out "[t]he increasing life expectancy disparity between Socio-economic classes should continue to increase the disparity in value between ILI and retail priced alternatives." Furthermore, the article does an eye-opening comparison between alternative choices of taxable investing, retail variable universal life products, retail indexed universal life products, and RIA priced ILI.

As the Whitelaw brothers point out, "institutional life insurance is different because the economic driver is the longevity profile of highly compensated white-collar individuals" and combined with the tax advantages of life insurance, ILI is "[n]ot a revolutionary advancement in HNW planning, but rather evolutionary."

About Charles M. "Mark" Whitelaw

Mark Whitelaw is Head of Design at Winged Foot Partners (WFP) and is a Registered Representative with World Equity Group, Inc., Member FINRA and Securities Investor Protection Corporation. WFP is not owned or controlled by World Equity Group, Inc. WFP provides institutionally priced life insurance access, analytics, and administrative services to accredited investors, the financial services sector, and trustees.

Mark has been managing the design, funding, communication, implementation, and administration of non-qualified benefit plans for more than 35 years. Mark's unique expertise is the investment analytics and administration of life insurance-funded executive benefits, trust-owned life insurance (TOLI), and individually owned institutional life insurance (ILI) plans.

He has served in management positions with The Equitable, The Whitelaw Group, Custom Administration Services Co. L.P., Rivenet, Valley View Consultants, Inc., and WFP.

Mark is a 1977 graduate of University of Missouri–Columbia with a B.A. in Economics. He and his wife Joyce live in Edwardsville, Illinois.

About E. Randolph Whitelaw

E. Randolph Whitelaw is Managing Director of Trust Asset Consultants, LLC (TAC), a trust-owned life insurance (TOLI) risk management consulting firm, and The TOLI Center, LLC (TTC), a life insurance policy administration and risk management firm. TAC's clients are trustees, beneficiaries, professional advisors, and affluent family groups. TTC provides professional fiduciaries, professional advisors, affluent families, and businesses with a service-based life insurance plan administration and policy risk management platform.

A leader in the TOLI risk management counseling and restructure marketplace, he is frequently engaged by professional fiduciaries and estate planning professionals to provide expert opinion and testimony in dispute and litigation matters and in FINRA arbitration. He lectures nationwide and regularly authors in-depth peer-reviewed articles that illustrate his comprehensive knowledge of the ever-changing life insurance and life settlement markets. He was engaged by the American Bar Association to co-author a book titled *The Life Insurance Policy Crisis: The Advisors' and Trustees' Guide to Managing Risk and Avoiding a Client Crisis* that was released for sale in September 2016.

Mr. Whitelaw has a corporate finance and capital markets background. He spent 15 years with a major bank holding company managing public corporation, larger private business, and affluent family group relationships. His lending experience includes coordination of multi-lender "work-out" borrowing arrangements. As Executive Vice President, he managed the holding company's middle market business and private client group including the cross marketing of trust, investment, and life insurance services. His management experience included interface with the Office of the Comptroller of the Currency (OCC) bank examiners.

In the mid-1980s, he co-founded a consulting firm to specialize in the unique management and business continuity planning issues of larger family businesses, affluent family groups, and family offices. His company offered investment advisory, life insurance, and family office support services as well as the design, implementation, and management of non-qualified deferred compensation plans for public corporations. In 1993, he co-founded and served as managing partner of a fee-based third-party TOLI policy administration company that developed a national reputation and clientele among regulated trustees and estate planning professionals. In 2001, he founded TAC to provide corporate trustees, professional advisors, and insurance trust beneficiaries with "single source" TOLI fiduciary risk management consulting services.

A member of the National Association of Estate Planners & Councils (NAEPC) and the Society of Financial Service Professionals (FSP), Randy, as he is known to his friends, has extensive expert witness experience that includes being the lead expert witness for the plaintiff in the infamous case *In re Stuart Cochran Irrevocable Trust*, 901 N.E.2d 1128 (Ind. Ct. App. 2009), better known as *Cochran v. Key-Bank*. He is a prolific writer and speaker, having authored or co-authored numerous peer-reviewed articles and spoken at an uncountable number of professional seminars, webinars, estate planning councils, bar associations, and other professional education events, including the NAEPC Annual Conference and the Heckerling Institute on Estate Planning.

In 2013, Mr. Whitelaw was inducted into the NAEPC Estate Planning Hall of Fame® and simultaneously awarded by NAEPC the Accredited Estate Planner- (Distinguished) (AEP® (Distinguished)) designation.

Was Your Client Sold the Most Expensive Life Insurance Policy on the Planet?

Charles M. "Mark" Whitelaw

E. Randolph Whitelaw, AEP® (Distinguished)

At the time of this writing, we are approaching the four-year anniversary of the 2015 National Association of Insurance Commissioners Actuarial Guideline 49 (NAIC AG 49) regulating (1) the maximum illustration rate and (2) maximum policy loan leverage on Indexed Universal Life Insurance (IUL). What AG 49 did not address was:

- Equivalent return disclosure to the S&P 500 Total Return.
- IUL interest bonus/return enhancements.

Additionally, at this time:

- Regulators and associations are creating Best Interest conduct standards.
- All life insurance products are being repriced for the 1/1/2020 update to the 2017 Commissioners Standard Ordinary Mortality Table (2017 CSO) that is used for statutory legal reserve purposes.

That said, while the playing field may be changing, nothing is being proposed that will change the "win the illustration game" in the consumer's favor.

Equivalent Return Disclosure to the S&P 500 Total Return

Prior to the 2015 AG 49 calculation, life insurance companies were picking 20 to 25-year historical periods that would maximize the illustration rate based on their current 1-year Indexed Account cap—1-year ending periods typically sometime in December.

- Dates that would make it difficult for consumers to compare to traditional 12/31 reporting of alternatives.
- Illustration rates in the 8% to 10% range that may have 14% to 16% S&P 500 Total Return equivalents.

The result was a non-security product illustration based upon market total returns that exceeded the 12% maximum hypothetical illustration rate on securities and 10% maximum when being compared to other alternatives [FINRA Rule 2210(d) (4)(C) defining "hypothetical illustrations of mathematical principles"].

NAIC AG 49 provides a defined annual calculation that:

- Determines the maximum IUL illustration rate for a given Indexed account methodology.
- Utilizes a 65-year lookback encompassing every 1-year period and further segments those returns into every 25-year segment.
- When applied to the S&P 500 Total Return, provides the common starting point for comparison to a VUL policy.

For 2019 the S&P 500 Total Return (dividends included) AG 49 equivalent rate is 10.95%.

Hence, for 2019, when a consumer asks the simple question "how does this AG 49 rate illustration compare to investing in a S&P 500 index fund in a ____?" the basis of that comparison should be the alternative illustrated with a 100% allocation to the alternative's S&P 500 index fund at 10.95% before fund fees (gross). We say "should" because:

- A "total return" discussion could violate state regulations regarding unlicensed investment advice.
- 10.95% would violate the 10.00% FINRA maximum.

To date we have not seen anything from regulators or insurance companies that would (1) help consumers understand the benefits and trade-offs of going from an index fund based alternative to an indexed account based insurance product or (2) provide the equivalent return information to securities licensed agents so they can conduct themselves in a FINRA consistent manner.

IUL Interest Bonus/Return Enhancements

Initially, IUL utilized traditional policy pricing:

- Lowest costs possible (policy risk costs plus indexed account costs).
- Issuers were marketing either (1) low costs that often had lower Indexed caps, or (2) high Indexed caps that had higher cost of insurance (mortality rates) and expense costs to pay for the higher caps.
- A few policies offered small fixed bonus credits, formula bonuses or persistency dividends starting in year 10 consistent with the features offered on their UL or VUL products.
- Policies offered a limited number of Indexed account options/formulas.

AG 49 reduced IUL illustration rates. To make-up for those reductions the issuers added:

- Fixed Bonus credits—Fixed returns commencing in a policy year regardless of market/consumer's selected Indexed account return.
- Formula Bonus credits—Bonus formulas based on what the consumer's selected Indexed account earns.
- Return Enhancements—Undisclosed issuer managed programs whose enhanced return is based on the consumer's selected Indexed account return.
- Multiple Indexed account options, formulas for consumers to anticipate market performance the next 1–5 years (monthly and annual performance).

Depending upon the specific IUL policy with various insurers, and we are certain this survey is typical although limited in scope to major insurers, we have seen with the same carriers cost of insurance (mortality rates) and expense costs for IUL that are 1,500% to 3,000% greater than a UL or VUL policy illustrated in a consistent policy management manner (No . . . that is not a typo!).

Most recently, issuers have turned these types of programs into account options or policy riders:

- Option to choose lower cap Indexed accounts that have a bonus or higher cap accounts that do not.
- Riders that may increase lifelong illustrated value 20% in return for a 750% increase in cost of insurance (mortality rates) and other policy costs.

Currently the NAIC is reviewing the post-AG 49 IUL issues.

Applying AG 49 Principles to Consumer Planning Assumptions

On the positive side, NAIC AG 49 includes all 252 1-year ending returns within a calendar year. The following summary:

- Provides a 25-year summary of all 1-year return averages within calendar years.
- Includes the minimum and maximum return within those years.
- Assumes a 7.00% consumer long-term S&P 500 index return assumption and applies 25-year return differentials to calculate equivalent illustration rates for different products and management assumptions.

MA-200—200 Day Moving Average management.

- Remain in the S&P 500 fund when the current share price is *greater* than the 200-day average.
- Move to cash when the current share price is *less* than the 200 day average.

Moving Average typically utilizes 30, 50 or 200 day averages. A management strategy that can be applied to variable insurance products (VA & VUL) utilizing end-of-month share price averages to determine monthly management options within the 12 no-cost reallocations offered by most products.

Utilizing this methodology, the 7.00% planning rate would equate to comparing:

- IUL policy with 10% 1-yr point to point (PtP) cap at a 5.27% illustration rate.
- Planning alternatives (VUL, VA [variable annuity], IRA, Roth IRA, 401(k), Roth 401(k), etc.) allocated 100% to the S&P 500 index fund at 8.70% before fund fees (gross).
- IUL policy to planning alternatives at a 3.96% AAA bond return.
- Pros and cons of using Indexed account vs the Moving Average index fund management alternative.

Indexed insurance products provide an important consumer planning option, and have also evolved into a level of complexity that is *extremely* difficult for consumers and professional advisors to separate financial "sizzle" from financial "steak."

Best Interest

"Best Interest" has become a widely used term:

- The SEC has drafted regulations that would encompass Best Interest standards for both qualified and nonqualified assets.
- The CFP Board has included Best Interest in its Code of Ethics and Standards of Conduct effective 10/1/2019.

Best Interest also has a complement—Dispute Defensible Practice Management. Advisors and fiduciaries must be able to document their recommendations and purchases in anticipation of being questioned in the future. If the provider is not providing adequate information to say "yes," we believe you are obligated to say "no."

25-Year Annual Minimum - Maximum - Average Returns
Based on all 1-year ending returns between 1994-2018.
Annual Range of Return

S&P 500 Total Return vs Sample Indexed Return Alternatives

#	Year	Variable 0.15% Fund Fee — S&P 500 TR Index Fund Min	Max	Average	S&P 500 TR MA-200 Mgmt Min	Max	Average	Indexed UL 10.00% Cap, 0.00% Floor Capped 1-Yr P4P Min	Max	Average	Gross Index Average Returns — Vanguard Total Bond (Bond) Average	Index Return Average	S&P 500 Total Return Average	MA-200 Tot Return Average
1	1994	-1.48%	13.22%	4.72%	3.02%	12.03%	7.92%	0.00%	10.00%	2.36%	0.52%	2.00%	4.87%	8.07%
2	1995	-0.22%	41.79%	20.86%	2064%	25.30%	10.40%	0.00%	10.00%	8.20%	9.49%	17.76%	21.01%	10.55%
3	1996	14.01%	40.54%	26.83%	24.04%	32.15%	29.00%	10.00%	10.00%	10.00%	7.83%	24.07%	26.98%	29.15%
4	1997	16.67%	52.29%	32.33%	22.60%	34.39%	27.60%	10.00%	10.00%	10.00%	7.65%	29.91%	32.48%	27.75%
5	1998	-0.11%	52.78%	26.71%	23.23%	37.13%	31.64%	0.00%	10.00%	9.52%	10.18%	24.86%	26.86%	31.79%
6	1999	9.85%	40.92%	24.04%	18.83%	23.38%	21.18%	10.00%	10.00%	10.00%	3.44%	22.50%	24.19%	21.33%
7	2000	-11.73%	20.95%	8.89%	7.99%	22.53%	15.36%	0.00%	10.00%	7.30%	4.33%	7.75%	9.04%	15.51%
8	2001	-33.43%	1.30%	-15.35%	-0.15%	7.92%	2.91%	0.00%	0.29%	0.00%	12.50%	-16.23%	-15.20%	3.06%
9	2002	-33.50%	3.93%	-15.96%	-0.96%	-0.13%	-0.80%	0.00%	2.67%	0.03%	6.74%	-17.03%	-15.81%	-0.65%
10	2003	-30.41%	35.99%	0.81%	-0.98%	13.86%	3.34%	0.00%	10.00%	4.66%	7.06%	-0.83%	0.96%	3.49%
11	2004	6.81%	43.57%	19.00%	14.00%	25.08%	20.84%	5.13%	10.00%	9.67%	3.67%	17.89%	19.95%	20.99%
12	2005	2.65%	18.37%	8.59%	7.59%	14.45%	9.26%	1.00%	10.00%	6.51%	3.59%	6.82%	8.74%	9.41%
13	2006	2.28%	18.90%	10.50%	8.11%	10.45%	9.26%	0.54%	10.00%	7.53%	2.19%	8.61%	10.65%	9.41%
14	2007	1.82%	27.78%	14.88%	10.46%	16.45%	13.83%	0.08%	10.00%	9.05%	5.86%	12.89%	15.03%	13.98%
15	2008	-45.79%	4.02%	-15.62%	-0.16%	14.21%	5.55%	0.00%	2.16%	0.02%	5.86%	-17.23%	-15.47%	5.70%
16	2009	-47.65%	48.63%	-16.56%	-5.91%	7.64%	-0.93%	0.00%	10.00%	2.25%	6.61%	-18.56%	-16.41%	-0.78%
17	2010	3.75%	72.11%	24.33%	7.84%	29.29%	20.84%	1.86%	10.00%	9.36%	7.90%	21.90%	24.48%	20.99%
18	2011	-1.53%	33.48%	13.59%	12.45%	17.29%	14.97%	0.00%	10.00%	7.39%	5.14%	11.49%	13.74%	15.12%
19	2012	-1.63%	34.34%	11.52%	5.81%	13.21%	9.33%	0.00%	10.00%	5.88%	6.51%	9.25%	11.67%	9.48%
20	2013	11.84%	35.63%	21.83%	12.75%	23.37%	18.09%	9.46%	10.00%	9.99%	0.31%	19.28%	21.98%	18.24%
21	2014	10.28%	28.65%	19.99%	18.73%	24.94%	22.74%	8.20%	10.00%	9.98%	2.53%	17.67%	20.14%	22.89%
22	2015	-4.75%	20.04%	9.65%	0.22%	10.09%	14.55%	0.00%	10.00%	6.89%	3.23%	7.58%	9.80%	14.70%
23	2016	-9.82%	18.93%	3.66%	2.42%	9.16%	4.68%	0.00%	10.00%	2.92%	3.11%	1.59%	3.81%	4.83%
24	2017	13.08%	29.20%	19.35%	7.54%	18.86%	14.87%	0.00%	10.00%	10.00%	8.84%	17.03%	19.50%	15.02%
25	2018	-10.84%	27.71%	14.48%	13.19%	19.59%	17.91%	0.00%	10.00%	8.69%	-0.57%	12.42%	14.63%	18.06%
	Average:	-5.59%	30.60%	10.95%	8.97%	18.85%	13.77%	2.25%	9.00%	6.73%	5.06%	8.94%	11.10%	13.92%
	Std Dev:	18.48%	16.85%	14.25%	0.17%	0.03%	0.00%	3.00%	2.77%	3.50%	3.28%	13.95%	14.25%	8.97%
	Average vs. S&P 500 Index Return:			22.60%			54.13%			-24.72%	-43.37%		24.27%	55.81%

Hypothetical Illustration Rates utilizing 25-Year Average Differentials and 7.00% S&P 500 Index Return Planning Rate

	Net of Fund Fee	8.55%			10.76%				5.27%	3.96%			8.70%	10.91%
	Std Dev								2.74%	2.57%			11.17%	7.03%
	2019 Maximum Permitted Illustration Rate								6.12%		Variable Products		12.00%	Maximum

What's Coming Down The Pipe?

The next 12–24 months should be very interesting, to say the least:

- Greater access to $0 agent commission, $0 surrender charge products for the direct access and fee-based planning "space."
- More insurance policies with just placement commissions—elimination of lifelong policy commission structures.
- More insurance policies that differentiate agent placement and ongoing TPA services compensation.
- Differentiation of highly compensated, accredited investor socio-economic risk class and life profile.
- More VUL policies offering Indexed accounts as asset allocation alternatives.

And, hopefully, recognition by the insurance companies that different types of distribution have different disclosure responsibilities or the advisor needs to say "no." Remember, the first life insurance decision is an investment decision.

Both of us entered the insurance business in the early 1980's with the introduction of universal life based (UL, VUL, AL [adjustable life], etc.) policies—"buy term and invest the rest" products where the first agent and consumer decision was how they wanted to invest the cash values that pay the monthly term insurance costs.

Today, thanks to medical advancements extending life expectancy, many products offer greater living benefits than comparable investing in taxable structures (brokerage account or nonqualified annuity) while offering the consumer a planning gain at death for their heirs.

Regardless, the policy structure, cost structure and cost curve remains the second life insurance decision. For example, what costs have to be paid when the return is low, zero or negative? As shown in our 25-year summary, 60% of the time someone received a 0% IUL crediting rate.

The lapsing policy crisis of policies issued in the past are primarily the result of *not* applying reasonable investment return assumptions to life insurance purchases. Declared interest rates are no longer in the 8% to 11% range—but the same issues are facing consumers today:

- IUL policies with 6% to 7.5% illustration rates that assume a 10.95% S&P 500 Total Return.
- IUL policies with bonus interest and performance enhancements that typically do not get paid when markets correct.
- IUL policies with cost of insurance (mortality rates) and other expense pricing of $30,000 to $45,000 compared to $1,000 to $1,200 for the same amount of protection in a VUL policy.

To wrap up, Agents / Advisors / Trustees . . . can you explain why you considered a $30,000 cost of insurance, rather than a $1,000 cost of insurance, was in the clients Best Interest?

High Net Worth (HNW) Access to Institutionally-Priced Life Insurance for Personal Asset Diversification

Charles M. "Mark" Whitelaw

E. Randolph Whitelaw, AEP® (Distinguished)

Overview. In the early 1980s, a life insurance revolution commenced with the introduction of flexible premium non-guaranteed death benefit products (Accumulation Life, Universal Life, Variable Universal Life, etc.), described as "buy term and invest the difference." Over time, the policy pricing, investment options and cash surrender value enhancements expanded and became ideally suited for Corporate Owned Life Insurance (COLI) and Bank Owned Life Insurance (BOLI) usage due to their balance sheet presentation and annual lifelong risk management. More recently, Institutionally-Priced Life Insurance (ILI) has become the product of choice for corporate, bank, trust and individual owners for reasons to be discussed.

The 2018 Investment Company Institute (ICI) Fact Book reports that Americans own $9.9 trillion dollar of mutual funds in taxable structures—$8.8 trillion in taxable structures and $1.1 trillion in non-qualified variable annuities. What is unknown is:

- How much is held by individuals with $1+ million net investable assets?
- How many family members are age 18+, healthy and expect to live longer than we do today?

Institutionally-priced life insurance (ILI) is the leading alternative investment and asset diversification "container" for businesses to fund supplemental retirement benefits to executives as well as multiple business continuity obligations. The primary "value-driver" as compared to retail life insurance and taxable investing is the superior longevity of highly compensated white-collar risks resulting in ILI costs having less impact and "drag" on investment gains than taxes. Access to ILI is typically limited to professionally administered multi-life COLI/BOLI/Bonus 162 programs, or third party administered (TPA) sponsored employer facilitated programs for direct executive personal access.

Recently ILI support services have been expanded to the fee-based registered investment advisors (RIAs) supporting America's 13.5 million high net worth families and their trustees:

- TPA sponsored ILI investment, cash, tax and risk management programs.
- RIA authorized for asset allocation management.
- ILI issuer streamlined underwriting to age 60.

Not buying a life insurance policy in the traditional sense but participating in a collaboratively monitored and administered program consistent with ILI best practices.

Evolution of the ILI Value Proposition

ILI was created in 1986 as an alternative investment, cash, tax and risk management container for corporations (COLI) and banks (BOLI) to informally fund nonqualified retirement benefits to executives capped-out of tax-qualified plans.

- 1986—The policy cash value could fund about 75% of an executive benefit. The policy death benefit was needed to cost-recover the balance.
- 2002—Executives were living so long, reducing costs to the point where the policy could fund 100% of the executive benefit. The excess policy death benefit represented pure keyperson protection at $0 incremental cost when compared to taxable investing alternatives.

Since 2002:

- COLI/BOLI has been an investment alternative driven program—cost-shifting from the cost-of-taxes to the lower cost-of-ILI while receiving added financial protection at $0 incremental cost when compared to taxable investing alternatives.
- A handful of specialty ILI TPA firms appeared offering TPA sponsored and administered individually-owned ILI—moved the ILI plan sponsor role from the employer to the TPA firm for the participant's lifelong support. Executives could personally access these programs, but the programs competed with the executive's investment advisor or retail insurance agent.
- 2015—The first ILI brokerage general agency (BGA)/TPA, making the TPA sponsored and administrated ILI program available to investment advisors and agents through the life insurance BGA distribution system—TPA acts as a HNW (High Net Worth) support unit for the BGA and their advisor/agent members.
- 2018—BGA/TPA model enhanced for RIA collaboration—BGA/TPA serves as the LOA (Licensed Only Agent) as the policy pays $0 writing agent level compensation and RIA approved by policyowner for asset allocation of the policy separate accounts.

Rather than the advisor selling a life insurance policy in the traditional retail manner, the advisor is sitting on the consumer's side of the table assisting in the due diligence of participating in the TPA's ILI management plan.

Today there are three levels of life insurance product and consumer:

1. **Retail**—General purpose protection with net investable assets of less than $1 million. "LIRP" Life Insurance Retirement Plan acronym for maximum funding a retail policy for cash accumulation purposes.

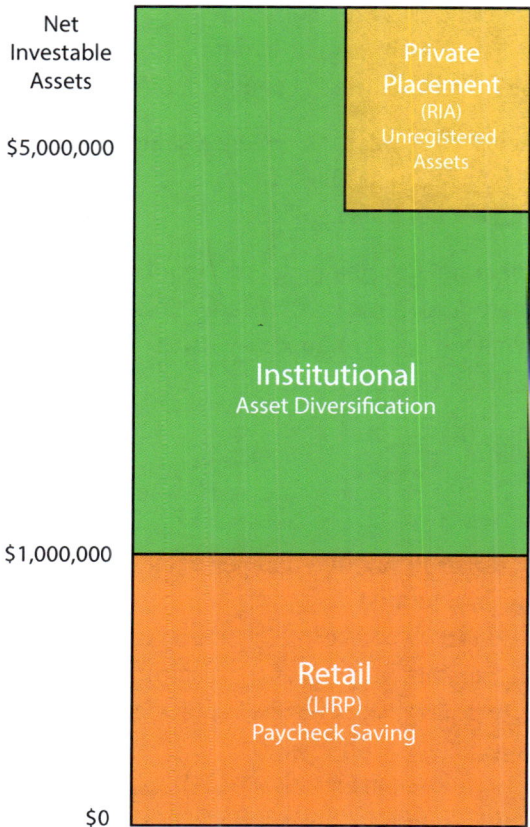

2. **Institutional**—Registered asset investment driven lifelong protection products for those with $1+ million net investable assets. Alternative to taxable investing for those capped-out of tax-qualified investment accounts.

3. **Private Placement**—RIA controlled investment driven policy that includes registered and unregistered assets for those with $5+ million net investable assets. Alternative to taxable unregistered asset investing.

Institutional/Private Placement (PP) products are designed to minimize the financial protection and related costs to maximize cash value accumulation and income tax-free value to heirs when it's needed the most—average life expectancy and beyond. Because the ILI/PP VUL decision is based on the policy lifetime benefits vs. taxable investing, the added financial protection is viewed as (1) a planning enhancement for those that do not believe they need life insurance, and (2) a cost-savings to those that do—reduces the amount of protection the individual needs to "buy" in the traditional/retail sense.

Agents/Advisors Can Finally Address Structural Suitability

The primary financial risk for highly compensated, high net worth individuals is living.

- The Socio-economic classes that live the longest due to lifestyle, white-collar roles and pro-active healthcare utilization.
- Minimal value of tax-qualified accounts due to plan caps and restrictions.

Many retail policies offer riders to enhance short-term cash values similar to a COLI policy—often referred to as "Diet COLI"—but are structurally unsuitable for this alternative investment container role:

- General population risk pricing and risk-pool cost exposure.
- Limited Separate Account (fund) or Indexed account offerings.
- Policy cost management limitations—artificially restrict how low the protection can be reduced to reduce costs.

What distinguishes ILI?

- Defined contribution offered policy—How much contribution capacity do you want?
- Limited to insuring highly compensated "white-collar" risks—Those expected to live the longest.
- Serves as an alternative investment, cash, tax and risk management container—Protect against living plus terminal illness and death.
- Value proposition enhancements are medical science driven—the longer we live, the greater the value proposition.
- $0 initial assets under management (AUM) exposure—Year 1 cash surrender value comparable to a Taxable Brokerage Account.

Retail life insurance products typically do not offer the structural capacity to serve in this alternative investment management container role.

Investment Container Comparison

All life insurance decisions are investment alternative decisions. The only difference is whether the measurement is life or death. Medical science extending life expectancy, lowering life insurance costs, has allowed investment driven policies to evolve into a lifelong investment, cash, tax and risk management alternative to taxable investing. Not a "buy term and invest the rest" equalized protection analysis, but which pricing and tax container offers you the better total value proposition for life, illness and net value to heirs.

Two regulations provide the basis for preparing consumer comparative illustrations:

- FINRA Rule 2210(d)(4)(C) (2013) specifying how a registered representative prepares "hypothetical illustrations of mathematical principles"—illustrations of different investment and tax structures.

- NAIC Actuarial Guideline 49 (AG 49) (2015) specifying how a life insurance company annually calculates the maximum illustration rate on Indexed Universal Life (IUL) indexed accounts—complex calculation encompassing every 1-year return of the past 65-years.

These two regulations provide:

- A FINRA methodology for preparing illustrations of different investment and tax structures.
- A NAIC calculation that can be extended to the S&P 500 Total Return to provide comparable comparatives between IUL illustrations and other life insurance and investment structures.

For 2019 the S&P 500 Total Return AG 49 equivalent rate is 10.95%. If an agent is illustrating an IUL policy at the current AG 49 rate the comparable would be alternatives illustrated at 10.95% to a S&P 500 index fund before fund fees. This is the "apples to apples" *starting point* before other considerations.

Following are two comparatives of illustrated values of (1) taxable brokerage account (TBA) at different average tax assumptions to (2) RIA priced ILI (VUL) to retail VUL and (3) a retail IUL policy managed to minimize protection and maximize lifelong values. Retail VUL & IUL illustrations assume policy mix is 50% term rider to reduce agent compensation expenses 50% and increase policy values. Illustrations assume a male age 50 contributing $100,000 annually for 7 years and demonstrate after-tax/income tax-free cash flow for 35 years from age 65 to age 100.

AG 49 Equivalent Value Summary—10.95% S&P 500 Total Return

TBA Tax Rate	15%	20%	35%	RIA - ILI	Retail - VUL	Retail - IUL
Year 1 AUM/CSV	$109,061	$108,536	$106,936	$107,770	$55,829	$29,857
Annual Net Cash-flow at Age 65	$175,899	$158,091	$113,262	$214,183	$186,511	$73,897
Total Net Cash-flow to Age 100	$6,156,471	$5,533,176	$3,964,165	$7,496,405	$6,527,885	$2,586,395
Net Values to Heirs at Age 100	$1	$1	$1	$380,819	$324,546	$516,532
Planning Solvency to Age	100	100	100	121	121	112
Total Economic Value	**$6,156,472**	**$5,533,177**	**$3,964,166**	**$7,877,224**	**$6,852,431**	**$3,102,927**
	-22%	**-30%**	**-50%**		**-13%**	**-61%**

8.00% S&P 500 Total Return Equivalent Value Summary—IUL illustration rate adjusted using AG 49 differentials.

TBA Tax Rate	15%	20%	35%	RIA - ILI	Retail - VUL	Retail - IUL
Year 1 AUM/CSV	$106,562	$106,176	$105,018	$104,191	$53,286	$28,641
Annual Net Cash-flow at Age 65	$104,462	$95,961	$73,774	$116,376	$102,963	$15,877
Total Net Cash-flow to Age 100	$3,656,167	$3,358,633	$2,582,102	$4,073,160	$3,603,705	$555,695
Net Values to Heirs at Age 100	$1	$1	$1	$223,944	$191,080	$112,094
Planning Solvency to Age	100	100	100	121	121	100
Total Economic Value	$3,656,168	$3,358,634	$2,582,103	$4,297,104	$3,794,785	$667,789
	-15%	-22%	-40%		-12%	-84%

Observations:

- ILI provides comparable or greater lifelong value as taxable fund investing using comparable assumptions.
- ILI's greater value is for higher risk/return objectives due to its relatively fixed annual cost.
- Life insurance commissions are designed for sales and service functions, not plan/planning administration and investment management.
- Removal of writing agent compensation increases the ILI value proposition as the impact on lifelong consumer value typically is $3–$4 of cash value per $1 of agent compensation.
- Retail IUL requires increased advisor analysis due to (1) its 300%–400% greater lifelong cost of insurance (mortality rates) and other expense costs attributed to pricing due to increased caps and fixed or formula bonus credits and (2) complexity of indexed account selections designed to provide active reallocation to address changing market conditions.
- There is one Institutional IUL policy in the COLI/BOLI marketplace that is priced consistent with an institutional VUL policy (defined contribution policy with low costs and multiple indexed alternatives) but currently is not accessible outside the employer sponsored COLI marketplace.
- Parameterized Return Monte Carlo Simulations are available to stress-test these different pricing and tax structures per advisor mean return and standard deviation assumptions.

- Comparative analysis is based on lifetime values with the cost drivers being the cost of taxes on a TBA vs. the cost of insurance. Hence, the added lifelong protection (illness and death) has $0 incremental cost applied to the analysis when viewed in light of the taxable investment alternatives.
- The increasing life expectancy disparity between Socio-economic classes should continue to increase the disparity in value between ILI and retail priced alternatives.

Personally-owned ILI, like its COLI/BOLI counterparts, is an asset diversification decision in a similar role for non-qualified assets as the Rollover IRA is for tax-qualified assets—complementary planning tools.

Different Perspective of Dispute Defensible and Exposures

Medical science has added another element of Dispute Defensible practices—especially when serving those that currently hold the $9.9 trillion of mutual funds in taxable structures (ICI 2018). "How's your health?" has been elevated from a traditional life insurance death benefit question into a lifelong investment management question.

- Comparable or greater lifelong investment, cash, tax and risk management.
- Positioning for lifelong tax grandfathering on a single life or multi-generational basis.
- Increased value to heirs at $0 incremental cost-of-investing with respect to taxable investment alternatives.

Access to RIA priced ILI provides advisors and fiduciaries a longevity priced alternative that increases in efficiency the longer we live. Who doesn't think medical advancements will continue to let us live longer?

Conclusion

The investment management "math" for those expected to live the longest changed sixteen years ago. And every time you read about another medical advancement that math improves.

It took sixteen years, but RIA's, Trustees and Accredited Investors finally have access to specially-priced ILI and integrated lifelong plan administration support—access to the math their career and life choices made possible.

The increasing longevity disparity between Socio-economic classes continues to increase the value proposition disparity between institutional and retail priced life insurance. Many leading retail IUL issuers devalued their policies in early 2017 by increasing cost of insurance (mortality rates) and other expense costs and adjusting bonus formulas resulting in increased consumer policy solvency risk if market returns or consumer indexed account allocation don't result in returns consistent with as-sold illustrations.

John Mauldin (Mauldin Economics) uses the term "Catastrophic Success" to describe the catastrophic consequences on governments of medical science extending life expectancy—the longer we live, the greater the need for tax revenue for funding Social Security and Medicare.

This expression also applies to what we have seen with protection based TOLI and the lapsing policy crisis—in addition to declining fixed interest & dividend returns, HNW insureds are living longer than policy funding expectations.

As we've described, ILI is different because the economic driver is the longevity profile of highly compensated white-collar individuals. ILI is the only alternative that turns the Economics of Longevity into an increasing comparative financial advantage and presents an opportunity for advisors to respect the career and life achievements of those that make the ILI value proposition possible.

Wealth management firms and trustees need to implement dispute defensible practices that either (1) include ILI as an investment management alternative or (2) clearly discloses to prospects and clients that they do not offer ILI or life insurance-based investment management services.

TOLI converted from a High Net Worth (HNW) convenience into a lapsing policy crisis because trustees didn't extend their investment and market forecasting and planning assumptions to death benefit driven life insurance. ILI is more consistent with traditional investment management alternatives—simply a more efficient pricing and tax structure for lifelong wealth management while receiving added financial protection. ILI is not an unknown asset in the institutional Trust world as 64.0% of U.S. banks and savings associations own ILI across the hall. (Equias Alliance/Michael White Report BOLI Assets Grew 2.7% to Over $171 Billion as of September 30, 2018)

Not a revolutionary advancement in HNW planning, but rather evolutionary. And all indications point to medical science continuing to increase the financial advantage of longevity-based investment management.

Today, the greater financial risk to HNW individuals is life. This risk is exacerbated by tax-qualified plan limitations, retail products priced for different socio-economic financial needs and ongoing changing perspectives of the fair tax treatment of the "rich." Given today's alternatives for healthy successful individuals, RIA priced ILI offers the greater value proposition, financial protections and tax preferences should life go as planned, better than planned, or not—Total Protection Management.

The Lapsing Life Insurance Policy Crisis— The Need for Dispute Defensible Advisor Practices And A Glidepath to Safety, Especially for Seniors

E. Randolph Whitelaw, AEP® (Distinguished), and George P. Whitelaw

Introductory Comments by Gary Flotron

E. Randolph Whitelaw, AEP® (Distinguished), and **George P. Whitelaw** are pioneers in the administration and risk management of trust-owned life insurance (TOLI). They are the founders and co-managing directors of The TOLI Center, LLC (TTC) a fee-based, independent third-party life insurance policy evaluation, administration, and risk management firm that provides services for professional and personal trustees, advisors, and policy owners. The TTC clientele includes many national trust companies, affluent family groups, businesses, attorneys, and other advisors. E. Randolph Whitelaw, known as Randy, is also the managing director of Trust Asset Consultants, LLC (TAC). TAC is a fee-based life insurance consulting firm to family groups, businesses, trustees, and attorneys. TAC specializes in formalizing each client's life insurance planning objectives and implementing the plan and policy administration, risk management, and participant communication. Further, TAC specializes with impaired risk underwriting, life insurance portfolio management, viatical and life settlements, and family meetings. TAC and TTC work hand in hand as "big picture" issues are addressed by TAC and life insurance policy management is addressed by TTC.

One of the major themes of this book is "the risk transfer paradigm shift that precipitated a policy crisis." Indeed, this book alludes to the crisis in Chapters 1 and 2. At the end of Chapter 2, the book touts the lesson "that with flexible premium non-guaranteed life insurance products we cannot rely on the use of **constant and continuous** assumptions [used in policy illustrations for either prospective purchase or in-force policies] in predicting the performance of the policy." However, while the linear policy illustration for non-guaranteed values is in itself extremely flawed, combined with inadequate disclosures or proper communication of the policy illustration limits, or just plain deceptive advisor practices, the illustration is a complete disaster. Additionally, combined with the common practice of using the linear, constant assumption policy illustration to determine the minimum funding premium for flexible premium non-guaranteed products—to say nothing of the failure to monitor and risk manage these policies—there is no wonder why there is a lapsing policy crisis.

In their contributed article, "The Lapsing Life Insurance Policy Crisis—The Need for Dispute Defensible Advisor Practices and A Glidepath to Safety, Especially for Seniors," Randy and George Whitelaw examine the causes of the lapsing life insurance policy crisis and provide "A Glidepath to Safety." Basically, the Whitelaw brothers postulate that the life insurance policy crisis is caused by a combination of illustration abuse, unwarranted policy replacement, lack of advisor due diligence, lack of product disclosure and suitability determinations, lack of policy monitoring and risk management, and sales agent practices that "can be described as deceptive, misleading and, occasionally, predatory."

The article goes on to describe the proper roles of the parties to a life insurance policy purchase and subsequent policy administration, monitoring, and risk management. Most importantly, the article describes creditable life insurance policy risk management and actuarially defensible policy evaluation. This latter topic parallels the process and evaluation techniques contained in Chapter 4 and, especially, Chapter 5—namely, actuarial evaluation using policy benchmark standards and Monte Carlo simulation.

This is a very intriguing and thought-provoking article that in many ways summarizes the material in Randy's book, *The Life Insurance Policy Crisis: The Advisors' and Trustees' Guide to Managing Risks and Avoiding a Client Crisis*, co-authored with Henry Montag and published by the American Bar Association. Full disclosure: the author was the peer reviewer and technical editor for this book.

In fact, while there are numerous differences, there are a lot of similarities between this book and Randy and Henry's book. For example, one concentrates on the external forces causing the policy crisis while the other is an internal "under the hood" perspective. However, in many ways these two books complement each other.

About E. Randolph Whitelaw

E. Randolph Whitelaw is Managing Director of Trust Asset Consultants, LLC (TAC), a trust-owned life insurance (TOLI) risk management consulting firm, and The TOLI Center, LLC (TTC), a life insurance policy administration and risk management firm. TAC's clients are trustees, beneficiaries, professional advisors, and affluent family groups. TTC provides professional fiduciaries, professional advisors, affluent families, and businesses with a service-based life insurance plan administration and policy risk management platform.

A leader in the TOLI risk management counseling and restructure marketplace, he is frequently engaged by professional fiduciaries and estate planning professionals to provide expert opinion and testimony in dispute and litigation matters and in Financial Industry Regulatory Authority (FINRA) arbitration. He lectures nationwide and regularly authors in-depth peer-reviewed articles that illustrate his comprehensive knowledge of the ever-changing life insurance and life settlement markets. He was engaged by the American Bar Association to co-author a book titled *The Life Insurance Policy Crisis: The Advisors' and Trustees' Guide to Managing Risk and Avoiding a Client Crisis* that was released for sale in September 2016.

Mr. Whitelaw has a corporate finance and capital markets background. He spent 15 years with a major bank holding company managing public corporation, larger private business, and affluent family group relationships. His lending experience includes coordination of multi-lender "work-out" borrowing arrangements. As Executive Vice President, he managed the holding company's middle market business and private client group including the cross marketing of trust, investment, and life insurance services. His management experience included interface with the Office of the Comptroller of the Currency (OCC) bank examiners.

In the mid-1980s, he co-founded a consulting firm to specialize in the unique management and business continuity planning issues of larger family businesses, affluent family groups, and family offices. His company offered investment advisory, life insurance, and family office support services, as well as the design, implementation, and management of non-qualified deferred compensation plans for public corporations. In 1993, he co-founded and served as managing partner of a fee-based third-party TOLI policy administration company that developed a national reputation and clientele among regulated trustees and estate planning professionals. In 2001, he founded TAC to provide corporate trustees, professional advisors, and insurance trust beneficiaries with "single source" TOLI fiduciary risk management consulting services.

A member of the National Association of Estate Planners & Councils ((NAEPC)) and the Society of Financial Service Professionals (FSP), Randy, as he is known to his friends, has extensive expert witness experience that includes being the lead expert witness for the plaintiff in the infamous case *In re Stuart Cochran Irrevocable Trust*, 901 N.E.2d 1128 (Ind. Ct. App. 2009), better known as *Cochran v. KeyBank*. He is a prolific writer and speaker, having authored or co-authored numerous peer-reviewed articles and spoken at an uncountable number of professional seminars, webinars, estate planning councils, bar associations, and other professional education events, including the NAEPC Annual Conference and the Heckerling Institute on Estate Planning.

In 2013, Mr. Whitelaw was inducted into the NAEPC Estate Planning Hall of Fame® and simultaneously awarded by NAEPC the Accredited Estate Planner® (Distinguished) (AEP® (Distinguished)) designation.

About George P. Whitelaw

Mr. Whitelaw is a Director and Chief Executive of The TOLI Center, LLC (TTC), a policy administration and risk management consulting firm to regulated and personal trustees and individuals. Administrative managers who coordinate daily administrative activities report directly to Mr. Whitelaw.

Mr. Whitelaw received his B.A. degree from St. Lawrence University in 1972. He spent ten years in commercial banking specializing with closely held corporations. In 1986, he co-founded a closely held insurance sales and consulting company and managed its executive and employee benefits practice until June 1998. In 1998, he founded Glenwood Consultants, LLC, an insurance sales and consulting company to individual and small-business clients.

In 1992, he co-founded Custom Administration Services Co., an insurance administration firm specializing in non-qualified plan administration to corporations and trust-owned life insurance administration to regulated trustees. In 2000, he formed TrustBuilder Services, LLC to purchase Custom Administration Services Co. and in 2012 he merged the operations and services of TrustBuilder into TTC.

In 2014, he formed The TOLI Resource Center (TRC), a fee-based insurance consulting firm that develops and licenses custom insurance administration software applications to manage trust-owned life insurance portfolios.

The Lapsing Life Insurance Policy Crisis—The Need for Dispute Defensible Advisor Practices And A Glidepath to Safety, Especially for Seniors[1]

E. Randolph Whitelaw, AEP® (Distinguished)
George P. Whitelaw

How Could This Happen?

In recent years, much has been written concerning escalation of the lapsing life insurance policy crisis, "illustration abuse," "unwarranted replacement," increased

---

1. E. Randolph Whitelaw is co-author of *The Life Insurance Policy Crisis: The Advisors' and Trustees' Guide To Managing Risks and Avoiding A Client Crisis* published by the American Bar Association. Many of the prudent practices discussed in this article are also discussed in more detail in this book.

carrier litigation, and continued sales agent promotion of questionable policy administration and risk management schemes for flexible premium non-guaranteed death benefit policies. Cautionary warnings with corrective action guidance have been directed to all policy owners mindful that illustration abuse adversely impacts insureds of all ages and life insurance programs of all types. Special attention should be given to senior insureds as well as to trustees, both skilled and unskilled, of policies owned in Irrevocable Life Insurance Trusts, to seek creditable, dispute defensible policy risk management consulting. A glidepath to safety is readily available—creditable consulting just needs to be used.

The scope of illustration abuse is significant—every flexible premium policy type has been impacted by illustration abuse. The degree of impact is directly related to the policy investments and, secondarily, the insurance costs (also described as cost of insurance or COIs). After 40 years of cautionary warnings, the known questionable and problematic sales and risk management practices still persist, despite the fact that dispute defensible policy sales and management practices have been available for most of this time to safeguard the policy owner's best interests. Throughout this time period, many sales agents have promoted policy replacement, thus generating a new commission; however, creditable policy risk management and policy rehabilitation typically are more favorable for the policy owner, assuming the planning objectives have not changed significantly.

Today's lapsing policy crisis brings into question Advisor due diligence, product disclosures and suitability determinations at the time of policy issue. For example, "sales" agents typically overlooked the disclosure of annual policy administration and risk management evaluation services needed to maximize the probability of a favorable planning outcome.[2] The usual response to this "How Could this Happen?" question is that agents are paid to sell new policies, and carriers do not offer policy risk management services appropriate for flexible premium products. Further, carriers financially benefit when policies are surrendered (a surrender charge is obtained and a death benefit is not paid) or lapsed (a death benefit is not paid).

What is The Purpose of This Article? To Provide Practical Advice and Explain the Obligations of the Parties.

The purpose is to review both the "illustration abuse" questionable practices creating the lapse problem as well as the "dispute defensible" (litigation-tested) advisor practices that maximize the probability of a favorable planning outcome. Informed and experienced advisors play a value-added role in the prudent practices process, and this role is direly needed.

---

2. 35% of universal life (UL) and variable universal life (VUL) policies are currently estimated to lapse prior to insured life expectancy or 5 years thereafter based upon The TOLI Center (TTC) client policies.

It should be noted from the outset of this article that creative destruction of the traditional agent distribution channel was predicted almost 40 years ago, and it has happened as predicted. Further, "The life insurance industry has endured a flood of litigation the last three years because of the changes the life insurance companies have been attempting to make in the non-guaranteed elements of cost of insurance (COI) and expenses. The amount of litigation is clear evidence that illustrations mislead. The cost of that litigation will be passed on to the consumer within the cost of future life insurance."[3]

Who are the Parties to a Life Insurance Policy Purchase and Subsequent Policy Administration and Risk Management, in addition to the owner? Given the lapsing policy crisis and accompanying litigation, this seems a timely question, to say the least.

- **Legal and Tax Advisors**: These advisors typically assist their clients in determining the need for life insurance, the face amount, the coverage time period (either period-certain or lifetime), and the beneficiaries. If the policy is to be owned in a trust, the legal advisors usually draft the trust agreement and any related documents. The trustee should be selected prior to policy purchase and delivery so that the trustee is fully aware of the reasons for the policy selection, the risks that need to be managed, and the post sales role of the sales agent in coordinating ongoing policy administration and risk management. If the agent confirms his/her role does not include post-sales policy administration or risk management, the grantor and advisers should delay policy acceptance until the sales agent confirms how the annual management function will be provided in a form that safeguards the purpose of the trust and avoids illustration abuse.

- **Sales Agent**: The agent is responsible to understand the policy purchaser's need for life insurance, risk tolerance and medical history. Additionally, the Agent is responsible to communicate his/her carrier appointments, product type knowledge/expertise, and the need for and form of post-purchase policy administration and risk management. Finally, the agent has a fiduciary responsibility to make a suitability determination as the basis for his or her carrier, product type and policy design recommendation. A copy of this suitability summary should be provided to the policy purchaser, including the

---

3. Ben G. Baldwin, Jr., "Between a Rock and a Hard Place: NAIC Regulators—Life Insurance Intermediaries—State and Federal Regulators," *Estate Planning Review—The Journal*, 2018, CCH Incorporated and its affiliates. **Related article comment**—"In general, life insurance advisors do not consider post-sales policy performance reviews to be their responsibility, unless such review can result in a commissionable policy replacement or additional policy sale. Post-sale policy performance reviews were not a condition of agent appointment by the issuing carrier, although some carriers promoted such reviews as a replacement opportunity. It is important to note that agents who are not securities licensed are limited in what information they can communicate to their clients to avoid allegations of unlicensed investment advice."

trustee of an irrevocable life insurance trust (ILIT), and clarify how post-sales policy management services will be provided.

- **Policy Administration and Risk Management Advisor**: Sales agents are compensated by life insurance carriers to sell life insurance policies. Concerning post-purchase administration and risk management, it is the responsibility of the policy owner (or ILIT trustee) to clarify the post-sales role of the sales agent. If the agent affirms that he/she will not provide post-sales policy management services, then the owner or trustee should engage a third-party to perform the administration and policy management functions. These functions are critical to achieving a successful planning outcome over a 10 to 40-year (or longer) time horizon. Further, these functions are usually delegated to third-party specialists. Hence, it is important to request assistance from legal and tax advisors in obtaining the names of these specialists, and in preparing a Request for Proposal (RFP) for submission to these specialists. This RFP should require, as a minimum, an explanation of the specialist's dispute defensible policy risk management methodology.

What is "Illustration Abuse"?

Illustration Abuse[4] refers to the use of insurance policy sales illustrations that appear to promise future financial performance levels that are unrealistically higher than the levels guaranteed by the underlying insurance contract. These illustrations are based on assumptions that are not creditable. Abuse occurs when the prospective policy owner is permitted or encouraged to believe that the unrealistic numbers in the illustration reflect reality or is given reason to expect that the illustration is a promise that will or must be fulfilled by the insurer.

Illustration abuse can be avoided by advising prospective policyowners that ultimate policy performance is not influenced by sales illustrations. It has been observed that for the most "competitive" insurance products there is less than 10% probability that the product's actual performance will meet or exceed its illustrated values.[5]

Why is there a Lapsing Policy Crisis?

Flexible premium non-guaranteed products are ideally suited for individual and family planning, corporate benefit programs, multi-generational wealth management and transfer planning programs; however, credible annual policy risk management has been typically overlooked. Carrier illustrations make full disclosure that

---

4. Burke A. Christensen. "The Perils of Life Insurance Sales Illustrations," *Probate & Property*, 1993.
5. Ibid.

illustrations for these products only show how the product works, and do not serve a predictive value purpose. Hence, annual policy risk management has always been necessary to maximize a favorable planning outcome.

The current lapsing policy crisis in part reflects the fact that non-guaranteed products have been serviced by Advisors and Agents with the same minimal attention to annual risk management as is customary for guaranteed products. It should be noted that the Universal Life "family" includes Guaranteed UL which warrants annual policy administration attention that is typically overlooked because the scope of the "guarantee" is either not explained by the sales agent or not understood by the policy owner, especially if the policy is owned in an Irrevocable Life Insurance Trust having an unskilled trustee.

"Illustration Abuse" warnings and guidance have been provided not only by the issuing life insurance carriers, but also the Society of Actuaries, American College of Trust and Estate Counsel (ACTEC), Financial Industry Regulatory Authority (FINRA), State Insurance Licensing Departments, Life Insurance Associations, the Society of Financial Service Professionals (FSP) and National Association of Insurance Commissioners (NAIC).

As noted, carrier illustrations make full disclosure that non-guaranteed policy illustrations only show how the product works and do **not** serve a predictive value purpose. In turn, an agent's misuse of non-guaranteed life insurance policy illustrations in suitability determinations and sales presentations can reflect "illustration abuse" and can be described as deceptive, misleading and, occasionally, predatory.

Why is there a lapsing policy crisis? The simple answer is questionable "sales" agent practices[6] over the past 35 years combined with questionable policy owner "due diligence" practices and advisor reliance. The creditable use of carrier illustrations combined with creditable analytics is needed to provide dispute defensible suitability and prudent risk management determinations.

For example, flexible premium non-guaranteed death benefit products have been marketed from the outset as "buy term and invest the difference" products. The purchase of Variable Universal Life and Equity Indexed Universal Life products is an investment decision mindful that the policy owner should consider target return, asset allocation, policy premium protection and investment management. The same Monte Carlo investment analytics used for investment modeling are available for flexible premium products.

---

6. E. Randolph Whitelaw and Henry Montag, *The Life Insurance Policy Crisis: The Advisors' and Trustees' Guide to Managing Risks and Avoiding a Client Crisis*, American Bar Association, 2016, includes an in-depth discussion of creditable practices, litigation-tested practices, and litigation warranting reader consideration.

What is Actuarially Defensible Policy Evaluation?

A credible dispute defensible option has been available for over 20 years but not offered by life insurance carriers or the traditional sales agent, brokerage general agent, most producer groups, and third-party illustration-based administrators distribution channels. Actuarial Evaluation uses generally accepted actuarial methods, impartial analysis and objective data to assess the probability that an illustration's scheduled premiums for non-guaranteed flexible premium life insurance will successfully sustain the policy to contract maturity or insured life expectancy, as a minimum.

Annual or periodic performance monitoring and risk management should address the following questions:

Premium Adequacy: What is the probability that the current scheduled premium will sustain the policy to insured life expectancy and contract maturity? If the probability is less than 100%, what is the risk-appropriate correcting premium adjustment?

Lapse: Assuming timely payment of the scheduled premium, what is the age of the insured person when the policy is projected to lapse? Actuarial evaluation combines with Monte Carlo simulation using 1,000 randomized trials to calculate earliest lapse age and age range for the concentration of projected lapses.

Policy Expenses: How do either the proposed or inforce policy's costs compare to the product standards benchmark for that product type? Are they higher or lower, and if so, by what percentage?

Policy Comparison: If a policy warrants restructure, actuarial evaluation facilitates a creditable analysis of carrier-illustrated restructure options, specifically the premium appropriate for the selected duration period, typically the insured s life expectancy at a minimum or life expectancy plus "X" years. That said, it is important to remember that the annual life insurance mortality costs increase with age, and the increase is significant over age 70. A life expectancy report should be obtained to help determine the duration period.

The History of Flexible Premium Non-Guaranteed Policies (aka The Buy Term and Invest the Difference Transition)

In the late 1970s and early 1980s, fixed income interest rates were in the 16 to 17 percent range. The S&P 500® annual return for 1980 was 31.74%. Because of the portfolio crediting and blending approach applied by carriers to whole life products, the value proposition provided by traditional whole life products was questionable at best. As a result, the owner of a whole life contract, with an accumulated cash value of $100,000, earning 3 to 5 percent interest, had the ability to borrow cash value at 6 to 8 percent interest and invest in a money market or savings account earning 15%. Thus, without assuming more risk, the owner could earn an additional 7 to 9 percent.

The life insurance industry watched the withdrawal and transfer of billions of dollars in their cash value coffers. In response to this outflow, life insurance carriers introduced Universal Life with illustrations showing an annual crediting rate of 15% or higher. "The economic conditions of the early 1980s were a perfect incubator for the universal life variation of whole life."[7] With the introduction of this new product, life insurance transitioned from a Buy-and Hold financial asset to a Buy-Fund-Manage financial asset . . . but the requisite manage services were not provided then and still are not provided by the issuing carrier.

As investment returns and fixed income rates subsequently declined, most UL owners had no idea the "as sold" policy values would never be realized unless corrective action was taken. This disclosure was rarely communicated by the sales agents prior to or at the time of policy delivery. Moreover, it is questionable what post-sales policy performance monitoring services were provided by the sales agent or what guidance the agent may have provided the buyer concerning how to obtain these needed services.

Several years ago, the policy "crediting rate" of Universal Life policies sold in the 1980s and 1990s was reduced by issuing carriers to the contractual minimum rate. Additionally, issuing carriers have increased the "cost of insurance" charge. As a result, the probability of policy lapse has increased, especially for seniors, meaning a credible (dispute defensible) performance review should be a priority for flexible premium products insuring seniors.

Post sales policy "risk management" services have been minimal. Policy owners, in general, were not notified that the scheduled policy premium needed to be reset at a higher amount and future resets considered as the crediting rate declined and/or the Cost of Insurance charges increased. Today, the crediting rate for policies issued prior to 2005 is the contractual 4% to 5% guaranteed minimum before consideration of increased Cost of Insurance (COI) charges. Creditable "Risk Management" services are essential to implementing a "glidepath to safety."

Life Insurance Distribution Channels

There are four basic channels. Two are ideally suited for the prospective policy owner, one is highly questionable and one is not. The second and fourth channels should be avoided unless the sales agent has clarified or will clarify how creditable (dispute defensible) annual or periodic policy risk management can be obtained that avoids illustration abuse and maximizes the probability of a favorable planning outcome.

---

7. Edward E. Graves, Editor, *McGill's Life Insurance*, 9th Edition, The American College, Bryn Mawr, Pennsylvania, 2013, pages 5.17–5.19.

1. **The Traditional Retail Channel** that markets Fixed Premium Guaranteed Death Benefit policies. Most of these sales agents have long-standing contracts with carriers such as Northwest Mutual, The Equitable, Prudential, etc. and many may be described as "captive" agents depending on their carrier contract.

2. **The Institutional Channel**—Producer Groups comprised primarily of "specialty producer groups"[8] having relationships with several larger carriers who offer specialty products and support services based upon the specific needs of each producer group.

3. **The Institutional Channel**—Policy Administration Companies consist of third party administration companies that primarily serve Fortune 500 companies and have access to high-performing products similar to the "specific producer groups" but provide the necessary supporting policy management requirements as well. This channel marketed the introduction of COLI (Corporate-Owned Life Insurance) and BOLI (Bank-Owned Life Insurance) programs. In recent years, it has commenced marketing "Institutional" Life Insurance to affluent families and family groups, a product that is significantly more efficient and favorable to policy owners than traditional products.

4. **The "Fire and Forget" Channel** (also described as the "Churn and Burn" Channel) markets flexible premium products to individuals and family groups to generate a commission and move on. Suitability is questionable and policy management assistance unavailable unless an agent believes the analysis will justify purchase of another policy and payment of another commission.

Policy Performance Review and Risk Management Process[9]

The TOLI Center in talking with legal and tax advisors, skilled and unskilled ILIT trustees, businesses and family groups concerning credible inforce policy evaluation, recognizes that most know very little or nothing about life insurance; hence, they discuss with policy owners the following steps to be pursued:

- Establish simple defensible policy performance criteria, starting with policy sustainability (typically insured life expectancy at a minimum or life expectancy plus "X" years depending on risk tolerance).

---

8. While the producer group concept enhanced the perceived professionalism of life insurance and investment advisors, it also opened the door for "churn and burn" advisors to take advantage of the producer group's reputation, marketing materials, and attractive commission comp arrangements. However, the expected post-sales scope of services was often <u>not</u> provided unless the sales agent expected policy replacement and availability of a new commission.

9. Flexible premium life insurance products can be described as sophisticated "buy and manage" products, assuming the "manage" function is both creditable and dispute defensible. Mindful of the lapsing policy crisis, flexible premium policy owners and their "trusted" advisors should request a copy of the sales agent's suitability determination and assure the "manage" function is dispute defensible.

- Understand that carrier illustrations show how the product works and provide the "source" data for actuarial evaluation.
- Evaluate every flexible premium policy using Monte Carlo Simulation[10] and Actuarial Evaluation to calculate the needed premium to sustain the policy to the sustainability objective.
- Set the policy administration and performance review frequency (typically every year).
- Communicate with trust parties, typically trust beneficiaries.
- Document corrective action taken for underperforming policy decisions. For example, premium increases or death benefit reductions should be expected as well as life settlements for policies likely to lapse because increased premiums are needed but not affordable.

Actuarial Evaluation (AE) Reports

Sample Actuarial Evaluation 1. An inforce $1,200,000 universal life policy current illustration for a male attained age 61 shows that the scheduled $18,368 annual premium will only sustain the policy to insured age 77, 11 years prior to the insured's estimated age 87 life expectancy. Actuarially-certified evaluation calculates policy lapse between insured ages 77–81, and calculates a $24,854 correcting premium is needed to sustain coverage to insured life expectancy. Also, the evaluation calculates the In-Force policy COI (Cost of Insurance) is less favorable (more expensive) than the Policy Standards average.

Actuarial Evaluation of $1,200,000 In-Force Universal Life Policy		1,000 Random Illustrations
Asset Allocation Criteria (equity/bond):	N/A	
Average Return/Projected Crediting Rate:	5.69%	
Actuarial Premium Adequacy Percent:	18%	In-Force
Current Funding Assumption Earliest Predicted Lapse Age:	77	▣180
Current Model Premium Concentration of Predicted Lapse Age(s):	77 – 81	820 ▪Sustain ▪Not Sustain
Policy Standards Pricing Deviation (+/-)	-.73	
Correcting Modal Premium to Sustain Death Benefit at Premium Adequacy Risk Tolerance:	$24,854	

10. Flexible Premium Non-Guaranteed Death Benefit life insurance products have been described from their introduction as "buy term and invest the difference" products. They are described as investment products with the policy cash accumulation account allocated to either fixed income, equity, or index accounts. **Monte Carlo Simulation**, or probability **simulation**, is a technique used to understand the impact of risk and uncertainty in financial, project management, cost, and other forecasting models. Uncertainty in Forecasting Models (www.solver.com). Hence, Monte Carlo Simulation combines with actuarial evaluation to provide for the creditable and dispute defensible risk management of these "buy term and invest the difference" products.

Sample Actuarial Evaluation 2. Trust-Owned Life Insurance (TOLI) policies often warrant more expanded evaluation especially if the trustee is unskilled, the sales agent does not provide post-sales service, the ILIT grantor (insured) wants to assure trust gifting is adequate to pay annual premiums and the family attorney is expected to "quarterback" timely premium payment and communication with all parties. The following sample report shows how an AE Report can provide information to differing life expectancy ages. The sample report pertains to a Variable Universal Life policy and assumes an equity/bond asset allocation of 80%/20%. It should be noted that differing asset allocations can be evaluated no different from differing life expectancies.

The inforce $4,000,000 death benefit policy issued in 2011 was reviewed as of its 2018 policy anniversary date. The insured is currently age 74 with a life expectancy of age 84. The carrier-provided inforce illustration showed the current $92,596 annual premium would only sustain the policy to insured age 80. In turn, we evaluated the premium amount needed to sustain the policy to age 84 as well as various other life expectancy dates for informational reasons. (Note. Other equity/bond asset allocations such as 60%/40% can be included so that all risk management options are reasonably considered. Also, a life expectancy report can be obtained, based upon the insured's medical records. To determine the age-appropriate reset/age 84.)

	Age 80	Age 84	Age 90	Age 100
Asset Allocation Criteria (equity/bond):	80%/20%	80%/20%	80%/20%	80%/20%
Average Return / Projected Crediting Rate:	9.37%	9.41%	9.46%	9.39%
Actuarial Premium Adequacy Percent:	73%	1%	0%	0%
Current Funding Assumption Earliest Predicted Lapse Age:	78	78	78	78
Current Modal Premium Concentarion of Predicted Lapse Age(s):	78–82	78–82	78–82	78–82
Policy Standards Pricing Deviation (+/-):	+ 0.59	+ 0.59	+ 0.59	+ 0.59
Correcting Modal Premium to sustain current Death Benefit to Evaluation Criteria	$96,978	$122,233	$155,384	$193,245

Dispute Defensible policy evaluation in the form discussed in this article has been available for over 20 years. Illustration abuse has been a problematic discussion for approximately 40 years despite the ongoing caveat emptor warnings. As shown in these two sample cases, dispute defensible policy evaluation is readily available so that policy owners can initially evaluate and subsequently monitor and re-evaluate policy management alternatives consistent with initial and changing planning objectives.

Noted again for emphasis purposes, "The life insurance industry has endured a flood of litigation the last three years because of the changes the life insurance companies have been attempting to make in the non-guaranteed elements of cost of insurance (COI) and expenses. The amount of litigation is clear evidence that illustrations mislead. The cost of that litigation will be passed on to the consumer within the cost of future life insurance."[11]

After 40 years, how long will illustration abuse persist? Regulator guidance and creditable analytic tools have been and remain readily available.

New Department of Labor Guidelines

Finally, as set out in the new DOL guidelines, the advisor must comply with the Impartial Conduct Standards that:[12]

- Provide advice that is prudent, meeting a professional standard of care;
- Operate in the best interest of the client rather than any competing interest of the advisor or financial institution;
- Charge no more than reasonable compensation, and
- Make no misleading statements about the investment transaction, compensation and conflicts of interest.

Conclusion

Flexible premium non-guaranteed life insurance products remain ideally suited for personal, business and trust planning purposes. These "buy term and invest the difference" products have been the product of choice for almost 40 years, yet illustration abuse, unwarranted replacement, questionable sales agent and service practices persist.

Traditional-thinking life insurance advisors and investment advisors seem frozen in the "illustration abuse" era. Legal and tax advisors typically defer life insurance suitability and risk management determinations to a life insurance sales agent without obtaining a second opinion specific to the avoidance of illustration abuse in the suitability determination and ongoing risk identification and prudent management.

However, litigation has clarified "dispute defensible" practices and these matters have helped define a glidepath to safety. The tools for this glidepath are readily available to avoid questionable life insurance marketing practices as well as known

---

11. Baldwin, *supra* note 3.
12. Society of Financial Service Professionals "On the Call" program June 2, 2017.

illustration abuse in order to safeguard the interests of policy owners, beneficiaries and advisors. The tools just need to be used.

The lapsing policy crisis and its adverse implications for policy owners and their advisors seems an ideal incentive to adopt dispute defensible practices that safeguard the interests of all parties.

Index

AALU. *See* Association for Advanced Life Underwriting (AALU)

Accidental death benefit, 109

Actuarial evaluation (AE) reports, 85, 86, 88, 110, 123–124, 274–276

Actuarially certified policy standards analysis, 82–87

Adverse selection, 21, 21n36, 164

Aging, 163–164

Anderson, James C.H., 1n2

Asset mix, life insurance in, 103, 107–108

Association for Advanced Life Underwriting (AALU), 121

Associations, professional, 120–122

Baker, Guy E., 153–177

Baldwin, Ben G., Jr., 179–187

Ballsun, Kathryn, 12, 43, 45

Bank Owned Life Insurance (BOLI), 255

Beneficiaries, 96–98

Best Interest, as term, 252

Blattmachr, Jonathan G., 189–200

BOX, The, 164–177

Carrier insolvency risk, 43–45, 129–131

Carrier selection, 110–112

Cash value accumulation, 95–96

Cline, Christopher P., 12n23

Collins, Patrick, 12, 43, 45

Comdex, 44–45, 110–111, 129

Compound interest, 168, 170, 172, 203–208

Constant assumed rate of return, 30–31

Constant earnings assumption, 31

Contingent beneficiaries, 97

Convertibility, 102

Corporate Owned Life Insurance (COLI), 255, 258

Cost of Insurance Leveraging, 207–208

Credentials, of life insurance professionals, 119–120

Credit rate
  declared, 175–176
  indexed, 176

Disability waiver, 108–109

Dispute defensible, 3n8, 82n107, 261, 263–277

Distribution channels, 272–273

Diversification risk, 68–69

Dividend performance risk, 48–49

Dividends, 10n20

Duration planning, 75–80

Earnings crediting, 27–32

Education, of life insurance professionals, 119

Equity account volatility, 30

Equity indexed universal life insurance, 28

Estate tax, 64, 95, 97–99, 192–200, 196n20, 238

Evaluation
  credible, in perspective, 87–89
  creditable, 123–127
  extreme disconnect in, 81–82
  improper methods in, 82
  Monte Carlo simulation in, 82–87

Expenses, in pricing, 7, 170–171

Financial planner, 116–117

Financial Planning Association (FPA), 121

Fixed account volatility, 29

Flagg, Barry D., 12n23

Flexibility, 95

FPA. *See* Financial Planning Association (FPA)

Goals of life insurance, 91–92

Grantor trusts, 239–241

Graves, Edward E., 3–4, 11

Hause, Christopher, 8, 201–208

Health deterioration, 136–138

Health improvement, 136–138

Hidden rate, 176–177

High net worth (HNW), institutionally-priced life insurance for, 255–262

HNW. *See* High net worth (HNW)

ILITs. *See* Irrevocable life insurance trusts (ILITs)
Illustration abuse, 269
Illustrations, 181–186
Indexed credit rate, 176
Indexed policies, 28
Indexed universal life, 59–62
Inflation, 94–95
Institutionally-priced life insurance, for high net worth individuals, 255–262
Interest
    compound, 168, 170, 172, 203–208
    in pricing, 7, 171
Investment management, life insurance management *vs.*, 71–72
Investment returns, in pricing, 7
Irrevocable life insurance trusts (ILITs), 41, 68, 73, 209, 211–212, 241
Jansen, Donald O., 209–214
Jurkat, Dieter, 12, 43, 45
Kitces, Michael E., 215–234
Lapse rate, 8
Lapsing crisis, 263–277
Life expectancy, 17–20, 141
    personalized, 75–78
Life insurance
    goals of, 91–92, 156
    purpose of, 91–92
    as temporary *vs.* permanent, 93
    type selection, 102–110
Life insurance management. *See* Management, life insurance
Life insurance professionals, selection of, 112–123
Long-term care (LTC) rider, 109–110
Management, life insurance
    best practices in, 74–75
    delegation of duties in, 73–74
    duration planning with, 75–80
    personalized life expectancy reports in, 75–78
    policy statement, 73
    predatory practices in, 74–75
    traditional investment *vs.*, 71–72
Markowitz, Harry, 68
Mauldin, John, 262
MDRT. *See* Million Dollar Round Table (MDRT)
MEC. *See* Modified Endowment Contract (MEC)
Million Dollar Round Table (MDRT), 121
Modern portfolio theory (MPT), 68
Modified Endowment Contract (MEC), 174

Monte Carlo simulation, 82–87, 110, 124
Mortality, in pricing, 7, 170
Mortality cost waiver, 108–109
Mortality tables, 16–17, 18–19, 18n34, 158–159
Moving Average 200, 252
MPT. *See* Modern portfolio theory (MPT)
NAIC. *See* National Association of Insurance Commissioners (NAIC)
NAIFA. *See* National Association of Insurance and Financial Advisors (NAIFA)
National Association of Insurance and Financial Advisors (NAIFA), 121
National Association of Insurance Commissioners (NAIC), 16, 179–181, 184–187
Ownership, policy, 96–98
Paid-up additional insurance, 109
Par whole life policies, 51–52
Pasquale, Marc A., 189–200
"Pay as you go" life insurance, 22
Permanent life insurance
    assumptions in, 26
    assumptions *vs.* reality in, 27–36
    creation of, 23–25
    earnings crediting, 27–32
    mathematics of, 23–27
    policy interest in, 27–32
    whole life insurance and, 24–25
Persistence, 8, 171
Personalized life expectancy reports, 75–78
Planning horizon, 93–95
Policy interest, 27–32
Policy management statement, 73, 141–142
Policy monitoring, 123–127
Policy ownership, 96–98
Policy performance review, 268n3, 273–274
Portfolio, life insurance as part of, 103, 107–108
Predatory practices, in life insurance management, 74–75
Premiums
    determination of, 159–163
    inadequate, 133
    in level premium term life, 101
    nonpayment of, 138–141
    outlay of, *vs.* cash value and death benefit amount, 104–107
    transparency and, 9–10, 9n18
Pricing
    assumptions, 14–16
    factors in, 168, 169–171
    as integrated whole, 13–14
    overview of, 7–9
    retail, 174–175

Product suitability risk, 64–67
Product types, risks by, 47–50
Professional associations, 120–122
Purchasing power risk, 45–47
Purpose of life insurance, 91–92
Radix, 18n33
Rate of return, 32–36
Regulators, 179–187
Risk
    capacity, 220–225, 228–229
    carrier insolvency, 43–45, 129–131
    defining, 42–43
    diversification, 68–69
    dividend performance, 48–49
    indexed universal life and, 59–62
    net amount at, 32–36
    no-lapse guarantee universal life and, 57–59
    par whole life and, 51–52
    product suitability, 64–67
    by product types, 47–50
    profiling, 227–233
    purchasing power, 45–47
    term insurance and, 50–51
    tolerance, 102–103, 134–136, 219–225
    universal life and, 52–55
    in whole life insurance with blended base,
        with combination paid-up additions
        and decreasing term insurance dividend
        option, 62–63
Risk management, 123–127
Risk tolerance questionnaires (RTQs), 103, 217,
    222, 224, 226–234
Risk transfer, 39–41
    adverse consequences in, 41–42
    background on, 39–41
    history of, 39–41
    perspective on, 39–41
    trust-owned life insurance and, 41–42
Risk transfer assumptions, 14–16
RTQ. *See* Risk tolerance questionnaires (RTQs)
Schwartz, Richard A., 66
Section 702, 94
Shenkman, Martin M., 235–241
SLAT. *See* Spousal lifetime access trust (SLAT)
Spousal lifetime access trust (SLAT), 241
Statutory tables, 16
Taxes
    capital gains, 55, 95, 134
    death, 94

deferred acquisition charges, 9
    estate, 64, 95, 97–99, 196n20, 238
    income, 52, 92, 138n126, 239
Terminal reserve, 10n19
Term insurance
    characteristics of, 20–22
    estate tax and, 195–196
    mathematics of cost of, 20–23
    "pay as you go," 22
    riders, 109
    risk and, 50–51
Third-party ownership, 97–98
TOLI. *See* Trust-owned life insurance (TOLI)
Transparency, 9–13
Trust-owned life insurance (TOLI), 41–42, 73,
    209–214
Underperformance, 131–133
Underwriting considerations, 98–100
Uniform Prudent Investor Act (UPIA), 209,
    213–214
Universal life, 1–5, 166
    duration planning with, 75–80
    equity, 28
    indexed, 59–62, 105–106, 249, 251
    no-lapse guarantee, 57–59
    policy interest and, 27–31
    premiums in, 15
    product suitability risk and, 64–65
    risk and, 52–55
    transparency with, 13
    unbundling in, 11
    variable, 29, 55–57, 106, 212–213
    whole life *vs.*, 166–167
UPIA. *See* Uniform Prudent Investor Act (UPIA)
Variable market rate, 176
Verification, 123–127
Waiver
    disability, 108–109
    mortality cost, 108–109
Weber, Richard M., 8
Whitelaw, Charles M., 243–262
Whitelaw, E. Randolph, 243–262, 263–277
Whitelaw, George P., 263–277
Whole life insurance, 24–25
    blended base, with combination paid-up
        additions and decreasing term insurance
        dividend option, 62–63, 106–107
    par, 51–52
    universal *vs.*, 166–167